# OCR
# Sociology

Chris Livesey

HODDER
EDUCATION

OCR

Philip Allan Updates, an imprint of Hodder Education, an Hachette UK Company,
Market Place, Deddington, Oxfordshire, OX15 0SE

*Orders*

Bookpoint Ltd, 130 Milton Park, Abingdon, Oxfordshire, OX14 4SB
tel: 01235 827827
fax: 01235 400401

e-mail: education@bookpoint.co.uk

Lines are open 9.00 a.m.–5.00 p.m., Monday to Saturday, with a 24-hour message
answering service. You can also order through the Philip Allan Updates website:
www.philipallan.co.uk

© Chris Livesey 2012

ISBN 978-1-4441-7756-5

First printed 2012
Impression number 5 4 3 2
Year 2015 2014 2013 2012

Typeset by DC Graphic Design Limited, Swanley Village, Kent

Printed in Italy

OCR examination questions used with permission of OCR

Hachette UK's policy is to use papers that are natural, renewable and recyclable
products and made from wood grown in sustainable forests. The logging and
manufacturing processes are expected to conform to the environmental regulations
of the country of origin.

P2129

# Contents

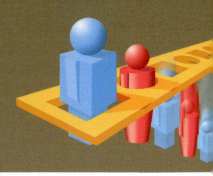

## Unit G672: Topics in socialisation, culture and identity

# Introduction

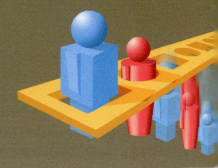

This textbook provides full coverage of all Unit 1 (G671) and Unit 2 (G672) modules in the OCR AS Sociology specification. It follows the specification logically and consistently in a way that makes it:

➤ easy to follow and map out
➤ easy to align with personal schemes of work and lesson plans

The text is an introduction to the main themes, concepts and theories of sociology at this level. Although each area of the specification is covered, it's important to see the content as *indicative*, rather than *prescriptive*. In other words, while the text gives students a good grounding in the various themes, concepts, theories, research methods and studies they need to understand if they're to successfully negotiate their AS exams, it's not the last word on content.

It's fully expected that teachers will supplement the text with other resources (including audio and video materials). The text should, therefore, been seen as a starting point or launch pad for teaching and learning rather than something that has to be religiously followed.

The OCR specification has a contemporary focus and this is reflected in the research studies highlighted throughout the text. Where relevant, however, a variety of historical theories and studies have also been cited — a historical perspective is frequently helpful and necessary if students are to understand the development of sociological thinking and its usefulness to contemporary ideas. The studies cited in the text are fully referenced in their own section at the end of the book.

## Features

The text has three additional features that require a little explanation:

### 'Quick-check' questions

Dotted throughout the text and indicated by a  **?**  are a variety of relatively simple questions that follow the 'Identify and explain…' or 'Suggest a reason…' OCR question format. These are designed to reinforce key points or ideas within the text.

### Exam-style questions

At the end of each chapter/section is a selection of OCR exam-style questions (some taken from past OCR papers). These are designed to help students practise answering real examination questions.

### Mnemonics

I wanted to include a revision technique that I've always found useful. Again, this is not something that teachers and students have to use in order to get the most from the text (the mnemonics are designed to be unobtrusive), but it's a feature that's there if you want to use it. Alternatively, if you want to practise using this technique, creating your own memorable mnemonics might be preferable to following those created by someone else.

# Unit G671

# Exploring socialisation, culture and identity

# Chapter 1

# The formation of culture

**By the end of this chapter you will be able to:**
- ➤ define key concepts (norms, values, status, culture and roles) in the formation of culture
- ➤ identify and define different types (high, popular, subculture, consumer and global) and aspects (diversity, multiculturalism) of culture

Sociology is the study of human relationships and behaviour or, as Ritzer (1979) puts it, 'the study of *individuals* in *a social setting*'. Like many others, such as psychologists and journalists, sociologists are interested in explaining the behaviour of individuals. However, unlike other social commentators, their focus is not 'the individual', but rather 'the social setting' — an idea that concerns how our membership of social groups, such as families, schools or the workplace, shapes our individual behaviours (the particular ways we relate to other individuals).

What interests sociologists, therefore, is not so much people *as* individuals (their particular psychologies, hopes, fears and so forth) but how we *acquire* these things. Why, for example, do we take for granted forms of science and technology that, to people 2,000 years ago, would have seemed magical, and how we *explain* them in terms of our relationships with others — our membership, in other words, of social groups.

# Culture

Although we're all unique individuals — no two people, not even genetically identical twins, ever behave in exactly the same way — we live in social groups. We choose to live our individual lives in the presence of others, but and to live among and fit in with others, to be 'part of the group', we have to give up some aspect of our individuality. We have, in other words, to stop thinking as an individual ('what's best for me') and start thinking as part of a group ('what's best for us'), and in this idea we can see how to resolve the tension between 'the individual' on the one hand and 'the society' on the other.

We need to live with others to obtain the means to exist as individuals — initially basic things like food and shelter but, in time, the more sophisticated things (like cars, computers and mobile phones) that make our lives easier and more pleasurable. In this way we all 'strike a bargain with each other': by becoming part of a social group, or society, we give up some of our individuality in exchange for the safety and security that allow us to express our individual hopes, fears, ideas and beliefs.

This is where the concept of **culture** — something we can initially, if crudely, define as a 'way of life' characteristic of a particular society — comes into the picture. Culture represents the way social groups are organised around a set of broadly agreed shared beliefs and values.

# Defining culture

Taking a more sophisticated view, Nieto and Bode (2010) define culture as consisting of 'the values, traditions, worldview and social and political relationships created, shared and transformed by a group of people bound together by a common history, geographic location, language, social class, religion or other shared identity'. While this sounds rather complex, we can think about it in the following way:

> People see themselves as having things in common, such as where they live or religious beliefs. These things help to bind them as a group.
> Groups develop certain relationships, such as being family members, employees or teachers.
> These relationships express the things people value, their beliefs about the world (worldview) and the like.

Initially we can identify two *dimensions* to culture:

> **Non-material** (or **symbolic**) culture consists of the knowledge, beliefs and values that influence people's behaviour. In our culture, for example, behaviour may be influenced by religious beliefs, such as those of Christianity, Islam or Buddhism, and/or scientific beliefs — your view of human development, for example, has probably been influenced by Darwin's theories of evolution.
> **Material** culture consists of the physical things ('artefacts') produced by a society, such as cars, mobile phones and books. These reflect levels of cultural knowledge, aptitudes, skills, interests and preoccupations.

Apple

Mobile phones are now a common feature of British material culture

These dimensions are, of course, closely related. First, material culture is created by and from non-material culture; the mobile phone had to be invented and this required a range of cultural knowledge. Second, physical artefacts have cultural *meanings* for the people who produce and use them. They have, in short, **symbolic significance**: it may not be enough just to have a mobile phone; it may be necessary to have the latest, most up-to-date mobile on the market. This leads us towards the idea that our culture provides us with something more than just things to use: it gives us a range of attributes that shape both how we think about and behave in society.

Being born and raised in a particular culture doesn't just give us a certain standard of life; it also equips us with **cultural ideas and attributes**:

➤ **community** — the idea that we have things in common with others ('people like us')
➤ **history** — both social (how our society has developed over time) and personal (such as being part of a particular family group)
➤ **identity** — how we define ourselves as individuals and as members of a particular society (our cultural identity)
➤ **language**

These ideas lead us to three further aspects of culture:

➤ **Transmission**: Culture is passed from one generation to the next.
➤ **Change**: Cultures are constantly developing through exposure to new and different influences and experiences.
➤ **Variation**: There are also cultural differences between societies based on **time** (the same society considered at different points in its historical development) and **space**.

> **?** Briefly explain one cultural difference between the UK and France.

# The cultural framework

All cultures develop from the same basic building blocks — which is not to say that all cultures are the same. Rather, culture itself is always based on four fundamental ideas that give us a framework for cultural development: social roles, social status, values and norms. These are discussed in the sections below.

## Social roles

This refers to people 'playing a part' in society: just as an actor performs a role in a play, people take on and perform various roles (such as student, sister, brother, friend and employee) in their day-to-day life. Roles are a basic building block of any culture for two main reasons.

The first reason concerns **sociality**. Roles are always played in relation to other roles. For someone to play the role of teacher, for example, others must play the role of student. This demonstrates how roles contribute to the creation of culture; they demand both social interactions — people have to relate to each other in order to successfully perform certain tasks — and an awareness of others. A teacher, for example, must understand how and why they are performing that role in relation to the needs and requirements of students (such as helping them pass exams).

Normally when we play a role we find ourselves at the centre of a range of related roles — something that further extends the idea of cultural relationships because we become locked into a range of expected behaviours. This is called a **role-set**. A sociology student, for example, plays this role (slightly differently in each case perhaps) in relation to a range of roles of other people:

➤ other sociology students
➤ students studying other subjects
➤ sociology teachers
➤ other teachers
➤ caretaking staff
➤ administration staff
➤ parents or guardians

The second reason that roles are central to culture concerns **expectations**. Every role is identified by a name (or **label** — such as 'sociology student') and carries with it a sense of expected behaviour in any given social situation. A teacher, for example, is expected to behave in certain ways towards their students (and vice versa). These common expectations give a feeling of order and predictability to our relationships because role play is governed by certain behavioural rules (a **prescribed aspect** of a role — general beliefs about how you should behave when playing a role). As we'll see later, these rules involve **values** and **norms**.

In this way — through the roles we play, the range of people we play them with and the social expectations about behaviour that they involve — we become woven into a cultural web of relationships that brings a sense of predictability and order to our lives.

We can distinguish two **types of role**:

➤ **Achieved roles** are those we choose or are allowed to play — but we need to have done something to earn the right to play them. Someone might, for example, only be allowed to play the role of an 'A-level student' if they have the required GCSE qualifications, whereas playing the role of 'friend' will involve a quite different set of 'qualifications'.

➤ **Ascribed roles** are those we're given or forced to play by other (usually more powerful) people. An example might be the role of a son or daughter since it is a role 'chosen for us' by our parents.

Roles such as mother, father, daughter are all ascribed in our culture

As suggested above, role play is a source of order and predictability in our *cultural* relationships; through role play we establish some basic ground rules for people's behaviour (for example, I expect the checkout operator at my local supermarket to make me pay for the things I buy). Without them the social world would be a very confusing place — imagine a situation where you could not remember what your relationship to everyone around you was supposed to be.

One benefit of role play, therefore, is that once we've learnt what's expected of us in particular situations, we can use this knowledge whenever we play that role. Teaching and learning, for example, are made easier if both teacher and student behave towards each other in ways appropriate to their roles. It would be difficult to learn if the teacher was unable to stop students misbehaving.

Although roles are hugely useful to both the individual and society, we play so many of them simultaneously that there are occasions when they create problems. **Role conflict** occurs when the demands of one role prevent us from behaving in accordance with the demands of another role. Consider, for example, these two roles:

➤ a student role demanding you to be in class at 3 p.m. on a Friday
➤ an employee role demanding you to start work at 2 p.m. on a Friday

Role conflict occurs here because it's impossible to successfully combine these roles. If you obey the demands of the student role you cannot conform to the demands of the employee role (and vice versa).

## Social status

Social status refers to the 'level of respect' we're expected to give someone when playing a particular role. Different roles have different statuses, and different levels of status apply to different people within a **role-set** (the status of a student, for example, may be similar to that of other students in a class, but different from that of the class teacher). As with the concept of role, there are two basic **types of status**:

➤ **Achieved statuses** involve doing something to earn a particular position and level of respect. A teacher's status is initially earned, for example, because they have the required qualifications and training to play this role. Students will afford their teacher an initial level of respect based on this knowledge, although this may be modified through subsequent social interaction.

➤ **Ascribed statuses** are those given to you by others (whether you want them or not), such as a teacher's judgement about whether you are a 'good' or 'bad' student. Since the teacher is the sole judge here, the best you can do is try to influence their decision by your behaviour.

**?** Suggest one achieved and one ascribed status you currently hold.

Although status can be achieved in many ways in our society (from being rich and powerful to doing work that's useful and admired), it doesn't have a physical existence: we recognise it when we see it, but it's not something we can buy in the shops. We can, however, *demonstrate* its existence by using things that do have physical substance as **indicators**. For example, people use a range of indicators called **status symbols** (some of which can be bought in shops). These are objects that symbolise (or represent) social status. For example, a mobile phone functions partly to tell other people something about you (which may or may not be what you intended, depending on how fashionable or otherwise your choice of mobile).

## Values

Values have two important characteristics:

➤ They are beliefs about how something *should* be. For example, the belief that someone is 'innocent until proven guilty' is the expression of a value, as is the idea that 'a woman's place is in the home' (because it argues women *should not* go out to work). Values, therefore, reflect beliefs about matters like right and wrong or good and bad. In this respect, the strongest beliefs in any culture are **morals** — fundamental beliefs that are generally reserved for behaviours of which we strongly approve or disapprove.

➤ They are **general behavioural guides** because they reflect ideas about how people performing a particular role or living in a particular culture should behave. In an educational context, a teacher should teach their students, mark their work and so forth, while students should listen attentively, hand in work for marking and the like.

Values can be **cultural** (widely shared by the people of a specific culture) or **personal** (particular to an individual), an idea we can illustrate with the example of capital punishment:

➤ A widely held **cultural** value in our society is that people who commit murder *should not* be put to death by the state. This is reflected in the legal system, where capital punishment was abolished in 1965. In other societies (such as some US states and China, where capital punishment is still carried out) the reverse is true.

➤ On the **personal** level, many people in our society believe capital punishment for murder is right.

Personal and cultural values frequently coincide because the latter can influence the development of the former. For example, 'queuing in the supermarket' is a cultural value in our society (people should form an orderly queue when paying for things) and we're generally taught (or learn through experience) that it is expected behaviour when we play the role of customer.

Values, by definition, always involve *judgements* about behaviour (both our own and that of others). Whenever we express our values we're choosing to believe one thing rather than another.

## Norms

Norms are specific guides to our behaviour in that they indicate *expected* forms of behaviour in a given situation. Norms are closely related to both values and roles. While values tell us how something should be (people should form orderly queues when waiting to pay), norms tell us exactly how to express the value — people must stand in a line, one behind the other, and wait patiently to be served. If they don't (if they break or **deviate** from the norm by trying to push into the queue), they can expect to be punished (or 'negatively sanctioned'). Norms, therefore, are basic behavioural rules we use to perform roles predictably and acceptably. When playing the role of customer, for example, it is a norm in our society to queue to pay.

Norms, as Goffman (1959) suggests, are much more open to **negotiation** than either roles or values and this makes them more flexible behavioural guides that can adapt to changes in the social environment. People playing related roles, such as teacher and students, may be able to discuss the norms that will apply to their respective roles. For example, a teacher may allow students in their class to leave early if they have completed a set amount of work.

A further dimension to normative negotiation is that it's possible to play the same role (such as a student) differently in different situations, depending on how a teacher, for example, interprets the norms associated with this role. The teacher of one class may interpret the student role narrowly, enforcing all kinds of rules and restrictions (such as working in silence). The teacher of another class may interpret the role more broadly, allowing their students to behave in ways unacceptable to the first teacher.

We can further note that norms operate on two levels:

➤ **Informal norms** are used to guide individual behaviour when playing a particular role.

➤ **Formal norms** are usually expressed as laws — the strongest type of norm in any society.

Negative sanctions for breaking these norms are prosecution and/or a fine

TA Craft photography/Fotolia

**?** What are two norms associated with the role of 'student'?

# Types of culture

So far we've looked at culture in terms of a society having certain beliefs, values and norms that apply to the majority, if not all, of its members. While this is initially useful as a way of understanding the concept, we can develop these ideas by thinking about different **types of culture**, starting with the idea that groups within a society may develop quite distinctive roles, values and norms *not* shared by the majority.

## Subcultures

Subcultures are groups that exist within a large culture or society and have two main characteristics:

➤ **Distinctiveness**: Members share a distinctive set of roles, values and norms that are different in some way from those shared by the cultural majority. In our society, for example, we can identify a wide range of different subcultural groups such as football supporters, train-spotters and A-level students. The members of a subculture are not always wholly separated from wider cultural membership; rather, they tend to share features of the wider culture and can claim membership of both. It's unusual for subcultural groups to be wholly opposed to the norms and values of a wider culture, although they may distance themselves from these norms and values (as with some religious groups, such as Jehovah's Witnesses).

➤ **Identity**: Members have a sense of their own subcultural identity; that is, individual members partly define themselves in terms of their group membership ('I am an A-level student', for example) while also defining themselves in terms of wider cultural connections (such as family membership).

Sociologically, subcultural groups generally conform to one of two types: **reactive** (or **oppositional**) and **independent**.

## Reactive subcultures

A particular group of people come together as a reactive subculture when they develop norms and values that are both a response to and opposition against the prevailing norms and values of a wider culture. In other words, this kind of subculture develops when a group reacts to the actions of some other cultural group.

This type of development is common in schools, for example, where pupils form a subcultural group because of the way they are treated by teachers. Hargreaves (1967) found the boys in his study were labelled as failures on the basis of their poor academic performance; this gave them both a feeling of having things in common and something against which to react (being written off and disrespected by teachers).

Willis (1977) found a similar process at work among a small group of working-class boys who were similarly seen as failures by their teachers. The boys developed subcultural behaviours that gave them a sense of the status they were generally denied by the wider school culture. Their **reaction** turned to **opposition** through the development of a shared set of norms and values that stressed the importance of 'having a laff' and 'mucking about', and brought them into conflict with the school.

### Laddishness

More recently Jackson's research into 'laddish' behaviour has extended the above ideas. Jackson (2006) argues laddish behaviour is a defensive mechanism — adopted, initially, by some young males and, more recently, by some young females — that guards against the 'fear of failure'. Laddishness, in other words, is a **reaction** to what some pupils see as the overbearing demands of the education system.

Laddishness has, Jackson (2002) argues, three dimensions:

➤ overt rejection of academic work
➤ messing around in class
➤ prioritising social over academic pursuits

The rejection of academic work is a crucial component of laddishness because it allows 'lads' to behave 'in ways currently consistent with hegemonic forms of masculinity in their schools'. In other words, it's a valid way of behaving that has some resonance with both masculine peer group norms (that 'real men' don't have much time or need for academic work) and teacher perceptions (the idea that 'boys' education' needs to appeal more to masculine ideals).

Such behaviour does, however, 'provide an excuse for failure and augments success'. If boys fail academically they can claim it was because they 'couldn't be bothered'; if they succeed, their achievement is heightened because of the appearance of 'never having done any work'.

Jackson (2002) also argues that these specific 'protection strategies' developed for both psychological and sociological reasons:
➤ as protection of the lads' social worth (their standing in the eyes of their peers, for example)
➤ through fear of academic failure
➤ through fear of the 'feminine' (where educational success has come to be seen as a feminine quality — to succeed educationally becomes associated with a loss of male identity)

As Jackson (2003) argues,

> Fears of academic failure are relatively common in contemporary secondary schooling; the high value attached to academic ability combined with the current, regular, high-stakes ability testing programmes in schools is a potent recipe for fostering fears of academic failure. These fears may then prompt a range of defensive strategies that act to protect a student's self-worth by providing 'explanations' for academic 'failure' that deflect attention away from a lack of academic ability onto other, less damaging, reasons. For example, students can explain 'failure' in terms of lack of effort rather than lack of ability.

### Independent subcultures

An independent subcultural group forms around a particular set of **shared interests** (classic examples are hobby or leisure groups, such as train-spotters, joggers or dog owners). Group norms and values reflect the focus of the group's interest and will necessarily be different from those of the wider culture. However, the crucial difference from reactive subcultures is that such groups don't develop in reaction or opposition to other social groups or cultures (although their behaviour may, at times, bring them into conflict with the wider culture — as when a dog owner fails to pick up their dog's excrement). Usually, they simply reflect the interests and preoccupations of a distinctive group within a wider culture.

**?** Using an example to illustrate your answer, how do reactive and independent subcultures differ?

# Cultural diversity

'Diversity' means difference, and the existence of subcultural groups within a wider culture is one example of cultural diversity. However, we can expand this idea to think more widely about cultural differences within and between societies.

## Intercultural diversity

Intercultural diversity involves differences *between* societies. There are broad cultural differences between Britain and France, for example, in language, social history, and political organisation and representation (Britain has an unelected monarch as head of state, while France is a republic with an elected president). There are, of course, many further differences, ranging from the things we eat, through the cultural products (such as films, books and magazines) we create and consume, to the side of the road on which we drive.

Another example of intercultural diversity concerns **personal space**. In our society we like to maintain a circle of space that extends roughly 60 cm all around — and we feel uncomfortable if people enter this space uninvited. Although many other cultures have concepts of personal space, they differ from society to society. In Hungary personal space extends around 40 cm while in Argentina it can be so small as to be almost non-existent.

In the United Arab Emirates, holding hands is a sign of mutual respect

Another example concerns acceptable forms of touching. In Saudi Arabia it is a sign of mutual respect for a man to hold another man's hand in public. In Britain it would be assumed that the two men were (sexual) partners. In Uganda they would be arrested and imprisoned (homosexuality is a criminal offence).

## Intracultural diversity

Intracultural diversity involves differences *within* the same culture. Differences are found across a range of social categories (to be further considered when we examine the concept of **identity**): gender, region, age, class, ethnicity and sexuality.

### Gender

Males and females display wide differences in their cultural behaviours and tastes. McRobbie and Garber (1976) argue that female cultures are less socially visible than male cultures, mainly because of different **cultural attitudes**. Young female lifestyles, for example, are more likely to conform to the 'culture of the bedroom — experiments with make-up, listening to records [music], sizing up boyfriends', whereas young male lifestyles are traditionally played out in public (in the street, sometimes literally).

The development of home entertainment (through personal computers and consoles such as PlayStation and Xbox) has arguably diminished some of these differences — young male behaviour is arguably more home-centred now. However, gender differences exist in the use of these systems: boys generally prefer fast-paced action and fantasy gaming, while girls tend to be more involved in social networking and social gaming (Facebook games like Farmville). Alderman (2011) notes:

> Games companies are increasingly creating products aimed at older women, a demographic that tends to be more interested in simple 'casual' games, which can be played in short bursts and don't require too much attention...games are being sold as a way to relax, to indulge in 'me-time' and, above all, to connect with others. Farmville, with its extremely simple gameplay and emphasis on social connection, has tapped into this market.

## Region

Within Britain we can identify specific **national** cultures (English, Scottish and Welsh) based around a range of different traditions and customs. Although each nationality celebrates New Year's Eve, for example, the Scottish tradition of Hogmanay is a more involved celebration focused around friendship ('Auld Lang Syne') and good luck. The custom of 'first footing' involves being the first person after midnight on New Year's Eve to cross the threshold of a friend or neighbour's house carrying a symbolic gift, such as whisky or fruitcake.

Similarly, a range of **regional** cultures, such as Cornish, exist in Britain. Wood et al. (2006) note that:

> London is now more diverse than any city that has ever existed. Altogether, more than 300 languages are spoken and the city has at least 50 non-indigenous [non-British-born] communities with populations of 10,000 or more. Virtually every nation, culture and religion in the world can claim at least a handful of Londoners.

And London is not alone; they note that there are:
➤ 25,000 Indians in Leicester
➤ 600 Portuguese in Bournemouth and Poole
➤ 650 Greeks in Colchester
➤ 370 Iranians in Newcastle

Each of these cultural groupings contributes to the overall sense of diversity in Britain through the expression of their own particular traditions, beliefs, practices and lifestyles.

### Age

Youth lifestyles are more likely to be played out in public (pubs and clubs), whereas those of the elderly are generally played out in private (the home and family). There are a wide range of cultural differences among these groups based around **taste** — in music, clothing, activities and language, for example.

> **?**   Give two ways in which the cultural tastes of young and elderly males differ.

### Class

We can identify distinctive class groupings in our society (working, middle and upper classes, for example), each of which has particular cultural attributes and differences in areas like work, education and lifestyle:

- ➤ **Work**: Manual occupations (plumber, road sweeper) are largely working-class, while professional (non-manual) occupations (dentist, accountant) are middle-class.
- ➤ **Education**: Different classes have different levels of educational achievement. Middle-class children, for example, are much more likely to have a private education and attend university than their working-class peers.
- ➤ **Lifestyle**: Middle-class cultural lifestyles are more likely to include things like opera, theatre and fine dining; working-class cultural pursuits are more likely to include gambling (such as betting on horses), cinema and eating at McDonald's. While lifestyles are related to income derived from higher levels of education and work (we can note clear status differences here, with the middle classes in middle and senior managerial positions), they are also based on the idea of **taste** ('**taste cultures**' are explored in more detail later).

### Ethnicity

Ethnicity refers to cultural differences between social groups in areas like religion, family structures, beliefs, values and norms. As Winston (2005) suggests, ethnicity involves people 'seeing themselves as being distinctive in some way from others' on the basis of a shared cultural background and history. Song (2003) develops this idea to argue that an **ethnic group** is a group within a larger society that has a 'common ancestry' and 'memories of a shared past'; it has a sense of shared identity based around a variety of 'symbolic elements…such as family and kinship, religion, language, territory, nationality or physical appearance'.

Intracultural diversity

**G** ender
**R** egion
**A** ge
**C** lass
**E** thnicity
**S** exuality

   When we think about cultural diversity we tend to think in terms of different ethnic groups (such as English, Asian, Black African or Caribbean). This is certainly an important source of cultural diversity though not, as we've seen, the only source. We can further explore this form of diversity in terms of multicultural societies.

### Sexuality

We can identify different cultural groupings based on gay and lesbian identities and lifestyles. This could be further extended into areas like transvestism (wearing clothes traditionally associated with the opposite sex) and different types of sexual behaviour, both heterosexual and homosexual (such as sadomasochism).

# Multicultural societies

A multicultural society involves two or more different cultures. England, for example, contains a variety of distinctive cultural groupings — from English, Scots, Welsh and Irish, through Afro-Caribbean, Asian (e.g. Indian, Pakistani, Sri Lankan, Bangladeshi), East European (e.g. Polish, Romanian), West European (e.g. French) to Australian, Canadian and American. 'English society' can therefore be broadly characterised as 'multicultural' in the sense of containing a number of different and distinctive ethnic groups.

**Multiculturalism** is a related but slightly different concept that reflects a set of beliefs about the *relationship* between different ethnic groups within a society. A multicultural society can display a range of different relationships between ethnic groups, from:

➢ **domination** of one group over all others (in Saddam Hussein's Iraq, for example, the Kurdish minority was subjected to a variety of assaults, including a poison gas attack in 1988)

➢ **toleration** of some minority customs and traditions, but not others (France, for example, introduced a ban on women wearing niqab or burqa veils in public in 2011)

➢ **equality**, respect and tolerance between different groups ('**multiculturalism**')

Multiculturalism refers, therefore, to the idea that separate and distinctive cultures can coexist in the same society, such that each cultural grouping broadly retains those features — values, customs, traditions and so forth — that are a unique and distinctive part of their cultural background and heritage, while also being part of a much wider cultural grouping (or society).

Multiculturalism is a perspective (or **ideology**) that argues ethnic groups should be able to maintain their distinctive cultural attributes within a host society, with the different groups interacting with one another respectfully and peaceably (such as a predominantly Christian culture respecting the different religious traditions and behaviours of Muslim or Jewish cultures).

Multiculturalism in Britain has focused on what Favell (1998) suggests are a number of key political and legal features:

➢ **Managing** the relationship between majority and minority populations.

➢ **Encouraging** minority languages, religions and cultural practices.

➢ **Discrimination** on the basis of race being outlawed. In 1965, for example, the first Race Relations Act (there have been

Multiculturalism

**M** anaging
**E** ncouraging
**D** iscrimination
**I** ntegrating
**A** llowing

further Acts and Revisions) made racial discrimination on 'grounds of colour, race, or ethnic or national origins' unlawful 'in public places' (although shops were excluded at this time).

➤ **Integrating** various minority rights and freedoms into law, in areas like citizenship and freedoms relating to religious practice, political association and protest.

➤ **Allowing** and encouraging ethnic cultures and practices, such as religious festivals.

Manning (2011) summarises these ideas thus:

> The essence of multiculturalism is the idea that, if one makes immigrants feel welcome by allowing them to retain their culture and by seeking to address discrimination against them, they will reciprocate by embracing a British identity and the values needed for a harmonious society.

**?** What are three key political and legal features of multiculturalism in British society?

# Global culture

While we've largely concentrated on cultural diversity and multiculturalism in the context of *British* society, in the contemporary world we don't live in total isolation from other societies — and this has led to the idea that we increasingly experience and embrace a global culture.

The idea of **cultural globalisation** relates to the free and rapid movement around the globe of different cultural ideas, styles and products that can be picked up, discarded and, most importantly, *adapted* to fit the needs of different cultural groups. The variety of available cultural products (both material and non-material) is vast and people are no longer restricted to local or national cultural choices.

Cultural products are **malleable** (open to manipulation and change). In situations where people are exposed to a huge range of cultural influences and choices it is possible to develop a '**pick and mix**' approach to culture — choosing elements of one cultural tradition and mixing them with elements of one or more other cultures to create something new and different — a process called **cultural hybridisation**. In Britain, examples might include new forms of music, film, food and individuals:

➤ **Music**: Bhangra is Asian (Punjabi) music transformed into dance music that combines traditional rhythms and beats with Western electric guitars and keyboards.

➤ **Film**: Bollywood films combine traditional Asian stories and themes with the Western (Hollywood) musical tradition.

➤ **Food**: Britain's favourite dish — chicken tikka masala — is not authentically Indian in origin, but rather a hybrid of Indian and British cuisine.

➤ **Individuals**: Burke (2009) suggests children of parents from different cultures are culturally hybrid individuals.

Although global influences on local and national cultural behaviour aren't new (different cultural practices and products have influenced 'British culture' for many hundreds of years), the *scope and speed* of cultural diversity and change have indisputably increased over the past 25 years — a process hastened by technological developments such as cheap air travel, the telephone and the internet. What is more disputable, however, is the *direction* of change.

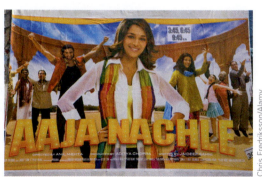

Bollywood films: a recent example of cultural hybridisation

Chris Fredriksson/Alamy

There are three general views about the nature and extent of global culture, which can be labelled 'different and mixed', 'similar *and* different', and 'disappearing'.

### 'Different and mixed'

This view suggests that the ebb and flow of different cultural ideas and influences creates **hybrid cultural forms** that represent 'new forms of difference'; culture is not simply something given to people but rather something actively constructed and reconstructed. **Globalised culture**, therefore, refers to the way local or national cultural developments can spread across the globe, being picked up, shaped and changed to suit the needs of different groups within and across different societies — and to how developments like the internet have changed the nature of cultural movements.

A good example is **social networking**. Internet sites such as Facebook (facebook. com), YouTube (youtube.com) and Flickr (flickr.com) are **social spaces** actively constructed and reconstructed by the people who use them — to share videos and pictures, play social games (e.g. Farmville, Mafia Wars) or connect with family and friends. An interesting aspect of this development is how the idea of **culture as a commodity** fits with the notion of freeing individuals to both produce and consume cultural ideas and products. While global commercial enterprises provide the tools through which cultural ideas and products can be exchanged, it's the millions of individuals around the world *using* these tools who provide the content that makes such virtual spaces vibrant and attractive, to both users and advertisers (Facebook, for example, registered its 500 millionth user in 2011).

### 'Similar *and* different'

The second view argues for:

> **Convergence and similarity** *within* global cultural groups: At the global level cultures are increasingly becoming much the same: sharing the same language (such as English), doing similar things (watching American films, visiting similar websites and using the same small number of networking sites) and consuming similar products (Big Macs, Pepsi or Coke).

➤ **Diversity** *between* such groups: Groups of like-minded individuals share certain cultural similarities across national boundaries, but these groups are potentially many and varied. Cultures come to resemble 'strands of influence'; some young people in Britain, Japan and India, for example, may develop **common cultural bonds** around sport, music or computer games, whereas others may develop cultural bonds based around Pokémon cards or manga comics.

Sklair (1999) suggests that to understand global cultures we need to think about two processes:

➤ **Localised globalism**: the idea that some forms of globalised culture are adapted and changed by particular (local) cultural behaviours. Regev (2003) argues that 'rock music' — a global product of American origin — is now consumed and filtered through many different cultural influences to produce new and different 'local varieties of rock'.

➤ **Globalised localism**: some features of local cultures (such as their uniqueness and individuality) become part of globalised cultures. Rather than seeing the globalisation of culture as making everything the same we should see it in reverse — globalisation involves the spread of different cultural ideas in ways that create new and diverse cultural forms.

An illustration here is the idea of **Disneyisation** — what Bryman (2004) calls 'the process by which the principles of the Disney theme parks are coming to dominate more and more sectors of American society as well as the rest of the world'. This involves the following closely related features:

➤ **Themes**: Different 'consumption experiences' are created. A burger in the Hard Rock Cafe probably tastes much the same as a burger from Planet Hollywood — what differ are the themed surroundings.

➤ **De-differentiation** (the removal of differences): Consumers are offered related products which provide a seamless 'lifestyle experience'. A particular perfume, for example, is associated with a particular style of clothing and footwear.

➤ **Merchandising**: By consuming cultural products people take 'themed lifestyles' into their homes and social groups.

While Disneyisation celebrates 'diversity' (in consumption, lifestyle, notions of 'freedom' and 'choice'), it invariably presents standardised, almost homogeneous, versions of these things (just as Disney World itself presents a rather sanitised version of 'the Wild West', for example).

### 'Disappearing'

The third view argues that the trend is for cultural differences to gradually disappear as all societies start to adopt ideas and attitudes broadly similar in style and content. Plumb (1995), for example, argues that culture has become a **commodity** for people to buy.

Lechner (2001) suggests that the economic behaviour and power of global companies (like Coca-Cola, Nike and McDonald's) create a **consumer culture** where standard commodities are promoted by global marketing campaigns to 'create similar lifestyles', an idea we can connect to **McDonaldisation**. Ritzer (1996) argues that contemporary corporate cultural products are standardised, homogenised and formulaic. Everyone who buys a McDonald's hamburger gets the same basic product, made to the same standard formula and tasting much the same; where Disneyisation seeks to create variety and difference, McDonaldisation focuses on

The taste and the experience are the same, wherever in the world it's consumed

likeness and similarity — and cultural products are increasingly predictable, safe and unthreatening.

Products must be created to appeal to the widest possible range of tastes across the widest possible range of cultures — from Britain to Bosnia and Bangalore. Berger (1997) characterises this as **McWorld Culture** — global (popular) culture is increasingly Americanised:

> Young people throughout the world dance to American music...wearing T-shirts with messages...about American universities and other consumer items. Older people watch American sitcoms on television and go to American movies. Everyone, young and old, grows taller and fatter on American fast foods.

However we actually theorise the precise impact of global culture on local (or national) cultures, its development pulls into sharp relief a distinction that's frequently made in our society between 'high' and 'low' (or 'popular') culture.

**?** List two ways people 'buy culture' in our society.

# High culture

This involves the idea that some cultural products and practices are **superior** to others: classical music, opera, the works of Shakespeare and so forth are high cultural forms whereas pop music, cinema and the works of J. K. Rowling (*Harry Potter*) or Stephenie Meyer (*Twilight*) are not. As Gans (1974) puts it, high culture relates to 'the art, music, literature, and other symbolic products that were (and are) preferred by the well-educated elite...[as well as] the styles of thought and feelings of those who choose these products — those who are "cultured"'.

This distinction also means that those who prefer high cultural products are 'superior' to those who do not: the 'cultured' (a relatively small, exclusive **elite**) have more refined tastes than those who are 'uncultured' (the **masses**). The elite see themselves as being at the very top of society. In the past they could separate themselves from 'the masses', who could be expected to 'know their place', and **status distinctions** between rich and poor, master and servant could be easily (if sometimes forcefully) maintained. Contemporary societies, however, give far greater opportunities (for example through mass education and the development of highly paid, high-powered professions) for the lower classes to work their way up the social scale (in both economic and political terms).

This increasing economic and political fluidity — making it possible for someone of lowly social origins to become hugely wealthy — leads to an **identity crisis** among elite groups; they are increasingly unable to maintain their sense of superiority over the masses on the basis of wealth and income, since these are something that 'anyone' can have. This is where 'taste' comes into play because, from this exclusive viewpoint, 'taste' can't be bought or learnt; it is something that, rather conveniently, is bred into an elite over many generations. In a society where it's increasingly difficult to maintain status distinctions on the basis of how one speaks, lives or dresses, differences can be maintained through the consumption of cultural products and ideas.

Katz-Gerro et al. (2007) suggest that this view of high culture sees societies as 'culturally stratified' in terms of a basic division between a small, cultured elite at the top and a large, **acultured** mass at the bottom ('acultured' meaning literally 'without culture' in the sense of not being able to appreciate high culture).

**Elite cultural identity**, therefore, is not only reflected in the things consumed, but also involves questions of leadership, since elites see themselves as 'determining what happens in society'. An elite group identifies those aspects of culture that are 'the best in thought and deed' (a judgement that happily coincides with the cultural products they consume) and separate them from (as they see it) the worthless, the mass-produced and the artificial.

By taking ownership of these cultural forms and elevating them to a position of cultural superiority, an elite group does three things:
➤ asserts its own cultural identity ('this is who we are and who you are not')
➤ establishes its **cultural hegemony** (leadership) over questions of taste (the elite decide what is high culture and what is not)
➤ creates a strong 'taste barrier' between an elite and the masses (most importantly, those of the latter who might aspire to elite membership)

> **?** Apart from those given in the text, suggest two examples of high culture.

# Popular culture

Giddens (2006) defines popular culture as 'entertainment created for large audiences, such as popular films, shows, music, videos and TV programmes' — the very opposite of high or elite culture. It is the **'culture of the masses'** — a term often used in a disparaging way to suggest a culture that is shallow, worthless and disposable. Popular culture is, however, a wide-ranging concept (it takes in a vast range of cultural ideas and products), and we can examine it using two contrasting viewpoints: critical and progressive.

### Critical view

This view sees popular culture as having the following characteristics:

➤ It is **manufactured**, in that it is created by 'culture professionals' (record and film producers, television executives and so forth) on an industrial scale; it is, in other words, **mass-produced** (the opposite of the 'individual crafting' of high culture). As Fiske (1995) argues: 'The cultural commodities of *mass culture* — films, TV shows, CDs, etc. are produced and distributed by an industrialized system whose aim is to maximize profit for the producers and distributors by appealing to as many consumers as possible.'

➤ It is also manufactured in the sense of being **artificial** (those who create it have no great interest or emotional investment in their cultural products) and formulaic — once a cultural product becomes a popular success the 'winning formula' is simply reproduced in order to churn out increasingly pale copies.

➤ It is **bought and sold**. It is a purely commercial enterprise — the only objective is to make money.

➤ It has **mass appeal**. Cultural products are aimed at the widest possible audience — not to enrich their lives but to achieve commercial success. In order to be as inclusive (and profitable) as possible these products must appeal to the **lowest common denominator** (LCD). To appeal to 'the uncultured masses', products have to be safe, intellectually undemanding and predictable — in other words, bland, inoffensive and simple to understand. Davis (2000), for example, notes that **high culture** is 'the preserve of very few in society' and that it involves 'art, literature, music and intellectual thought which few can create or even appreciate. **Popular culture**, by contrast, is regarded as the mediocre, dull, mundane entertainment to be enjoyed by uneducated and uncritical "low-brow" hordes'.

➤ It is **accessible**. Popular culture must be easy (and relatively cheap) to buy and easy to consume (in the sense of being intellectually undemanding).

➤ It is **transient**. If popular culture is to be accessible it must be undemanding, shallow and above all else entertaining — and so can't involve anything of lasting value.

➤ It is **disposable**. Where the objective is to make money, old cultural products have to be discarded and new products introduced in the constant search for profit. If high culture must be unchanging and challenging, because it represents the pinnacle of cultural achievement in a society, popular culture must be the reverse.

➤ Its consumers are **passive**. They play no part in its production; their role is simply to buy whatever is produced by culture professionals. 'The masses' are simply passive consumers of an artificial, disposable, junk culture.

Mass consumers, therefore, are seen as:

➤ **undifferentiated** — people like much the same kinds of things.

➤ **manufactured** — cultural tastes are created by the media.

➤ **uncritical** — audiences generally accept whatever they're given and choice is restricted to a narrow range of popular products.

➤ **uncreative** — popular culture is created by professionals, not consumers.

> **?** What are two features of popular culture?

## Progressive view

Technological developments such as personal computers, mobile phones and the internet have changed the way at least some elements of popular culture are characterised. Where the critical view sees mass audiences as 'willing dupes', the progressive view has a different take on the nature of audiences and the production and consumption of cultural products.

This view challenges some of the assumptions about **audiences** made by the critical approach by arguing that the audience for cultural products is:

➤ **differentiated** — rather than being a mass with similar tastes, audiences differ hugely in terms of their tastes.

➤ **critical** — audiences are active in seeking out new cultural products and increasingly selective of the cultural products they consume. Audiences don't just uncritically accept whatever 'culture professionals' serve up for popular consumption.

➤ **creative** — new digital technologies allow consumers to become producers. For example, a social network such as Facebook only exists because consumers create it through their day-to-day interactions.

A combination of simple-to-use technology and more critical and creative audiences has led to the development of contemporary forms of popular culture with three distinguishing features:

➤ **new places and spaces** for the production and consumption of popular culture, such as the World Wide Web.

➤ **fragmentation** — the audience for cultural products has fragmented into **niche consumers** with different tastes, desires and cultural motives. Fragmentation suits small-scale producers and consumers by providing markets for cultural products that are too small to be adequately (or profitably) addressed by commercial producers.

> **placelessness** — although audiences are fragmented, they are not necessarily small; the internet connects niche consumers to create a global mass that is 'placeless' in the sense that it only exists as a mass in cyberspace.

Whichever viewpoint you favour, it is clear that the development of global cultures has changed the way a mass consumer audience relates to cultural products. While elites have frequently used cultural products as symbols of both status and identity, global cultural development has created similar opportunities for 'the masses' through the agency of consumer culture.

**?** How are critical and progressive views of popular culture different?

## Consumer culture

Boris Roessler/dpa/Corbis

Boden et al. (2005) suggest that consumption involves ideas about 'how we shop, where our purchasing "needs" come from, how we treat the products we buy and how consuming shapes our lives'. The slogan 'I shop, therefore I am' neatly captures the flavour of the relationship between consumption, culture and identity.

**Consumption** (in the form of shopping) is culturally significant behaviour that has the added bonus of saying something important about — and perhaps actually defining — 'who we are'. The significance of **consumer culture** is, in this respect, twofold.

First, there has been a change in the nature of consumption in recent years, away from shopping as a 'chore' (something that is necessary, routine and mundane) and towards the idea of shopping as something we do for **pleasure** — a leisure and lifestyle choice.

Second, it expresses the idea that, in contemporary Western societies, we 'shop for **identities**'. The *objects* we buy or consume tell us something about who we think we are and want to be. **Conspicuous consumption** — buying things to use as a sign of higher social status — is also used to project an image about our identity to others. *Ideas* are also involved: as 'identity consumers' we have an expanding range of choices about 'who to be' and how to express our sense of self.

**?** Suggest two features of consumer culture.

Sangherd (2006) identifies some key features of consumer culture that can be related to identity in contemporary society:

➤ **Consumption** is the most important organising principle in society: everything, from work through education to family life, is related to the need and desire to consume.

➤ **Market** values (everything is a commodity, has a price and can be bought or sold) become the dominant values. Identities too become commodities to be worn, altered and discarded in favour of something new, different and more exciting.

➤ **Choice** — not just over what to buy but also 'who to be' — is seen as important. Identity construction becomes a private choice over which others have no control or input — society, in the shape of social identities, can no longer tell you your place in the great social scheme of things and expect to be obeyed. The consumer (or individual) is sovereign and identities are negotiated and negotiable.

➤ **Never-ending needs** are created. A consumer society continually changes; consumption feeds itself. Never-ending needs mean never-ending consumption, which means never-ending profits.

---

**Exam-style questions**

**1** Define the concept of status. Illustrate your answer with examples.    (8 marks)

**2** Outline and explain any two aspects of high culture.    (16 marks)

---

# Chapter 2

## The process of socialisation

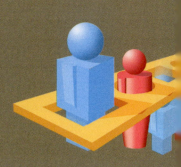

**By the end of this chapter you will be able to:**
- ➢ understand the process of socialisation and how it links to cultural formation
- ➢ identify and explain different types of socialisation (primary and secondary) and social control (formal and informal)
- ➢ explain the role of a variety of agencies in the socialisation process
- ➢ understand the difference between structure and action approaches and the different sociological perspectives that flow from this distinction

This chapter examines the question 'How is culture created?', first by outlining a non-sociological ('**nature**') approach and then by considering a general sociological ('**nurture**') approach focused around examining different **types** and **agencies** of **socialisation**. We will also examine a range of different **sociological perspectives** on cultural development, grouped in terms of **structure** and **action** approaches.

# Nature or nurture?

Personal experience shows that life is not simply a series of random, purposeless or unstructured events. Wherever we look we're surrounded by **patterns of behaviour** (in families, schools, workplaces, and so on). A **social institution** (such as the family, marriage or the education system) is defined as a 'pattern of shared, stable behaviour that persists over time'. The existence of **institutionalised behaviour** suggests it must have a cause — something that encourages people to behave in ways that are generally predictable on a day-to-day basis. We can predict, for example, that a certain percentage of people will go to school or to work each day.

While the existence of patterns of broadly predictable behaviour is a necessary component of culture, this doesn't explain *why* people act in predictable ways. We consider two possible explanations for this — one ('nature') non-sociological, the other ('nurture') sociological.

## Nature (instinct)?

One explanation is that human behaviour is guided by our genes. The idea is that human beings naturally have **genetic imperatives** (commands that cannot be ignored). In other words, people are born with certain instinctive abilities and capabilities, which are part of human nature.

At one extreme, **instincts** are seen as fixed human traits — things we are born knowing (such as a 'mothering instinct'). The cultural environment into which we are born plays little or no significant role in individual development.

A less extreme view is that people are born with certain **capabilities** that are realised through environmental experiences. Nature gives us 'strong hints' about cultural organisation, but people are free to ignore those hints. For example, if women have greater child-nurturing capabilities it 'makes sense' for them to take on a caring role within a family.

One problem with both views is that they suggest instinctive behaviour is somehow natural — that we are born with certain abilities we either have no choice but to use (instinct) or ignore at our peril (capabilities). But does the evidence of human behaviour actually support either of these positions? One way to test them is to look at feral children.

### Feral children

Evidence of human infants raised by animals 'in the wild' is rare and not always reliably documented (one exception being Saturday Mifune, discovered in 1987, aged 5, living in a pack of monkeys in South Africa). However, evidence of children raised with little or no human contact is more common. A well-documented example is 'Genie', a 13-year-old Californian girl, discovered in 1970. Pines (1997) notes that Genie had been 'isolated in a small room and had not been spoken to by her parents since infancy'. Although she 'seems to have been a normal baby...she was malnourished, abused, unloved, bereft of any toys or companionship'. The result of this experience was that, when found, 'she could not stand erect...she was unable to speak: she could only whimper'. Feral children are significant for two main reasons. The first concerns **development**. When children are raised by animals or in the absence of normal human contacts, they invariably fail to show the level of social and physical development we would expect from a conventionally raised child. For example, they do not develop the ability to talk.

The second reason concerns **recovery**. If behaviour was instinctive we would expect that, once a feral child had been returned to human society, they would relatively quickly and easily pick up those things we consider part of being human (talking, walking upright, eating with utensils and so forth). This, however, is not the case — and for this reason we have to look at a different form of explanation for the development of human cultures, based around the ideas of choice and diversity.

### Choice and diversity

Instincts, by definition, involve a lack of **choice**; their purpose, after all, is to create order by removing choice from our behaviour. Human behaviour, however, involves an almost limitless set of choices, some of which are fairly banal ('Should I do my sociology homework or play 'Call of Duty' on the PlayStation?') and some of which are not ('Should I buy or steal this PlayStation game?').

The fact that we can make behavioural choices contributes to the **diversity** of our behaviour: people develop different (or diverse) ways of doing things. Sometimes these are relatively trivial — Billikopf (1999), for example, found out the hard way that 'In Russia, when a man peels a banana for a lady it means he has a *romantic* interest in her' — but at other times they are more fundamental. Wojtczak (2009) notes that in Victorian Britain most women:

> ...lived in a state little better than slavery. They had to obey men, because in most cases men held all the resources and women had no independent means of subsistence... A woman who remained single could not have children or cohabit... Nor could she follow a profession, since they were all closed to women. Girls were barred from universities, and could obtain only low-paid jobs. Women's sole purpose was to marry and reproduce.

This is not a situation we would recognise in contemporary Britain.

These intercultural and intracultural comparisons are important because if human behaviour was simply based on instinct we would expect to see much the same sort of behaviour anywhere in the world and at any time in history. Sociologists, therefore, suggest an alternative explanation for human behaviour, based on the idea that 'culture isn't something we're born with, it is taught to us' (Podder and Bergvall, 2004).

**?** How do feral children illustrate the idea that human infants need to be socialised?

### Nurture?

For sociologists, culture is learned through **socialisation** — a process whereby we are taught the behavioural rules we need to become members of a particular culture. Sociological explanations for patterned behaviour, therefore, focus on culture as **learned behaviour**, for two reasons:

> ➤ **Shared rules**: To live in social groups people must define behavioural rules shared with others.
> ➤ **Flexibility**: The exact form of these rules differs from culture to culture, mainly because people live in different physical and social environments. Cultural rules, therefore, have to be sufficiently flexible to cope with these different environments (unlike instinctive behaviour).

# Types of socialisation

We can distinguish two broad types of socialisation: primary and secondary.

## Primary socialisation

Primary socialisation occurs, according to Cooley (1909), within **primary groups** that involve 'intimate face-to-face association and cooperation' and which are fundamental to the development of those behaviours we recognise as 'fundamentally human' (such as walking upright and talking). The first primary relationship we form is usually with our parent(s), followed by primary attachments to people of our own general age (our **peers**) and, subsequently, to other adults (such as work colleagues).

Primary socialisation is necessary because human infants require the assistance of other members of society to develop both as human beings and as members of a culture. We don't just need to learn 'general human behaviours', we also have to learn about social relationships, how to play roles and so forth. Primary socialisation within the family, for example, teaches us some of the basic skills and values we will need in adult life.

Most importantly, it does this in the context of a family group governed, according to Parsons (1951), by **affective relationships** (relationships based on love, affection, responsibility and duty), where mistakes can be made and lessons learned without too much harm being caused. Much of this type of learning is **informal** (there is no set curriculum for primary socialisation).

> **?** Name two things you were taught through primary socialisation.

## Secondary socialisation

Secondary socialisation involves **secondary groups** and is characterised, according to Berger and Luckmann (1967), by 'a sense of detachment...from the ones teaching socialisation' — it doesn't necessarily involve close, personal face-to-face contacts. One of its main purposes (or functions), Parsons (1951) argues, is to 'liberate the individual from a dependence on the primary attachments and relationships formed within the family group'. In other words, where the majority of people we meet are strangers it would be impossible and undesirable to treat them in the same way we treat people we love or know well.

For this reason we must learn how to form **instrumental relationships** — how to deal with people in terms of what they can do for us and what we can do for them in particular situations (the opposite of the **affective relationships** we find in primary groups). Berger and Luckmann (1967) suggest that, while primary socialisation involves 'emotionally charged identification' with people like our parents, secondary socialisation is characterised by 'formality and anonymity' — you don't, for example, treat a stranger who asks you for directions as your closest friend.

> **?**  Why do we have to be taught 'instrumental relationships'?

### Other types of socialisation

In addition to these two main types of socialisation, we can note some related forms that apply in certain situations:

> **Anticipatory socialisation**: It's quite rare to go into a social situation (such as a job interview) with no knowledge about that situation. Even if someone has no personal experience of job interviews they will be able to imagine what it involves (because they've read about other people's experiences, watched television programmes about interviews and so forth). An individual may, therefore, anticipate the demands of the role ('how to be an interviewee') and rehearse in their mind how to play the role correctly in normative terms — the appropriate way to dress, to talk and the like.

> **Resocialisation**: There are times when we have to learn to play new roles. For example, someone promoted to a position of authority over their former colleagues must learn how to deal with this change of situation — from being one among 'equals' to having to manage, organise and perhaps discipline people. A change like this can be a culture shock, which may be resolved by a resocialisation process, such as attending a training course on how to manage others. In some situations, such as joining the armed forces or going to prison, an individual is forced to undergo a radical form of resocialisation that Goffman (1961) calls **mortification**: they are subjected to procedures, such as being dressed identically, only being allowed to speak when spoken to by someone in authority, designed to kill off ('mortify') everything they've previously learned and taken for granted in their life prior to their new role. Once this process is complete the individual can be resocialised into the norms and values of their new role.

> **Developmental socialisation** reflects the fact that socialisation is a lifelong process — we are constantly being forced to adapt to changing situations and circumstances.

# Social control

Socialisation represents a way in which any society tries to bring order, stability and predictability to people's behaviour. If a child is socialised into a 'right' way to do something (such as eat with a knife and fork), there must also be a 'wrong' or 'deviant' way (such as eating with fingers) to be discouraged. Socialisation, in other words, involves **social control** — a relationship Pfohl (1998) characterises thus:

> Imagine *deviance* as noise — a cacophony of subversions disrupting the harmony of a given social order. *Social control* is the opposite. It labours to silence the resistive sounds of deviance…to transform the noisy challenge of difference into the music of *conformity.*

Social control has two related elements:

> **Rules**: Human behaviour involves a lifelong process of rule-learning. We may not always agree with those rules (nor always obey them) but we have to take note of their existence — mainly because rules, whether **informal** (norms) or **formal** (laws), are supported by sanctions.

> **Sanctions**: These are things we do to make people conform to our expectations. **Positive sanctions** (or rewards) are the nice things we do to make people behave in routine, predictable ways. Examples range from a smile, through words of praise and encouragement, to gifts and the like. **Negative sanctions** (or punishments) are the nasty things we do to make people conform. These range from not talking to people if they annoy us to putting them in prison. The ultimate negative sanction, perhaps, is to kill someone.

The distinction between formal laws and informal norms is mirrored by a distinction between formal and informal social control.

## Formal social control

Formal social control involves written rules:

> **laws** (legal rules) that apply equally to everyone in a society and cover both individual and organisational behaviour

> **organisational rules** (non-legal rules) that apply to everyone playing a particular role in an organisation (such as a school or factory)

Sanctions are enforced by:

> **agencies of social control** (such as the police)

> **agents of social control** — individuals (such as teachers) within each agency who take responsibility for social control

Table 2.1 outlines examples of legal and non-legal rules, control agencies and sanctions.

Table 2.1   Agency rules

|  | **Legal rules** | **Non-legal rules** |
|---|---|---|
| Examples | Theft<br>Assault | Dress codes<br>Attendance rules |
| Control agents | In contemporary societies law enforcement is carried out by government agents (such as the police or traffic wardens) and, in some cases, private agencies employed by the state. | Enforcement is the responsibility of those in a position of organisational authority (such as a teacher or employer). |
| Control agencies | The main agencies of formal social control in Britain are the police and the judiciary (the legal system), although the armed forces are, on occasion, used as formal control agents. Some private agencies supply prison officers. | These include any organisation — from businesses through schools and colleges to libraries and social clubs. |

| | **Legal rules** | **Non-legal rules** |
|---|---|---|
| Sanctions | Formal prosecution procedures that may entail arrest, charge and trial. Penalties for breaking the law vary depending on the nature of the offence: examples include fines, community orders, antisocial behaviour orders (ASBOs) and imprisonment. | Formal disciplinary procedures (that may involve verbal and written warnings). Sanctions vary between organisations: showing disrespect to a teacher might lead to detention; being disrespectful to an employer might lead to sacking. . |

Formal written rules and controls tell everyone within a group exactly what is and is not acceptable behaviour. Rule infringement ('deviance') brings with it the threat of formal sanction. While laws are applicable across the whole of a society (including organisations), organisational rules only apply when an individual plays a particular role within a group.

**?** Suggest some formal rules operating within schools.

## Informal social control

Informal controls similarly exist to reward acceptable behaviour or punish unacceptable behaviour. They cover a vast array of possible sanctions that may differ from individual to individual, group to group and society to society. Such controls relate to informal norms and may involve the use of ridicule, sarcasm, disapproving looks, personal violence and so forth.

Informal controls operate between people in everyday, informal settings, such as the family, and don't normally involve written rules and procedures. These controls work through **informal enforcement mechanisms**, their object being the type of informal normative behaviour we find between family members, friends or indeed strangers (for example when buying something from a shop).

Generally, informal social controls apply to the regulation of primary relationships and groups, although there are many exceptions to this rule (because primary relationships can occur in secondary groups). To take an exceptional example: calling your partner 'Honeybuns' may be perfectly acceptable in private; but if your partner also happens to be your employer, calling them 'Honeybuns' in front of work colleagues may not be considered acceptable.

Generally, informal social controls relate to 'unofficial rules' — the behavioural rules we create in informal groups. Although every social group is governed by norms, these can vary from group to group; while some might be generally applicable (punching people in the face is probably universally unacceptable — unless you're in a boxing ring, when such behaviour is encouraged), the majority are specific to particular groups. Swearing when with friends, for example, will probably not invite sanction; swearing at your mother or father might, however, invite negative sanction.

A further general aspect of social control is **self-control**. We don't need to be constantly told where behavioural boundaries lie because we learn the norms that apply in certain situations and what will happen if we deviate from them. If you continually skip your sociology class you may be asked to leave the course and, since you don't want this to happen, you (indirectly) control your behaviour to obey the norm.

> **?** What informal rules operate within the family or the school?

# Agencies of socialisation

In this section we will take a more detailed look at the organisation of cultural behaviour through a variety of **primary** and **secondary agencies of socialisation**.

## Primary agencies

**The family** is one of the most influential socialising agencies in any society and the main agents are parents, although immediate relatives such as brothers and sisters and less immediate relatives such as grandparents may also be involved. We can consider the family in terms of roles, values, norms and sanctions.

A family — one of the most important socialising agencies

**Roles**: The relatively limited range of roles within the family (both for adults and children) hides a complexity of **role development** (how roles change depending on the way a group develops — something that may involve **resocialisation processes**). Adults, for example, may learn roles ranging from husband or wife to parent or step-parent while children have to come to terms with being a baby, infant, child, teenager and, eventually perhaps, an adult with children of their own.

**Values**: Parents represent what Mead (1934) calls **significant others** — people whose opinions we respect and value deeply — and they are influential in shaping both our basic values, such as manners and moral values, such as the difference between right and wrong.

**Norms**: Although these differ between families, basic norms normally taught within the family include, for example, how to address family members (Mum, Dad); when, where and how to eat and sleep; and definitions of 'good' and 'bad' behaviour.

**Sanctions**: These are, as we've seen, mainly informal. **Positive** sanctions range from facial expressions (smiling) through verbal approval or reinforcement ('You are a good boy/girl') to physical rewards (such as gifts). **Negative** sanctions are similarly wide-ranging — from showing disapproval through language (shouting at someone) to physical punishment.

To some extent children are socialised by copying behaviour. For example, Hartley (1959) argues that **imitation** of adult family behaviours (e.g. girls 'helping mum' with domestic chores) is a significant part of a child's socialisation. However, while we often see primary socialisation as a one-way process (from parents to children), socialisation is generally more complicated than simply teaching behaviour that is then adopted without question. Children are also actively involved in negotiating, to some extent, their socialisation: for example, they don't always obey their parents. They may also receive **contradictory socialisation** messages from differing agents — another relative may reward behaviour a parent would punish.

> **?** Suggest two values people are taught within the family group.

## Secondary agencies

Secondary socialising agencies include schools, religious organisations and the media; agents include teachers, priests, television personalities and pop stars. In some cases, such as in school, we are in daily, face-to-face contact with the people socialising us, without ever developing a primary attachment to them. In others, such as admiring a particular actor or musician, we may never meet them yet are influenced by their appearance or what they say and do.

Below we will look at secondary agencies of socialisation within education, the media, religion, peer groups and the workplace.

### Education

School is one of the first times children in our society are separated from their parent(s) for any length of time and it provides both opportunities (to demonstrate your talents to a wider, non-family audience) and traumas — in learning how to deal with people who are 'not family' or **authority figures** such as teachers.

**Behaviour**: One function of education is to teach things required for adult life. These include:

➤ knowledge — for example of history (giving us a sense of our society's past) and geography — of both our own and other societies
➤ skills, such as learning to read and write or solve mathematical problems

In addition to the **formal curriculum** (the subjects we go to school to learn) children are also exposed to a **hidden curriculum** — what Jackson (1968) called the things we learn from the experience of attending school (such as how to deal with strangers and deference to adult authority).

**Roles**: A number of roles are played within the school (such as teacher and pupil) and these, as we've seen, fit into a range of further roles that are part of a teacher's or student's **role-set**.

**Values**: Schools project a range of values, from the idea that pupils should work hard to achieve qualifications to a range of ideas about:

- individual competition for academic rewards
- conformity to authority (not questioning what is being learnt and why it is necessary to learn it)
- achievement on the basis of merit ('you get what you deserve')

**Norms**: Bowles and Gintis (2002) argue for a correspondence between school norms and workplace norms: 'Schools prepare people for adult work rules by socialising people to function well, and without complaint, in the hierarchical structure of the modern corporation.' This **correspondence theory** is evidenced through school norms like the daily need to attend and register and the right of those in authority to give orders they expect will be obeyed.

**Sanctions**: Positive sanctions include the gaining of grades, qualifications and prizes, as well as more personal things like praise and encouragement. On the negative side, teachers use sanctions like detentions, suspensions and exclusions; failure to achieve qualifications or gaining a reputation for 'stupidity' also function as negative sanctions, at least from the viewpoint of teachers, if not always from that of the pupil.

**?** What is the difference between the formal school curriculum and the hidden one?

### The media

This is a slightly unusual secondary agency because our relationship with it is impersonal; we may never actually meet those doing the socialising.

**Behaviour**: There's very little hard evidence that the media have a direct long-term effect on behaviour, although there may be short-term effects — advertising, for example, aims to make short-term changes in our behaviour by encouraging us to try different consumer products. Potter (2003) suggests that **short-term effects** include:

- **learning**, when we are introduced to novel ideas and places
- **imitation**, such as copying behaviour seen on television
- **desensitisation**, whereby our emotional reaction to something (such as violence or poverty) is lowered through constant and repeated exposure

Media effects

**S** hort-term
**L** earning
**I** mitation
**D** esensitisation

There is stronger evidence for *indirect* long-term effects. Chandler (1995) argues that 'Television has long-term effects, which are small, gradual, indirect but cumulative and significant.' **Long-term effects**, according to Potter (2003), include the following:

- **Consumerism**: Repeated exposure to affluent lifestyles and desirable consumer goods suggests 'happiness' is something that can bought.
- **Fear**: 'Heavy exposure to negative and violent' media leads some people to overestimate things like the extent of crime and their likelihood of being a victim.
- **Agenda-setting**: Philo et al. (1982) argue that the media determine how something will be debated (for example, immigration is currently framed and discussed in

terms of numbers of immigrants, and Islam is frequently discussed in the context of terrorism).

**Values**: The extent to which the media can *impose* its values on our behaviour is uncertain, but it does represent a potentially powerful force in terms of supporting or marginalising certain values. For example, the media have a (loud) voice in debates over nationality (what it means to be 'British'), and many English newspapers take an anti-European Union stance. Potter (2003) suggests that this involves a process of **habituation** — the more we are exposed to certain images and ideas, the greater the likelihood we will incorporate them into our personal value systems.

**Norms**: The media have what Durkheim called a **boundary marking** function; they publicise acceptable and unacceptable forms of behaviour to reinforce perceptions of expected behaviours. This idea does, of course, work both ways — the media can try to preserve particular ways of behaving (through anti-paedophile campaigns, for example, that highlight 'abnormal sexuality' and, by so doing, underline 'normal sexualities') or promote changes in behaviour (e.g. through campaigns against racism).

**Sanctions**: Positive sanctions involve the use of praise, flattering pictures and uncritical treatment, whereas negative sanctions may involve the use of unflattering pictures, criticism or public ridicule.

### Religion

Whether or not we see ourselves as 'religious', religious institutions have played — and continue to play — a significant role in the general socialisation process in our society.

**Behaviour**: Religions play an important indirect socialising role in terms of both influencing general social values ('Thou shalt not kill') and performing certain ceremonial functions (such as marriages, christenings and funerals).

**Values**: Many of our most important **moral values** have been influenced by religious values; many of the Ten Commandments of Christianity, for example, are reflected in our legal system. In terms of moral beliefs, few people would argue you should be allowed to kill people or that theft is desirable.

**Sanctions**: In some respects the power of religions to apply positive and negative sanctions probably turns on the extent to which you are a believer in the god — or gods — being promoted. Hinduism, for example, involves a belief in reincarnation (once you die you are reborn into a new life) based on how well you observed religious laws in your previous life; the reward for good behaviour in one lifetime is being reborn into a higher social position. Similarly, Christian notions of sin can be significant in religious control.

### Peer groups

'Peer group' typically refers to a group of people of a similar age (although friends can usually be included among our peers). Peer groups can exert considerable socialising influence.

**Behaviour**: Peers are influential on both a *primary* level (close friends, for example, who influence what we wear or how we behave) and a *secondary* level (as a **reference group** — what Hughes et al. (2002) call 'the models we use for appraising and shaping our attitudes, feelings and actions'). In both cases, peer groups provide 'both normative and comparative functions' — the former in terms of direct influences on our behaviour and the latter in terms of how we compare ourselves with others, such as friends or people we see on television. This illustrates **peer pressure** as a form of social control.

**Roles**: We play a range of peer-related roles, depending on our age group and situation. 'Friend', for example, expresses very personal role play, whereas at school or work we may have a variety of 'acquaintances'. In the workplace we are also likely to play the role of 'colleague' with at least some of our peers.

**Values**: The values we're taught within a friendship or peer group vary with age and circumstances. However, something like the value of friendship will probably be carried with us throughout our life.

**Norms**: Peer group norms involve issues such as age-appropriate behaviour. Young children, for instance, are not allowed to smoke or buy alcohol. Conversely, it's generally not considered age-appropriate for the elderly to take part in extreme sports or wear clothes considered more appropriate to younger age groups.

**Sanctions**: These are informal and the norms of different peer groups can vary considerably. The same behaviour in different situations may also produce different responses. Swearing at your grandmother, for example, will probably be met with disapproval, whereas swearing in the company of friends may actually be a norm. Approving gestures and language, laughing at someone's jokes and seeking out their company may represent positive sanctions; refusing to speak to someone, rejecting their friendship and physical violence are negative sanctions.

> **?** How is people's behaviour shaped by their peers?

### The workplace

Although the workplace has primary socialising elements, such as the relationship between close colleagues, it also has important secondary characteristics.

**Roles**: The two main workplace roles of **employer** and **employee** hide a range of differences in terms of how such roles are performed; an employee may be a professional worker (such as a lawyer) with an associated high status or they may perform a low-skill, poorly paid role with few, if any, prospects. A professional employee may also occupy a position of trust and responsibility that involves controlling the behaviour of other employees, whereas a casual manual labourer or shop assistant may experience high levels of boredom, frustration and control by others.

**Values**: One clear work-related value concerns **payment** — we should get money in exchange for our labours. Less obvious values include competition and the belief that hard work and competence should be rewarded by promotion, increased responsibility, control over the working environment and so forth.

**Norms**: We expect to be paid for work, although some types of work, like housework and voluntary work, don't involve money. Similar norms to those in the education system apply here — attendance, punctuality, obedience and the like.

**Sanctions**: Employers have a range of positive sanctions at their disposal — pay increases, more responsibility, freedom (to work from home or at your own pace, for example) and control over both your working day and the work of others. On the other hand, disciplining, demoting or sacking someone constitutes the main negative sanctions available.

> **?** Suggest one value we learn in the workplace and one norm associated with that value.

# Sociological perspectives

In the 'nature–nurture' debate sociologists come down squarely in favour of the latter; human behaviour is built around a combination of **structures** (such as families and education systems) and **choices** (whether to have children, how to raise them and so forth). On the one hand social structures clearly place limits and restraints on our individual behaviours (we all, for example, have to attend school between the ages of 5 and 16), while on the other hand the choices we make (such as bunking off school) are also a significant part of 'being human'.

These two behavioural dimensions are also important within sociology itself, with some sociologists arguing that **social structures** are the most important influence on our behaviour and others arguing that **social actions** (how and why we express individual choices) are more significant. It would, therefore, be useful to outline these two general positions.

## Social structure

It sometimes helps to visualise social structures as a '**framework of rules**' — a rule being something you're supposed to obey and a framework being the way such rules are created, maintained and policed. We can illustrate this general principle by thinking about how everyday behaviour is governed by laws — we can talk about a *legal framework* (or structure) involving:

> politicians making laws (formal, legal rules)
> police enforcing these rules
> judges deciding whether you've broken the law
> prisons in which to lock up the guilty

This is a useful way of visualising the concept of a social structure, for a couple of reasons:

➤ Even though we may never 'break the law', this doesn't mean our behaviour isn't influenced by legal rules; we may *choose* not to break the law precisely because we understand the possible consequences.

➤ Although 'legal rules' have no physical existence (we can't see, smell or touch them), we know they exist because we experience their *effect* if we're caught breaking the law.

If you think about the different ways behaviour is governed by norms, the idea of a social structure should become a little clearer. As we've seen, every relationship involves:

➤ role play
➤ values relating to the role
➤ norms expressing a value

Every time we play a role, therefore, we experience (however unwittingly) the effect of social structures — rules that shape our behavioural choices.

## Social action

The social action perspective focuses on our ability to make behavioural **choices**. Just as we make choices about our friends, so too, ultimately, we make choices about the rules we obey or disobey — although, because social structures exist, there will be punishments (negative social sanctions) for choosing to disobey. Regardless of how social structures try to influence our behaviour, we always have a *choice*. To put this another way, our behavioural choices are potentially unlimited — we can act in whatever way we choose.

However, by and large, we don't. Most of us follow 'the rules' most of the time and this is because our *actual* behavioural choices are limited by the effects of social structures — by the framework of cultural rules that make group behaviour possible.

We can understand these ideas a little more clearly by thinking about society as a game, such as chess:

➤ **Structure**: Chess, like a society, has certain *physical boundaries* (the playing area). It also has *rules* governing how it's played: these are both *technical* (relating to the basic mechanics of the game: the starting position of each piece, how different pieces are allowed to move, taking it in turn to move) and *cultural* (it's a competitive situation, the objective being to beat your opponent). This is the basic *framework of rules* (social structure) within which the game is played.

Society, like the game of chess, has a framework of rules

> **Action**: Each player is free to choose their particular *strategies* and *moves*, based on an assessment of how to successfully play to win.

In chess, therefore, structure and action combine in the sense that each player's behaviour (action) is limited, in some ways, by rules and conditions:

> **Rules**: If one player decides to break the rules, their opponent will react to this deviant act (by protesting or refusing to continue playing).

> **Conditions**: Each player must, in this competitive environment, take note of how their opponent is playing — by responding to certain moves or moving in ways that produce particular responses from their opponent.

Structure and action are both important, in terms of understanding the relationship between society and the individual, and complementary. Just as we can't imagine society without individuals, we can't think about people without society. Ideas about structure and action are, therefore, fundamental to sociologists — but the question is, which is more important: the structures that influence actions, or the actions that create structures?

**?** What are two differences between social structural and social action approaches in sociology?

# Structure perspectives

For sociologists who take a structure perspective, society is, as Jones (1985) argues, 'a structure of (cultural) rules', telling us how to behave appropriately in any given situation, and what to expect in terms of others' behaviour. Individual behaviour is considered relatively unimportant — structuralists are not really concerned about why some individuals don't like going to school; all that really matters is that enough people do go to school. This perspective (or way of seeing the social world) takes two different forms: consensus and conflict.

## Consensus perspectives

The focus here is on how social order is created and maintained through agreement (by developing shared norms and values). One of the main consensus perspectives is **functionalism**.

### Functionalism

Functionalists explain how **social order** and **stability** are created and maintained by looking at how societies are organised at the level of the **social system** (sometimes called the 'systemic level of analysis').

This involves the idea that the various parts of a society (family, education, work and so forth) work in harmony, such that each part is dependent on other parts of the system. This idea is expressed using an **organismic analogy** (society is like a human body). The different parts of the human body are interconnected — the heart, lungs, brain and so forth work together to form something greater than the sum of their individual parts (a living body). In a similar way, the interconnected parts of a society work together to form a social system. Just as a human body has vital organs that, if damaged, can lead to death, so, according to Parsons (1937), does society.

Just as the human body requires the various organs of the body to be connected and working together (the heart pumps blood containing oxygen to the brain and so forth), a functioning social system requires connections between its various 'parts', such as the family, school, work and government, on the basis of **purpose and need**. Social systems fit together on the basis of *institutional* purposes and needs.

For example, for a *family institution* to exist (and perform its *functions*) its members *need* to survive. The *work institution* performs this function by allowing family members to earn the money they need to buy the food (among other things) they consume; conversely, to fulfil this *purpose*, work *needs* families to produce human beings who understand cultural rules; in more complex societies, such as contemporary Britain, an *education system* is also needed to provide the skills, such as literacy and numeracy, required by more advanced work processes.

For these reasons, functionalism focuses on **consensus**; each part of society must work in cooperation with other parts. Everything that exists, therefore, has both *purpose* (what it exists to do) and *needs* (things it requires from other parts of the system to fulfil its purpose or functions).

Functionalists like Parsons (1937) explain how individuals fit into the overall structure of society on the basis of **functional prerequisites** — the things that *must* happen if society is to function properly. For individuals to survive and prosper they need to be part of larger cooperative groups — they must *combine* to solve a number of fundamental problems. Every social institution (such as an education system), therefore, must develop ways (through roles, values, norms and rules) of ensuring that individuals conform to the needs of both institutions and society as a whole.

Social institutions, therefore, can only function if people do not simply pursue their own individual self-interests; if millions of individual human beings did that, things would fall quickly apart. We must, therefore, be compelled to behave in ways that are reasonable, consistent and broadly predictable if societies are to function for the overall benefit of everyone.

**Socialisation**, from this perspective, serves a number of purposes for both the individual and society:

➤ **Culture**: People are born into a culture that they must learn in order to take their place in society and, by so doing, contribute to the continued functioning of that society. Socialisation, from this viewpoint, is the 'process of acquiring culture'.

➤ **Participation**: The individual must learn the general and specific roles, values and norms required for full participation in the political, economic and cultural life of the society in which they live.

> **Primary socialisation** is normally taught in the family group, where the individual learns the behaviours expected from them in a generally supportive environment. Primary relationships in the family are based on affection (**affective relationships**) and involve close, personal relationships, such as those between children and parents, siblings and so forth.

> **Secondary socialisation**: In contemporary societies we have to learn how to deal, dispassionately, with people who are 'not family' and with whom we are not particularly close. For functionalists this involves learning secondary or **instrumental relationships** through socialising agencies such as schools or the workplace.

> **?** How is society like a living organism?

### Evaluation

> **Social change**: It's difficult to explain why anything in a society should change if it already performs an essential function. In this respect, functionalism is often seen as a politically conservative perspective that lends its support to the status quo (the desire to 'keep things as they are').

> **Dysfunction**: Functionalists place too much emphasis on the beneficial aspects of social institutions and downplay dysfunctional tendencies (things that can be damaging to the individual or society). Schools, for example, may be places where children learn many useful things — but they're also places where bullying, sexism and racism can exist.

> **Tautology**: This a statement that contains its own proof and functionalists are sometimes accused of producing such arguments to justify their ideas. For example, the claim that 'If something exists in society, it has a function' is supported by the argument that 'It has a function because it exists'. A tautological statement, in other words, cannot be disproved.

## Conflict perspectives

For the conflict perspective, societies are generally stable and orderly because powerful groups impose their ideas on other groups (the powerless). Therefore, conflict theorists argue, some groups benefit from the maintenance of the status quo far more than others. Below we discuss two types of conflict perspective: Marxism and feminism.

### Marxism

The fundamental conflict from this perspective is different economic groups (**social classes**) constantly battling against each other. For Marxists work is the most important form of activity in any society because other social activities (politics, family, culture and the like) can only exist if people have first secured the means for survival (if you don't have enough to eat or a roof over your head, then the lack of interesting television programmes is not going to be your most pressing concern). Thus, how work is socially organised (who does it, what they do and who benefits from it) is the key to understanding how all other social relationships are organised.

*Conflict*

The workplace is a key area of conflict because of how it is organised. Marxists argue that, in our capitalist society, the '**means of economic production**' (things like factories, machinery and land) are owned by one **class** of people (the **bourgeoisie** or ruling class). The vast majority of people own little or nothing, and so are forced to sell the one thing they do have — their ability to work (their '**labour power**'). This creates a situation where:

➤ a small number of people own the means of production — in capitalist societies they become very rich because they keep **profits** made from producing goods and services

➤ a large number of people own nothing but their ability to work for wages — these people (the working class or **proletariat**) are relatively poor (when compared with their bourgeois employers)

Conflict occurs in this type of society because:

➤ owners want to keep as much of their profit as possible (the less you pay in wages, the more you have to buy desirable things)

➤ non-owners want a larger slice of the economic pie. The working class also want the desirable things society has to offer — it's in their interests, therefore, to demand more from employers.

*James Boardman/Alamy*

*Competition*

Competition is not merely encouraged in capitalist societies; it is also considered desirable since it's through competition, capitalists argue, that wealth is created and

Strikes are one form of economic conflict

progress made (through the constant invention of new ways of doing things, for example). Competition — between businesses for customers or workers for jobs — also inevitably leads to conflict. With competition there will always be winners and losers. Although, for Marxists, economic competition and conflict are most significant, competition occurs throughout society — between businesses, different groups of workers, men and women, and so on.

*Social class*

Social class involves grouping people according to their 'relationship to the means of production'. As we've seen, two basic classes exist in any capitalist society:

> the **bourgeoisie** (the ruling or upper class) — those who own the means of production
> the **proletariat** (the lower or working class) — people who own nothing but their ability to work

The picture is not as simple as this, of course; there can be many different relationships to the means of production — managers (sometimes called the middle class or petit bourgeoisie) may not own a business but they belong to a different social class from non-managers.

*Power*

Given the emphasis on conflict, you could be forgiven for thinking our society is engaged in a war of all-against-all; this, however, is clearly not the case. Marxists explain this by suggesting that those at the 'top' of society (the ruling class) are not only **economically powerful**, but also **politically powerful**: they control how laws are made (through politicians identifying with the interests of a ruling class) and they can use force (the police and the army, for example) to minimise conflict. Althusser (1968) characterises these methods of social control as '**Repressive State Apparatuses**' because they are a way of compelling people to conform.

A ruling class is also able to influence how people generally *think* about the social world through their control of **ideological institutions** (such as the media and the education system) that deal in ideas (what Althusser calls '**Ideological State Apparatuses**').

**Socialisation** from this perspective involves looking at how individuals are socialised into roles and behaviours that help to maintain and reproduce capitalist societies and economic relationships:

> **Culture**: Like their consensus counterparts, conflict theorists note the various processes of primary and secondary socialisation involved in 'learning the culture' of the society into which people are born. For Marxists, however, the difference is not so much in the nature of the process (learning certain roles, values and norms, for example) as in the ultimate objective.
> **Objective**: People are not simply socialised 'into society'; rather, they are socialised into their particular place in society. A working-class child will, for example, experience a different form of primary and secondary socialisation from an upper-class child. For Marxists, therefore, the primary purpose of socialisation is to reproduce capitalist social relationships (future owners, managers and workers).
> **Participation**: The role of socialisation is to control how future generations are raised to replace those who have died or who are too old or sick to work. People must be taught to respect:
>   > **processes** — such as the rule of law or the way political leaders are elected
>   > **ideas** — such as the notion that social inequalities are not only acceptable but desirable

? How do those who 'own the means of production' and those who do not differ?

## Evaluation

- **Conflict**: Marxism overstates the level of conflict in society and underplays the significance of non-economic types of conflict (gender or ethnic conflict, for example). Some feminists (see below) are especially critical of the emphasis on work-based conflicts.
- **Communism**: Class conflict can only end once capitalism is replaced by communism — a type of society where work is not organised around private profit. Whatever the shortcomings of capitalist societies, communism does not appear imminent.
- **Economic determinism**: Marxism assumes work is the most important institution in any society. While this may (arguably) have been true in Britain in the past, some writers (especially postmodernists — see below) argue this is no longer the case. They question both the significance of social class as a source of people's identity and, consequently, the view that class conflict is the key area of conflict in any society.

## Feminism

This conflict perspective has a number of varieties: we'll look at liberal, Marxist and radical feminism, and at post-feminism. One theme common to most varieties is the belief that society is **male-dominated** — that the interests of men have always been considered more important than the interests of women.

## Liberal feminism

The key ideas of liberal feminism are as follows:

- **Equality of opportunity**: Liberal feminists are mainly concerned with equal opportunities for men and women (not 'equality', as such, but the chance to compete equally with men); in broad terms, they want an end to **sexual discrimination**.
- **Legal reform**: Liberal feminists have been active, in Britain and America for example, in promoting a range of **anti-discriminatory laws** which, they argue, are needed to redress the historical gender imbalance. UK examples include the Equal Pay Act (1970) and the Sex Discrimination Act (1975; updated in 2003), which made discrimination in the workplace illegal.
- **Dual role**: The situation where women increasingly play a dual role (as both carers within the family and paid employees) is seen as a major area of inequality that needs to be addressed, by changing male attitudes to family life and through the continued development of anti-discriminatory laws and practices, such as the introduction of child-care facilities for working women, maternity and paternity leave, and so forth.

Liberal feminism
**O**pportunity
**L**egal
**D**ual role

*Criticisms*

➤ **Status inequality**: Legal equality is not the same as status equality (women having equal status to men). Women are still treated in ways that assume they are inferior to men; in Britain, for example, women can expect to earn, on average during their working lifetime, 70–80% of male income — even when they do comparable work.

➤ **Class differences**: By lumping all women together as a 'class', liberal feminism ignores differences in life experiences. Working-class women don't have the same advantages as upper-class women — they face far greater difficulties in securing equal opportunities. In addition, black women, in general, have different life experiences and chances from white women.

> **?** Do men and women have equality of opportunity in our society?

*Marxist feminism*

This applies Marxist ideas to gender relationships and involves the following key ideas:

➤ **Class inequality**: Marxist feminists see class inequality as the main cause of female oppression, exploitation and discrimination. In a competitive, capitalist society men are encouraged to exploit any 'weaknesses' in women's market position (the fact that women may be out of the workforce during and after pregnancy, for example) to their own advantage.

➤ **Patriarchal ideology** (ideas that support male domination of women): Although patriarchy is an important concept, Marxist feminists use it to show how the social and economic exploitation of women is justified (by both men and women) through powerful ideas about masculinity and femininity. Ideas of men as 'natural breadwinners' and women as 'natural homemakers' can be strong influences on people's behaviour.

➤ **Social class**: Men and women are not separate (sex-based) classes; upper-class women, for example, have very little in common with working-class women apart from being biologically female. Men and women have a common interest in creating a form of society (communism) in which all are treated equally.

➤ **Gender socialisation**: Patriarchal ideas, attitudes and practices (such as sexual discrimination) are the product of cultural differences in the way males and females are raised. Men are not naturally exploitative of women; rather, it is the economic system (capitalism) that encourages and rewards sexist attitudes and behaviour.

*Evaluation*

➤ **Patriarchy**: Radical feminists argue patriarchy is a feature of all known human societies, not just class-based (capitalist) societies. Patriarchal relationships, therefore, should be given more emphasis than economic (class) relationships.

➤ **Patriarchal exploitation**: Marxist feminism assumes (rightly or wrongly) that men and women have similar 'long-term' interests: the replacement of an unequal, patriarchal, capitalist society with an equal, non-patriarchal, communist society.

Such a development doesn't, however, look a very likely prospect in our society for the foreseeable future.

➤ **Social change**: Marxist feminism ignores the extent to which society, and the respective positions of men and women, have changed and continue to change. Female lives, for example, have altered quite dramatically over the past 30 years, when considered in terms of family responsibilities, educational achievements (where women now out-perform men at just about every level) and work opportunities.

**?** **How are women exploited by men in our society?**

### Radical feminism

Radical feminism has a number of key ideas:

➤ **Patriarchy**: The source of female oppression, for radical feminists, is that all known societies have been male-dominated — and improvements in female lives can only come about through the overthrow of the patriarchal ideas and practices on which such domination is based.

➤ **Sex class**: Males and females are viewed as sex classes, with fundamental psychological differences; in crude terms, men are naturally aggressive and confrontational whereas women have qualities of cooperation, caring (nurturing) and so forth. Women form a class, based on both a common biology and gender, whose experiences and interests differ significantly from those of men. Just as Marxist perspectives see the overthrow of the ruling (economic) class as the way to achieve human liberation, radical feminists argue that female liberation involves overthrowing the ruling sex class (men).

➤ **Matriarchy** (female domination of men): Men are the enemy of women because they have always exploited women. For this situation to end women must establish a matriarchal society in which the current (patriarchal) roles are reversed; instead of men dominating and exploiting women, women are to dominate men.

➤ **Sexuality**: Rich (1980) developed the term 'compulsory heterosexuality' to express the idea that male–female relationships are the basis of patriarchy (and therefore the source of male domination), and radical feminists often advocate lesbian relationships and women-only support groups as a way of both developing matriarchal ideas and practices and rejecting their patriarchal counterparts.

➤ **Public and private spheres**: Discrimination against women takes place in two main areas: the Public (the workplace, for example, where women are paid less and have lower status) and the Private (the home, where women carry out the majority of unpaid domestic work). This is a dual form of female exploitation not experienced by men.

### Evaluation

➤ **Sex class**: As we've noted, female life chances, considered across categories like class, age and ethnicity, are not necessarily very similar. ('Life chances' refers to our ability to get the desirable things in life, such as money, health and happiness, while avoiding the undesirable, such as ill health or going to prison.)

➤ **Psychologies**: Differences in male and female psychologies — if they actually exist — can be the product of gender socialisation rather than innate (fixed and unchanging) differences. Given the right conditions, women appear as capable as men of aggressive behaviour, for example.

➤ **Relationships**: Not all gender relationships are characterised by oppression and exploitation, and the relative position of women in our society has improved over the past 30 years.

**Socialisation** from this general perspective involves understanding how individuals are socialised into the following:

➤ A **culture** that assigns males and females different social and psychological characteristics. Socialisation, therefore, involves understanding how primary and secondary socialisation involves a process of 'acquiring gender' — the various ways boys 'learn how to be boys' and girls 'learn how to be girls'. Central to this process is the learning of gender roles.

➤ **Gender roles** involve the various ways we learn the range of behaviours our society associates with males and females. For both Marxist and radical feminists the focus of gender socialisation is:

 ➤ **Patriarchy** — males and females are socialised in very different ways to reflect their different positions and statuses in adult society.

 ➤ **Primary socialisation** involves learning a range of sex-roles and relationships — the ways males and females are *supposed* and *expected* to behave in terms of their *ascribed gender*. The family is an important agency here, for reasons we will develop later.

> **?** How are the life chances of a young, black, working-class woman likely to be different from those of an elderly, white, upper-class woman?

### Post-feminism

The newest form of feminism is based on the idea that the 'battle for sexual equality' has been fought and largely won; feminists should, therefore, focus on understanding (and to some extent celebrating) the diversity of female identities: how they are constructed and how they impact on female lives. The key ideas of this general position include the following:

➤ **Anti-essentialism**: The concept of essentialism involves the idea of fundamental ('essential') differences between males and females. These relate not simply to biology but, most importantly, to psychological differences in the way men and women think, act and feel. Butler (1990) argues this essentialism is mistaken for the following reasons:

➢ Women are not a sex class — they are too diverse a group for this.

➢ Categories such as 'male' and 'female' now involve more differences than similarities. Gay and lesbian identities, for example, have little in common with their heterosexual counterparts.

➢ **Gender is not biology**: Butler (1990) sees 'gender' in terms of how it's performed: that is, things we do at different times rather than something we 'always are'. Her solution to gender essentialism is the subversion of separate 'male' and 'female' identities. She argues we should no longer see men and women as distinctive sexes; rather, we should see gender as a range of social processes, some of which are similar, such as some gay men who display traditional female traits and women who display traditional masculine traits, and some of which are different.

➢ **Choice**: This idea, central to **postmodern perspectives**, reflects the fact that men and women have a range of choices open to them in contemporary societies that were denied to all but the (rich) few in the past. One choice is expressed in terms of how we define ourselves (our personal identity) — people have greater freedom to construct gender identities in almost any way they choose. For post-feminists, this 'personal construction' often involves 'reclaiming femininity' in the sense that women can be both 'feminine' (whatever that means in practice) and able to pursue what in the past were almost exclusively masculine roles —a full-time education, a career and so forth.

➢ **Interchange**: Choice leads to an interchangeability of gender roles and relationships; behaviours once considered masculine may now be incorporated into female identities (and vice versa). Traditional ideas about masculinity and femininity are, therefore, no longer valid. Post-feminism argues that **identity transgression** occurs when, for example, women choose to adopt ways of thinking and behaving which have traditionally been seen

Are some young women now adopting 'traditional' masculine behaviour?

as 'masculine'. Examples here range from 'ladettes' (young women who mirror the outrageous behaviour of young males — 'booze, bonking and the beautiful game') to transgendered individuals who define themselves as 'neither male nor female'.

*Evaluation*

➢ **Choice**: The idea of all women being able to exercise choice in their lives is questionable. For the rich (whether male or female) a massive range of behavioural choices exist. For the poor, behavioural choices are far more restricted (not least by patriarchal ideologies).

➤ **Class**: Concepts such as social class, age and ethnicity have a serious impact on the range of choices open to both men and women. Post-feminists are accused of assuming that the freedoms and behaviours enjoyed by a very select (and usually very rich) group of women are available to all women.

➤ **Individualism**: Post-feminism has been accused of downplaying the problems faced by the majority of women because most women's lives are not characterised by unlimited choice, freedom and individual self-expression (just as the same is probably true for most male lives).

# Action perspectives

Although there are a number of social action perspectives, for our current purpose we can use the catch-all category of **interactionism**, where the emphasis is on how we construct the social world through our everyday relationships. Unlike structuralists who focus on the way society pushes and pulls the individual in various directions, 'making' us form family groups or develop educational systems, interactionists reverse this picture. Society, in this view, is created and recreated on a daily basis by people going about their lives. The objective is to understand how people constantly, if not always consciously, produce and reproduce the social world through their individual and collective behaviour.

From this perspective society is an 'elaborate fiction' that people create to explain the limits they place on their behaviour — it doesn't actually (or *physically*) exist anywhere; it does, however, 'exist' *mentally* (inside our heads). We act *as if* society exists. For this reason, interactionists question the idea — fundamental to consensus and conflict structuralism — of society as a vast, invisible, all-pervading force acting on people in ways that propel them into particular forms of behaviour.

Interactionists changed the sociological focus — from social structures to social actions — by examining the **socio-psychological processes** through which people constructed both social groups and, by extension, a sense of society. Writers such as Garfinkel (1967) have demonstrated just how precarious our 'taken-for-granted' beliefs about the social world actually are by disrupting social norms and observing how agitated, confused and angry people become when this happens.

For interactionism, therefore, social life is a series of **encounters** — separate, but linked, episodes that give the appearance of order and stability, not something imposed on us ('from above', by society). Order and predictability exist for as long as we *act* in ways that maintain them.

**Social interaction** is a key idea for this perspective: the social world is created by interactions between people, a process that involves **meanings**. Interactionism stresses the importance of meaning (what we each understand by something) on two levels:

➤ **Definitions**: First, to interact socially we must develop shared 'definitions' of a situation. For example, if a teacher defines a situation as 'education' and her student defines it as a skateboard park, this is probably a recipe for confusion (unless and until the teacher simply *imposes* her definition of the situation by excluding the skater dude from her class).

➤ **Negotiations**: Meanings can easily change; the meaning of 'gay', for example, has changed dramatically over the past 50 years (once it meant 'carefree', now it means homosexual). In terms of gender, the meanings of 'masculine' and 'feminine' have also changed over the past few years.

Society and culture are not 'things', fixed or slow to change. On the contrary, because meanings are argued over (**negotiated**) the social world is a fluid and flexible space that can rapidly change. If society is not a 'thing' acting on our behaviour (since it has no objective reality outside of social interaction) it becomes a convenient label we give to the pressures, rules and responsibilities that arise from our relationships. The idea of labelling (or naming) is important because it suggests how interactionists view social structures as forms of social interaction.

**Labelling theory**, for example, argues that when we name something (e.g. categorising people as 'young' or 'old') we associate the name with a set of characteristics, our knowledge of which is used to guide our behaviour. For example, the characteristics we assign to the label 'student' lead us to expect certain things from a person so labelled, in the same way we would expect something quite different if they were labelled as a 'criminal'.

**Socialisation** from this perspective is conceptualised in a very different way from the structural perspectives we've previously outlined. There is, as might be expected, *greater* emphasis on socialisation as a:

➤ **Two-way** (or **reciprocal**) **process**: Just as parents try to socialise their children, the reverse is also true — children socialise their parents in a variety of ways. This leads to the idea of socialisation as a negotiated process.

➤ **Negotiated process**: rather than being, as structuralists suggest, something imposed on the individual, interactionists see socialisation as a process of negotiation, in the widest sense, between those being socialised and those doing the socialisation. While structuralists portray socialisation as a relatively smooth and untroubled process of social control, interactionists note how socialisation can be **contradictory**. Children, for example, may receive different socialising messages from different agencies; the efforts of parents to socialise their children in a particular way may be counteracted by the messages children receive from their friends or the media.

*Evaluation*

➤ **Overemphasis** on individual meanings and interactions ignores the impact of social structures on our lives. Meighan (1981), for example, uses the concept of **haunting** to show how social actions are always surrounded by the **ghosts of social structures**. We are all haunted by things we cannot see but which nevertheless affect our behaviour; when teachers and students enter a classroom the interaction between them is haunted by things like the knowledge that can be taught (because it reflects what our culture values).

> **Patterned behaviour**: By focusing on the **social-psychological** aspects of social life, interactionist sociology fails to explain why people seem to behave in broadly similar ways (such as living in families, obeying the law, going to school or work and so forth).

> **Social structures**: Interactionism doesn't explain how individual meanings, definitions and interpretations are affected by social structures. For example, if I define a situation as one thing (a fancy-dress party, for example) and others define it as something else (a game of cricket), this will have serious consequences (and not just in terms of the fact that I can't bowl properly in my chicken outfit) — which introduces the idea of power as an important concept. We are not equal in our ability to define situations — some groups (or classes) have greater power than others when it comes to defining a situation as 'real'.

**?** **What labels have been given to you by your family, teachers or peers?**

## Postmodernism

Postmodernism is a relatively new sociological perspective, developed over the past thirty years or so. While it doesn't always fit neatly with action perspectives, it has more in common with these perspectives than their structural counterparts — hence its inclusion in this section. The key ideas of postmodernism concern narratives, metanarratives, globalisation, identity and uncertainty, discussed below.

Our lives are seen as a seamless web of interlocking **narratives** (stories) which we define and move between at will. For example, when I'm with my wife the narrative I construct is one of a loving, helpful, dutiful husband, alert to her every need, whim and desire. However, when I'm in the pub with my mates the narrative I construct is somewhat different. I have no problem moving between these narratives and I am always the person I believe myself to be in each (which means I'm either a fantastic person or a very good liar).

**Metanarratives** are 'Big Stories' we construct either individually or, more usually, as a culture to explain something about the nature of the world. Examples include:
> religions (such as Christianity or Islam).
> political philosophies (such as socialism or conservativism)
> social sciences such as psychology or sociology (and, within sociology, perspectives like functionalism, Marxism and feminism)

For Lyotard (1979) postmodernism involves an 'incredulity towards metanarratives'. Big Stories about the world cannot be sustained any more because their claims to explain 'everything about something' are increasingly challenged. Christianity and Islam can't both be 'right' since they explain the same thing (religion) in different ways, just as political philosophies like conservatism or socialism offer competing explanations and solutions for social problems. We are, according to the postmodern view, increasingly cynical and sceptical about the claims made by metanarratives.

**Globalisation** is another key idea of postmodernism. We live in a global society that transcends national boundaries; the way we think about and interact with people is changing rapidly. Email, social networks and internet phones all enable instant global communication that broadens our cultural horizons — and opens our eyes to new and different ways of doing things.

This has impacted on **identity**. In the past identities were more likely to be **centred**: clear, relatively fixed and certain. For example, people in our society once had a much clearer idea about what it meant to be 'a man' or 'a woman' because there were relatively limited ways to play these roles. The same is true for categories like age, class and ethnicity. In postmodern society, however, things have changed (perhaps) to such an extent that we now have a wide range of possible choices about identity (in terms of sexuality, for example, I can choose to be heterosexual, homosexual, bisexual, asexual, transsexual...).

This leads to **decentred identities**. As the range of possible meanings expands, people become less certain about how they are supposed to behave. Under the influence of globalisation, categories like class, gender, age and ethnicity are easily combined to create a new range of identities (such as some young British Asians defining themselves as Brasian — a mix of British and Asian cultures and identities).

The downside to the wide range of choices from which we 'pick and mix' our identities is **uncertainty** and confusion about who we are and how we're supposed to behave. The old certainties of class, gender, age and ethnicity no longer have much currency in terms of telling us how to behave appropriately. While this is neither a good nor a bad thing, it does cause us problems since we lack the reference points we once had that told us how to play roles successfully.

**Socialisation** from this approach further extends interactionist ideas in the sense that while people are still socialised into a variety of roles, values and norms, their content is not 'imposed from above' — by 'society' setting certain standards of belief and behaviour — but 'emerges from below'. In other words, postmodern approaches focus on the way that individuals attempt to shape their own lives through the development of **personal identities** that are always unique is some way, shape or form. While our individual development (or **personal narrative**) is clearly influenced by the people around us, it is in no sense *determined* by these relationships. Rather, socialisation is shaped by the particular circumstances of an individual's life.

Whereas for structuralists socialisation is a bit like satellite navigation — something that guides the individual every step of the way, from their unsocialised home to their fully socialised destination — postmodernists see socialisation as a **kaleidoscope of possibilities** — every time choices are added to the socialising mix the pattern of socialisation changes. In this sense, even very small changes to an individual's life can produce major changes in outcome and this helps to explain how and why individuals who may be socialised in the same family in apparently very similar ways often develop into quite different adult personalities.

| ? | What is the difference between a centred and decentred identity? |

*Evaluation*

➢ **Choice**: While choice is an important concept, postmodernism overestimates the levels of choice that can be and are exercised by the majority of people in contemporary societies. While a relatively small minority have the money, power and resources to exercise choice in meaningful ways, this has probably always been the case.

➢ **Identity**: Many people still define themselves (or are defined by others) in fairly traditional ways when it comes to categories such as class, gender, age and ethnicity. While these identities are now more fluid and changeable, the significance of these changes is not as great as postmodernists claim; inequalities based around class, age, gender and ethnicity are still important and impact directly on our sense and understanding of identity.

➢ **Metanarratives**: While postmodernism is right to point to widespread scepticism concerning Big Stories about the world, it can be argued that postmodernism itself is just one more metanarrative competing for our attention.

**Exam-style questions**

**1** Define the concept of socialisation. Illustrate your answer with examples.     (8 marks)

**2** Outline and explain any two mechanisms of social control.                    (16 marks)

# Chapter 3

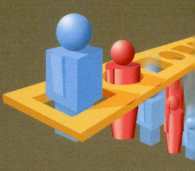

## The role of socialisation in the creation of identities

**By the end of this chapter you will be able to:**
➤ explain the role of socialisation and culture in the creation of identities
➤ explain how gender, class, ethnic and age identities are created and reinforced by agencies of socialisation

'Identity' refers to how we define ourselves (how we answer the question 'Who am I?'). Any response to this question will probably include references to **social characteristics** like:

➤ **Family** (name and general background)
➤ **Age** (whether you are, for example, young or old)
➤ **Nationality** (such as English or Scottish)
➤ **Gender** (whether you are male or female)
➤ **Sexuality** (whether you are heterosexual or homosexual)

Identity

**F** amily
**A** ge
**N** ationality
**G** ender
**S** exuality

In other words, answers will typically be expressed in explicitly social terms. This illustrates two ideas:

➤ To describe (or identify) ourselves we draw on a range of **sources of identity** (such as class, age, gender and ethnicity) — that is, a range of social characteristics we use to construct a sense of 'who we are'.
➤ To define ourselves as *individuals* we draw on *cultural* ideas and beliefs — something that illustrates the central importance of both **culture** and, by extension, **socialisation** in the identity-creation process.

**Identity** in this respect involves understanding the things that are 'important to us' and, by extension, the culture into which we are born and socialised. This suggests that our identity is at the very least shaped — and possibly determined — by culture *and* socialisation. The difference between them is as follows:

➤ When we consider **socialisation and identity** the focus is on how we're socialised into various identities (such as male or female).

➤ Considering **culture and identity**, on the other hand, involves looking at the various ways a particular culture defines identities, such as male or female.

**?** How would you answer the question 'Who are you?'

Before we examine these relationships in more detail, it will be helpful to identify two dimensions of identity: social and personal.

## Social identities

Every culture classifies behaviour in some way; it groups similar types of behaviour under a particular name and, most importantly, assigns various meanings to that behaviour. Interactionist sociologists like Hayes (1997) call this a process of **labelling** and an example might be gender. Our culture generally recognises two biological sexes (male and female) and assigns to each a set of social characteristics; these, being cultural in origin, may change over time or differ from society to society. In this respect social identities relate to the attributes we are given when we play different roles (achieved or ascribed); men and women, for example, are expected to take and show, respectively, the masculine and feminine traits that our society associates with biological sex (Table 3.1).

Table 3.1    Gender stereotypes

| Men are: | Women are: |
| --- | --- |
| Strong | Gentle |
| Brave | Timid |
| Rational | Emotional |
| Standoffish | Attached |
| Providers | Carers |
| Aggressive | Passive |
| Impulsive | Reflective |
| Dominant | Submissive |
| Independent | Dependent |
| Insensitive | Sensitive |

As this list shows, the stereotypical social characteristics assigned to biological opposites tend to mirror each other — which tells us something about how our culture theorises gendered social identities.

## Personal identities

Personal identities relate to what we each *believe* ourselves to be, considered in two ways. The first is how we *interpret* the particular role we're playing at any given time. 'Being male', for example, can mean something different (or personal) to me than to some other men, just as the concept of masculinity can have different interpretations and meanings — for some men (and women) it involves traits of toughness, ruggedness, aggression and so forth, whereas for others it has a completely different meaning.

The second way involves what Marshall (2003) defines as 'a unique core or essence — the "real me" — which is coherent and remains more or less the same throughout life'. Personal identity can relate to deep beliefs about who we are when we strip away our social pretensions (the person we present to others, for example, when we're trying to impress or influence them).

# Culture and identity

Concepts of culture and identity are linked because one presupposes the other. We can only have a 'sense of our self' through our ability to interact culturally with others. Culture and identity, therefore, presupposes what Smith (1996) terms **communities of identity** — the idea that *social identities* based around class, age, gender, ethnicity and the like represent sets of culturally developed ideas about how to 'behave appropriately' when we assume particular identities. *Personal identities*, on the other hand, can only develop in a cultural context as people 'express their individuality' by drawing upon a selection of identity sources which they then shape in particular ways.

Alcoff (2000) suggests that 'Identity categories are cultural negotiations' in that what it means, for example, to be young or female differs both *historically* (in the same society over time) and *cross-culturally*, between different societies. Differences in the way societies interpret the meaning of 'being female', for example, suggest such meanings are neither inherent (we are not born knowing how to be or behave as 'a man or woman' — something that once again relates to *socialisation*) nor unchanging. The general idea that identity is 'culturally negotiated', however, hides a range of sociological arguments about the nature and purpose of identity we can explore in terms of two broad approaches we outlined in Chapter 2: those emphasising **social structures**, and those emphasising **social actions**.

## Social structures

Although there are differences of interpretation between, for example, functionalists and Marxists, this general approach argues that **structural forces**, such as the socialisation process, shape identities in ways that push people into behaving in an orderly and broadly predictable fashion. Socialisation, therefore, is viewed as a powerful guiding force in terms of how people are made into self-aware beings and categorised into particular forms of cultural identity. As in Chapter 2, we can divide structure perspectives into two types: one stressing consensus structures and the other stressing conflict structures.

### Consensus structures
**Functionalism** focuses on how people are socialised into the norms of pre-existing social identities because it is only by learning cultural rules that social interaction

becomes both possible and manageable. Social identities (such as class) structure people's behaviour, channelling it in some ways but not others, and the emphasis here is on the way individual identities and behaviours are *constrained* and *controlled* by the rules governing the performance of social identities. Identities, therefore, function at an **institutional level** of society and ultimately social identities such as age or gender develop as a means of:

➤ establishing a sense of **order** in an unpredictable (individualistic) world
➤ providing the means by which broadly **predictable** behaviour can take place (through role play and the adoption of particular identities), an example being the way **gendered social identities** are constructed to complement (or mirror) one another in our culture
➤ limiting conflict in our relationships by specifying clear behavioural boundaries

For Parsons (1951) the significance of social identities is that when people take on certain identities they necessarily **internalise** the basic 'rules of society' (behavioural norms are incorporated into our **personal value system**; we don't question them because they appear self-evident, natural and normal). Thus, once the label 'male' or 'female' is applied to a child they are subjected to a socialisation process that reflects how a culture interprets and applies the meaning of these categories. Individual identities, therefore, are shaped by socialisation and people are a product of their cultural upbringing.

### Five functions of identity

We can contextualise these ideas by looking at a contemporary application of the way identity is functional for the individual and society. Adams and Marshall (1996) have suggested five functions of identity that focus on what identity *does* 'rather than how identity is constructed':

➤ **Structure**: Identities provide a 'framework of rules', used to guide behaviour when playing certain roles, that helps us understand our relationship to others.
➤ **Goals**: We develop a sense of purpose by setting goals for our behaviour. A 'student identity', for example, involves the desire to achieve goals like educational qualifications.
➤ **Personal control**: Identities provide a measure of 'active self-regulation' in terms of deciding what we want to achieve and how we plan to achieve it. An A-level student, for example, understands the need to take notes to help them remember the things they might be tested on in an exam.
➤ **Harmony**: When adopting a particular identity (such as that of a

Andrew Fox/Alamy

The goal of exam success

teacher or student) we have to ensure the commitments we make (the things others expect from us) are consistent with our personal values and beliefs. A teacher or student who sees education as a waste of time is unlikely to be able to successfully perform this particular role.

➤ **Future**: Identities allow us to 'see where we are going' in terms of likely or hoped-for outcomes (what we want to achieve). A student identity, for example, has a future orientation: the role may be performed to achieve the goal of going to university, which requires the passing of A-level exams.

> **?** Give one example for each of the 'five functions of identity'.

## Conflict structures

Conflict approaches focus on the different ways identities are used for social action: they examine how *primary* forms of identity (such as **social class** in Marxist sociology and **gender** in feminist sociology) form the basis for both personal and social change. We will illustrate this by looking briefly at the implications of Marxist and gendered (feminist and masculinist) approaches.

Both approaches focus on particular forms of **conflict** as the basis for **primary identities** (sources of identity that are so powerful that all other forms of identity are *secondary* to, or dependent on them). Identities, in this view, are both formed and given meaning through relationships based around exploitation, domination and subordination.

### Marxist approaches

Marxist approaches see identity formation in terms of the fundamental conflict between **social classes**, defined in *economic* terms. Economic production is organised so as to produce distinctive social classes (upper, middle and working classes), with attendant identities, based on their relationship to the **means of production**.

We can distinguish two ideas concerning class in this situation. The first is that of a **class-in-itself** — the idea of a distinctive class based on its relationship to the means of production. The second is that of a **class-for-itself** — the idea that the members of a particular social class may develop a sense of their common group identity and interests.

This approach to culture and social identity, therefore, argues that classes involve people who have:

➤ particular roles to play in the production of goods and services
➤ a particular relationship to other classes in society
➤ class interests they are organised to pursue

Wood (1995) argues that a sense of class identity (a belief that one belongs to a particular class group) is forged through different experiences of 'exploitation and domination'. Working-class identities are based around the experience of being exploited and dominated in the workplace, while upper-class identities are forged through the experience of doing the exploiting and dominating. Primary identities develop from these two very different economic experiences, since they condition the way we see the world and our respective positions in that world.

### Gendered approaches

Gendered approaches also see identities as being forged through conflict, although both **feminists** and **masculinists** (in their different ways) see **gender** as the key source of identity in contemporary societies.

**Feminist approaches** start from the assumption of female inequality as the fundamental form from which all other inequalities flow. In patriarchal societies, where women are considered inferior to men, this lowered relative status is translated into areas like *family life* (where women perform the majority of household tasks) and the *workplace* (where women, on average, earn less than men and the latter occupy many of the higher-status positions of power and influence). Different feminist approaches put forward slightly different explanations of how gender differences are exploited by men, as discussed below.

#### Liberal feminists

Liberal feminists see female inequality as enshrined in general day-to-day male behaviours and practices. Hammer (1997), for example, argues that 'gendered language… symbolically excludes women' from male-dominated spheres. The masculine pronoun 'he', for example, is often used in the media in reference to both men and women, and adult women are frequently referred to as 'girls' whereas adult males are rarely called 'boys' (outside of sporting events or the armed forces). Women also routinely suffer **sexual discrimination** in the family and the workplace.

For liberal feminists, however, biological differences do not automatically translate into gender differences — male domination and exploitation can be limited through the legal system and enlightened social policies (in the UK, for example, the Sex Discrimination Act (1975) made it illegal to discriminate on the basis of sex).

#### Marxist feminists

Marxist feminists point to **class inequalities** as the main cause of female oppression, exploitation and discrimination. Traditional forms of male economic dominance, such as higher status and pay, exist, and women are encouraged to see their main identities as 'mothers and carers' within the home (making them economically dependent on men).

This male domination of women is supported by **patriarchal ideologies**. An example is the belief that 'a woman's place is in the home' — that men are 'natural breadwinners' and women 'natural carers'. The development of distinctive masculine and feminine identities is reinforced through primary and secondary socialisation processes that encourage men to exploit women in all areas of society.

### Radical feminists

Radical feminists similarly view female identities in terms of patriarchal ideas and practices, but a major difference here is the emphasis placed on gender identities being based around fundamental *psychological* differences. Women are seen as having cooperative and caring qualities that set them apart from men as a **sex class**.

Female identity develops out of the experiences and interests women share, such as the experience of sexual discrimination, and is forged through the experience of patriarchal practices in both the *private sphere* of the home and the *public sphere* of the workplace — a dual form of exploitation not experienced by men.

### Post-feminism

For post-feminists, the battle for gender equality in contemporary societies has, by and large, been fought and won. Unlike in the past, women have complete legal equality and are free to make the same choices as men — to work, develop a career, attend university, marry, start a family, remain childless, engage in heterosexual or homosexual relationships, and so on. There is no area of contemporary society closed to women simply on the basis of gender.

Post-feminists are highly critical of other feminist perspectives for misrepresenting women's achievements and for denying women **choice**. In their view, contemporary female identities are built around a wide range of choices opened up by global cultures and postmodern societies. Personal choices have been freed from the constraints of past (patriarchal) social identities. Postrel (2003), for example, argues that 'the idea that women must choose between intelligence and beauty, mind and body, substance and surface' reflects 'the stereotypes of an earlier era'.

Both sexes have a range of choices open to them in contemporary societies, one being how we define ourselves (our 'personal sense of social identity'): men and women have the freedom to construct gender identity in any way they choose. For post-feminists this 'personal construction of femininity' often involves 'reclaiming femininity' in the sense that women can be both 'feminine' (whatever that may mean) and able to pursue their education and career independently of men.

**?** List three differences between feminist approaches to understanding identity.

### Masculinist approaches

Traditionally men have been able to draw on a wider range of social and personal identities than women for two main reasons:
- **Power**: Men have, to greater or lesser extents, occupied the most powerful positions in society (e.g. in the economic and political system, and in the traditional role of 'head of the household').
- **Spheres of influence**: Where, traditionally, female roles have centred on the private sphere of the family, men have had greater freedom in the public sphere and, consequently, have been better positioned to create a wider range of identities

because of their greater involvement with significant others outside the restrictions of home and family.

Male abilities to move easily *between* these spheres, coupled with higher levels of power *within* each sphere, have meant that men potentially have a wider range of economic, political and cultural sources of identity.

One (extreme) aspect of a masculinist perspective is the Men's Movement in America. Their argument is that rigid, fixed biological sex differences translate into cultural (gender) differences. Bly (1990), for example, has argued for a version of masculinity that, according to Wolf-Light (1994), is 'authoritarian and autocratic, impersonal, contemptuous and violent. In short, the very image of patriarchy'.

# Social actions

**Interactionist approaches** focus on how people construct and make sense of the social world, where identities are used to establish a sense of order and predictability in potentially chaotic situations. Such identities develop for two main reasons:

➤ **Social**: A 'female identity', for example, keys into a general set of roles, values and norms that provide guidelines for behaviour. Interactionists, however, take this idea of 'structure' one step further by arguing that, first, social structures can't exist independently of the people who create them; a 'woman', for example, is not automatically a prisoner of what others associate with this identity. Second, therefore, social identities are spaces within which we have the scope to interpret and negotiate the actual personal meaning of any identity; someone can be 'a woman' in a wide variety of ways.

➤ **Personal**: Identity structures provide, in Goffman's (1959) terms, a means for the presentation and expression of 'Self'. This idea is based around a **dramaturgical model** of self and identity, where social life is a series of dramatic episodes and scenarios. We participate as actors: we write and speak lines (expressing our personal identity) or repeat lines written for us (under the influence of social identities that tell us how we should behave in particular situations and roles). As Barnhart (1994) puts it: 'Interaction is viewed as a performance, shaped by environment and audience, constructed to provide others with impressions' that match 'the desired goals of the actor'.

This involves us in **impression management**. When we adopt a particular identity we 'perform' in ways that tell others something about who we are. We try, in Goffman's words, to 'manage the impression others have of us'. Identity performance is directed at achieving desired ends (what we want from others); when you want to create a favourable impression on someone, for example, you 'act' in ways you believe they will like. Every social encounter, therefore, is just one more part of the act.

This isn't to say we simply 'use people' for our own particular ends; we're not always as cool and calculating as this might suggest. Rather, in the majority of our social encounters we use people as a **looking-glass self**: people are like mirrors that reflect 'our self as others see us'. When we 'look into the mirror' of how others behave towards us, we see reflected an image of the person *others* think we are. Depending on how significant these people are to us, this may or may not affect our sense of personal identity.

For Goffman, the '**presentation of self**' always involves:

➤ **Interpretation**: Identities are broad social categories whose meaning can differ (historically and cross-culturally).

➤ **Negotiation**: Identities, because they are socially created, are open to discussion. What it means to be male, female, young, old and so forth is constantly changing as people 'push the negotiated boundaries' of these identities.

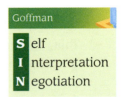

Goffman

**S** elf
**I** nterpretation
**N** egotiation

> **?** How do people try to 'impression manage' their identity?

## Postmodernism

Postmodernist approaches take up the theme of '**identity as performance**' and develop it in relation to ideas of centred and decentred identities.

**Centred identities** are clear, fixed and certain in terms of what is expected by others when we adopt (or are given) them. In the past, people had a much clearer (*centred*) idea about what it meant to be 'a man' or 'a woman' because there were relatively few *choices* available to them for the interpretation of this category:

➤ Social groups and communities were much smaller and more close-knit.

➤ Travel to and from other countries was only available to a select few.

➤ People were not exposed, as we are now through media like television and the internet, to new and different ideas about how to be male or female (or a range of other identities).

For these reasons **social identities** (whatever rules a culture developed to govern how to play a particular identity) were incorporated wholesale into **personal identities**. The rules governing 'how to be young or old', for example, were clear, consistent and rigidly enforced, and we sometimes see echoes of this 'centred past' when both young and old are criticised for 'not acting their age'.

For postmodernists a key change has been the development of *global* economic and cultural influences that have opened up societies, communities and individuals to new and different experiences, behaviours, ideas and consumption patterns. Just as we now eat food from America, wear clothes from China and listen to MP3 players from Japan, we've also imported a range of cultural ideas, styles and fashions from around the globe.

This has resulted in **fragmented identities** — a concept that involves two main ideas:

➤ **Sources of identity**: Primary sources of identity such as class, age and gender have become significantly less important as ways of defining 'our Self', while other sources, such as consumption, the Green movement and cyberspace, have become increasingly significant.

➤ **Heterogeneity**: Under the cultural onslaught of exposure to different ways of living, behaving and being, traditional identity sources like gender, age or class can no longer be sustained as monolithic entities (with the idea that there is only 'one' correct way to be 'female' or 'elderly'); there are, in contemporary societies, such a diversity of ways to be these things that relatively simple, centred social identities can no longer be supported, sustained, policed and controlled.

Consequently, the rules once governing the *correct* way to play out these identities ('Big boys don't cry') are relaxed as people develop the freedom to both invent and adapt identity sources to their own personal tastes and styles. Identity categories such as class, gender, age and ethnicity are easily and effortlessly combined to create a whole new range of **hybrid identities**. We can, for example,

A Gay Pride march

mix masculine and feminine styles to create an identity that is neither quite one nor the other. In terms of sexuality, where in the past a form of **compulsory heterosexuality** was the norm (with homosexuality hidden from view and criminalised), we now have a range of sexualities from which to choose — heterosexual, homosexual, bisexual, transsexual, asexual.

This leads to the idea of **decentred identities**. One outcome of fragmentation is that people become less certain (*decentred*) about how they are supposed to behave in a particular identity; if there are many ways to be 'middle class', for example, which is the 'right way'? The downside to the new range of choices is uncertainty and confusion about who we are and how we should behave. The old certainties of class, gender, age and ethnicity no longer have much currency in terms of telling us how to behave appropriately.

**?** Give an example of one hybrid identity in modern Britain.

### New identities

The discussion above suggests that identities in contemporary society are changing. We can identify two examples of new forms of identity that have arguably arisen as a consequence of consumer society: Green identities and cyber identities.

**Green identities** have developed around the environmental movement and reflect an increasing concern about consumption and the environment. For example, some people have become **ethical consumers**, who 'tend to buy environmentally friendly products when possible, who will not buy products for political reasons and will boycott certain labels' (Brusdal and Lavik 2005). Wray (2007) notes how companies have experienced consumer boycotts for the way they allegedly use child labour in products like trainers and footballs.

**Cyber identities** are another recent phenomenon. The development of the internet has brought us the World Wide Web, email, blogging, peer-to-peer (file-sharing) communication such as BitTorrent, and social networks such as MySpace, Facebook and Twitter. All this has opened up possibilities for identity formation, development and change on an unprecedented scale.

Sometimes these identities are real. **Social networking** is a recent but rapidly growing cyberspace development that provides the tools for people to create an online presence and, by so doing, network with like-minded individuals. In terms of identity, social networking is a space where the real and virtual worlds intersect; people generally use networks to present their real-world, conventional identities to an invited audience. Of course, as with real-world interaction, people may attempt to **impression manage** by presenting an **ideal self** for public consumption.

Very frequently, however, identities are **anonymised**. The ability to connect and converse 'anonymously' with a huge potential network across the globe provides opportunities for identity experimentation, allowing people to construct and play with a variety of different identities in different situations in online forums and chatrooms.

## Transformations

Although the virtual world is an obvious place for different forms of identity **transformation**, Phillips (2003) notes ways in which personal identities are transformed through consumption in the real world:

➤ **Surgical transformations**: The body may be altered by surgery for cosmetic reasons (e.g. to gain a 'new nose') or medical reasons (e.g. to repair damaged limbs). Changing the appearance of one's body can have symbolic significance for identity because changes to our body image impact on our self-concept, making us more comfortable in the identities we've already developed or allowing us to create a new identity, such as changing gender through surgery (transgenderism).

➤ **Landmark events**: Events such as childbirth or divorce encourage identity changes through changes in consumption practices, such as discarding the clothing we associated with a past identity (being married, for example) and buying a new wardrobe to reflect our changing sense of identity.

➤ **Transition periods**: When we undergo transitions, such as the move from childhood to youth, consumption patterns and preferences may change to reflect our newfound sense of identity.

# Soc

## Gender identity socialisation

The following sections outline how a range of agencies help to construct gender identities.

### The family

Some examples of identity socialisation include assumptions, associations and reinforcements.

#### Assumptions

Parents assume boys are different from girls, so they treat them in different ways, as was clearly evidenced in Will et al.'s (1976) experiment described by Giddens (2006):

> Five young mothers were observed in interaction with a six-month-old called Beth. They tended to smile at her often and offer her dolls to play with. She was seen as 'sweet', having a 'soft cry'. The reaction of a second group of mothers to a child the same age named Adam, was noticeably different. The baby was likely to be offered a train or other 'male toys' to play with. Beth and Adam were actually the same child, dressed in different clothes.

#### Associations

Parents develop identities in their children through the way they associate different things with each gender:
- **Colours** (pink for girls, blue for boys in our society, which Wagner (2007) suggests 'is a fairly modern, even a 20th-century, convention') and **styles**: Shakin et al. (1985) found strangers were able to identify the sex of very young babies through the cultural clues given by how parents dressed each sex.
- **Toys** reinforce both gender ideas (girls are associated with dolls and domestic toys because it reflects a future caring role) and performance — the things males and females do. Boys are, for example, associated with active, mechanical and scientific activities; girls with reflective, non-mechanical pastimes.
- **Demands**: Girls are more likely to be required to do domestic chores, for example.

#### Reinforcements

Hartley (1959) suggests that ideas about gender norms and values are reinforced in a range of ways:
- **Imitation** of adult family behaviours: For example, girls 'helping mum' with domestic chores leads to gender-typing; children come to see different ideas, behaviours and practices as being associated with different sexes.
- **Identification**: Children, by seeing themselves reflected in their parents, come to understand the essential features of their different gender identities.
- **Role learning**: By adopting roles in line with adult gender expectations, children understand how it is 'normal' for men and women to behave.

➤ **Conditioning**: Adult understanding of gender identities is passed down to children through several means:

  ➤ **Language**: Praising a girl for being pretty, for example, not only rewards her, it teaches her that if she wants to continue to receive praise she must reproduce behaviour that gains parental approval.

  ➤ **Canalisation**: Boys and girls are channelled into different activities and behaviours, reinforcing both a sense of difference and the idea that certain ways of behaving are masculine or feminine.

  ➤ **Identity maintenance**: Parents act in routine ways to maintain a child's gender identity — through things that either are themselves gender-specific (clothes, jewellery and toys) or contain gender-specific messages (such as books and films).

The processes Hartley identifies remain applicable to modern families (even though her research is over 50 years old), but the *outcomes* of this gender reinforcement are much less certain in contemporary societies for two reasons:

➤ **Changing social identities**: Both girls and boys have many more gender identity options than in the past, making it more difficult for parents to channel children into clearly defined gender identities.

➤ **Exposure**: The media, for example, intrude into the family group far earlier and more forcefully now than in the past, making it difficult for parents to limit their child's exposure to different ideas about gender identities. The 'mental maps' about gender held by parents are less clear and decidedly more confused than in the past, and processes of gender identification can be further blurred by the intrusion of media messages that contradict parental messages.

Although the ideas, attitudes and behaviours surrounding gender identity within the family are significant, we should see this in terms of broad tendencies (pointing boys and girls in different gender directions) rather than specific, clearly articulated, received and understood messages about masculinity and femininity. In other words, while we can identify **gendering processes**, **gender outcomes** are much less easy to predict.

> **?** What reasons explain why girls and boys might grow up to be like their parents?

### Education

Murphy and Elwood (1998) argue that boys and girls start school with some general understanding of gender identity — but the question here is the extent to which schools reinforce or call into question cultural ideas about masculinity and femininity. Eichler (1980) has highlighted how, in the past, the education system built on family experiences to influence educational experiences because girls saw their primary adult role in terms of the **private sphere** whereas boys saw their primary adult role as being in the **public sphere** (perceptions that reflect gendered ideas about identity introduced in the family group).

The problem here is that over the past 30 years social changes have contributed to a widening of female horizons and a narrowing of male expectations. Economic changes have meant a decline in traditional male work in manufacturing and engineering, allied to the expansion of service industries employing large numbers of women. Cultural changes mean it's no longer simply assumed that women will marry, have children and spend their life raising them.

The question, therefore, is the extent to which traditional assumptions about masculinity and femininity have been weakened. One way to objectively test this is through subject choice. If traditional notions of masculinity and femininity still hold strong, we would expect to see significant gender differences in these choices — and there is evidence that subject choice at the higher (non-compulsory) levels is broadly **gendered** (more boys, for example, study technical subjects, as shown in Table 3.2).

Table 3.2   UK A-level or equivalent entries for young people

| Subject | Males (%) | Females (%) |
|---|---|---|
| physics | 76 | 24 |
| computer studies | 73 | 27 |
| economics | 70 | 30 |
| design and technology | 65 | 35 |
| mathematics | 60 | 40 |
| biology | 38 | 62 |
| English literature | 30 | 70 |
| social studies | 30 | 70 |
| modern languages | 30 | 70 |
| drama | 30 | 70 |
| art and design | 30 | 70 |
| home economics | 06 | 94 |

Source: Babb et al. 2006

The evidence in higher education is less clear-cut (many subjects show no real gender difference) but Hughes and Church (2010) note some gendering:
> **Male-dominated subjects**: engineering and technology, computer science, architecture and, to a lesser extent, physical sciences.
> **Female-dominated subjects**: education, sociology, psychology, law, medicine and dentistry, and agriculture.

Educational choices are further reflected in adult career choices (engineering, for example, is male-dominated while nursing and secretarial work are female-dominated) and these patterns point us towards the idea of underlying social and educational processes that contribute to this gendering process.

Overall the relationship between subject choice and gender identity is perhaps weaker than might be expected. Myers (2000) for example argues, 'There is no doubt that things have changed. Attitudes about what is possible for men and women, boys and girls to do and aspire to are more open. Girls are doing even better and in a wider range of subjects in schools.' This is not to say schools are unimportant in terms of some aspects of identity formation; a range of studies suggest otherwise:

➤ Lobban (1974) showed how reading schemes in early-years education represent a readily available source of sex-role socialisation.

➤ Mahony (1985) demonstrated how girls were frequently marginalised in the classroom by both boys and teachers. Staffing structures also reflected male importance in the workplace (the highest-status teaching jobs were — and still are — occupied largely by men). Mirza et al. (2005), for example, noted, 'Women make up over half (53%) of the secondary teaching population, but are still under-represented in secondary school senior management positions, particularly headships' (around 30% of secondary heads are women).

➤ Kelly (1988), who explored female under-representation in science, concluded that science was seen as difficult and demanding and that the image of scientists was considered by girls to be unflattering and unfeminine.

> **?** **Does the evidence from subject choices suggest that traditional assumptions about masculinity and femininity have been weakened?**

## Peer groups

Martin and Ruble (2004) observe that 'From an early age, children are like "gender detectives", searching for clues about gender, such as who should and shouldn't engage in certain activities, who can play with whom, and why girls and boys differ.' Among young children, peers shape and reinforce gender identities by drawing on and reproducing existing social identities in play, games, activities and pastimes.

Play is semi-structured in that children adopt a theme (such as 'doctors and nurses') and improvise around it — which means they have to draw on ideas about masculinity and femininity in order to maintain their play.

Games are structured forms of play (they have rules) and have gender associations in terms of who can and cannot play them. Particular sports (such as football and cricket) have masculine associations — participating may reinforce notions of masculinity (if you can play them to an acceptable standard).

Activities and pastimes also have gender connotations and expectations because they act as focal points for participation and inclusion (both of which are important in terms of peer groups). Thus, common interests in areas like cars, motorbikes, heavy and death metal music (boys) and fashion, cosmetics and shopping (girls) help to both create bonds and reinforce identity barriers. Individuals who cross those invisible boundaries (the girl who likes bikes and death metal, the boy who likes fashion and cosmetics) risk being negatively sanctioned for breaking identity norms.

This involves **peer pressure** — trying to make others conform to group norms, to fit in with the crowd. Children who fail to conform to gender norms face a range of negative sanctions — from being bullied to exclusion from valued peer and friendship groups.

Peer groups can also function as **reference groups** or sounding boards, used to explore various aspects of gender and identity. Looking for clues about how to behave appropriately from people of our own age and gender leads to a kind of 'collective mentality' in the establishment of age and gender norms. To be part of the group we need to like what our friends like, wear what they wear and, to some extent, behave as they behave — all things that serve to reinforce gender ideas, attributes and identities.

> **?** How can peer pressure influence our behaviour?

## The media

In a society as thoroughly media-saturated as our own (with 24/7 television, 24-hour news, hundreds of television stations, web-enabled mobile phones, social networks...) it's easy to forget that as recently as 50 years ago the media in Britain were far smaller (two television channels, one public and one private, broadcasting for a few hours each day — in black and white), less diverse and resolutely non-interactive (not a red button in sight).

British society was also very different, at least in terms of gender relationships — homosexuality was illegal, relationships outside marriage were still seen as 'living in sin', and divorce, if not exactly uncommon, was by no means as simple, straightforward and relatively risk-free as it can be today. This distinction between (relatively recent) past and present is important because mainstream media — television, radio, magazines and newspapers — were not only a major source of information, but were also far less diverse in terms of ideas about gender. The 'gender scripts' pushed by the media were very similar and very limited: gendered social identities were **centred** around traditional notions of masculinity and femininity. These ideas are confirmed by research examples from 20 to 30 years ago:

➤ McRobbie (1977) argued that young female identities — as depicted in the pages of *Jackie*, the best-selling teenage magazine of the time — were shaped by a 'narrow and restricted view of life', marked by 'romance, problems, fashion, beauty and pop', coupled with an 'idealised and romanticised' view of boys. The *Jackie* girl inhabits a world of 'romantic individualism' where the objective is to find and keep 'her man' — and, by so doing, escape the 'bitchy, catty atmosphere of female company'.

➤ Ferguson's (1983) analysis of women's magazines over a 30-year period described a 'cult of femininity' revolving around traditional female values of caring for others, marriage, concern with appearance and the like. The general message, as far as female identities were concerned, was that women should define themselves in terms of male needs.

➤ Sharpe's (1976) study of teenage girls found female identities were shaped around 'love, marriage, husbands, children, jobs and careers, more or less in that order'.

➤ Cumberbatch (1990) found that television advertisements used male and female identities in very different ways — older men and younger women were more likely to be used than other age groups. Older men featured heavily when an advertiser wanted to convey authority (especially when technical expertise was involved) while young women were used to convey sexiness.

Although these studies are informative and interesting, their current relevance to gender identity as anything more than historical documents is more debatable — partly because of significant economic and cultural changes in our society and, more importantly, changes in the range of the media over the past 15 to 20 years. In addition, our relationship to media has not remained static; we don't consume media in the way we did 5 years, let alone 30 or 50 years, ago. In this respect we can note two ideas:

➤ As audiences have changed so too have the media. Not only has the range of male and female portrayals changed, even fairly traditional gender portrayals are subtly different from what they once were.

➤ Access to and consumption of media have changed — not only in terms of the range of available media (Cumberbatch's study was based on the two commercial television stations at the time; there are now hundreds of commercial channels) but also in terms of how we use them.

Just as they always have, the media still send a range of gender socialising messages. Kraeplin (2007), for example, notes how 'Popular teen magazines link appearance and consumerism. Women are constantly being made aware of their imperfections, then offered products that will help them attain the socially constructed ideal' (something increasingly true of men, too, as advertisers attempt to exploit the largely untapped 'male grooming market').

However, we shouldn't assume women (or indeed men) treat these kinds of media messages uncritically — that the media tell us to do something and we blindly obey. While the relationship between the media and behaviour may, in the past, have been much closer — because of the limited range of media all saying much the same thing about gender (the idea of **agenda setting** we noted earlier), the limited range of gender roles played and, most importantly, the limited number of gender scripts — this is arguably not the case now. As Butler (1990) suggests, gender scripts are no longer limited, but many and varied; there are now many more ways to 'perform gender'.

Contemporary style magazines, for example, aimed at different age groups (from pre-teens to adults) and genders, offer a range of information about gender performance and while some of it undoubtedly reflects fairly traditional gender concerns and behaviours (magazines aimed at women tend to focus on the **individual self** and how it can be 'improved' through practical advice and tips on make-up, sex, partnerships, love, career and so forth), much of it does not.

We are more 'media-literate' now than in the past (we know how they work and what they are trying to do). Gauntlett (2002), for example, suggests:

> Teenagers were well able to think critically about the magazines they read. Although some young and not-quite-so-young readers found the repeated sex themes to be rather claustrophobic, most readers recognised that they were useful in information terms, and also somewhat empowering, particularly when considered in contrast with gender roles and attitudes of the past.

Different ways of accessing, consuming and using media (mainly brought about by the development of the internet and mobile technology) have led to a change in the range of gender scripts — from the very traditional to the more radical — presented through the media. Macdonald (2003), for example, argues, 'gender is not static and women are permitted to take on certain masculine behaviours in certain situations'.

The key idea here is 'certain situations'; while gender identities are not as clear-cut and fixed as they once were, this doesn't mean the media don't attempt to both exploit and reinforce 'traditional stereotypes' in their use of **sexuality** and representations of male and female bodies. Female sexuality is often used to sell consumer goods and a particular form of (hetero)sexuality is frequently emphasised, one combining particular body shapes (thin, large-breasted and so forth) with patriarchal notions of 'availability'. 'Normality', in terms of gender concepts and relationships, is usually represented by heterosexuality.

While representations of male and female **bodies** have changed in some ways (images of sexualised male bodies — the 'sixpack', for example — are held up as sexually desirable for women and culturally desirable for men), they have in other aspects stayed the same, such as the way female bodies are displayed through the media to sell everything from cars to camping equipment.

The contemporary relationship between gender identities and media representations is one where men and women are represented in many different ways — from traditional gender stereotypes to ways that confront, challenge and break down these stereotypical representations (the powerful and dominant female, the happy resourceful gay couple). This reflects the fact that both gender and media are no longer simply homogeneous (all the same).

Gender is arguably more **fluid** in contemporary societies: people see themselves (their personal identities) in new and different ways. This sometimes involves identities that have little or no apparent permanence but which change from day to day and situation to situation. This, in turn, involves the idea that gender identities are more

**fragmented** now than at any time in the past — there are no longer clear, simple ways to be male or female. This makes it harder — if not impossible — to talk about 'men' or 'women' as simple gender categories. Rather, we may need to think in terms of the different ways it is possible to be 'a man' or 'a woman' in our society.

In terms of current relationships between the media and gender identities, Gauntlett (2002) suggests that *'within limits*, the mass media is a force for change'. He argues that traditional views of women have been replaced by 'feisty, successful "girl power" icons', while male representations have changed from 'ideals of absolute toughness, stubborn self-reliance and emotional silence' to a greater emphasis on emotions, the need for help and advice and the 'problems of masculinity'.

> **?** How does the media influence gender identities?

## Religion

An initial problem with tracing the influence of religious beliefs on identity formation is that, in Britain at least, there is increasing evidence that the majority of the population are not particularly religious (something that is certainly true in terms of religious practice, such as attending church). Religious beliefs and practices for the majority may not extend much beyond the (secular) celebration of religious festivals such as Christmas, a general 'belief in God' and the odd silent prayer. Among those who *do* hold strong religious beliefs, the effect on gender identities tends to be more marked, partly because of the **patriarchal** nature of many of the world's major religions (including Christianity and Islam). This is expressed in two main ways: through structure and through language.

### Structure

Religions tend towards a 'top-down' pyramid structure where men hold positions of power and authority and women occupy a variety of supporting roles. Different religions have different levels of **gender segregation**: for example, the Catholic Church — characterised by Morgan (1970) as 'an all-male hierarchy' — doesn't allow women to occupy any positions of power and authority, whereas the Church of England increasingly does.

Such power imbalances between men and women have **symbolic significance**, in terms of demonstrating differences in male and female power (and hence identity). They also have **practical importance** because female identities may be defined and controlled by men. Islam, for example, is particularly clear on things like gender relationships, associations and even dress (with some forms of Islam insisting on female bodies being hidden from view in public) which, in the main, reflect male power over women. Christianity too has beliefs about gender relationships, such as 'sin originating in women' and women being requested to 'love, honour and obey' their male marriage partner (although many women choose not to utter these words nowadays).

### Language

Religious texts are generally patriarchal in tone (the male God of Christianity, for example) and teaching. Elliott (2009), for example, argues, 'The Bible itself is a handbook for the subjugation of women. But then the Bible, like religion, was created by men for men, and has been used ever since its inception as a tool to keep women in their place.'

**?** How is religion patriarchal?

## Work

The workplace is an important source of male identity. Men have traditionally used occupation to establish their identity, in terms of both paid work (something that has traditionally differentiated male and female identities) and particular occupations within the workplace (from plumber through accountant to managing director). *Within* the workplace gender identities are reinforced through **stratification**. This can involve vertical or horizontal segregation.

### Vertical segregation

Within many occupations, the positions with highest status and pay are still mainly filled by men — something we can explain in terms of four related concepts:

➢ **The glass ceiling**: Even where overt forms of sex discrimination do not exist, women are still, in the main, unable to reach the top positions in companies. They can, however, 'see' others in these positions.

➢ **The glass trapdoor**: This more sophisticated concept suggests that those few women who reach higher occupational levels do so on the basis of adopting male organisational behaviours, practices and identities. Once in higher managerial positions such women effectively 'close the trapdoor' to prevent other women following in their footsteps.

➢ **The glass cliff-face**: This involves 'the tendency for women who break through the glass ceiling to be placed in more precarious leadership positions than men' (Ryan and Haslam 2005). They are, as Henderson (2004) reports, 'much more likely than men to be given "poisoned chalice" jobs in which they struggle to succeed'. This solidifies perceptions of both male and female identities because frequent 'female failures' reinforce the idea that higher managerial positions are a male preserve.

➢ **The concrete ceiling**: This expresses the idea that higher occupational levels are simply 'closed off' to women, so that they have no real prospect of attaining them or interest in trying.

### Horizontal segregation

Many occupations are sex-segregated in the sense of being mainly performed by either males or females. Female-dominated occupations include teaching, nursing, shop and secretarial work — occupations that frequently involve a 'caring and support role' that reinforces traditional notions of female (and by extension male) identities.

This type of segregation is further reflected in **dual labour markets** that involve a **primary sector** with high levels of profitability, job security, promotion, career prospects and wages and a **secondary sector** with lower levels of each. The primary labour market, as Sommerlad and Sanderson (1997) argue, is male-dominated and also 'conceptualised as male and characterised by male ways of working and career norms'.

# Masculinities and femininities

Historically, the relationship between gender and identity in our society has turned on the way each biological sex is socialised into what Connell (1995) calls two forms of **dominant** gender identities:

> **Hegemonic masculinity**: In the past, 'traditional' masculinity centred around a variety of male physical and mental characteristics that Gauntlett (2002) expresses in terms of **role modelling** — the idea that primary and secondary socialisation processes defined a clear set of roles for men and women (the former as paid workers and providers, the latter as homemakers and carers) from which an equally clear set of identity characteristics could be read. In terms of physical characteristics, men were encouraged to adopt a particular body shape that, ideally, emphasised physical strength and physique. In terms of mental characteristics, men were supposed to be 'leaders' and 'providers' (a source of authority in society), and to lack emotion (to be rational, calm, cool and calculating).

> **Emphasised femininity**: Female identities were defined in terms of 'accommodating the interests and needs of men' and the dominant identity was one that 'matched and complemented' hegemonic masculinity. Women were supposed to be essentially passive, emotional beings whose identity was expressed in the service of others (either within the family or, where work was involved, through similar 'caring' roles — nursing, teaching, social work and the like). Kitchen (2006) suggests this is a type of **complicit femininity** — one that is defined by male needs and desires.

Connell and Messerschmidt (2005) argue that, even in a society where different masculinities exist, one is always dominant — and it need not be the 'traditional' type we've just outlined. Given that gender identities are closely associated with the work people do (the traditional idea, for example, of men doing paid labour and women doing unpaid domestic labour), changes to working arrangements mean that contemporary forms of hegemonic masculinity should differ from those of the past. Such changes *should*, according to Gauntlett (2002), generally mean that gender identities in contemporary Britain exhibit the following qualities:

> **Fluidity**: A range of male and female identities are now available and the meaning of these identities changes over time. What it means to be a woman in 2011 is quite different from its meaning in 1961.

> **Non-conformity**: Economic and social changes (on both a national and global level) weaken the hold of cultural traditions on people's behaviour. Without strong,

traditional gender reference points, it becomes possible for people to develop new and different forms of gender identity (as described in the next point).

➤ **Knowing construction of identity**: In the past, male and female identities were largely *ascribed*; people were socialised into a relatively narrow, fixed set of ideas about masculinity and femininity. In contemporary societies, exposed to different cultural ideas about gender, the individual plays a more central role in the construction of their personal identity.

> **?** Briefly explain what is meant by 'hegemonic masculinity'.

## Masculine identities

If one form of masculinity is always dominant, it follows that alternative forms must exist. Schauer (2004) identifies examples of these 'multiple masculinities':

➤ **Subordinate**: Subordinate masculinities generally relate to gay men, with homosexuality being, at worst, criminalised and, at best, tolerated as an example of a 'lower' form of masculinity.

➤ **Subversive**: However, gay identities can also undermine 'traditional' forms of masculinity because they are in complete opposition to hegemonic masculinity.

➤ **Complicit**: Connell (1995) suggests that 'as women have become more powerful, male identities have begun to change'. One form of possible change is reflected in 'newly feminised' masculinities such as the new man — an identity arising in the 1980s (especially in advertising) based around men who are willing to combine paid work outside the family with their share of unpaid work within the home. Lewis (1999), however, wryly notes, 'There are few sightings of the new man.'

➤ **Marginalised**: Willott and Griffin (1996) discovered 'marginalised masculinities' among the long-term unemployed working class as traditional beliefs about 'the good family man' providing for wife and kids collided with the reality of an inability to provide for their partner and children.

Writers such as Mac an Ghail (1994) and Benyon (2002) have suggested a **crisis of masculinity** in contemporary societies caused by a combination of factors:

➤ unemployment
➤ loss of traditional male employment in manufacturing industries
➤ lower educational achievement relative to girls
➤ female-friendly service industry work

Where men once 'knew where they stood' in terms of the kinds of masculinity they were expected to display (the traditional masculine features outlined above), this is no longer the case. For example, 'marginalised masculinities' are unable to demonstrate traditional male qualities because they no longer control the economic resources (such as regular income) on which such masculinity was based. The response to this crisis has been the development of a variety of **exaggerated masculinities**.

**Retributive** masculinities aim to 'reclaim' (from their 'emasculated peers') traditional forms of masculinity. An example is the **new lad** — someone whose (young) life centres around 'birds, booze and the beautiful game'. In this instance the emphasis is on a late twentieth century 'reinvention' and reinterpretation of a more traditional form of masculine identity. In this respect 'laddishness' embodies a form of exaggerated masculinity, expressed in a range of behaviours (drinking to excess, smoking, fighting, womanising, 'loutish' behaviours and the like) that draw on an idealised version of a 'traditional' form of (sexist) hegemonic masculinity — when 'men were men and women were glad of it'. This type of masculinity is:

➢ patriarchal — with 'birds' considered merely as adornment to masculinity
➢ centred around a relatively small range of acceptable male behaviours
➢ aggressive in both thought (the idea that masculinity is bound up in fearlessness) and deed (being prepared to use violence to solve problems if necessary)
➢ oppositional, in the sense of going against contemporary norms of 'feminised masculinity'
➢ reclamational — involving the idea of 'reclaiming masculinity' as an identity

**Hypermasculinity** represents a version of masculinity that Wolf-Light (1994) characterises as 'authoritarian and autocratic, impersonal, contemptuous and violent. In short, the very image of patriarchy.' Hypermasculinity is, in some respects, a logical extension of 'laddishness' although, as Robinson (2006) argues, it is a form particularly but not exclusively found in America, with 'a substantial following amongst white, middle-class and middle-aged men primarily because of its ability to provide a degree of certainty about what it means to be a man...a belief in an essential and unchanging "deep masculinity"'.

**?** Why do some sociologists argue that there is a 'crisis of masculinity'?

### Feminine identities

There are a variety of ways for women to express their identity in contemporary society.

#### Contingent femininities

Contingent femininities involve a variety of identities which are shaped around male beliefs, behaviours and demands.

➢ **Normalised identities** are those where women learn to play a secondary role to men: identities (such as mother, girlfriend, partner) that play a supporting role for their 'male leads'. Normalised identities, Chambers et al. (2003) argue, continually struggle with the problem of 'producing a femininity that will secure male approval'.
➢ **Sexualised identities** inhabit the other extreme in that they are largely fashioned through male eyes and fantasies. Women are reduced to sexual objects that exist for male gratification.

### Assertive identities

Assertive identities reflect the changing position of women in society, partly as a result of feminist political and cultural ideas and partly as a reflection of changing economic circumstances. They involve women 'breaking free' from traditional ideas about femininity while not completely setting themselves apart from their male counterparts. Froyum (2005) suggests that assertive femininities are adopted to 'resist male power without actually threatening to overthrow such power'. Examples include the following:

How does girl power resist male power?

> **Girl power**: This identity has become available to women in recent times. Hollows (2000) suggests that, while the emphasis on 'sex as fun', 'girls behaving badly' ('ladettes') and the importance of female friendship may represent one way of 'coping with masculinity', older women are largely excluded from adopting 'the new femininity'.

> **Modernised femininities**: These relate to a slightly older age (and class) group by locating new-found female economic and cultural power within a relatively traditional context of family relationships (the assertive aspect here being a desire for personal freedom and expression within the context of traditional gender relationships). For McRobbie (1996), modernised femininities involve attributes like the pursuit of a career, 'individualism, liberty and the entitlement to sexual self-expression'.

> **Ageing femininities**: Older female identities have generally been stigmatised as objects of pity and charity. Alternative identities as fashionable, active and sexual beings are a more recent development and reflect both the general ageing of the UK population and higher levels of disposable income in this age group.

### Autonomous identities

Froyum (2005) suggests that autonomous identities are characterised by female attempts to 'establish power by negotiating within their heterosexual relationships'; they involve *competition* with men, on female terms. Where women have greater choice over how to live their lives and express their femininity, Evans (2006) points to **female individualism** as part of a 'new gender regime that frees women from traditional constraints' (such as pregnancy and child care). Autonomous women are likely to be:

> highly educated
> successful
> professional
> career-focused

In terms of relationships, Evans suggests that they tend to form non-committal heterosexual attachments that may involve marriage, but are unlikely to involve children.

**?** List three contemporary forms of femininity.

# Class identities

The idea of **social class** implies that we can identify very large groups based on a range of indicators such as occupation, values, norms and lifestyle. Some writers have questioned its usefulness in contemporary society: for example, Bauman (1990) argues that we should think instead about **in-groups** ('people like Us') and **out-groups** ('people like Them'). However, class remains a widely used sociological concept.

## Class identity socialisation

### Work

Crompton (2003) notes that 'Employment position has long been used as a proxy for class.' We can outline the relationship between identity and class in terms of a distinction between three conventional categories: working class, middle class, and upper class.

### Working-class identities

Working-class identities have changed as the nature of employment has changed in our society.

**Traditional** working-class identities are centred around manual work and manufacturing jobs — both of which were in reasonably plentiful supply even into the latter part of the twentieth century. In Willis's (1977) study of working-class boys, for example, 'the lads' looked forward to leaving school at the earliest opportunity to enter the adult world of paid manual work.

Writers such as Crompton (2003) have suggested the emergence of a **new** working class. This contrasts a traditional working-class identity (male, associated with manual work and work in traditional industries such as mining or manufacturing) with a new form of class identity first found in Goldthorpe et al.'s (1968) study of affluent car workers. The study questioned the belief that class identities were converging into a general 'middle-classness' (expressed by Zweig's (1961) *Embourgeoisement* thesis' — the idea of people 'becoming middle class' in terms of both their lifestyles and identities).

Goldthorpe et al. demonstrated that even those members of the working class who had good, well-paid jobs were sufficiently different from their middle-class peers in terms of identities, attitudes, values and behaviours to make traditional class distinctions valid. They did, however, argue that 'affluent manual workers' represented a new development in working-class identity, one that was increasingly **privatised** (focused on the home and the family) and **instrumental** (with work seen as a means to an end — the creation of a comfortable home and family life — rather than an end in itself).

In terms of class identity there were still important differences between the new working class and the middle classes; Devine (1992), for example, notes the former still showed a strong sense of 'being working class'.

> **?** What is one difference between 'old' and 'new' working-class identities?

### Middle-class identities
Self and Zealey (2007) note that those employed in 'middle class occupational positions' (both at the higher, managerial and professional level and at the lower, sales and customer service level) now account for around 65% of the UK employed workforce. This involves a range of 'occupational identities':

- ➤ **Professionals** such as doctors: This kind of identity combines high levels of educational achievement with personal **autonomy** (freedom of action) in the workplace and in decision making.
- ➤ **Managers** involved in the day-to-day running of private and public companies: This identity, as Brooks (2006) suggests, combines career progression, decision making, power and control over others, and the organisation of work routines.
- ➤ **Intellectuals** (such as university lecturers): This group has an academic identity dealing with knowledge and information services.
- ➤ **Consultants**: This identity is focused on selling knowledge, information and skills across both national and global markets.
- ➤ **Service workers** (such as shop assistants or care staff): This identity group represents workers at the bottom end of the middle-class scale. They may have lower earnings and levels of skill than those in some higher working-class occupations, but qualify as middle class on the basis of their non-manual work and (in occupations such as nursing) higher levels of social status (a significant factor in their class identity).

> **?** Give two reasons why middle-class identities differ from one another.

### Upper-class identities
This relatively small but immensely powerful class consists of two major identity groupings:

- ➤ **Landed aristocracy**: The traditional source of this group's power is their historic ownership of land and their political connections to the monarchy that, in the past, made them the most significant section of society. Over the course of the twentieth century their economic power and influence have arguably declined but they remain a not insignificant 'upper-class cultural rump'.
- ➤ **Business elite**: This group is characterised by their ownership of significant national, international and global companies. They can be subdivided into **financial elites** (involved in the provision of banking, insurance and knowledge services) and

**industrial elites** (focused around manufacturing). Of the two it can be argued that, in a contemporary context where service industries predominate (the 2008 global banking crisis notwithstanding), financial elites are now the most significant class identity in terms of wealth, power and political influence.

## Education

Occupational class identities are supported by a range of educational identity indicators and markers:

➢ **Type of school**: Around 7% of the school-age population attend private, fee-paying schools. These schools contribute to a distinctive sense of identity by setting a certain class of children apart (those whose parents can afford private education). Grammar schools, although far fewer in number than thirty years ago, attract large numbers of middle-class pupils and contribute to middle-class identities through educational attainment.

➢ **Types of study**: Although the distinction doesn't hold true in all instances, class identities do fit reasonably well with the educational divide between vocational education and training (mainly associated with the working class) and the academic studies leading to higher-status (middle-class) occupations.

➢ **Type of university**: Different universities have different levels of status and, while university students are overwhelmingly middle class, a grading 'system within the system' applies: universities such as Oxford and Cambridge have greater status than many others, and attract a disproportionate number of wealthy and privately educated students.

The association of education with class and identity is evidenced by Aries and Seider's (2007) study of privately and publicly educated students: they found that 'affluent students regarded social class as significantly more important to identity than did the lower income students'. Heath and Payne (1999) further argue that upper-class identities are maintained by restricting and closing access to 'economic and political networks of mutual self-interest'. Such networks develop through a pattern of attending an expensive, high-status public school (such as Eton) and a high-status university (such as Oxford or Cambridge).

> **?** Think of one way a private school education contributes to class identity.

## Family

The family is an important source of identity across all classes and general class identity is expressed in terms of:

➢ **Background and history**: Although these give most of us some kind of fix on our personal and family identity (at the very least giving us a family name), they can be particularly important as identity markers for the upper classes (especially some of the aristocracy) since they locate the individual in a historical continuum that, in some cases, extends over many hundreds of years.

➤ **Location**: Where you live and how you live is an important identity marker because it says something about you to others and also cements a sense of identity to a physical location — as evidenced, perhaps, by the difference between those who live on council estates and those who live on landed estates.

The family is also an important arena of **consumption**. Here we are concerned not only with the physical objects that contribute to our personal sense of identity, but with cultural changes in taste and consumption. It is argued that there has been a general *convergence* of working- and middle-class tastes, such as to make class distinctions increasingly blurred. Fenster (1989), for example, notes that 'even into the 1980's class-based *taste cultures* (defined in terms of a recognisable group "of similar people making similar choices") could be relatively easily identified'.

Working-class identities were reflected in cultural **orientations** such as:

➤ **present orientations** (a concern with **immediate consumption** — because you might not get the opportunity later)

➤ **immediate gratification** (leaving school at the earliest opportunity to take paid employment, for example)

➤ **tastes** such as pop music, football, television, not 'eating out'

**Middle-class identities** were reflected in orientations such as:

➤ **future orientation**

➤ **deferred gratification** (staying in education to obtain qualifications that give entrance to professional careers, for example)

➤ **tastes** such as 'popular' classical music, theatre and 'eating out'

Taste cultures as indicative of distinctive boundary lines between working- and middle-class identities have, however, changed dramatically in recent times. Prandy and Lambert (2005) suggest 'there is a gradual shift amongst the population from seeing themselves as working class to middle class'. Savage (2007) argues that although people generally still use traditional class categories as a source of identity, the *meaning* of this identity has changed over the past fifty years: greater emphasis is now placed on *individual*, rather than collective, experiences. Savage argues that people now talk in terms of **hybrid class identities**, which involve a mixture of traditional working- and middle-class tastes. For him this reflects the idea that social class is a **fluid identity** based on the 'ability of people to make some kind of choice'.

Brooks (2006) identifies three general cultural themes contributing to **middle-class identity**:

➤ **Not working class**: Brooks argues, 'The construction of middle class identities has primarily been related to the claim that one is "not working class"' — expressed in contemporary society by the idea that middle-class identities involve taste cultures (the consumption of music, food, literature, film, clothing and so forth) qualitatively different from those of the working class (the difference, perhaps, between shopping in Waitrose and Lidl).

> **Disgusted subjects**: Lawler (2005) argues, 'expressions of disgust at perceived violations of taste [and] white working-class existence' are a consistent and unifying feature of middle-class identities. An example here is the idea of **chav culture** — that large sections of the white working-class lack taste. Although 'chavs' may buy expensive clothes (brands such as Burberry that were once exclusively middle class), their lack of taste (involving cheap flashy jewellery, for example) marks them out for (middle-class) ridicule. The 'ownership of taste' allows the middle classes to distinguish themselves from those below and, to some extent, those above (who can be categorised in terms of 'vulgar and tasteless shows of wealth'). As Bourdieu (1984) puts it, 'Social identity lies in difference, and difference is asserted against what is closest, that which represents the greatest threat.'

> **Social capital**: This involves the ways in which people are connected to (or disconnected from) **social networks** ('who you know') and the value these connections have for what Putnam (2000) calls 'norms of reciprocity' (what people are able and willing to do for each other). Middle-class families are better positioned to tap into significant social networks (such as those found in schools or the workplace) that reinforce their sense of identity and difference. One important aspect of this is what Bourdieu (1986) calls **cultural capital** — the various (non-economic) resources, such as family and class background, educational qualifications, social skills and status, that give people advantages over others.

Cohen and Prusak (2001) argue that social capital involving 'the trust, mutual understanding, shared values and behaviours that bind the members of human networks' produces a distinctive set of **upper-class identities** that are continually reinforced by both mutual self-interest and cooperation. Such identities are based around:

> **Privilege regimes** whereby the upper classes tap into top-level social networks that give access to the most powerful decision-makers, high-ranking politicians, top civil servants and so forth. From a Marxist perspective Milliband (1969) argues that upper-class identities are based around common cultural backgrounds that develop out of family relationships and networks and continue through the secondary socialisation process of (private) education.

> **Privileged networks** and, in particular, **personal private networks** (such as the so-called **old boy network**, forged through a common educational experience and exploited for mutual benefit). For Heald (1983), private personal networks originate within the family — family name and connections give access to wider upper-class social networks which are closed to other classes.

> **Privacy**. As Galbraith (1977) puts it, 'Of all classes the rich are the most noticed and the least studied.' Upper-class identities are cemented through **social distance**: members of this class live, work and socialise predominantly with members of

their own class. Privacy extends from private education and healthcare, through employing professionals (such as tax lawyers) to shield their economic activities from close inspection, to creating physical distance — gated communities, country estates and mansions where access is tightly controlled, patrolled and regulated.

**?** Suggest two ways in which social capital contributes to middle- and upper-class identities.

## Peer groups

Peer groups are significant for class identity in a range of ways, partly because of their use as reference groups and partly because of the tendency for people of similar social class and status to live in close proximity.

In the past, an important source of working-class identity was traditional **communities** — largely urban, relatively close-knit in terms of social relationships and further characterised (unlike their middle-class peers) by a lack of home ownership. With this 'sense of community', people of a similar background, occupation and general social outlook could have their cultural identities and beliefs continually reinforced through personal experience and socialisation. 'The (working-class) Self' could be contrasted with 'the (middle-/upper-class) Other' (those who lived in the suburbs or the countryside).

Traditional working-class culture revolved around what McKibbin (2000) calls:

a fairly distinctive lifestyle and cultural life; industrial villages such as those around coal mining or the industrial areas of the big cities typified this lifestyle with their terraced housing, pubs and working men's clubs, keenness on sports and...a rigid sexual division of labour.

Traditional working-class female identities were largely constructed around marriage, child-rearing and the home.

New working-class identities underwent a radical change into what Goldthorpe et al. (1968) called a **privatised** working class, centred around the private sphere of the home, family life and children. A further change, noted by Peele (2004), was that 'affluence had affected working-class attitudes, making workers more *instrumental* and less solidaristic'; in other words, new working-class identities were less likely to form around shared experiences in trade union membership and close-knit communities, and were more likely to involve expressions of an individual desire for personal and family advancement.

More recently, Peele argues, traditional class divisions (especially between the working and middle class) have become less clear — the result of 'The shrinking of Britain's *manufacturing* base and the rise of the service economy [that] created a different social environment even from that of the 1960s'. Global economic changes (such as manufacturing industries moving to countries where labour costs were significantly lower) have drastically reduced the number of manual, manufacturing jobs, replacing them with service employment: both low-skill, low-pay, low-prospects work (in shops and restaurants) and more highly skilled and well-paid work in areas like finance, investment and information technology. Where the latter reflect conventional middle-class areas of employment, this has resulted, Peele argues, in 'a blurring of traditional class identities'. As traditional sources of shared working-class occupational identity gradually disappeared, so too did the strong, centred identities based around these occupational certainties.

## The media

Class identities are reflected and reinforced through the media in a number of ways.

### Desirability

Skeggs (2004) argues that television representations of the working class devalue them relative to the middle class. In other words, the media function to uphold 'desirable' middle-class attributes, traits, ideas and behaviour by contrasting them with 'undesirable' working-class attributes, such as tastelessness. A recent media phenomenon, reflected in both mainstream media and the World Wide Web, is the mocking persecution of 'chavs' — young working-class men and women seen to be deserving of ridicule for their tasteless and vulgar behaviour and personal adornment.

### Morality

Skeggs et al. (2007) discuss reality television shows that highlight **moral failures** among the lower classes (in areas like childcare, employment or personal care) and, by extension, the **moral superiority** of the middle classes, in the form of professionals charged with correcting these failures:

➤ supernannies who demonstrate how to control unruly (lower-class) children
➤ 'benefit busters' finding gainful employment for 'workshy' lower-class layabouts
➤ secret millionaires — a modern-day version of private help for the 'deserving poor', whose lives are changed by the intervention of middle-class benefactors

In this respect, repeated media demonstrations of working-class 'lifestyle failures' (from their lack of taste to their cultural failings) serve to reinforce middle-class identities by devaluing working-class identities. Conversely, mainstream media shape middle-class identities by presenting them as the norm, in two main ways:

➤ **Virtues**: They are presented in terms of their positive attributes: resourceful, self-reliant, practical in their ability to solve 'social problems' and, above all, successful.
➤ **Vices**: Middle-class virtues are contrasted with stereotypical representations of those *below* (the working classes who lack middle-class attributes and are consequently in need of their help) and those *above*, portrayed as eccentrics (Channel 4's *The F***ing Fulfords* of 2004, for example) or as part of sinister and shadowy upper-class cliques

who use their power and influence in selfish, frequently corrupt and self-serving ways (which contrasts with middle-class virtues of help and advice for others).

> **?** How does the media shape working- and middle-class identities?

# Ethnic identities

When thinking about ethnic identities, we need to avoid the misconception that '**race**' and '**ethnicity**' have the same meaning.

➤ **Race** involves the belief that we can distinguish between people on the basis of things like physical characteristics (such as skin colour) — what Ossorio (2003) terms 'simple divisions of people...that are deep, essential, somehow biological or even genetic, that are unchanging, [involving] clear-cut, distinct categories of people'.

➤ **Ethnicity**, as we've previously seen, refers to **cultural differences** between social groups in areas like religion, family structures, beliefs, values and norms.

This distinction is important in terms of understanding how and why ethnic identities develop because it rejects the idea that 'racial identities' are somehow inherent, natural and definable independently of the cultures in which they exist.

Ethnicity is not, as Modood et al. (1997) argue, always easy to define; it can be difficult to precisely identify the cultural differences that mark one ethnic group apart from another because ethnic identity, as Burton et al. (2008) put it, 'is a multi-dimensional concept'. Song (2003) suggests that investigating ethnic identity involves discovering whether people are 'conscious of belonging to the group'; as Self and Zealey (2007) suggest, 'Membership of an ethnic group is something that is subjectively meaningful to the person concerned'.

## Ethnic identity socialisation

As with other identities, a range of socialising agencies contribute to the formation of ethnic identities.

### The family

This group is an important source of ethnic identity in terms of **markers**. Song (2003) suggests that an ethnic group is a group within a larger society that has a 'common ancestry' and 'memories of a shared past'; the group has a shared identity based around a variety of 'symbolic elements' that include:

➤ family and kinship
➤ religion
➤ language
➤ territory
➤ nationality
➤ physical appearance

The family is a crucial **reference group** for the construction and maintenance of ethnic identities in terms of **cultural markers**:

➢ **Traditions and customs**: This involves a range of unique cultural practices that mark one ethnic group off from another (which may also include things like a shared language).

➢ **History**: The family group contributes to the maintenance of unique ethnic identities by drawing on a range of oral histories and testimonies about shared experiences, such as being victims of white slavery in the case of black Caribbean and African identities.

➢ **Origins**: This involves country of origin and the sense of a common geographic location. Mehrotra and Calasanti (2010) suggest that first-generation immigrants (people relocating to a new country) use the family group to maintain their previous ethnic identity in the face of a changed geographic and cultural situation.

➢ **Religion**: The beliefs, celebrations and traditions associated with different religious backgrounds also help to bind people together on the basis of shared cultural practices, such as common forms of worship.

Cultural markers

**T** raditions
**H** istory
**O** rigins
**R** eligion

## Peer groups

The peer group also acts as a significant **reference group**, especially in situations where ethnic identities in contemporary, globalised cultures are not fixed and unchanging. Ethnic identities are, in this respect, **negotiable**: their nature and meaning, Song (2003) suggests, change through both external stimuli (contact with other cultures) and internal stimuli, such as a clash of ideas and experiences between different age, class or gender groups within a particular ethnic identity. Ethnic identities involve:

➢ **Constant maintenance**: The peer group and community offer various forms of support: from collective activities (festivals, celebrations, religious gatherings and the like) to a variety of material and symbolic cultural artefacts. These might include traditional forms of dress, food and crafts.

➢ **Choice**: There is choice in how a particular ethnic identity is interpreted and constructed. There is also the choice of identity itself (e.g. whether to style oneself British and Asian, Brasian, British, Asian or whatever). Although these are personal choices, such identities usually require the support of a peer group of like-minded individuals if they are to be maintained.

Wimmer (2008) argues that an important aspect of ethnic identities is the ability to define them in relation to other ethnic groups by constructing a sense of difference that establishes boundaries for a particular identity. While these oppositions can be positive, by conferring a sense of belonging to a definable cultural group and identity, they can also be **defensive** (a means of combating or lessening the effects of racism and discrimination, for example) or **imposed** through cultural stereotypes about ethnic groups and identities (which also have the unintended consequence of reinforcing a stereotyped group's sense of identity).

Ethnic identities can also be reinforced by **segregation** between different ethnic groups. Phillips (2006) argues that in some areas of Britain two forms of segregation are taking place:

➤ **Hard segregation** involves ethnic separation in schools ('faith schools', for example, whose intake is restricted to followers of a particular religion) and residential districts that are 'on their way to becoming fully-fledged ghettoes'. Tyler (1999) found clear ethnic segregation in and around Leicester with the maintenance of 'white enclaves' in the context of black and Asian settlement.

➤ **Soft segregation** occurs when 'outside work, people confine their social and cultural lives to people of their own background and seldom make friendships across ethnic boundaries'.

 Briefly explain what is meant by the idea that 'peer groups are important reference groups'.

## Education

Within the education system ethnic identities are reinforced in a number of ways:

➤ **Faith schools**: The development of minority ethnic 'faith schools' based around religious preferences may contribute to the maintenance of ethnic identities in a multicultural society; it can also lead to the **segregation** of children from different cultural backgrounds.

➤ **Labelling**: Both positive and negative labelling within the education system contribute to ethnic identities. Indian and Chinese ethnicities generally attract positive labels based on their perception as academic and hard-working; black Caribbean pupils (boys in particular) generally attract negative labels based on a perception of low achievement levels.

➤ **Curriculum**: In both the National Curriculum (1988) and recent pronouncements by the education secretary Michael Gove (2009), the emphasis in history teaching is on British identity. Gove argues that 'There is no better way of building a modern, inclusive, patriotism than by teaching all British citizens to take pride in this country's historic achievements', involving a 'proper narrative of British History'. Within this narrative, outside of passing reference to 1950s black Caribbean immigration, there is little or no reference to a British history as being anything other than white (although non-white ethnicities do appear as 'victims' or 'benefactors' of British imperialist history). Many schools, however, now recognise various aspects of minority ethnic cultures, such as celebrating different 'holy days' in addition to Christmas and Easter.

? Think of two ways ethnic identities can be reinforced through the education system.

## The media

One feature of ethnic representation is the change from the *crude* forms of stereotypical, negative and demeaning representation prevalent in even the recent past (such as in the hugely popular television sitcom *Love Thy Neighbour* in the early 1970s, where black people were described as 'sambos' and 'nignogs') to forms of representation that are less negatively stereotypical and more positive — at least in some parts of the media. (We need to keep in mind that 'the media' cover a wide and diverse range of outlets.)

While black and Asian characters feature more frequently and positively in television programmes (from comedy to drama), there's also evidence that black actors are beginning to feature more frequently in prime-time starring roles. The BBC, for example, is currently (in 2011) featuring two black British actors in leading roles in programmes aimed at a mainstream British audience (Idris Elba in *Luther* and Chiwetel Ejiofor in *The Shadow Line*).

However, while representations are clearly changing, two qualifications should be noted. First, the baseline for measuring change was one where black and Asian actors rarely appeared on television other than in minor supporting roles or as the object of white derision, fear and stereotyping: any move away from this situation, however small, would represent a large increase. Second, across the media as a whole, black and Asian actors are

Idris Elba: proof of changing media attitudes to black British actors?

under-represented. Cassidy (2011) reports, 'Actors from black, Asian or other ethnic minorities appeared in just 5.3 per cent of UK TV ads screened in 2010'.

### Inferential racism

Hall (1995) argues that, while ethnic stereotyping has changed, it has not disappeared. Rather than the **overt** (or '**crude**') **racism** of the past, ethnic groups face **inferential racism**. While representations are now less overtly and crudely racist, ethnic groups are still represented in ways that stress their *difference* (usually in cultural rather than biological terms) and their *problematic nature* (debates about immigration, for example, centred around ethnic groups as the source of social problems and terrorism). A recent (2011) example of this idea was Brian True-May (producer of *Midsomer Murders*) describing the programme as the 'last bastion of Englishness'; he didn't feature black and Asian actors because 'it wouldn't be an English village with them'.

**?** What is the difference between 'crude' and 'inferential' racism?

### Stereotyping

Sreberny (1999) suggests that ethnic minorities are 'represented by two dimensional characters, and...often negatively stereotyped'. Examples noted include *Coronation Street* introducing a black character who promptly helped burgle a house and an Asian family who took over the corner shop.

Ethnic stereotyping in comedy is more difficult to assess because of the fine line between 'laughing with' ethnic stereotyping and 'laughing at' crude ethnic stereotypes. Ravichandran (2010) argues that the BBC comedy *Come Fly with Me* crossed that line in featuring:

> ...a middle-aged black woman played by a 'blacked-up' white man, who utters 'Praise the Lord' at the end of every sentence, is too lazy to run her coffee shop and who spends her time shopping for cheap bargains at the airport and, of course, the token sexist Muslim who calls every female 'a bitch' and sexualises anything in a skirt.

### Labelling

Klimkiewicz (1999) points to three areas where ethnic minorities are negatively labelled in the media:

➤ **Crime**: They most frequently feature as agents of both domestic criminality and international terrorism.

➤ **Victims**: A 'victim identity' is established through the news reporting of natural disasters in places like Africa, and of ethnic minorities in Britain as victims of racism and discrimination.

➤ **Problems**: Non-white immigration is frequently discussed in terms of the 'problems' it creates for the host country. In a relatively new twist, however, ethnic groups such as Poles and Romanians have attracted negative newspaper labelling in terms of 'benefit tourism' — the idea that various Eastern European ethnic groups are able to freely enter Britain and live off 'generous State benefits'.

### The gaze

Ethnic minorities and their lives are generally viewed through a white, largely middle-class gaze (with notable exceptions such as the comedy programme *Goodness Gracious Me*, featuring an all-Asian cast — the title is an ironic reference to film and television stereotypes of Asian speech). Carrington (2002) notes how apparently 'positive' black identities are constructed around cultural spaces like sport, fashion and music (rap and hiphop, for example), based around a concept of **hyperblackness** — representations that promote stereotypes of 'black bodies' that reflect white perceptions of race conceived in terms of 'athleticism and animalism' (the idea these are somehow 'natural' features of black excellence).

### 'The Other'

Ethnic minorities are frequently discussed in terms of their 'otherness' — how 'They' are different from 'Us'. Representations are produced against a social background that constructs ethnic identities in terms of not just difference but also social problems.

### Threat

Ethnic minorities are often characterised in the media as a threat: a **cultural threat**, presenting challenges to a 'British' (by implication, 'white') way of life through cultural practices like 'arranged and forced marriages'; or a **physical threat** — classically expressed in terms of the connection between 'Muslims' and 'terrorists' following the terror attacks of 11 September 2001 in the USA.

## Religion

Religion promotes a sense of ethnic identity through:

➣ shared experiences, such as worship and cultural activities
➣ customs and traditions associated with religious festivals
➣ 'cultural rules' that describe how to be a good Christian, Muslim or whatever

Religious identities can be used as **defensive identities** by drawing ethnic groups into a much stronger cultural grouping that becomes a vehicle for fighting racism, discrimination and social exclusion from mainstream society.

## Work

One aspect of work-related identity noted by Song (1999) is 'the importance of small family-based businesses as a key form of immigrant adaptation' in two ways. The first involves the significance of 'the family as workplace' for some ethnic minority groups (such as Chinese, Italian and Asian groups). The second concerns the way in which children are co-opted into the family work space. In the case of Chinese families running takeaway restaurants in Britain, Song notes how 'children contribute their labour [and] come to understand and believe in "helping out" as part of a "family work contract"'.

# Hybrid ethnic identities

In considering hybrid ethnic identities, we can contrast conventional and contemporary hybridisation.

### Conventional hybridisation

Conventional hybridisation suggests that the mixing of distinctive ethnic identities produces new and unique identities. In the main this mixing tends to take place on the margins of identity, involving the combination of specific *features* of different ethnic identities, rather than a complete identity interchange. Examples include:

➣ food (where Indian, Chinese and Italian cuisine have become embedded in British culture, often with subtle changes that give them a unique 'British' identity)

> dress (where American jeans and T-shirts become incorporated into a variety of ethnic identities)
> music (displaying crossover styles that produce unique musical fusions and genres)

### Contemporary hybridisation

In modern societies ethnic identities undergo frequent maintenance, change and development under the influence of two main processes: **mass immigration**, where different ethnic groups physically meet, and **cultural globalisation**, where agencies such as the internet bring increasing exposure to different cultural influences. The key feature of contemporary hybridisation is that cultural changes, rather than creating a new and different hybrid identity (something that is actually quite rare), produce gradual changes to an *established identity*.

Ethnic identities, in this view, are constantly drawing on new influences, re-establishing old constants in the face of new challenges and so forth. An obvious example is white English youth identities that have variously *incorporated* aspects of other cultures:

> music (rock, pop, rap, hiphop)
> food (hamburgers, Asian cuisine, German beer)
> language (especially slang terms)
> clothing (blue jeans, T-shirts)

While these cultural imports have undoubtedly changed these identities, this has been by way of **incorporation** and **modification** to an existing sense of cultural identity and style, rather than through a conventional form of hybridisation.

> **?** Give two examples of how the mixing of distinctive ethnic identities produces new and unique identities.

# Age identities

We can understand the idea of different age identities in terms of **life-course** — the idea that we can identify major phases in our biological development (such as childhood, youth, adulthood and old age) associated with different cultural meanings and identities. Although we can trace ways that socialising institutions such as the family, peer group and media help to establish, maintain and change age-related identities, we need to remember that age categories are **transgressive** — they cut across such institutions (family groups, for example, help to establish adult age identities as well as those of children and these, in turn, are influenced by media and the workplace).

A complicating factor in age-related identities is the lack of clear *historical* or *cross-cultural* agreement about the age at which the individual loses one identity and takes on another (when, for example, does adulthood begin?).

Settersten (2006) suggests that age identities are significant in contemporary societies for three reasons:

➤ **Salience**: Age identities have a formal, organisational importance (salience) for societies as a way of structuring 'rights, responsibilities and entitlements' (between, for example, adults and children). Informally, individual age identities 'shape everyday social interactions', such as those between a parent and child and provide a basic structure to these exchanges.

➤ **Anchorage**: The passage of *biological time* is a way of fixing the passage of *social time* in that we give certain age-related events (an eighteenth or twenty-first birthday, retirement from work and so forth) social significance as markers (see next point).

➤ **Markers**: These denote the transition from one phase in the life-course to another, such as from child to adult. These processes are called **rites of passage**; they take different forms in different cultures, but in contemporary Britain include things like christenings, marriage ceremonies and funerals (with birthday celebrations also being part of the age ritual). Significantly, Settersten suggests that biological age itself is relatively unimportant here: 'What matters is what the age *indexes* — the important experiences that happen at those times.'

We can note two further aspects of age identities related to the above:

➤ **Mapping**: Age identities come bundled with normative expectations (concerning the types of behaviour expected from different age groups) that we use as a 'life map'. Polkinghorne (1991), for example, suggests 'Individuals construct private and personal stories linking diverse events of their lives into unified and understandable wholes...They are the basis of personal identity and they provide answers to the question "Who am I?"'. In other words, I come to understand 'my self' by linking a range of age-related experiences to create 'the story of my life'.

➤ **Strategies**: Riach (2007) suggests that, by understanding how age identities are organised, we can use this knowledge to both upset normative expectations (of age-appropriate behaviour, for example) and 'pre-empt possible forms of marginalization'. For example, in situations where **ageism** is at work, people may take conscious steps to avoid 'embodying the older worker'.

> **?** Think of two ways in which age identities are significant in modern British society.

# Age identity socialisation

### The family

Family groups can be important in the fixing of adult age identities (by having responsibility for children, for example). However, the family is particularly important for **childhood**, which, according to Woodson (2000), 'is the manner in which we understand and articulate the physical reality of biological immaturity' and, as such, is arguably the first social identity consciously experienced by 'immature humans'. During this period we're first exposed to *primary* socialising influences from adults (mainly parents) and, increasingly, *secondary* influences from sources such as the media.

Jenks (1996) argues, 'childhood is not a natural but a social construct' and is associated with a variety of meanings — from the idea of 'innocence' to the need for adult care, supervision and protection. Childhood also involves socially constructed ideas about **permissions** (children are 'allowed' to exhibit behaviours — such as play — discouraged in adults) and **denials** (children are not allowed to do a range of things — such as marrying — open to adults).

The family group is also important for age identification in the following ways. It's where we're first introduced to a range of different age groupings (from baby, through child, youth, adulthood and old age); our first practical experience of age gradations comes through contacts with parents and relations who fall into different age groups. In addition, it introduces age expectations and norms — different age identities are associated with different behaviours (the way we dress, relate to one another, talk to each other, exercise varying levels of social control and the like).

## Education

In Britain the education system is **age-grouped** — children of similar ages are always placed together in classes. This contributes to a sense of age identity in two ways. First, children learn age-related differences, in terms of the different behaviours expected of different age groups. Second, children have age-related things in common; this is reinforced by age-grading and subcultures:

➤ **Age-grading**: This involves testing children at different age-related stages in their school career (culminating with GCSE at the age of 16). Each of these key stages reinforces the association with age identities and cultural knowledge (the things our society expects children of a specific age to know).

➤ **Subcultures**: Although youth subcultures tend to have wider associations with peer groups (and class and gender identities), school subcultures are a significant dimension of age identities, given that they tend to arise in particular (mainly teenage/youth) age groups. Francis (2000), for example, argues that teenage boys use 'laddish' behaviour in the classroom as a way of offsetting the generally low levels of esteem they received from both teachers and (female) pupils. Power et al. (2003) found a subcultural labelling process at work when they noted how successful middle-class students labelled themselves as failures for their inability to match the achievements of some of their highflying peers.

## Peer groups

Shields (1992) rejects the notion of 'youth subcultures' and instead suggests that age identities can be characterised by:

➤ **fragmentation**: lots of different identities co-existing within different age groups, for example, rooted in 'fleeting gatherings' rather than rigid groups

➤ **consumption**: the things people buy and use — in the physical sense, or in the metaphorical sense of buying into a particular **lifestyle**

Lifestyle and consumption differences seem to be particularly important in contemporary societies among **youth** which, like childhood, reflects a range of identities, such as pre-teens or 'teenies', teens and young adults, that have recently come into existence to reflect changes in areas like education, work and consumption patterns. Hine (2000), for example, argues that 'teenagers didn't make much of an appearance in Britain until the mid-to-late 1950's', with the development of this identity reflecting changes like the extension of education and the development of consumer goods (music and fashion in particular) aimed at a specific post-child, pre-adult market.

Baron et al. (1999) note that functionalists have argued that **youth cultures** and **subcultures** (spectacular versions of which include skinheads, punks and goths) function to provide a '**period of transition**' between childhood (the narrow family) and adulthood (the wider workplace). In other words, societies create 'youth identities' as a way of allowing young people to gradually move away from childhood and into adult identities.

Do youth subcultures help young people to manage the transition to adulthood?

### Age-appropriate behaviour

Within and between peer groups generally (from childhood through youth to adulthood and old age), different age groups reflect different cultural assumptions about how it is appropriate for people of a particular age to behave. These assumptions reflect back onto individual identities:

➤ through a process of **identification** with people of a similar biological age. This creates a sense of belonging (**social solidarity**) to a specific grouping with its own particular values, norms and forms of behaviour.
➤ through **peer pressure** to conform to an **ascribed** age grouping. Children, for example, are denied some of the opportunities open to adults in our culture while the elderly are similarly denied opportunities to behave in 'age-inappropriate' ways (in terms of sporting activities, sexuality and so forth).

In this respect, strong age identities act to control behaviour both within and across age groups. Young peer groups, for example, are generally sensitive both to consumption patterns within their group (wearing the right clothes, owning the latest mobile and so forth) and to the 'age-inappropriate' behaviour of other peer groups, such as the acute embarrassment created when an adult tries to 'get down with the kids'.

**Give some examples of what some might consider 'age-inappropriate behaviour' in modern Britain.**

## The media

The significance of how different age groups are represented through the media relates to two ideas:

➢ **Self-concept**, where members of an age group come to define themselves in terms of how they're represented in the media. This is a form of **self-fulfilling prophecy** — a claim that, by being made, brings about the predicted behaviour. For example, if we expect 'teenagers' to be moody and introverted, we look for evidence in their behaviour to support this belief. When we find it, this confirms the original prediction.

➢ **Other-concept**: This is the idea that how we expect others to behave is based less on personal knowledge and experience and more on how we see them represented in the media.

**Children**, as Buckingham et al. (2004) note, 'have always been seen as a 'special' audience in debates about broadcasting — an audience whose particular characteristics and needs require specific codes of practice and regulation'. This group is subject to particularly strong forms of **censorship** (what they're allowed to watch and when it can be viewed). This reflects how children in our society are seen as a particularly vulnerable group, easily influenced by the media.

**Youth** identities are often represented in terms of being 'a problem' — rebellious, disrespectful, ungrateful, sex-obsessed and uncaring. A dominant form of representation over the past 40 years has been the distinction between 'normal' and 'abnormal' youth, with the former being largely defined in opposition to various spectacular forms of youth subcultures. Teddy boys (ask your grandparents), mods and rockers, skinheads, hippies, punks, emos and, indeed, chemos (emo chavs) have all featured heavily in the media as examples of abnormal youth.

**Elderly** people have also traditionally been represented as social problems (a burden on the young). They have often been portrayed unsympathetically, as being senile or forgetful, ill (mentally and physically) and unattractive (physically and sexually). Willis (2003) notes, 'older people were often crudely stereotyped in drama, with fictional portrayals showing them as grumpy, interfering, lonely, stubborn and not interested in sex. Older women are often seen as "silly", older men as "miserable gits"'. However, the changing nature of television audiences — with more elderly viewers, who demand programming that reflects their identities, interests and abilities — means that representations are also gradually changing. In some situations, middle-aged or elderly men (in particular) are used to add a sense of seriousness or moral gravity to a situation.

It's also interesting that different age groups are neatly compartmentalised into discrete (separate and self-contained) categories. The conflicts that supposedly arise when adults meet youth, for example, are an unending source of inspiration for media writers (from *The Simpsons* onwards). Connor (2001) also points to the way ghettos exist *within* age groups and media: 'In print...youth magazines are often split along gender lines and it is difficult to find any popular magazine that crosses the gender divide.' Willis (2003) notes, in terms of television, 'Everyone over the age of 55 tends to be lumped together as if they were a completely homogeneous group'.

## Religion

Religion is potentially an important source of age identity because it provides a clear set of ideas, beliefs and practices that both bind believers together and give them a shared sense of identity based around religious certainties. The problem with this relationship, however, is twofold:

➤ O'Beirne (2004) found little evidence of religious belief or practice forming a significant part of self-identity in any age group. Across all ages only 20% of her respondents considered religion 'an important part of their personal description' — but even among these people religion was considered less important than family, age, work and interests as sources of identity.

➤ There is no clear evidence that religious beliefs and practices are closely tied to particular age groups. While the elderly, for example, tend to show the greatest levels of religious commitment, this is not true of the elderly *as a whole*. Similarly, while young adults generally show the *least* religious commitment, *some* young adults show *more* religious commitment than other age groups.

While there is no *general* relationship between religion and age identity, religion can be a significant identity source for particular groups *within* age groups. Gans (1971) suggests membership of a religious group may provide certain benefits to individuals (by defining who they are, promoting clear moral guidelines and satisfying psychological, social and spiritual needs) — but as Perry and Perry (1973) note, this may only be important 'in times of rapid social change, in which problems of identity are critical'.

In other words, when social groups experience rapid changes that challenge their world view and make them anxious about the future, religious certainties can act as an important source of identity. Two groups that, for different reasons, are more likely to experience the dislocating effects of social change are the young and the elderly.

> **?** Suggest two ways in which religion contributes to centred age identities.

### Youth identities

Traditional religions have less appeal to the young (as one of Robins et al.'s (2002) respondents put it, 'It's not cool to be a Christian'). However, smaller sects and cults can have greater appeal, one based, for Zimbardo (1997), on the idea that they offer comfort and certainty at a point in people's lives where these things may be in short supply:

> Imagine being part of a group in which you will find instant friendship, a caring family, respect for your contributions, an identity, safety, security, simplicity, and an organized daily agenda. You will learn new skills, have a respected position, gain personal insight, improve your personality and intelligence. There is no crime or violence and your healthy lifestyle means there is no illness...Who would fall for such appeals? Most of us, if they were made by someone we trusted, in a setting that was familiar, and especially if we had unfulfilled needs.

For those without 'unfulfilled needs', Hunsberger (1985) argues, religious belief doesn't increase with age — those who were nonbelievers in their youth don't become believers as they get older.

Although the absolutes and certainties of religion can be attractive for some young people, as a source of social and psychological stability, the reverse may also be true: prescriptive moral codes (such as the anti-abortion, anti-contraception and anti-gay teachings of some religions) may, in the words of another of Robins et al.'s (2002) young respondents, become 'a big turn-off '.

### Elderly identities

Jowell and Park (1998) argue, 'All the differences between age groups...are minor in comparison with those on religion. The fact is the young are overwhelmingly less religious than their elders'. Cumming and Henry (1961) suggest one reason for greater religious involvement among older people is that religious belief is a means of psychologically coping with the trauma of death.

De Geest (2002), however, relates religion to age identity on the basis that the elderly in our society progressively '**disengage**' from the world (retirement forces them out of workplace relationships, families no longer live together, friends start to die). Religion can help them form new group connections.

### Work

For Magolda (1999), adulthood represents a shift in individual identity focus, away from the various forces that shape children and young adults and towards a sense of 'what to make of themselves within the context of the society around them'. The workplace represents a **symbolic separation** between adult and youth identities — even in terms of young adults being paid less than their older counterparts. The workplace can be central to the construction of age identities — something negatively evidenced, perhaps, when the individual is excluded from work through retirement.

In contemporary societies 'old age' is both separated from general notions of adulthood (although the old do, of course, retain certain aspects of adult identity) and an identity in its own right — one becoming increasingly significant in Britain through the twin trends of an **ageing society** (where the elderly outnumber the young) and **longer life expectancy**.

Retirement from work can, therefore, be a significant **rite of passage**, marking the transition from an adult to an elderly identity — a **diminished** identity resulting from the loss of status when retirement is enforced. Mutran and Burke (1979) note that 'old people have identities which, while different from middle-aged persons, are similar to young adults: they see themselves as less useful and less powerful than middle-age individuals'.

> **?** Give two examples of age 'rites of passage' in modern British society.

In addition, elderly identities can be **stigmatised** by seeing old age as an inevitable process of decline, senility, helplessness, withdrawal from society and loneliness. The elderly, in other words, are reconceptualised as a **deviant minority group**. Gianoulis (2005) argues that the **medicalisation** of old age contributes to this process: 'Medicine defines and manages individuals deemed undesirable by the broader culture...and instead of viewing the disorientations of older people as being the result of personal and social change, they are viewed as symptoms of "senility".'

Conversely, we could note the contemporary **reinvention** of elderly identities based around longer life expectancy and more affluent lifestyles. This involves:

➤ the fragmentation of elderly identities (distinguishing between the old and the very old, for example)
➤ changing patterns of consumption and leisure (especially among the middle classes)
➤ different interpretations of the meaning of 'being old', whereby the elderly refuse to conform to conventional stereotypes and social identities

---

**Exam-style questions**

**1** Define the concept of femininity. Illustrate your answer with examples.     (8 marks)

**2** Outline and explain how any two agents of socialisation influence age-related behaviour.     (16 marks)

**3** Answer **one** of the following questions:
  **a** Explain and briefly evaluate the reasons why males adopt a laddish culture.
  **b** Explain and briefly evaluate the ways in which ethnicity may shape a person's identity.
  **c** Explain and briefly evaluate the ways in which class may shape a person's identity.     (24 marks)

- research problem
- research review
- research hypothesis or question
- respondents
- data collection
- data analysis
- presentation of completed research

# Research problem

This is the initial stage at which the sociologist decides such things as:

- what topic to study (education? health? family life?)
- what aspect to study (having decided on, for example, education, decisions have to be made about what exactly will be researched — 'attitudes to education', say)

# Research review

Depending on the aims of the researcher, the research review may serve a number of purposes, such as:

- generating ideas about what to study
- replicating ('exactly repeating') previous research
- avoiding errors made in previous research
- becoming more familiar with research on a topic

# Research hypothesis or question

The hypothesis or question is the focus of the research and will set the basic theme for that research. For example, if a **research hypothesis** is used it will have to be **tested** and this means using research methods suitable for this purpose. If, on the other hand, a **research question** is used, this may be sufficient as a means of guiding the research in a particular (possibly descriptive) direction.

## Hypothesis

For many sociologists the hypothesis is the starting point and it's easiest to think of a hypothesis as a question we want to answer or statement we want to explore. A hypothesis has one very important characteristic: we must be able to test it (to discover if it's true or false) and to do this we have to look at the relationship between two or more things. For example, if we're interested in researching 'Why do people steal?' a simple hypothesis could be: 'People steal because they are poor'. In this way we can eliminate or confirm 'reasons for stealing' because we've tested a possible relationship.

Ginn and Arber's (2002) analysis of how motherhood impacts on the lives of graduate women was based on the following research hypothesis: 'Is the effect of motherhood on full time employment minimal for graduate women?'

? Suggest a possible hypothesis for any of the following research topics:
➤ reasons for male underachievement in our education system
➤ the most common type of family structure in our society
➤ why people believe in God

### Research question

Other sociologists begin with a research question they want to answer by collecting evidence. Although not directly tested, the answer to a research question can be supported (or not as the case may be) through research. An example could be: 'What are people's attitudes to theft?' Here the researcher would be gathering evidence about peoples' views on a particular form of behaviour.

Conway's (1997) examination of parental choice in secondary education was based around the question of whether such choice 'helped to strengthen the advantage of the middle classes over the working class'.

## Respondents

These are the people who 'respond' to the sociologist's research by answering questions, agreeing to be observed and so forth. Although it would be ideal to select and study everyone who might have a contribution to make to a piece of research (the '**target**' or '**general' population**), this isn't always possible or desirable. For example, if the target population was 'every secondary school teacher in England and Wales' (around 450,000 people) the size and geographic distribution of such a group would make it difficult to observe or question everyone personally. For this reason sociologists frequently take a sample of a target population.

A **sample** is a relatively small proportion of the people who belong to the target population. In the above case the researcher might choose 100 teachers and, by studying their behaviour, try to say something about all teachers. This involves the issue of **representativeness**, which is arguably more important than the size of a sample because it concerns whether the sample characteristics accurately reflect those of the target population. For example, if 60% of the target population are female then 60% of our sample should also be female.

If the sample group is representative then anything discovered about them can also be applied to the target population — an idea called **generalisation**. A representative sample allows the researcher to generalise the behaviour and opinions of this group to a target population — they can, in other words, make statements about a group they haven't studied (the target population) based on the behaviour of a group they have studied.

To construct a representative sample a researcher needs some way of identifying the people in a target population, for two reasons:
➤ If a researcher can't identify everyone in their target population their sample may not be representative; it will not accurately reflect the characteristics of the target population.

➤ To contact people in their sample (to interview them, for example), the researcher needs to know who they are.

To do this a researcher uses a **sampling frame** which, at its most basic, is a list of everyone in a target population. Examples include:

➤ electoral registers — lists of everyone eligible to vote
➤ school registers — lists of children attending school
➤ professional membership lists (e.g. the register of all doctors in Britain kept by the British Medical Association)
➤ company payrolls — lists of employees

However, a researcher will not always have access to such sampling frames. Access may be denied for various reasons:

➤ **Legal reasons**: A school, for example, may not give unauthorised individuals access to their registers.
➤ **Confidentiality**: A business organisation may not give access to its payroll records.
➤ **Secrecy**: Some groups (such as religious organisations, political parties or criminal gangs) may not want to be studied.

**?** Why might a researcher not be able to get access to a sampling frame?

## Types of representative sampling

### Simple random sampling

Simple random sampling is based on the *probability* that the random selection of names from a sampling frame will produce a sample representative of a target population. An important characteristic of this type of sampling is that for it to be truly random everyone in the target population must have an equal chance of being chosen. A simple random sample, therefore, is similar to a lottery:

Feradz/Fotolia

Random samples are based on chance distributions

➤ Everyone in the target population is identified on a sampling frame.
➤ The sample is selected by randomly choosing from the frame until the sample is complete.

A 30% sample of a target population of 100 people, for example, would involve the random selection of 30 people.

### Systematic sampling

A variation on simple random sampling — often used when the target population is very large — is to select names *systematically* by taking the sample directly from a sampling frame. For a 25% sample of a target population containing 100 names, a systematic sample would involve choosing every fourth name from the sampling frame.

Although this technique is not truly random (in this example the fifth name on the list could never be included in the sample so not everyone has an equal chance of inclusion), it is 'random enough' for most samples.

### Advantages of simple random and systematic sampling

➤ **Time**: They are relatively quick and easy ways of selecting samples, especially when the target population is very large.
➤ **Expense**: Both are reasonably inexpensive to create using a sampling frame accurate for the target population.
➤ **Information**: Other than some way of identifying people in the target population (a name for example), the researcher doesn't require any knowledge about this population.

### Disadvantages of simple random and systematic sampling

➤ **Sampling frame**: This may not be available for a target population.
➤ **Unrepresentative**: Chance doesn't always produce a representative sample.

**?** Give one advantage and one disadvantage of simple random sampling.

### Stratified random sampling

A problem with simple random or systematic samples occurs when the target population is **diverse**, consisting of lots of small groups whose views are all important to the research (for example, different age groups within the target population). A **biased sample** can easily occur because with random samples some groups may be **over-represented** and others **under-represented**.

Stratified random sampling avoids these problems, while keeping the idea of sample selection based on chance, by dividing (**stratifying**) the target population into groups whose characteristics are known to the researcher (such as males and females, or different age groups). Each group is then treated as a random sample in its own right.

For example, imagine a target population of 100 people (80 females and 20 males) where the researcher wants a 10% sample. To exactly represent the gender balance of the target population the researcher needs a sample of 8 females and 2 males. This might be achieved by chance, but it's easier to give chance a helping hand by splitting the target population into two groups — the 80 females and the 20 males — and then selecting 10% of each (8 females from the female-only group and 2 males from the male-only group). If we then combine the two samples we get a final random sample fully representative of our target population.

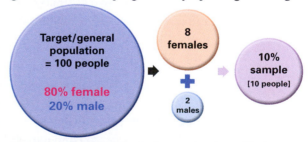

Figure 4.1 A simple worked example of stratified random sampling

### Stratified quota sampling

This variation involves the same technique as stratified random sampling, with two main differences:

➤ **Sampling frame**: Although a sampling frame is always useful, it's not strictly necessary here. It's usually enough just to know the characteristics of respondents — and their associated quotas — in order to construct a sample.

➤ **Non-random selection**: Using the previous gender example, the selection of 8 females from the female-only group and 2 males from the male-only group is done on an 'opportunity basis'; the researcher, for example, works through the group of 20 males, asking each in turn to be part of the sample. Once 2 males have agreed, the '**quota**' for the male-only sample is complete and no further males can be selected — which means this technique isn't truly random in its sample selection because not everyone in the target population has an equal chance of being selected (the first person asked has a greater chance than the last).

### Advantages of stratified sampling

➤ **Focus**: The researcher can focus the sample on relevant distinctions in the target population (age, gender, class, ethnicity, etc.) and ignore irrelevant factors.

➤ **Representativeness**: Known differences in the target population will be accurately reflected in the sample; the researcher can, therefore, be sure the sample will be broadly representative.

➤ **Assets**: In terms of resources, quota samples are usually cheap and quick to construct accurately (which is partly why they're used by political polling organisations).

➤ **Generalisation**: It's possible to generalise from the sample to the target population, even when the sample is relatively small in relation to the target population.

➤ **Size**: Stratified samples can be relatively small, since it's possible to make certain that the sample has accurately reflected the target population.

### Disadvantages of stratified sampling

➤ **Information**: Accurate information about the target population isn't always available, which means a representative sample can't be constructed.

➤ **Uncertainty**: When using a team of researchers to construct a quota sample you can't be certain they have correctly placed everyone in the right quota category. If, for example, your research assistant cannot find '100 men over the age of 65' to fill their quota, there may be a temptation to fill it using men under that age — which would affect the representativeness of the sample.

> **?** Give one advantage and one disadvantage of stratified sampling.

## Non-representative sampling

Although researchers generally find it useful to make their sample representative of the target population, there are times when they might not use a representative sample.

### Choice

For some types of research the sociologist might not want to make generalisations about a large group based only on a sample of that group. They might, for example, simply be interested in the behaviour of the group itself, rather than what they may or may not represent. An example of this type of non-representative sampling is a **case study**. The objective here is to study, in great detail, the characteristics of a particular group (or case). Although a case study is technically an example of a **research method** (see below), it illustrates how a non-representative sample works.

The researcher doesn't care whether the group is representative of any other similar groups and the sample in this type of research *is* the target population. This is perfectly acceptable as long as the researcher doesn't try to **generalise** their findings (the group being studied is representative only of itself). An example of a case study is Ward's (2008) research into drug selling among 'rave' dance participants in London.

### Necessity

Circumstances sometimes make it impossible to create a representative sample and the researcher may be forced to settle for **opportunity sampling**, a general type of non-representative sampling that has two main subdivisions: 'best opportunity' sampling and snowball sampling.

'**Best opportunity**' **sampling** involves deliberately choosing a sample that gives the best possible opportunity to test a hypothesis. If the hypothesis is false for this group, it will probably be false for any other similar groups. Goldthorpe et al. (1968), for example, wanted to test the claim that the working class in Britain was becoming indistinguishable from the middle class. Their best opportunity sample consisted of highly paid car assembly workers in Luton, chosen on the basis that if any working-class group was likely to show lifestyles similar to their middle-class peers it would be this group of 'affluent workers'.

Just as a snowball rolling downhill gets larger as it picks up more snow, a **snowball sample** picks up more and more people to include in the sample over time. A researcher, for example, identifies someone in the target population who is willing to be part of their research. This person then suggests another two or three (perhaps more) people who are also willing to participate. These then suggest further possible participants until the researcher has a usable sample.

Although this technique doesn't produce a representative sample, it may be the best that can be achieved in certain situations. Wallis (1977), for example, used this technique to contact (ex-) members of the Church of Scientology when his request to interview current members was rejected by the Church authorities. This technique is useful when:
➤ no sampling frame is available
➤ the researcher knows little or nothing about the characteristics of their target population

While this technique is not ideal (and runs a real risk of being unrepresentative), it may be the only way a researcher can construct a sample. Charlton et al.'s (2001) study of young children's mobile telephone ownership used an opportunity sample of schoolchildren in the absence of any available sampling frame. For Sappleton et al.'s (2006) analysis of gender segregation in the audio-visual industries, 'Respondents were enlisted through personal referrals, prior contacts and cold calls'.

### Advantages of non-representative sampling

➤ **Availability**: A researcher can construct a sample in situations where it would be impossible to use any other sampling technique.

➤ **Resources**: It can be a cheap and quick method of sampling (although this depends on both sample size and the speed at which the researcher is able to contact respondents).

### Disadvantages of non-representative sampling

➤ **Representativeness**: It's unlikely the sample will be truly representative and there is no way of checking its representativeness.

➤ **Resources**: It can be a relatively expensive and time-consuming sampling technique (especially if the sample is large and/or widely dispersed across a large area, and respondents are reluctant or unable to suggest further potential respondents).

➤ **A self-selected sample** is a distinct possibility because this type of sample effectively 'picks itself' rather than being selected by the researcher.

A good example of a self-selected sample is Hite's (1976) investigation into female sexuality that claimed to uncover a range of interesting sexualities and practices 'representative of the population of America'. Her respondents, however, were self-selected because she chose anyone who responded to her advertisements asking for people to talk openly about their sexual behaviour. In this respect, therefore, the responses of a small number of unrepresentative people who wanted the world to know about their sexual behaviour came to represent 'general public behaviour in America'.

This research also illustrates a further potential problem (not exclusively related to opportunity sampling): that of **statistically inadequate samples**. A sample that is too small to accurately represent a target population, such as a couple of people in the street who are asked what they think about the education system, will be inadequate for research purposes. As a general rule, the larger the sample as a *proportion* of a target population the greater the *probability* it will be statistically adequate. This may improve the chances of your sample being representative, but a large sample is no guarantee of a representative sample.

**?** Why might a self-selected sample be unrepresentative?

# Data collection

Once the researcher is ready to start collecting data, a range of **methodological considerations** arise. 'Methodology', Browne (2000) notes, 'is concerned with the choice of research methods for collecting, analysing and interpreting data'.

## Pilot studies

It is sometimes useful to conduct a pilot study. Van Teijlingen and Hundley (2001) refer to this as a 'mini version of a full-scale study'; it is, in other words, a small-scale exploratory piece of research, carried out prior to the actual research, designed to test and tweak the research design. The purposes may include:

- convincing funding bodies of the research team's competence and demonstrating that a study is both possible and worth funding
- identifying any problems that might occur in a full study (such as establishing access to respondents)
- testing the research methods (e.g. by trialling questions to eliminate possible sources of bias, checking for misunderstood questions and collecting preliminary data)
- establishing whether the sampling frame, technique and size are appropriate
- determining the level and extent of resources (such as finance and staff training) needed for a study

## Concept operationalisation

A researcher always needs to define, test or measure (or '**operationalise**') the various elements involved in the hypothesis or research question. In the poverty hypothesis we used previously, a researcher would need to be clear about how poverty is defined — otherwise it would be impossible to test the relationship between poverty and stealing. We can operationalise the concept of poverty by using one or more **indicators**. In this instance income would be a useful indicator: we could specify that, for the purpose of the research, anyone with an annual income of less than £10,000 would be considered poor.

Most research involves concepts that can't be easily defined or measured because they don't physically exist. We therefore need to use indicators of their existence, such as income in the case of poverty, which can be measured.

> **?**
>
> Suggest a possible indicator we could use to measure each of the following:
> **1** educational achievement
> **2** religious beliefs
> **3** the extent of crime in the UK

## Choosing a research method

Although all research methods have their strengths, weaknesses, uses and limitations, we can identify two methodological concepts that also influence the researcher's choice of method in terms of data collection: reliability and validity.

### Reliability

Reliability refers to the *consistency* of the data collected in any research process. We can check the accuracy of data by repeating the research to see if we get the same, or very similar, results (we may have to allow for possible changes over time). In general, data are reliable if similar results are gained by different researchers (or the same researcher at different times) asking the same questions of similar people.

A simple example might be a researcher cross-checking the reliability of a response within a questionnaire by asking the same question in a different way:

➢ How old are you?
➢ When were you born?

If they get two different answers, the data are unreliable — and if data are unreliable, any conclusions we draw from them are going to be of limited use.

We need, therefore, to be aware that data reliability is affected by such things as:

➢ **Researcher bias**: Are there opportunities for the researcher (consciously or unconsciously) to influence or distort the data collection process?
➢ **Definitions**: When comparing data over time, is the same definition used for whatever is being measured?
➢ **Replicability**: If another sociologist attempted to exactly repeat a piece of research, would similar results be achieved?

### Validity

Validity refers to the extent to which data actually measure or describe what they claim to be measuring or describing. For example, if we were interested in the extent of crime in our society, we could use official crime statistics (a **secondary data** source published by the government — see below). We would need to be aware, however, that the validity of these statistics may be limited because they only record reported crimes — and people may not report crime for many reasons.

Validity is a useful concept because it reminds us to consider the accuracy of different data types — primary, secondary, qualitative and quantitative. While some forms of data (such as official statistics) may be *reliable*, their *validity* may be questionable for two reasons:

➢ **Representativeness**: They may not apply to everyone in a particular group. In Britain, for example, 'unemployment statistics' represent only those registered for unemployment benefit, not all those without a job. To achieve representativeness, the information we collect must be sufficiently comprehensive to accurately embody whatever the research claims to represent. Official crime statistics, for example, are unrepresentative of all crimes committed in our society so anything a piece of research says about crime on the basis of this data source needs to be *qualified* by saying that some types of criminal behaviour may not be fully represented in the statistics.

> **Depth**: They may lack the depth and detail required to accurately represent the views of a particular individual or group (and so fails to measure what they aim — or claim — to measure).

When evaluating the validity of a particular research method, data type or data source we always need to question whether they actually measure what they claim to be measuring. If they do, however limited their scope may be, they are valid. If they don't then validity is likely to be low.

## Primary and secondary data

The actual mechanics of data collection is an important element in research design. There are two basic types of sociological data: primary and secondary.

### Primary data

Primary data involve information collected personally by a researcher (or their research team). Sociologists use a range of research methods, such as questionnaires, interviews and observational studies, as *sources* of primary data.

#### Advantages

> **Data control**: The researcher is responsible for collecting data and this gives complete control over how they are collected, by whom and for what purpose (there is no need to rely on other people to collect the data accurately).
> **Reliability, validity and representativeness**: The ability to exercise a measure of control over how data are collected doesn't guarantee their reliability, validity or representativeness — a badly designed piece of research can be unreliable, invalid and unrepresentative. However, it's much easier for the researcher to deal with these issues when designing and carrying out the research themselves.

#### Disadvantages

> **Time**: It is time-consuming to design, construct and carry out research which collects primary data. If the group being studied is large and if individual interviewing is involved, the collection will take considerable time and resources.
> **Expense**: The cost of a researcher's time (among other things) may be a factor in the design of the research.
> **Access**: Having designed a piece of primary research, you need access to the people you want to study — and this may involve both *material problems* (your plan to interview the 100 richest people in the UK will come to nothing if they refuse to be interviewed) and *immaterial problems* (with historical research, for example, potential primary sources may be dead).

### Secondary data

Secondary data involve information *not* personally collected by the researcher. Sources include newspapers, books, personal documents (such as letters and diaries), official documents (such as government reports and statistics) and even the research of other sociologists.

### Advantages

➤ **Resources**: It may be unnecessary or impractical to create some forms of data (using primary methods) when they already exist. The British government, for example, collects and distributes a huge amount of statistical data each year. For the price of a book, a visit to library or an internet search, the researcher has immediate access to data — such as national crime or marriage statistics — that would cost an enormous amount of money, time and effort to collect personally. In addition there may be situations where secondary data are the only available resources (for example, the primary data sources may be dead, as in some historical research or research into suicide).

➤ **Comparisons**: Secondary data can be useful for historical and/or comparative purposes. Aries (1962), for example, used historical data, such as paintings and documents, to support his argument that childhood was a relatively recent invention.

➤ **Reliability**: Some (but not all) forms of secondary data can be highly reliable. Official statistics (those produced by the UK government, for example) are generally considered reliable because:

  ➤ They are collected regularly and consistently in the same way from the same sources. Education statistics, for example, are regularly collated by the Office for National Statistics from a variety of government sources and surveys.

  ➤ They generally measure, within reason, the same things each time they're collected; comparisons made between different years are, therefore, comparing 'like with like'. Official statistics measuring educational achievement at GCSE, for example, consistently use the same definition of achievement (grades A*–C).

➤ **Validity**: Some kinds of secondary source (biographies and personal documents such as diaries, for example) provide highly valid data because they give detailed, well-rounded insights into people's thoughts and behaviour — something that may be especially useful in circumstances where individuals are dead or have written contemporary accounts of long-past historical events.

➤ **Representativeness**: Where data are produced by the British government there is normally a high level of representativeness because the resources (e.g. funding, number of researchers) committed to collecting data mean that large samples can be accurately constructed. The census (a questionnaire distributed to every household in the UK every 10 years), for example, draws on a highly representative sample of the UK population. Its reliability is also high because it must, by law, be completed by every household.

*Disadvantages*

➤ **Data control**: This may be difficult because secondary data are not always produced with the needs of sociologists in mind. For example, the way governments measure social class may differ from sociological ways of measuring class.

➤ **Reliability**: The range and variety of secondary data make generalisations about reliability difficult — some sources, such as official statistics, may be reliable whereas others, such as a diary or newspaper article, may be unreliable. To assess the reliability of secondary data we always need to ask questions about:

> ➤ **who** produced them
> ➤ **how** they were produced
> ➤ the **objectives** behind their production

➤ **Validity and representativeness**: Do the data represent the viewpoint of just one individual or a much wider range of views? A newspaper article, for example, can express the personal and unrepresentative view of a single journalist. Similarly, historical documents may reflect the views of particular social classes, because it was generally the upper classes in Britain who, until quite recently, recorded their particular view of the world. Conversely, the only surviving record of something may provide a valid insight into that event, but without supporting evidence (a question of *reliability*) we can't be certain of either its validity or representativeness. As with reliability, the range and scope of secondary data make it difficult to generalise about their validity — some forms, such as eyewitness descriptions of an event, may have greater validity than official statistics that simply focus on quantifying something.

Reliability

**H** ow
**O** bjectives
**W** ho

> **?** Give two reasons why a sociologist might collect secondary rather than primary data.

## Quantitative and qualitative data and methods

Primary and secondary data can be subdivided into two types: quantitative and qualitative.

### Quantitative data

Quantitative data are data expressed *statistically* or *numerically*. We could, for example, count the number of people in Britain who live in poverty or vote Conservative; such data are usually expressed in one of three ways:

➤ **Number**: For example, the total number of people who live in poverty could be stated.

➤ **Percentage** (the number of people per 100 in a population): For example, 30% of British voters regularly vote Conservative.

➤ **Rate** (defined here as the number of people per 1000 in a population): For example, if the birth rate in a particular country is 1, this means that one baby is born each year for every 1000 people in the population.

Although raw numbers can be useful (e.g. knowing the number of children who will be starting school in 10 years' time allows the government to plan for the number of schoolteachers, school places and so on), data are often expressed as a rate or percentage because this allows **comparisons** between and within groups and societies. For example, when comparing unemployment between Britain and America, expressing unemployment as a raw number wouldn't tell us very much, since the population of America is roughly five times larger than that of Britain. Expressing unemployment as a percentage or rate allows us to compare 'like with like' by taking into account the fact that one society has more people than the other (so we might expect the larger society to, numerically, have more people unemployed, even though unemployment rates might be broadly similar).

> **?** Briefly explain, using an example to illustrate your answer, what is meant by quantitative data.

### Strengths

➤ **Comparisons**: Where the researcher wants to test a hypothesis, quantitative data allow for relatively simple 'True/False' distinctions to be made on the basis of statistical comparisons (the hypothesis will be either true or false). Similarly, cross-cultural comparisons (crime rates in different countries, for example) are made possible through the use of quantitative data. **Longitudinal studies** (where the same group may be questioned at different times to track changes in their behaviour) can also exploit this comparative feature of quantitative data. As Kruger (2003) argues, quantitative methods and data 'allow us to summarize vast sources of information and make comparisons across categories and over time'.

➤ **Objectivity**: Where the researcher has no direct, necessary and personal involvement with the generation of data, it is less likely (but not, of course, impossible) that personal biases will intrude into the process. This gives quantitative data collection what Kealey and Protheroe (1996) term the ability to 'eliminate or minimize subjective judgments'.

➤ **Reliability**: Quantitative data tend to be more reliable than qualitative data because it's easier to **replicate** (repeat) the data collection process. This is because **standardised questions** (questions that don't change) can be asked of different groups, or the same group at different times. Matveev (2002) notes that the ability to control the conditions under which data are collected (such as using standardised questionnaires) makes quantitative data more reliable.

➤ **Numbers**: The ability to express relationships statistically can be advantageous if the researcher doesn't particularly need or want to explore the reasons for people's behaviour. For example, if you simply need to know the number of murders committed each year or the number of students absent from the classroom in any given month then quantitative data satisfy this purpose more than adequately.

Strengths of quantitative data

**C** omparisons
**O** bjectivity
**R** eliability
**N** umbers

*Weaknesses*

> **Control**: Although the ability to quantify behaviour can be a significant plus factor for researchers, this situation is frequently achieved by placing the respondent in an artificial social setting. In other words, realism is sacrificed for control. In their everyday lives, for example, people rarely, if ever, encounter situations where they're asked to respond to a list of questions from a stranger; similarly, people are rarely placed in situations where their behaviour is observed (secretly or otherwise). The main question here, therefore, is the extent to which a researcher can capture people's 'normal behaviour' or 'real opinions' when they place respondents in a situation that is neither normal nor real.

> **Validity**: Quantitative methods only capture a relatively narrow range of data about people's behaviour — what Day (1998) calls the 'Who What When Where'. Although these can be interesting and informative questions, quantitative methods are relatively poor at capturing the *reasons* for such behaviour — something related to the problem of depth (see next point).

> **Depth**: The more detailed the data about behaviour, the more difficult they are to meaningfully quantify. One criticism of quantitative methods, therefore, is that they focus on relatively superficial aspects of behaviour while failing to address the complexities involved in even very simple forms of behaviour.

> **Meaning**: A lack of depth and detail leads to a further limitation — one noted by Kruger (2003) when he suggests it is 'difficult to get the real meaning of an issue by looking at numbers'. Although quantitative methods can ask people why they commit crimes or why they truant from school, their lack of depth and detail means they can't easily express the 'richness of meaning' behind their behaviour.

> **Prejudgements**: McCullough (1988) argues that a significant methodological limitation is the fact that 'issues are only measured if they are known prior to the beginning of the survey (and, therefore, have been incorporated into the questionnaire)'. In other words, in order to quantify behaviour the researcher must decide, in advance of their research, what is and what is not significant in relation to the behaviour being studied. There is little or no opportunity to develop the research outside of the original parameters decided by the researcher.

> **Reliability**: Although, as a general principle, quantitative data are usually considered both 'highly reliable' and 'more reliable' than qualitative data, this is not necessarily the case (reliability is not an automatic quality of any one particular research method). As Harvey (2002) argues, 'Many apparently quantitative data depend critically on the way in which they were collected, who collected them, where they were collected, when they were collected and from whom they were collected'.

We can also note the risk of **quantophrenia** in the choice of quantitative data. This term refers to what Sorokin (1956), partly tongue-in-cheek, terms a 'psychological compulsion to grasp for the numeric' — a 'condition' that leads to the use of quantification for its own sake, regardless of whether or not it tells us anything useful or interesting about the behaviour being quantified. As Eberstadt (2006) puts it, the 'victims' of this condition 'obsess over numbers as descriptors, no matter how dubious their basis or questionable their provenance'.

> **?** Briefly assess the strengths and weaknesses of quantitative data as a way of understanding people's behaviour.

### Qualitative data

With qualitative data the aim is to capture the *quality* of people's behaviour (what they feel, for example, about a sociologist asking them about crimes they may have committed). Such data say something about how people *experience* the social world and can be used to understand the **meanings** they give to behaviour. Boyle (1977), for example, studied the behaviour of a juvenile gang from the viewpoint of its members while Goffman (1961) tried to understand the experiences of patients in an American mental institution. Both were trying to capture and express the quality of people's behaviour — how they feel about and react to different situations.

> **?** What do sociologists mean by qualitative data?

### *Strengths*

- **Imposition**: If your research objective is to understand the meaning of people's behaviour, you must allow people the scope to talk freely. Qualitative data allow for this because the researcher doesn't *impose* their interpretation on a situation (by asking direct, quantifiable questions for example).
- **Depth**: Qualitative data provide greater depth and detail about behaviour since, as Day (1998) suggests, they are concerned with discovering 'the Why' — the complex reasons for such behaviour.
- **Prejudgements**: Qualitative methods avoid the problem of the researcher prejudging what are and what are not significant data prior to starting their research. Where the research objective is to describe or draw out people's opinions and the reasons for their behaviour, the respondent, rather than the researcher, is effectively the driving force — they lead and the researcher follows. The researcher can't tightly control the research process because respondents may start to talk about things they see as significant and take the research in directions the researcher had not originally thought about when the research was planned.
- **Rapport**: Many qualitative methods, such as observational methods where a researcher may live closely with those being researched, demand the researcher establish a close relationship with the people being researched (which doesn't mean they have to like them, only that they come to understand their situation). This has a couple of advantages:

> It means that everyone involved in the research is free to suggest new ideas and directions — the role of the respondent isn't limited to answering questions.

> Where the atmosphere is more relaxed and less clinical the researcher is more likely to get respondents to open up about their thoughts and feelings — which may improve research validity.

> **Validity**: Qualitative methods don't have a monopoly on validity (any poorly designed research can lack validity regardless of the methods used) but when we're dealing with the complexities of human behaviour it is much more likely that research methods that explore this complexity will score highly in terms of their validity — that they will measure what they claim to measure.

> **Naturalism**: Qualitative methods allow researchers greater freedom to study people in their everyday or 'normal' settings and this gives a greater chance of either observing or revealing what people 'really believe' or how they 'really behave'. This is a bit like the difference between asking people to remember and describe something they did last Monday and having been able to follow and observe them to discover exactly what they did. As Matveev (2002) suggests, qualitative methods allow the researcher to gain a 'more realistic feel of the world that cannot be experienced in the numerical data and statistical analysis used in quantitative research'.

*Weaknesses*

> **Comparisons**: Qualitative research is difficult to compare across time and space (because you're not comparing 'like with like'); it also tends to be structured in ways that make the research difficult to replicate.

> **Reliability**: Qualitative research methods generally produce data with lower levels of reliability:

  > Cassell and Symon (1994) argue that, where research evolves to take account of the input of different respondents, the original research objectives may change, making it difficult for subsequent researchers to replicate.

  > Where qualitative methods produce vast amounts of data relating to a wide range of issues, the researcher, as the initial interpreter, has a pivotal role to play in choosing which data are important and which are to be discarded. Different researchers could potentially arrive at different conclusions based on the data they choose to use, which means reliability will necessarily suffer.

  > Levy (2006), however, argues that reliability evidenced through the ability to replicate research is not a useful test for qualitative research methods. She suggests the concept of **trustworthiness** might be a more useful measure of the internal reliability of qualitative methods: 'it is up to the researcher to provide evidence of reliability by carefully documenting the data collection and analysis process...can we trust that the results are a 'true' reflection of our subject?'.

> **Abilities**: Qualitative methods require different skills from the researcher. The qualitative researcher may want to establish a close **rapport** with their respondents

while for their quantitative counterparts this is neither necessary nor desirable (since it would lower the **objectivity** of the research). In observational research the researcher needs to be able to convincingly and consistently 'play a role' within the group they are studying — and this requires a very different set of skills from those needed to deliver a questionnaire or structured interview.

➤ **Generalisations**: Qualitative research generally focuses on the intensive study of relatively small groups, so opportunities to generalise research findings may be limited.

> **?** Briefly assess the strengths and weaknesses of qualitative data as a way of understanding people's behaviour.

### Quantitative and qualitative data

There are occasions when a researcher may want to combine the two types of data — for example, collecting quantitative data about educational achievement or the number of people who visit their doctor each year alongside qualitative data that seek to explore the satisfaction levels of pupils or patients.

Alternatively, quantitative data are sometimes collected before starting qualitative research, as an **enabling study** to establish whether or not there is anything to qualitatively investigate. A researcher looking at reasons for school truancy in their locality, for example, may first carry out a quantitative analysis to discover whether or not pupils are actually absent from the classroom.

## Research ethics

Ethics refer to the morality of doing something. In sociological research there are ethical issues concerning what a researcher should or should not do before, during and after their research. It is necessary to consider both legal and safety issues (for the researcher, those being researched, and any subsequent researchers). These issues are discussed below.

### Legal considerations

➤ **Power**: It would be unethical to bully or blackmail people (emotionally or physically) into participating in research. In addition, especially when researching people who are relatively powerless, relationships need to be based on trust and personal integrity on the part of the researcher. For example, if the researcher promises anonymity when researching people involved in criminal or deviant activities, disclosing those identities to the authorities or the media would be unethical.

➤ **Illegal behaviour**: In Britain the collection, storage and retrieval of data are governed by acts and laws, such as the Data Protection Act, the Human Rights Act, copyright laws and the laws of libel. In addition, if research involves criminal or deviant activities, the researcher may have to consider the ethical question of participation in such behaviour or their responsibilities to both the perpetrators and their possible victims.

➤ **Research consequences**: Data can be used in many different ways (and not always in the way the researcher intended — media reports may seriously distort the research, for example) and participants should be aware of any possible consequences of their participation. In addition, if respondents feel they have been mistreated (physically or verbally, for example) or misled, this may have legal consequences for the researcher and create problems for any subsequent research.

➤ **Consent**: The researcher should always (at least try to) gain the informed consent of those being researched.

### Safety considerations

➤ **Rights and well-being**: Care should always be taken to ensure the physical and psychological safety of both the researcher and the respondents. The researcher needs to safeguard the interests, rights and general well-being of respondents. For example, the researcher should respect respondent privacy and minimise any anxiety or distress caused by the research.

➤ **Involvement**: Some types of research involve methods (such as covert participant observation — see below) that create high levels of involvement with respondents. Where close personal and/or intimate relationships arise, the researcher should ensure that, once the research is completed and contact diminishes, distress is not caused to potentially vulnerable people. For example, if your research involves visiting the elderly on a regular basis, it would be unethical to simply stop your visits once the research is completed.

### Code of practice

The conduct of sociological research is surrounded by a range issues that relate to what the British Sociological Association (2004) terms **professional integrity**. The behaviour of researchers is bound by a code of ethical practice that is an integral part of the professional research role. Pimple (2002) suggests three main ethical questions — Is it true? Is it fair? Is it wise?

### Is it true?

This relates to both the research process (how it is generally conducted) and, most importantly, the relationship between research findings and their implications. At its most extreme, perhaps, unethical behaviour in this category would involve the researcher deliberately *fabricating* ('making up') data or falsifying their results.

### Is it fair?

Unethical behaviour here relates to the different social relationships created during the course of a research study.

First, there is the relationship between the researcher and **other researchers**. This involves such issues as the **ownership** of a completed piece of research (who, for example, can ethically claim to be the author?). Authorship can be significant when career advancement (in a university, for example) depends on the ability to publish original research. One kind of unfair behaviour is **plagiarism** — passing off the work of others as your own.

Second, there is the relationship between researcher and **respondents**. This relationship is usually ethically straightforward, in terms of legality and safety for example. There are, however, 'moral grey areas' that sometimes arise during **covert** forms of research where the respondent is not aware they're being studied:

➤ Wallis (1977) wanted to study the Church of Scientology but the Church leaders refused to cooperate with his request for access to existing members, so he contacted ex-members instead and based his research around their opinions and experiences.

➤ Rosenhan (1973), who wanted to test if doctors could accurately diagnose schizophrenia, sent students displaying fake symptoms into hospitals to test his hypothesis that they could not — and the experiment discovered that doctors were unable to expose the fake patients.

➤ In Milgram's (1974) study of the effects of authority on people's behaviour, he investigated whether respondents were willing to inflict extreme levels of pain on innocent strangers when instructed to do so by an authority figure. Respondents were convinced they were administering electric shocks to 'learners' whenever the latter gave an incorrect answer to a question (in fact no shocks were administered and the 'victims' were under instructions to pretend they were being hurt). Such research raises important ethical issues about:

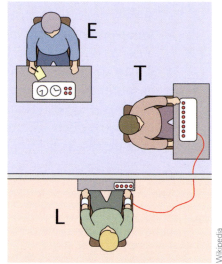

Illustration of the setup of a Milgram experiment. The experimenter (E) convinces the subject ('Teacher' T) to give what he believes are painful electric shocks to another subject, who is actually an actor ('Learner' L)

➤ tricking people into cooperating with research

➤ causing distress to respondents (some argued and protested about the instructions they were given and some broke down in the face of the pain they believed they were inflicting)

➤ experimenting on people who do not know they are being studied

> **Suggest two reasons to justify each of the following:**
> ➤ **studying groups who don't want to be studied**
> ➤ **deceiving people in the course of research**
> ➤ **secretly researching people**

**?**

OCR AS Sociology

*Is it wise?*

Here we are concerned with ethical questions about the relationship between 'the research agenda and the broader social and physical world, present and future':

➤ Can the research itself be morally justified?

➤ Would some other type of research have greater moral justification?

As Pimple puts it:

> Will the research improve the human condition, or damage it? Will it lead to a better world, or a worse one? Or less grandly, which of the many possible lines of research would we be better off pursuing? We have finite time and money for pursuing research, and the wisdom of research programs is a valid question in research ethics.

# Data analysis

Foucault (1970) argues that data 'can never speak for itself'; information has to be **analysed** and **interpreted**. Analysis involves bringing together and categorising related ideas, for example. Interpretation involves asking what the data and the overall research mean.

Analysis and interpretation take place on three levels:

➤ **Private or internal**: This level involves thinking about methodological concepts such as data reliability and validity (discussed earlier), to ensure data are logical and consistent.

➤ **Practical**: This level relates to the purpose of data collection: whether testing a hypothesis or answering a research question, the researcher must do something with the data. This might involve making **correlations** — noting how two or more things seem to occur at similar times. Wilkinson and Pickett (2009), for example, make extensive correlations between social inequality and crime, such that the more unequal a society is, the higher its relative level of crime. It might involve suggesting **causation** — that one thing occurs because something else has made it happen.

➤ **Public or external**: Whenever research is presented 'to the world' it represents the outcome of a process of social construction; at its most basic this means that not everything the researcher saw, heard or recorded is presented for public consumption, partly because it would make for very lengthy and unwieldy reports and partly because a great deal of collected data may be irrelevant to the overall research objectives. Decisions always have to be made about what to include (present to the world) and exclude.

**?** Why can data never 'speak for itself'?

# Presentation of completed research

Glaser and Strauss (1967) suggest that the presentation of research generally involves four related elements:

> **Patterns**: Is it possible to discover patterns in the data?
> **Analysis**: This involves analysing both current and related research to discover common themes and trends in the data.
> **Reflection**: This involves a questioning approach to understanding and interpreting the research. (Does it support or disprove the hypothesis? Does it answer research questions or raise further questions?)
> **Theory**: Does the research suggest ways the data can be linked to create an overall theory?

Presenting research

**P** atterns
**A** nalysis
**R** eflection
**T** heory

Finally, once the data have been analysed and interpreted they can be presented in terms of:

> **findings**
> **conclusions** about, for example, the hypothesis (has it been disproven?)
> **limitations** — this might include discussion of various research problems that impacted on the study
> **suggestions** for further research, improvements to the research design and the like

**Exam-style question**

Explain and evaluate the use of qualitative data techniques when researching the identities of young people who are seen as school failures. **(52 marks)**

# Chapter 5

## Exploring the use of quantitative data-collection methods and analysis in the context of research

**By the end of this chapter you will be able to:**

➤ define and evaluate quantitative data and primary and secondary research methods (including questionnaires, structured interviews, content analysis, and official and non-official statistics)

# Primary quantitative methods

In this section we will discuss two different kinds of primary quantitative method: social surveys and content analysis.

## Social surveys

Lawson and Garrod (2009) define a survey as 'the systematic collection of information about a given population', which could involve using any number of different research methods. However, we can think about surveys as involving the large-scale collection of data using a questionnaire (or some variation thereof, such as a structured interview) — a list of written questions normally completed in one of two ways:

➤ **Privately** (with the researcher not present): This is called a **postal questionnaire** (even though it is not necessarily posted). Respondents write their answers without verbal guidance from the researcher.

➢ **Publicly** (in the presence of the researcher): This is normally called a **structured interview** and respondents usually answer a researcher's questions verbally.

The same questions could serve equally as a postal questionnaire or a structured interview, the main difference being how they are administered.

## Questionnaires

Questionnaires are used to ask two types of question: closed or open.

### Closed questions

Closed questions are also called closed-ended or precoded questions. The researcher provides a set of questions with answers from which the respondent can choose one (or sometimes more) that best represents their situation, feelings, beliefs and so forth (hence the idea of questions being precoded — the researcher limits the responses that can be given). A (very) simple example is one that asks the respondent to choose between two options (although it's always useful to include a 'don't know' option for those who have no opinion either way):

| Do you own an iphone? | Yes | No | Don't Know |
|---|---|---|---|
| **Code** | **[1]** | **[2]** | **[3]** |

**Variations** can be a bit more adventurous. For example, the respondent could be allowed the (limited) opportunity to fill in an answer.

| What is your favourite subject? | |
|---|---|
| Sociology | |
| Physics | |
| Other (please specify) | |

The inclusion of an 'other' option avoids the need for long lists (in this instance, a list of curriculum subjects). It also means the respondent can add something the researcher may not have considered.

Alternatively, a researcher could measure respondent **attitudes**:

| How strongly do you agree/disagree with the statement 'Sociology is the best subject I have ever studied'? | | | | |
|---|---|---|---|---|
| Agree very strongly | Agree strongly | Neither agree nor disagree | Disagree strongly | Disagree very strongly |

There are further variations on the closed question theme, but their defining characteristic is that they allow respondents little, if any, scope to develop an answer beyond the categories preselected by the researcher. One advantage for the researcher is that the answer data are relatively easy to express statistically, hence such questions are used extensively to collect **quantitative** data.

### Open questions

Open (or open-ended) questions are different in that the researcher doesn't provide a set of answers from which to choose. Rather, the respondent can answer in their own words. A simple example of an open question is:

➤ What do you like about studying sociology?

This type of question can probe a little deeper into a respondent's opinions and produces a (limited) form of *qualitative* data (although the main objective with open questions in a questionnaire is usually to *quantify* responses in some way). Questionnaires can, of course, contain a mix of open and closed questions.

> **?** Write a closed question to find out how many GCSE qualifications someone has.

### Strengths of questionnaires

➤ **Validity**: Although postal questionnaires rarely have much depth, one aspect which may give them greater validity than some other methods is their anonymity: because respondents never meet the researcher, questionnaires can more easily explore areas which are potentially embarrassing (such as sexuality) or incriminating than can other methods. If people can anonymously admit to crimes they've committed, for example, they may answer questions more honestly than they would have done in the researcher's presence; this can lead to greater validity because the research potentially measures what it set out to measure.

➤ **Interview/interviewer effect**: This type of effect occurs when the relationship between the researcher and the respondent creates a situation that **biases** the responses (such as when a respondent gives answers they think the researcher wants to hear). Postal questionnaires — because they involve no personal (face-to-face) interaction — avoid this potential source of bias.

➤ **Coding and quantification**: The use of precoded questions makes it much easier to quantify data, since the options available are already known, limited in number and (relatively) easy to count. However, although closed questions are easy to codify, this is not necessarily the case with open questions. The researcher may receive a wide variety of very different responses, each of which has to be categorised, coded and quantified.

➤ **Analysis**: Postal questionnaires are relatively quick and easy to code and interpret (in some instances, 'interpretation' simply involves counting responses).

➤ **Reliability**: A questionnaire is easy to **standardise**, which increases reliability because everyone answers exactly the same questions.

➤ **Sampling**: Postal questionnaires are useful when the researcher needs to contact large numbers of people quickly, easily and efficiently. The respondents also do most of the

Questionnaire strengths

**V** alidity
**I** nterview effect
**C** oding
**A** nalysis
**R** eliability
**S** ampling

time-consuming work by actually completing the questionnaire before returning it (or not, as the case may be).

### Weaknesses of questionnaires

➤ **Anonymity**: This can work both ways — it may encourage honesty, but if someone other than the intended respondent completes the questionnaire then research **validity** and **representativeness** will be affected.

➤ **Reliability**: Where the researcher is not present it's impossible to know if a respondent has understood a question properly or to check that the questionnaire has been completed correctly. The researcher also has to trust that questions mean the same thing to all respondents. These problems can, to some extent, be avoided by conducting a pilot study, but they can never be totally eliminated (for example, does everyone understand 'the fear of crime' in exactly the same way?).

➤ **Responses**: Response rates are generally low for postal questionnaires (only a small proportion of those receiving a questionnaire tend to return it to the researcher) which may mean a carefully designed sample becomes unrepresentative. Research **validity** may also be affected by a low response rate because it increases the chances of a **self-selected sample**. In addition, people may fail to respond to particular questions (missing them out completely, for example), or they may respond incorrectly to a question (e.g. by ticking two choices when only one was requested).

➤ **Validity**: The questionnaire format makes it difficult to examine *complex* issues and opinions. Even where open-ended questions are used, the **depth** of answers tends to be more limited than with almost any other method. This may mean the researcher fails to collect potentially significant and informative data.

➤ **Bias**: While we have to assume that, for ethical reasons, sociological researchers do not intentionally bias their research data, questionnaires may introduce *unintentional* bias in terms of question phrasing and content — and this will impact on data reliability and validity. Some problems here include:

  ➤ **Ambiguity**: If a question has more than one meaning, people will effectively be answering different questions. For example, the question 'Do you agree that most people believe the prime minister is doing a good job?' is actually two questions; you could agree or disagree that the prime minister is doing a good job — but you could also agree or disagree with 'most people's belief'.

  ➤ **Leading questions**: This type of question is one that suggests a required answer (as in the above question; by saying 'most people agree' the question challenges the respondent to go against the majority).

  ➤ **Leading answers**: When giving respondents a range of possible answers it's important to ensure they are weighted equally. For example, the following possible answers are too heavily weighted in favour of a *positive* answer to the question posed.

| How do you rate sociology as a subject? | | | | |
|---|---|---|---|---|
| Brilliant! | Incredible! | Fantastic! | Marvellous! | Not bad |

➤ **Precision**: If an option isn't precisely defined it will mean different things to different people. Does 'occasionally', for example, mean the same thing to everyone?

➤ **Hypothetical questions**: These questions require respondents to imagine themselves in a position they do not actually hold ('If you were the prime minister how would you run the country?') — and imaginary questions invariably produce imaginary answers.

**?** How could a pilot study be used to test the reliability of a postal questionnaire?

## Structured interview

This involves respondents answering questions (both closed and, more rarely, open) read to them by a researcher.

### Strengths

A structured interview is more time consuming for the researcher than a questionnaire

➤ **Reliability**: Problems or issues surrounding the research can be discussed between the participants. The interviewer can, for example, explain the objectives of the research and resolve any problems with understanding or answering questions. If a respondent is unable or unwilling to provide an answer, the researcher will be aware of the reasons for this and may be able to resolve them.

➤ **Representativeness**: Structured interviews avoid unrepresentative research caused by low response rates or self-selected samples. Response rates are invariably high (they should be 100%) because the researcher rather than the respondent actually writes down answers given to a question.

### Weaknesses

➤ **Interview effect**: This occurs when a respondent tries to 'help' the researcher by providing answers designed to please or encourage — and if this happens research **validity** is lowered. Rather than answering honestly or accurately respondents simply provide answers they think the researcher wants to hear. This may not be done deliberately but may be caused by a **halo effect** — a situation Draper (2006) describes as occurring when the novelty of being interviewed, and a desire to reward the interviewer for giving the respondent the chance to experience it, may result in unintentionally dishonest answers.

➤ **Interviewer effect**: This refers to how the *relationship* between researcher and respondent may bias responses and lead to invalid data:

➤ An aggressive interviewer, for example, may intimidate a respondent into giving answers that don't really reflect their beliefs.

> Status considerations (based on factors such as gender, age, class and ethnicity) may also bias the data; a female respondent may feel embarrassed about answering questions about her sexuality posed by a male researcher and not answer honestly.

> **Prestige bias**: This occurs when a respondent gives an answer designed to not make themselves look bad. Opinion polls, for example, sometimes show respondents saying they would willingly pay more taxes if it helped to improve hospitals or care of the elderly — while actually voting for parties that promise to reduce taxes.

> **Prejudgements**: As with postal questionnaires, the researcher has decided, in advance of their research, what is and what is not significant in relation to the behaviour being studied.

> **Biased questions**: Again, the same types of biased questions noted in relation to postal questionnaires can be an unintentional feature of structured interviews.

**?** What are two validity problems associated with structured interviews?

# Content analysis

This research method is somewhat unique in terms of the methods covered here in that it has both **quantitative** and **qualitative** forms — the latter is outlined in the chapter on qualitative research methods (Chapter 6). What both varieties have in common is the study of texts (which for our purpose refers to data sources such as television, written documents and the like — a text is just a general term referring to data and is not restricted to written material).

**Quantitative** analysis of media texts involves using statistical techniques to do things like categorise and count the frequency of people's behaviour, as in the following examples:

> **Television**: Analysing *EastEnders* could involve creating two basic categories (men and women) and then counting the number of minutes each gender appears on screen. A more complex analysis might involve the use of categories like location (where each character is seen, such as in the pub as a customer or an employee, in their own home and the like) or activity (what each character does while they're on screen). Such analyses build up a picture of the **patterns of behaviour** that underlie the social interaction portrayed on screen.

> **Newspapers**: This could involve counting the number of column inches given to activities that focus on men as opposed to women — or counting the number of times men and women are pictured. A more complex analysis might involve analysing the prominence given to different stories featuring men and women.

Quantitative content analysis, therefore, is mainly concerned with categorising behaviour and its main 'tool of the trade' is a **content analysis grid** — a chart used to systematically collect statistical data. Table 5.1 is a very simple content analysis grid designed to analyse the behaviour of characters in a television programme.

Table 5.1  Sample content analysis grid

| Character | Male/female | Age | Place and purpose | How long on screen |
|---|---|---|---|---|
| Jo Banks | F | 37 | Pub (employee) | 15 seconds |
| Tom Ward | M | 56 | Pub (customer) | 43 seconds |
| Jo Banks | F | 37 | Home with ill child | 84 seconds |

This type of quantitative analysis can tell us something about the behaviour of a character (Jo Banks, for example, has two main roles — mother and employee) and although this is a simple example, content analysis can be complex and wide-ranging. Meehan's (1983) study of American daytime television used content analysis to identify and analyse the stereotypical roles played by female characters in soap operas. She discovered that women in soaps played a maximum of ten different types of role — 'the Good Wife', 'the Bitch' and so forth. More recently, Harwood (1997) used content analysis to demonstrate that television viewers generally prefer to watch characters of their own age.

> **?**  Briefly explain what is meant by content analysis.

### Strengths

➢ **Concept mapping**: Page (2005) argues that computer technology can be used to rapidly search texts (such as newspaper articles) for key words or phrases that indicate the use of similar ideas. Page was interested in understanding how the media portrayed global warming — as something naturally occurring, the result of climate variability, or as something created by human behaviour.

By tracking the way these concepts were used it was possible to create a concept map that demonstrated the ideological thinking of media professionals (whether 'the media' described global warming as having 'natural' or 'social' causes) on a worldwide basis. This, in turn, would tell us a great deal about how people generally understood the causes of global warming in terms of the information they received from media sources.

➢ **Analysis**: Quantification allows surprisingly complex conclusions to be drawn about people's behaviour on the basis of a relatively simple and straightforward data collection technique.

➢ **Reliability**: The use of a **standardised framework** (the grid) means data can be checked and **replicated** (although there are limits to the reliability of this technique).

➢ **Themes and patterns** of behaviour that may not be immediately apparent can be uncovered through relatively simple quantification. Recurrent themes (such as women being associated with housework) in complex forms of social interaction can also be identified using this method. Hogenraad (2003), for example, developed a computer-based content analysis program to search text-based historical accounts of war to identify key recurring themes that signify the lead-up to conflicts. This raises the interesting possibility of this method having predictive qualities; by identifying a pattern of past behaviour that always leads to war, it should be possible to predict the outbreak of future conflict on the basis of key themes appearing in newspapers or television news programmes.

### Weaknesses

➤ **Reliability**: Content analysis frequently involves making judgements about the categorisation of behaviour — the researcher decides which categories will or will not be used for analysis. The researcher must also judge which forms of behaviour fit which categories: can all observed behaviour be put neatly into a particular category, or does behaviour that cuts across different categories merit a category of its own? Data can be difficult to **replicate** because different researchers, studying the same behaviour, may not categorise them in the same way.

➤ **Reasons**: It doesn't tell us very much about how audiences receive, understand, accept or ignore uncovered themes and patterns (something called media **decoding** — how people make sense of (decode) the various messages pushed by the media.

# Secondary quantitative methods

In this section we will discuss methods using secondary data of two kinds: official and non-official statistics.

## Official statistics

In Britain, the two main sources of official statistical data are government **departments** (such as the Home Office) and **agencies** (such as the police). Governments produce **demographic data** (information about the behaviour of individuals and groups) for two main purposes:

➤ informing policy-making (e.g. how many teachers will be needed in 10 years' time)
➤ information/accountability purposes (e.g. how much is spent on defence or schooling each year)

### Strengths

➤ **Patterns** of behaviour may be picked up by statistical analysis because they can provide a broad overview of such behaviour across potentially wide areas (local, national and international). Durkheim (1897), for example, classically identified distinct patterns to suicidal behaviour that led him to argue that such behaviour must have social causes.

- **Representativeness**: As Marshall (1998) notes, statistical 'data are almost invariably nationally representative, because they are obtained from complete censuses or very large-scale national sample surveys'.
- **Availability**: Official statistics may be the only available source in a particular sociological area.
- **Cost**: Data that would be hugely costly, time-consuming and difficult to collect, such as statistics on marriage, divorce, crime and so forth, are freely available from government sources, such as the Office for National Statistics.

| Strengths of statistics | |
|---|---|
| **P** | atterns |
| **R** | epresentativeness |
| **A** | vailability |
| **C** | ost |
| **T** | rends |
| **I** | teration |
| **C** | omparisons |
| **A** | uthority |
| **L** | aunch studies |

- **Trends**: Using statistical data drawn from different years it's possible to see how something has changed over time ('longitudinal studies'). Education statistics, for example, can be used to track changes in levels of achievement between males and females over the past 50 years. Statistics can also be used to track possible changes in behaviour after the introduction of a new law, for example.
- **Iteration**: Many official statistical sources, in areas like crime, unemployment, marriages, births and divorces are backed by law (a marriage, divorce or birth must be legally registered, while the police have a legal duty to record reported crimes). Data are usually collected in the same way from the same sources ('iteration') which adds to their overall reliability because research can be **replicated**. Although definitions may change (the statistical meaning of 'unemployment', for example, has changed numerous times in the past 30 years), most statistical definitions, such as what counts as a birth or a murder, rarely change. This makes year-on-year comparisons possible.
- **Comparisons**: Statistics can be used for both **inter-group** comparisons, such as the differences in middle- and working-class family size, and **cross-cultural** comparisons. Bakewell (1999), for example, noted the significance of official statistics as a data source in his discussion of refugees; official statistics could be quickly and easily used to demonstrate the size and scale of an international social problem.
- **Authority**: Although some statistical data don't have high validity, this is not true of all official statistics. Demographic data in areas like marriage, divorce, births and deaths, for example, record all of these events with a very high degree of accuracy; these statistics measure what they

Legal registrations (e.g. marriages) increase the reliability of statistical data claim to measure. Even in areas where validity is much lower there are examples — such as the number of murders or car crimes committed each year — of higher validity; people are very likely to report car crime because they are insured against it.

➤ **Launch studies**: Official statistics can be useful for establishing the need for further research. They can, in other words, point to the existence of 'a problem' or issue that requires explanation.

### Weaknesses

➤ **Validity**: Official statistics, apart from not providing any great depth or detail, have validity problems associated with what governments include in — or exclude from — published data. The problem is that official statistics may only give us a **partial picture of reality**, for two main reasons:

  ➤ **Omissions**: For example, while official crime statistics provide valuable data about crimes that are reported to and recorded by the police, they tell us little or nothing about the **dark figure of crime**: crimes that are neither reported nor recorded. Young (2001) argues that around 75% of all crime in the UK 'is in the dark figure'.

  ➤ **Explanations**: Statistical data tell us little or nothing about the reasons for people's behaviour; while we have a reasonably precise figure for the number of year-on-year murders in the UK, this tells us very little about *why* people kill each other.

➤ **Interpretation**: Although quantitative data are normally considered more objective than qualitative data, the significance of any data must always be interpreted by the researcher — they have to decide what the data *mean*. A statistical rise in levels of crime, for example, may be the result of a real rise, the outcome of a different way of defining and counting crime, or it might result from the police targeting certain types of crime (and hence arresting more people).

➤ **Definitions**: Governments occasionally change the definition of key concepts (such as what counts as 'car crime' or, in Bakewell's (1999) analysis, how different governments define the concept of a 'refugee'). Such changes contribute to a potential **reliability** problem because to make statistical comparisons the researcher must ensure they are comparing 'like with like'. A further problem of definition can arise over the way behaviour is officially categorised; for example, in attempting to estimate the extent of 'knife crime' in our society, data are increasingly taken from hospital records (on the basis that victims of knife crime may not want to report their victimisation, because they fear reprisals or because to do so might involve incriminating themselves). While these official data give an insight into the general extent of 'knife wounding', they don't distinguish between things like deliberate and accidental wounding.

> **?** Suggest one use and one limitation of official crime statistics.

# Non-official statistics

Non-official statistical data are collected and published by a variety of public and private organisations. Mort (2006), for example, identifies more than 900 publications and services produced by non-governmental groups, including:

> ➤ trade unions (e.g. Unison)
> ➤ professional bodies (e.g. the British Medical Association)
> ➤ banks
> ➤ consultancies (such as management and accountancy firms)
> ➤ pressure groups (e.g. the Tax Payer's Alliance, Greenpeace)
> ➤ employers' federations (e.g. the Confederation of British Industry)
> ➤ charities (e.g. the Rowntree Foundation, which publishes statistics on poverty)
> ➤ quangos (e.g. the General Teaching Council, Audit Commission and Youth Justice Board)

These and many other organisations produce a wide range of statistical data (both national and international) that reflect a variety of interests and concerns (from the environment to mortgage lending).

### Strengths

While non-official statistics retain some of the strengths of their official counterparts (such as savings in time, money and effort), they have some additional advantages:

> ➤ **Sources**: They provide original data that are not available elsewhere.
> ➤ **Innovation**: Marshall (1998) argues that non-official statistics have opened up sources of information about areas of our society (such as consumption patterns, regional government and the environment) that are not covered in official statistics.

### Weaknesses

> ➤ **Sources**: Researchers frequently find it difficult to trace the sources used in compiling non-official statistics (especially, but not exclusively, when they're produced by private companies).
> ➤ **Reliability**: Information about how the data are compiled, such as adequate notes, definitions and details of statistical techniques, is frequently lacking — making it difficult to estimate data reliability.
> ➤ **Partiality**: Non-official data are frequently produced by organisations, such as trade unions, employer associations and pressure groups, to promote a particular aim or cause, which can lead to questions concerning:
> > ➤ **Completeness**: To what extent are statistics that don't chime with organisational aims ignored?
> > ➤ **Omissions and interpretations**: For example, The Tax Payers' Alliance (a right-wing pressure group that seeks to influence government spending) produced a list of 1,162 quangos in 2010 with the implication these were all 'unnecessary drains on the public purse' — but the list included 502 NHS trusts and 469 local

government authorities (which, in the case of the latter, stretches the definition of 'non-governmental' to breaking point).

> **?** How could the strengths of official statistics be used to overcome the weaknesses of non-official statistics?

# Quantitative research methodology

Choices about the use of particular research methods are not confined to simple practical questions, such as whether a questionnaire will provide the right level and type of data required for a research project. **Theoretical research considerations** are also important and perhaps one of the most significant of these is the methodological beliefs of the researcher.

Quantitative research methods have historically been associated with a very specific research methodology and design: **positivism**. 'Positivist' very loosely means 'scientific' and positivist sociologists argue that it's possible (and desirable) to study social behaviour in ways similar to those used by scientists, such as chemists or physicists, to study behaviour in the natural world.

## Positivist methodology

Positivist methodology has a number of basic features, described below.

The primary research goal is to **explain**, rather than describe, social phenomena. This involves **testing hypotheses** to either confirm or refute them (show them to be true or false). According to Firestone (1987): 'In quantitative research, the emphasis is on collecting data that lead to dependable answers to important questions.'

Sociology as 'science' involves the attempt to discover the general rules (or **laws**) that underpin all human behaviour. An example of a general sociological rule might be the idea that every child requires some kind of socialisation if they are to develop as a human individual.

To discover these general behavioural rules social scientists, like their natural scientific counterparts, must be **personally objective**. Research must not be influenced by a researcher's values, beliefs, opinions and prejudices — an idea sometimes called **value-freedom**. Science is concerned only with what is — rather than what we might want or personally believe something to be. To avoid biasing or influencing the data collection process the scientist shouldn't participate in the behaviour being studied. Rather, they must 'stand outside' that behaviour so they can study and observe it dispassionately.

Social scientists must also be **systemically objective**: the research methods used must be capable of producing objective data. Research methods, therefore, should not depend on the subjective interpretations of a researcher (what they may personally believe or feel about something) and research should be capable of exact **replication**. The greater our ability to replicate data, the higher the level of research reliability.

In this view, the social world has an **objective existence** — it exists in a way that can't be influenced by people's beliefs about it. For example, marriage rates have fallen consistently in our society over the past 25 years, regardless of how we personally feel about this statistic. If this is so, then **reliable and valid knowledge** can be discovered in the same way natural scientists discover knowledge: by systematic observation, critical questioning and experimentation.

Positivism leans towards **quantitative data** because of the fundamental belief in and desire for objectivity: as Firestone (1987) puts it, there is an assumption that 'there are **social facts** with an objective reality apart from the beliefs of individuals'. Because objectivity is seen as a crucial part of the scientific approach, positivist researchers choose methods that offer higher levels of objectivity and reliability.

To reliably and validly study behaviour, sociologists should use **empirical** methods: that is, methods involving the use of our senses (such as sight). **Evidence** about social behaviour, in other words, can only be considered reliable and valid if it is capable of being **observed** and **tested**. Anything not directly observable (such as people's thoughts) does not provide valid knowledge, since we can never objectively know what someone is thinking — the best we can do is make deductions or educated guesses on the basis of their actions.

Positivism focuses on **cause and effect**. If we can discover general behavioural rules it follows that the social world and the behaviour it involves are predictable: it should be possible to predict the various ways people will behave in particular situations.

Scientific research revolves around the ability to quantify and **measure** social behaviour. If something cannot be tested and measured it belongs to the realm of opinions, not facts. Positivism favours scientific forms of knowledge that are:
- factual
- objective
- evidenced-based
- tested

They are seen as more important, significant and worthwhile than non-scientific forms that are:
- based on opinion
- subjective
- based on unsupported interpretations
- untested

For positivists, knowledge consists of identifying facts about how and why people behave as they do and, eventually, making connections between different facts to produce **theories** that explain behaviour.

> **?** Briefly explain why positivist researchers are more likely to use quantitative research methods.

# Positivist research design: the hypothetico-deductive model

We can use Popper's (1934) classic example of how to design positivist social research, which was organised around two ideas:

➤ **'Hypothetico'** means 'starting with a hypothesis'. For Popper, the research process revolves around the ability to develop and clearly state testable hypotheses.

➤ **Deductive** logic is a way of making authoritative statements (proofs) about what is not known by a thorough analysis of what is known. The ability to make deductive statements becomes the basis for drawing logical conclusions about specific events from general events.

To simplify this idea, think about fictional detectives such as Morse or Lewis who solve crimes by:

➤ systematically investigating a case
➤ collecting and analysing facts
➤ identifying the guilty party on the basis of these facts

This is an example of deduction because they prove something specific that was not initially known (the identity of a murderer) on the basis of general observations about things that were initially known (the facts of the case, the clues identified and so forth).

A **model** is a small-scale representation of something (such as a research process) that helps clarify the relationship between the separate elements in the design by describing them in simplified terms. In this case, Popper's model suggests the various steps to follow in order to 'do research' and, as such, helps us to design the actual process itself.

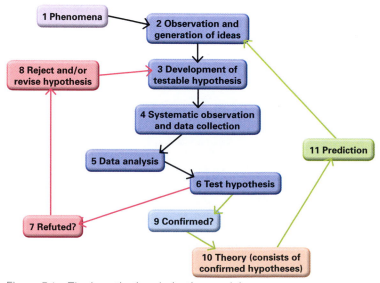

Figure 5.1 The hypothetico-deductive model

Here we will not consider the research design in detail, but will focus on two central aspects: a testable hypothesis, and systematic observation and data collection.

### Testable hypothesis

The model is organised around this fundamental principle of positivism: reliable and valid knowledge can be generated only through developing and rigorously testing a hypothesis. The hypothesis provides both a focus for the research and a clearly defined objective for data collection, since the researcher is locked into a systematic design for identifying, collecting and processing data. Once the hypothesis has been **operationalised**, using whatever **indicators** may be required, the researcher can arrive at an objective measurement of the behaviour being researched.

For example, in her review of research examining the educational properties of museums, Lindauer (2005) noted that the question 'Did the exhibition effectively communicate the main idea or message?' illustrates the idea of hypothesis testing within this type of research design. As she argues, 'The question...poses a cause-and-effect relationship — attending an exhibit will cause visitors to acquire particular knowledge or information' that can be measured and therefore tested (once the concept of 'effectively communicate' has been operationalised and quantified).

### Systematic observation and data collection

Systematic observation (something that covers a range of methods, from questionnaires through interviews to direct observation itself) is significant because the researcher's efforts are channelled towards testing the hypothesis; anything that deflects from this goal is a distraction, of no importance to the research, and can be ignored. Data are collected *after* the hypothesis has been developed precisely because they will be used to *test* the hypothesis.

---

**Exam-style question**

Explain and evaluate the use of postal questionnaires to research the importance of families in shaping people's identities. (52 marks)

---

# Chapter *6*

# Exploring the use of qualitative data-collection methods and analysis in the context of research

**By the end of this chapter you will be able to:**

➢ define and evaluate qualitative data and primary and secondary research methods (including semi-structured and unstructured interviews, focus groups, content analysis, non-participant observation, and covert and overt participant observation)

Many of the research methods outlined in this chapter are associated with the idea of **ethnography**. In sociology, this involves the study of people 'in their natural setting'. This can be done in a wide range of ways, from joining (either openly or secretly) the group you want to study ('participant observation') to engaging people in 'conversation' (semi-structured and unstructured interviews) designed to reveal their beliefs, values, norms, feelings and motivations.

Ethnography is not a research method as such (although the term is sometimes used interchangeably with 'participant observation'). Rather, as with the idea of social surveys, it's a general *research technique* involving an overall *philosophy* about how to study people in a reliable and valid way. It has a number of basic characteristics:

➢ **Depth**: The focus is on the depth and detail of data collection since the objective is to discover and understand as much as possible about people's beliefs and behaviours.

➢ **Interpretive**: One aim of this type of research is to uncover the *meanings* people give to everyday events, by closely observing or questioning them; this explains why qualitative data are seen as both desirable and useful, although this doesn't exclude the use of some forms of quantification. In some respects, therefore, the objective of ethnographic study is to provide a range of **narrative data**: that is, data which 'tell a story' about the people or behaviour being studied.

➤ **Small scale**: The focus is generally on small groups or individuals studied, as much as possible, in natural or normal settings and situations. Ethnographic research frequently involves case studies.

➤ **Understanding**: A major objective of ethnographic research is an in-depth understanding of how respondents see and understand the world in which they live. In other words, sociological understanding develops out of allowing respondents to describe and explain their thoughts and behaviours, with the sociologist's role being that of a channel through which these things can be drawn out. Cultural anthropologists call this an **emic account** — an attempt to get an 'insider' or 'native' view and explanation of behaviour; to let individuals 'speak for themselves' rather than impose an 'outsider' view on things (by trying to test hypotheses, for example).

➤ **Severity**: These studies make intense demands on both the researcher (participant observers, for example, may live for months or even years with their subjects) and the researched (as the subjects of extensive and detailed questioning, for example).

➤ **Empirical**: One objective of ethnography is to develop insights into people's behaviour based on a rigorous examination of their cultural beliefs and behaviours. The methods used to achieve this (e.g. observation, participating in the behaviour being studied) are similarly rigorous and based on objective standards of evidence, reliability and validity.

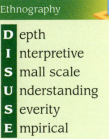

Ethnography

**D** epth
**I** nterpretive
**S** mall scale
**U** nderstanding
**S** everity
**E** mpirical

# Primary qualitative methods

## Semi-structured ('focused') interviews

Nichols (1991) defines this method as 'an informal interview, not structured by a standard list of questions. Researchers are free to deal with the topics of interest in any order and to phrase their questions as they think best.'

This involves the researcher setting up a situation (the interview) that allows the respondent to talk at length and in depth about a particular subject. The focus (or general topic) of the interview is decided by the researcher and there may also be particular areas they're interested in exploring. The interview has a structure (the things the interviewer wants the respondent to focus on), but it's not as tightly controlled as a questionnaire or structured interview (hence the term 'semi-structured interview'). There is no list of questions that must be asked and answered, and different respondents may be asked different questions on the same topic, depending on how the interview develops.

The objective is to understand things from the respondent's viewpoint, rather than make generalisations about people's behaviour. Open-ended questions are frequently used, some of which are created before the interview, while others arise naturally from whatever the respondent wants to talk about. There are a number of factors that can affect the conduct, reliability and validity of semi-structured interviews, discussed in the following subsections.

### Personal demeanour

This method requires certain skills of the researcher, such as knowing when to prompt for an answer and when to simply listen. Although these interviews are similar to conversations, they are not arguments; people are unlikely to open up to a rude and aggressive interviewer. Similarly, how researchers present themselves (how they dress, talk, appear interested or bored and so forth) can be significant factors. For example, respondents may restrict their answers if the researcher appears uninterested, and this may impact on research validity.

### Setting

It's important to build a rapport with people to get them to talk openly and at length; they should feel comfortable with the researcher, the interview and their surroundings. Unlike structured interviews, which can be conducted almost anywhere, semi-structured interviews can't be easily conducted on street corners. Gray's (1987) study of women's relationship to video recording technology used semi-structured interviews in a home setting because she needed to put her respondents at their ease and get them to talk at length about their feelings and experiences.

### Trust

Interviews may deal with matters of personal importance to respondents; they should feel that they are being taken seriously (whatever they may say or do) and that the information they give will be confidential. Building trust (**rapport**) may increase data validity because the researcher is more likely to get a detailed and well-rounded picture of whatever they're researching.

### Interview schedule

The interview schedule is a plan used to specify and track the progress of the interview. Although each one will be slightly different, they have the same general structure:

- **Introduction**: Schedules often start with an open-ended question about the major topic (or focus), designed to get the respondent focused and talking (e.g. 'Can you tell me about…').
- **Subsidiary questions**: These are questions or topics the researcher wants to explore and they may or may not be asked, depending on how the interview develops. If these questions are used they may not be asked in the order they originally appeared on the schedule (unlike a structured interview, which has a clear and rigid question order).

> **Exploratory questions**: The schedule can be updated with questions that arise during the interview — some suggested by the respondent and some which may occur to the researcher during the interview. These questions may or may not be used in subsequent interviews with different respondents (a development that will lower the reliability of the research, because it will be difficult to replicate, but potentially increase its validity).

### Hierarchical focusing

Tomlinson (1989) argues that the researcher should construct a schedule that starts with the most general question and gradually introduces more specific questions as the interview progresses (a 'question hierarchy'). General questions are used to encourage respondents to talk and specific questions are used as and when required to refocus the interview.

## Strengths

> **Prejudgement**: The problem of the researcher predetermining what will or will not be discussed is largely (although not totally) avoided, since there are few preset questions or topics.

> **Prior knowledge**: Where the interview allows the respondent to talk about the things that interest or concern them, it's possible to gather ideas and information that had either not occurred to the interviewer or of which they had no prior knowledge or understanding. This new knowledge can be used to inform subsequent interviews with different respondents; or the interview may form part of a **pilot study**, conducted to test how people respond to particular topics, issues and questions, and to generate new questions and lines of enquiry.

> **Validity**: By allowing respondents to develop their ideas and opinions the researcher tries to find out what they 'really mean, think or believe'. The focus on what the respondent sees as important and interesting produces a much greater depth of information and this, in turn, potentially increases validity by making it more likely that the research actually achieves what it set out to achieve. Oatey (1999) also suggests that 'Freedom for the respondent to answer how they wish to is important in giving them a feeling of control in the interview situation'.

> **Help and guidance**: Within limits, face-to-face interaction allows the researcher to help and guide respondents — to explain, rephrase or clarify a question or answer, for example — which may improve overall validity.

## Weaknesses

> **Skills**: Semi-structured interviews require certain skills of both the researcher (the ability to ask the right questions, establish a good rapport and think quickly about relevant question-opportunities as they arise) and the respondent (an inarticulate respondent will lack the skills to talk openly and in detail about the research topic). Oatey (1999) notes that open-ended questions, designed to get people to talk at length

find distasteful, disgusting or perverse. Covert observation goes some way to resolving this problem by allowing the researcher to understand the meaning behind people's actions because they experience such things for themselves.

➤ **Access**: Covert observation may be the only way to study people who would not normally allow themselves to be researched. Examples include:

  ➤ **Criminal or deviant groups**: Ward (2008) 'was a member of the rave dance drugs culture' when she began her 5-year study 'in London nightclubs, dance parties, bars and pubs and people's houses [where]...the social interactions and processes at the heart of rave dance drugs exchange were observed'.

  ➤ **Closed groups**: Lofland and Stark (1965) secretly studied the behaviour of a religious sect because this was the only way to gain access to the group.

  ➤ **Anonymous groups**: Ray (1987) covertly studied groups of Australian environmentalists in order to 'minimize defensiveness on the part of those studied and to avoid breakdowns in co-operation'.

➤ **Level of participation**: Although it's possible to argue that all sociological research involves some form of 'participation', in the sense of interacting with those being studied, with this method such participation is generally very high and, in some cases, almost total. The researcher may live, work and socialise with the people they're studying and, in consequence, produce data which are massively detailed, insightful, personally observed and experienced.

Covert participant observation strengths

**O** bserver effect
**V** alidity
**A** ccess
**L** evel of participation

### Weaknesses

Goffman's (1961) study of an American mental institution identified problems for the covert participant observer in three major areas: getting in, staying in and getting out.

#### Getting in

Problems here involve entry and access.

While gaining covert **entry** to any group can be problematic, some groups are more difficult to enter than others. There are three areas of potential difficulty for the researcher:

➤ **Characteristics**: If the characteristics of the researcher (age, gender, ethnicity and so forth) don't match those of the group, the researcher won't be able to gain access. A man, for example, could not covertly study a group of nuns.

➤ **Invitation**: Entry to some groups (such as the Freemasons) is by invitation only. Unless the researcher is invited, they cannot join.

➤ **Qualifications**: Some groups have entry requirements. To covertly study accountants or doctors, for example, the researcher would need to hold the qualifications required to practise these professions.

If the group is strongly hierarchical (divided into different levels) the researcher is unlikely to have **access** to all areas. A covert researcher posing as a student in a school would not have access to places (such as staffrooms) reserved for teachers. Parke and Griffiths (2008) also note: 'It's impossible to study everyone at all times and locations... Therefore it is a matter of personal choice as to what data are recorded, collected and observed...This affects the reliability and validity of the findings.'

Burgess (1984) notes that in some situations access to areas within a group is controlled by certain people ('**gatekeepers**'). As far as a group is concerned, a covert researcher may have no reason to want access to some areas (and may arouse suspicion by demanding it).

*Staying in*

Once inside, there may be problems concerning **level of participation**. A researcher has to quickly learn the culture and dynamics of a group in order to participate fully. This may require a range of skills — mixing easily with strangers, creating and maintaining a plausible 'back story', thinking quickly in unexpected situations. Parker (1974), for example, had to make decisions about whether or not to participate in the criminal activities of the gang of youths he was secretly studying.

In order to participate appropriately the researcher must have the **knowledge** and **skills** needed to fit into a group. Parke and Griffiths (2008), for example, noted the potential problems caused by 'lack of "street knowledge" about slot machine gamblers and their environments' (the terminology players use, machine features, gambling etiquette). If a researcher lacks the 'insider knowledge' appropriate to a group member, they risk exposure, which may jeopardise their ability to stay in the group.

The researcher may have to adjust to a situation in which the people being researched have greater expertise in certain situations. It can be difficult to 'relinquish control' to those you are secretly studying.

Another problem is that of '**going native**'. It can be difficult to separate the roles of participant and observer, especially in situations where the researcher becomes well integrated into a group. 'Going native', therefore, refers to a range of behaviours that may compromise the integrity of the research process.

At one extreme the researcher may have to choose to be an observer rather than a participant (such as when a group participates in criminal activities). At the other, the researcher may become so well integrated into the group that they cease to be an observer and effectively become a full participant. This would raise serious doubts about the reliability and validity of the research. Whyte (1943), for example, found that he became so involved with the lives of gang members that he progressively came to see himself as 'one of the gang' and not as a researcher.

Finally, pretending to be someone you're not carries the ever-present risk of **exposure** as a 'spy'. The consequences vary from group to group (the Women's Institute might write a letter of protest, whereas a criminal gang may take things a bit further) but the general consequence is the end of the research.

*Getting out*

It can be difficult to suddenly leave a group. A member of a criminal gang, for example, can't easily just 'stop participating'. For other groups, leaving may raise ethical problems, from the effect of leaving a group who may have grown to trust and depend on the researcher, to questions about whether covert observation as a research method is exploitative: does a researcher have the right to secretly spy on people (in Parker's (1974) terms 'pretend to be one of them') or use them for their own purposes?

Covert participation raises a further methodological problem in the shape of **reliability**. The study can't be replicated, we have to trust the researcher's observations (there's nothing to back them up) and recording data is frequently difficult; the researcher can't take notes or record conversations openly, for fear of exposure.

Goffman (1961) solved this problem by using a field diary to write up his observations at the end of every working day — although this still requires that the researcher remember things accurately and make decisions about the significance of events. Another possibility is to use modern technology, such as miniature cameras and voice recorders, to ensure data are accurately captured and recorded, but these not only risk exposure (how might a group respond if they discovered everything they did or said was being taped or filmed?) but also raise ethical questions about the extent to which it is permissible to secretly record people's behaviour.

> **?** **What problems might a researcher face gaining access to each of the following?**
> **1** a school
> **2** the police
> **3** a hospital

# Secondary qualitative methods: documentary sources

In our society there are a large number of documentary sources available to sociologists and classifying them in any meaningful way is difficult. Table 6.2 identifies a number of different types and sources and also suggests that documents can be either historical or current (contemporary). This is not intended as a hard and fast categorisation, but for organisational convenience, in terms of outlining different document strengths and limitations.

Table 6.2   Types and sources of documentary evidence

| Type | official | organisational | individual |
|------|----------|----------------|------------|
| **Possible sources** | government agencies and departments | private companies and organisations | personal documents created by individuals |
| **Historical and current** | official reports, court reports, academic studies, websites | newspapers (local, national), film, magazines, books, church records, academic studies | letters, autobiographies, diaries (paper and video), biographies, oral histories, photographs, personal websites, social networking sites |

Qualitative analysis of personal documents is often carried out using either of two types of **content analysis**:

➤ **Conceptual** (or **thematic**) analysis focuses on the concepts or themes that underlie documents (or 'texts'). In this respect such analysis can be considered an extension of the quantitative form of content analysis. Philo and Berry (2004), for example, identified a number of recurring themes in news reports of the Israeli–Palestinian conflict, such as language differences when referring to similar forms of behaviour (Palestinians were frequently classed as 'terrorists' while Israeli settlers were called 'extremists' or 'vigilantes'.)

➤ **Relational** (or **textual**) analysis examines how texts encourage the reader to see something in a particular way by relating one idea to something different. Hall (1980) calls this a **preferred reading**: the way text is constructed (how language, pictures and illustrations are used, for example) 'tells' the audience how to interpret the information presented (without necessarily appearing to do so). A brief glance through the sports pages of UK newspapers, for example, might lead you to think that sport is mainly a male activity.

## Strengths

➤ **Comparison**: Historical documents can be used for comparative purposes — contrasting how people once lived with how we live now is useful for tracking and understanding social change. Historical analysis also demonstrates the diversity of people's behaviour — things we now take for granted may have been seen differently in the past (and vice versa).

➤ **Resources**: The researcher gets access to data that would cost a lot of money, time and effort to collect personally.

➤ **Availability**: Documents can provide secondary data in situations where it's not possible to collect primary data (about things that happened in the past, for example). Documents about family life, education and crime may be the only available evidence for a researcher.

➤ **Validity**: There are a couple of aspects we can note:

   ➤ Documentary evidence may provide qualitative data of great depth and detail. For example, diaries can provide extensive and valuable details about people and their daily lives (examples are those of Samuel Pepys, who recorded life in England during the 1660s, and Anne Frank, who recorded her life in hiding from the Nazis during the Second World War).

➤ It's sometimes possible to compare accounts across time to test the validity of current accounts of social behaviour. We can, for example, compare past and present accounts of family and working lives to understand the continuities and changes in social behaviour. Pearson (1983) used media accounts going back over 100 years to demonstrate that 'hooligan' or 'yobbish' behaviour is not a recent phenomenon in our society.

➤ **Essence**: Documents can have two levels of meaning — **literal** (what they actually say) and **metaphorical** (what they tell us about the hopes, fears, beliefs and so forth of whoever produced them). Newspaper articles, for example, may frequently tell us more about their writers and how they see social problems than about the topic of the writing.

Strengths of documents

**C** omparison
**R** esources
**A** vailability
**V** alidity
**E** ssence

## Weaknesses

➤ **Reliability**: Aside from our ability to replicate qualitative data, documents have reliability problems in that they may be incomplete, inaccurate or partial (biased towards one viewpoint).

➤ **Representativeness**: When using documentary sources we need to know if they represent only one individual's view (as with a diary) or a range of views. Even in the latter case, such as an official government report, it is rare for documents to have high levels of representativeness — which makes generalisation difficult (if not impossible). While this may not be an issue if we have a large number of different sources, it will be a problem if there is only a single documentary source.

TopFoto

Anne Frank's diary provides a highly valid account of life under Nazi occupation

➤ **Authenticity**: With secondary documentary data there may be uncertainty over its source. Paper documents can be forged and we need to know whether they are originals or copies (which may have been changed by other authors). With electronic documents from the internet, similar considerations apply. Increasingly this applies to both photographic and video sources.

➤ **Credibility**: We don't always know why or by whom a document was created. Therefore we can't always be sure if the document is a credible source. Did the author have first-hand experience of the things they describe or are they simply repeating something at second or third hand?

**?** What reasons can you give for using personal diaries in sociological research?

# Qualitative research methodology

As we suggested earlier, when we looked at positivist methodology in Chapter 5, methodological beliefs are an important factor in deciding whether or not to use qualitative data. In this respect qualitative research methods can be associated with a specific research methodology and design: interpretivism.

## Interpretivism

This is a different way of looking at human behaviour and social research from the positivist approach we outlined earlier — one that argues that the social world is understood ('interpreted') by different people in different situations in different ways (for example, something you interpret as a 'problem' may not be a problem to someone else). Everything in the social world, therefore, is relative to everything else; nothing can ever be wholly true and nothing can ever be wholly false; the best we can do is describe reality from the viewpoint of those who create and define it — the people involved in particular types of behaviour, whether it takes place in an asylum, family, school classroom or prison.

Harris (2005) captures the distinction between the two methodologies when he notes that positivists use 'terms like "cause", "law" or "fact"' when talking about human beings as if they were 'snooker balls' being pushed around by some unseen force (social structures). Interpretivists, however, argue that people are very different from snooker balls because they have **consciousness** — an awareness of both themselves and the world. Whereas a snooker ball has no choice but to move when hit with a cue, human beings can make a wide range of choices (and responses) should someone try to do the same thing to them.

The ability to think, reflect and act makes people very different from inanimate objects in the natural world — and this means we cannot study them in the same way we study plants or rocks. Some key features of interpretivism are outlined below, in terms of description, social contexts, participation, validity and constructionism.

### Description

A major goal is to **describe** social behaviour, primarily in terms of the **meanings** and **interpretations** of those involved. While this involves some sort of explanation for people's behaviour, such explanations are 'developed from within' — in terms of the perceptions of those involved — rather than 'imposed from without' (in the sense of the researcher 'weighing all the evidence' and deciding which particular explanation among many is 'true'). By 'taking the role of the other' (using a method like participant observation) the researcher sees the world through the eyes of the people being studied;

the sociologist experiences what they experience, and, by so doing, gains an insight into why people behave in the way they do.

## Social contexts

Behavioural rules in any culture are context-bound; that is, they shift and change depending on the particular situation in which people find themselves. For example, if you slap me in the face, you have no way of knowing, in advance, how I'm going to react. I might do any of the following:

- cry (because you hurt me)
- not cry (because my friends are watching and crying doesn't fit with my carefully cultivated hard-man image)
- laugh at you
- run away
- slap you back

How I react will depend on a huge range of possible factors, relating to the overall social context of that behaviour.

Uncovering and describing behavioural rules, therefore, involves delving deeply into people's behaviour; it also involves the researcher gaining an intimate understanding of the context within which rules are created — hence qualitative research (and participant observation in particular) is frequently associated with this methodology because it involves exploring behaviour in this way. It also means that behaviour cannot be predicted — so there's no point trying to do the impossible.

## Participation

Humphries (1970) argues that participation is highly desirable; researchers get a deeper insight into people's behaviour because they may, for a time, actually *become* the people they're studying. Subjective involvement, rather than the objective detachment valued by positivists, is seen as the way to produce valid data. Research, from this viewpoint, is all about capturing the elusive qualities of human behaviour, which is not something that can be achieved using quantitative research methods and data.

## Validity

While data reliability is important, interpretivists place more emphasis on validity, partly because human behaviour is impossible to exactly replicate (so perfect reliability is impossible) and partly because, in their view, the objective of sociological research is to uncover the rules, meanings and interpretations people use as guides in their daily lives.

## Constructionism

Since, from this viewpoint, social reality is constructed and reconstructed by individuals on a daily basis, there is little or no interest in trying to discover 'wider behavioural laws' since these cannot exist — all behaviour is context-bound, which means that behaviour seen by one individual, group or culture as the norm may be seen as abnormal (deviant) by other individuals, groups or cultures.

# Interpretivist research design

Interpretivism uses what Oberg (1999) has characterised as an 'exploratory research design' consisting of four general stages: planning, information gathering, information processing and evaluation.

## Planning

A research issue is identified and a research question takes shape. This may flow from background reading or the researcher may want to 'come fresh' to the research to avoid being influenced by what others have said or written.

Figure 6.1   The stages in designing interpretivist research

## Information gathering

Although the general research process here is superficially similar to the hypothetico-deductive model, there are major differences in the way information is collected. This research design can be described as follows:

➤ **Non-linear**: Research doesn't begin with a hypothesis and end with it being confirmed or rejected. The objective is not to somehow discover definitive answers to a question; rather, it is to explore it from a variety of angles.

➤ **Exploratory**: The objective is to explore the behaviour being studied from a variety of different viewpoints, from those being observed to that of the observer. There can never be 'definitive answers'; the best we can do is uncover how people see and understand behaviour, both their own and that of others.

➤ **Oriented to subjective perceptions**: If, as Firestone (1987) suggests, 'reality is socially constructed through individual or collective definitions of the situation', the researcher needs to use a design and method that offers the greatest opportunities to capture this 'subjective sense of social reality'.

➤ **Holistic**: As much information as possible is collected, for two reasons. First, the researcher doesn't judge the significance of data at this stage in the process. Second, by casting the net far and wide the researcher involves those being studied in the research process (they may suggest ideas and issues that did not originally occur to the researcher).

➤ **Goal-free**: Hypothesis-based research designs are goal-oriented (the goal being to test whether a hypothesis is true or false). Lindauer (2005), however, argues that exploratory research designs are 'goal-free'. The researcher is free to explore whatever they — or the people they're studying — feel is important or interesting; these types of research design 'take shape as data collection and analysis proceed'.

➤ **Evolutionary**: Visualising the difference between doing questionnaire-based research and covert participant observation gives a good idea of the difference between positivist and interpretivist research designs. Where the hypothetico-deductive design framework is rigid and strong and directs the researcher clearly along every step in the process, the reverse is true of exploratory designs: the framework is flexible and weak, and bends to take account of new research ideas and developments. Rather than following an exact and predetermined path, interpretivist research design is open-ended; it can, for example, be expanded to cover areas suggested by those being studied.

> **Not researcher-focused**: While positivist designs are 'researcher-led and focused' (the needs of the researcher are considered more important than those of the researched), the reverse is true for interpretivist designs — the needs of the researched are more important than those of the researcher.

> **Active**: The participation and subjective involvement of the researcher in their research is actively encouraged. Venkatesh (2009), for example, spent around 8 years working with the gang he was studying while Ray (1987) lived covertly with a group of Australian environmentalists.

> **?** Why might interpretivists favour qualitative research methods?

## Information processing

While attempts may be made to categorise the data in various ways or sift and sort it into some form of readable (descriptive) narrative, such analysis, according to Schultz et al. (1996), is something that happens *throughout* the research process, rather than simply being completed after data have been collected. This is significant because this type of design involves a **feedback loop** between data collection and data analysis: the analysis of collected data is used to inform further data collection and this informs further analysis. Since there is no requirement to collect data for the express purpose of proving or disproving something, analysis is descriptive and can use the viewpoint of both the researcher and those being researched.

## Evaluation

Conclusions may be offered but it's more likely the reader will be left to draw their own conclusions. This highlights a further difference in research design between exploratory and hypothetico-deductive models. The latter model, by definition and design, involves the researcher making judgements (about what to research, what data to collect and, ultimately, the status — true or false — of the research hypothesis). The former, however, is **non-judgemental**: the objective of the research is not to decide things like 'truth' or 'falsity', 'validity' or 'invalidity'; rather it is to illuminate a particular issue by studying it from a multitude of possible viewpoints.

As Schwandt (2002) puts it, social research involves not so much a 'problem to be solved...as a dilemma or mystery that requires interpretation and self-understanding'. Firestone (1987) suggests that the main objective is to 'help the reader understand' how people see their world and situation, while Reason and Rowan (1981), in advocating a subjective, qualitative approach argue: 'There is too much measurement going on...in human inquiry it is much better to be deeply interesting than accurately boring.'

**Exam-style question**

Explain and evaluate the use of ethnography as a way of researching young children's ethnic identity. (52 marks)

# Chapter 7

# Exploring the use of mixed methods in the context of research

**By the end of this chapter you will be able to:**

➤ understand and evaluate the concepts of methodological pluralism and triangulation

➤ consider and evaluate ways that choice of research method and topic are affected by practical, ethical and theoretical research considerations

For the purpose of explanation in previous chapters, we've discussed:

➤ **research methods** in terms of quantitative or qualitative data

➤ **research design** in terms of positivist and interpretivist methodologies

➤ **research methodology** in terms of aligning positivism with quantitative and interpretivism with qualitative methods

While the split between positivism and interpretivism does have some basis in reality, there's a tendency to overplay both the distinction and the barriers between them. It implies that positivists would never use qualitative methods and interpretivists would never try to test a hypothesis. Positivism is frequently portrayed as a form of 'naive empiricism' where everything must be quantified and anything unquantified is sociologically worthless, while interpretivism is portrayed in mirror-opposite terms as insisting that no behaviour can or should be quantified and reducing sociological research to a kind of 'informed journalism'.

In the real world of sociological research things are not always this simple, clear-cut or crude. There is a strong argument that, outside of sociology textbooks, 'pure positivism' and 'untainted interpretivism' have little or no basis in reality, for two reasons.

First, these labels (positivism, interpretivism) are simply categories we create to help us make sense of the sometimes bewildering array of methods and methodologies used by sociologists. (Similarly, identifying 'sociological perspectives' like functionalism and feminism helps us to conveniently categorise an array of different ways of looking at the social world.) They are mental constructs we use for theoretical convenience. They are useful, for example in helping us to understand methodological principles such as reliability and validity. However, we shouldn't expect to meet them in their 'pure forms' in the messier world of real sociological research.

Second, sociologists routinely use a variety of quantitative and qualitative methods in their research. As Payne et al. (2004) argue, sociologists have generally taken the view that 'provided they were not forced into research using methods they personally found uncongenial, there was no absolute reason to prevent others from using alternative methods'.

On this basis, we can examine the use of 'mixed methods' in terms of two concepts: methodological pluralism and triangulation.

# Methodological pluralism

The term 'methodological pluralism' can be broken down in the following way:
- 'Methodological' refers to a general framework that specifies the various steps in the overall design of a piece of research (as exemplified in the hypothetico-deductive model we outlined earlier); in earlier chapters we've outlined two sociological methodologies, positivism and interpretivism.
- 'Pluralism' ('more than one') involves the idea of combining research methodologies — and more importantly research methods — so that the strengths of one methodology can be used to offset the weaknesses of another.

Methodological pluralism means that rather than stick rigorously to the principles of a single methodological approach (such as positivism or interpretivism) a researcher is free to combine these methodologies. As Payne et al. (2004) put it, 'sociological research methods are no longer characterised by "intolerance, indeed bigotry" toward rival styles. Many sociologists subscribe, at least in principle, to methodological pluralism', an idea they define as 'tolerance of a variety of methods in sociological research' that 'even extends to either side of the dubious dichotomy between "quantitative" and "qualitative" methods, a dichotomy that remains useful as a shorthand description but which is ultimately unsustainable'.

Methodological pluralism can also be justified on the grounds that quantitative and qualitative methods can be used to complement each other — to improve levels of reliability and validity, for example, by offsetting the weaknesses of one method against the strengths of another (as we suggested, for example, when we outlined the idea of focused extensions — quantitative questionnaires combined with qualitative group interviews). In other words, it recognises that no single research method is perfect — all have their strengths and weaknesses — so it would make sense to combine them, where necessary.

**?** Define 'methodological pluralism'.

# Triangulation

If methodological pluralism represents a theoretical justification for using mixed methods, the main question it asks is how to collect data that have the highest possible levels of reliability and validity (regardless of the actual methods or data types used). The practicalities of answering this question involve the idea of **triangulation**. This is the means through which the theory is put into practice and specifically refers to the various ways a researcher can attempt to improve research reliability and validity.

Conventionally, 'triangulation' refers to the use of two or more research methods — what Denzin (1970) has termed methodological triangulation. However, Denzin suggests that triangulation can also take other forms: researcher triangulation and data triangulation. Each of these concepts is discussed below.

## Methodological triangulation

One basic idea here is that the researcher can offset the weakness of one method with the strengths of another as a means of improving the reliability and validity of their research. For example, a general weakness of questionnaires is that the researcher must assume a respondent is telling us the truth. However, a researcher could offset this by using an observational method to check whether people actually do what they say they do. A combination of different methods can give a much more rounded picture of someone's life and behaviour; a researcher could, for example, observe a respondent's behaviour using participant observation and also question them about why they did particular things or behaved in one way rather than another.

Alternatively the researcher could compare the results from two different methods used with the same people (such as a semi-structured interview and a focus group): if the conclusions drawn are broadly the same this will help confirm the reliability and validity of the data. Hughes et al.'s (1997) examination of 'the appeal of designer drinks to young people', for example, used 'group discussions' (focus groups) and structured interviews, the data from one being used to cross-check and confirm data from the other (for example, each showed a strong pattern of age-related differences in attitudes to designer drinks).

We can divide methodological triangulation into two subtypes:

➤ **Within-method triangulation**: Bryman (2001) characterises this as 'the use of varieties of the same method to investigate a research issue'. On a simple level this might involve asking open and closed questions in the same questionnaire.

Observation can be used to check if people do what they say they do

> **Between-method triangulation**: Jick (1979) calls this 'the most popular use of triangulation' and Bryman (2001) characterises it as the use of 'contrasting research methods, such as a questionnaire and observation'.

## Researcher triangulation

In studies that rely heavily on researcher interpretations to generate data, one way to control reliability and validity is to use different researchers:

> If different researchers using the same research technique arrive at the same results, this will help to confirm data reliability.

> Using researchers from different ethnic, age, gender and class groups can help to guard against observer and interviewer bias.

## Data triangulation

Data triangulation involves gathering data through differing **sampling strategies**, such as collecting data at different times, in different contexts and from different people. This idea can be extended to include gathering data from both the individuals involved in a particular situation and the researcher's own experiences in that situation. Venkatesh (2009), for example, was able to make sense of certain forms of behaviour (such as dealing crack cocaine) and experiences (such as being black and poor) in ways that would not have been possible if he had not been involved in the world he was studying. He gathered data both from those involved (their understanding of what it meant to be black and poor, for example) and from his own experience of living in their world.

## Advantages of triangulation

### Compensators

While all research methods have their strengths and weaknesses, a researcher can use the strengths of one method to compensate for the shortcomings of another. Parke and Griffiths (2002), for example, argue:

> One obvious advantage of non-participant observation is that it relies only on observing behaviour. Since the researcher cannot interact in the behavioural processes, most data collected will be qualitative, interpretative, and to some extent, limited. However, by using other methodological research tools (e.g. structured interviews), suspicions, interpretations and even hypotheses can be confirmed.

### Aggregates

By gathering and aggregating different types of data (quantitative and qualitative) and sources (such as respondents and participant observers), the researcher is more likely to get a complete, fully-rounded ('holistic') picture of the behaviour they're studying.

### Reliability and validity

By using different methods and sampling strategies, a researcher can generally improve overall data reliability and validity. More specifically, data collected using higher-reliability methods (such as questionnaires) can offset reliability weaknesses in observational methods (with the reverse being the case for validity). Finlay (1999), for example, compared accounts of the same events given by different respondents in semi-structured interviews and added a further check by comparing 'the oral record of those events with the contemporary documentary record in...local newspapers'.

### Data confidence

A researcher's confidence in the accuracy of their data can be increased using triangulation. As Bechhoffer and Paterson (2000) argue: 'If we are...able to base part of an explanation on unstructured interview material, on documentary evidence and on the results of a survey, our confidence in our findings is likely to be greatly increased.'

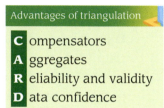

Advantages of triangulation

**C** ompensators
**A** ggregates
**R** eliability and validity
**D** ata confidence

## Disadvantages of triangulation

### Resources

Triangulation adds another layer of time, effort and expense to research, in terms, for example, of the time needed to analyse different data types created from a number of different methods, the need to employ more researchers and the general coordination of a much larger research project.

### Assumptions

While the principle of 'offsetting strengths with weaknesses' generally holds true, we should avoid the simple generalisation that quantitative methods are always highly reliable but low in validity while qualitative methods are the reverse. Official marriage statistics, for example, are both reliable (the definition of 'a marriage' doesn't change from year to year and every marriage is officially recorded) and valid (marriage statistics measure exactly what they claim to measure).

### Comparisons

Although collecting and comparing different types of data has its advantages, it also has its complexities; such data may not always be easily and neatly compared. As Bryman (2001) argues, 'Triangulation assumes that data from different research methods can be unambiguously compared and regarded as equivalent in terms of their capacity to address a research question.' This assumption may be incorrect: differences between the data from, for example, a structured interview and a focus group may have less to do with the reliability and validity of each method and 'more to do with the possibility that the former taps private views as opposed to the more general ones that might be voiced in the more public arena of the focus group'.

### Excess

As Bryman (2001) notes, triangulation is sometimes seen as a way of getting at 'the truth' by throwing a vast array of resources, methods and data at a problem, based on the (naive) idea 'there can be a single definitive account of the social world'.

### Reliability and validity

The issue of reliability and validity is linked to the point about comparisons above, in the sense that where a researcher gets contradictory data from two different sources it can be difficult, if not impossible, to disentangle 'truth' from 'falsity'. If the researcher receives two opposing accounts of the same thing, which account is true? And more importantly, how can the researcher tell?

**Disadvantages of triangulation**

**R** esources
**A** ssumptions
**C** omparisons
**E** xcess
**R** eliability and validity

### Examples of research using triangulation

Despite these disadvantages, triangulation (or methodological pluralism) has been used in a wide range of sociological research:

➤ Barker (1984) used **overt participant observation**, **questionnaires** and **semi-structured interviews** in her research with the Unification Church (or 'Moonies').

➤ Hey (1997) studied girls' friendships in two London schools using a (perhaps unique) combination of **participant observation** and **personal documentation** (some of the girls allowed her to read their diaries and she was also given access to the notes girls passed each other in the classroom).

➤ MacKeogh (2001) studied the 'micro-politics of family viewing' in relation to how young people used television and their parents' attempts to control how and what they watched. Her primary method was **overt participant observation** (she wanted to understand the critical awareness of young people about the media they consumed). Her observation notes were complemented by notes made by her respondents as well as **semi-structured interviews** used to explore some of the issues raised in the observations.

➤ Garforth and Kerr (2010) examined 'women's under-representation in science', using a mix of **interviews**, **focus groups** and **participant observation**.

**?** Why do sociologists use triangulation in their research?

# Fitness for purpose?

In this and preceding chapters we've outlined a range of primary and secondary, quantitative and qualitative research methods and sources of data within the general context of sociological research design. The underlying theme has been that sociological research is not a random process; rather, it is highly planned and structured in ways that reflect a range of ideas — from how individual sociologists see the social world (positivism and interpretivism), through their choice of research methods that reflect these broad theoretical preferences, to the likely impact of ethical considerations on individual respondents, researchers and the research process as a whole.

In other words, 'doing sociological research' involves more than simply choosing a topic, selecting a research method and focusing on your chosen hypothesis or research question. Sociological research — whether it's a large-scale, government-funded project lasting many years or a small-scale, personally funded piece of sociology coursework — is always surrounded by a range of **research considerations**. In this final section, we will draw these considerations together under the general heading of 'fitness of purpose'. For convenience, we can group research considerations into three categories: practical, ethical and theoretical ('PET').

# Practical research considerations: choice of method

Sociological research involves confronting and resolving a range of practical factors relating to choice of research method in the general context of an assessment of how and why these methods are 'fit for the purpose' of collecting data to test a hypothesis or answer a research question. As Dunican (2005) suggests, fitness for purpose 'reflects how well the chosen research method is suited to the context of study. This is measured in terms of how well it is suited to answering the issues posed in the research question.'

A good illustration is provided by (what ended up as) Venkatesh's (2009) overt participant observation study. He originally began 'armed only with a questionnaire and a desire to learn more about the lives of poor black people', but he got to ask only one of his questions — 'How does it feel to be black and poor?' — before realising that it was pointless to ask it; to understand what it was like 'to be black and poor' he had to experience these things and to do this he needed to participate in the lives led by the people he studied.

**Funding** is an obvious practical constraint. In a perfect world, money would always be available for research into any topic, using any method (my offer to study crowd behaviour at international football matches still stands), but in our imperfect world the amount of money you have to spend will directly influence the methods used. Questionnaires are generally cheaper than in-depth interviews, while interviews are generally cheaper than participant observation. The amount of

Venkatesh argued that he had to experience being 'black and poor' in order to really understand what it was like

funding available will also influence the size of any research team.

In this respect, therefore, 'fitness for purpose' is not always determined solely by the researcher. While Dunican's (2005) observation that 'It seems logical that the selection of any research method should be based on the nature of the research question' is, of course, perfectly reasonable, it's not always possible for the researcher to follow this line of reasoning. As Boaz and Ashby (2003) note, 'Sensitivity to the sponsor's requirements can, of course, contribute to the fitness for purpose of research but can equally well introduce biases that conflict with the aim of producing objective, good quality evidence.'

**Aptness** is another consideration. Some topics may lend themselves more easily to one type of method than another. Quantitative methods tend to be used when the researcher wants reliable data to establish statistical relationships, as in Kessler's (2000) fascinating study of the relationship between sponsorship and small business performance, where his main objective was to establish whether 'those who are sponsored are more successful than non-sponsored individuals'. Alternatively, with studies such as Diken and Laustsen's (2004) rather more racy analysis of tourist behaviour in Ibiza and Faliraki, a qualitative approach is more appropriate, given the descriptive nature of the research.

**Time** is an important practical consideration. Some methods are more time-intensive than others. Whyte (1943), for example, spent years on his overt participant observation study of an American street gang. Between 1937 and 1940 he gathered extensive information about the behaviour of one gang in a small area of the country (Boston).

The **size and composition of the group** being studied may be a factor in choice of method(s). Social surveys and questionnaires lend themselves easily to the study of large, widely dispersed groups. Participant observation, on the other hand, may be more appropriate for the study of small, geographically localised groups.

Method choice

**F** unding
**A** ptness
**T** ime
**S** ize

## Ethical research considerations

Ethics, as we've previously suggested, refers to the morality of doing something, and ethical issues in sociological research involve beliefs about what a researcher should or should not do before, during and after their research. Moral beliefs do, of course, extend into any consideration about whether a particular research method or practice is fit for purpose. Research ethics have been discussed in detail in Chapter 4.

## Theoretical research considerations

Although some research methods have greater fitness for purpose in some research situations than others, Ackroyd and Hughes (1992) argue that it's wrong to simply view methods as a set of 'tools' to be picked up and discarded on the basis of some objective measurement of fitness.

In this respect theoretical beliefs — that questionnaires are not a valid way of studying social behaviour, for example — play an important part. When collecting data, for example, a researcher has to make initial decisions about a range of factors:

➤ What counts as data (do they have to be quantitative or qualitative)?
➤ Should the data be statistical or descriptive?
➤ Do we try to test a hypothesis or simply report what respondents say?

Sociological research, in this context, involves confronting and resolving a range of theoretical questions, which we can express as the *how?* and the *why?* of choice of topic and research method.

## Choice of topic

➤ **Purpose**: The researcher's aims can be influential; if testing a hypothesis, for example, the topic is likely to be much narrower in scope than if the objective is to provide a descriptive account of something.

➤ **Focus**: Research often changes to meet new interests and concerns; while it's rare for a central topic to change during the research (e.g. from family life to education), aspects of the topic may well change. As research develops, changes may be made to quantitative questions or new areas of interest may open up in the light of respondent comments or researcher observations — all of which relates to constantly revising ideas about a method's fitness for purpose in the light of changing ideas, interests and needs.

➤ **Values**: What is considered 'worthy of being studied' will be influenced by a range of values. These are both **personal** (if studying poverty holds no personal interest then a researcher is not likely to choose this topic) and, importantly for real-world research, **institutional**. Given that institutions such as universities and government departments are likely sources of research funding, the topics they value are likely to be the ones researched in the way they want them researched. If a government sponsor values quantitative statistical data about some aspect of the education system, research involving in-depth qualitative data is not likely to be considered fit for purpose.

## Choice of method

**Theoretical perspective**: Although this influence is by no means as strong as some suggest, **interactionist** researchers tend to avoid using statistical methods, mainly because their objective is to allow respondents to talk about their experiences, rather than to establish causality. **Positivists** may take the reverse view, mainly because they're not particularly interested in descriptive accounts. There is, therefore, something of an association between interpretivist methodology and qualitative research methods, just as there is a similar association between positivist methodology and quantitative methods — but as we've noted, this relationship shouldn't be pushed too far.

**Reliability and validity**: These are always significant research concerns since beliefs about the reliability and validity of particular methods will affect decisions about whether or not they are fit for purpose — and these beliefs are related to the types of sociological methodology we've just noted.

**Values**: Researcher values are reflected in ethical beliefs about how something should be studied. If, like Polsky (1971), you believe that covert participation is unethical and methodologically invalid, you're not likely to choose this research method.

---

**Exam-style question**

Using the pre-release material (below) and your wider sociological knowledge, explain and evaluate the use of mixed methods to research the importance of the school in shaping gender identity.
(52 marks)

---

**Steve Taylor (2010) on Carolyn Jackson (2006)** *Lads and Ladettes in School: Gender and Fear of Failure*, **Open University Press**

Over the last 15 years there's been a mass of research looking at laddish masculinities and educational failure. For Carolyn Jackson, helpful though these theories are, they don't take us far enough: they don't explain hard-working boys and, of course, tell us nothing about laddishness in girls. They have also tended to ignore the role of school in 'encouraging' laddishness and in this context Jackson brings in social psychological theories about fear of failure and self worth protection. It's not failure itself that's stigmatising, it's being seen to be *trying* to succeed and still failing. *Lads and Ladettes in School* is, above all, a study of fear and the relationship between fear and laddishness.

Data in this study were obtained from Year 9 pupils in six secondary schools in the north of England, and schools were selected to reflect a range of class and ethnic backgrounds. The principal methods were structured questionnaire surveys and semi-structured interviews. Questionnaires were given to over 800 students, 153 of whom were followed up with 30-minute interviews. Thirty teachers were also interviewed. The questionnaires asked about different aspects of laddishness, popularity and different aspects of motivation and self-worth protection. The follow-up interviews probed student responses in more depth. As Jackson put it, 'questionnaires are good for covering the what questions, while interviews tell you more about the why questions'.

She found laddishness was motivated by two sets of fears — fear of social failure and fear of academic failure.

Social failure was the motivation not to be unpopular; the unpopular kids were the ones who were always in the library or hovering around the teachers, the geeky types who got their work in on time and who you didn't want to be seen hanging around with. In contrast the popular kids tended to be good looking and well dressed; they were good at sport (boys) and very thin and well groomed (girls); they had a full social life outside school and appeared to do little or no work in school.

Academic failure was the fear of being *seen* to be stupid, to have been seen to be trying and yet still failing. And it was here that laddishness came in. As Jackson explained, it served 'dual motives'; it could help students be popular and provide reasons for failure. If you didn't pass an exam it wasn't because you were stupid, it was because you'd been messing around in class or out with your mates every night. Laddishness was the 'insurance' that protected self worth and public image.

Students who wanted to do well academically and yet still be popular had to perform a delicate balancing act. They had to be seen messing around in class and spending time with their friends while doing enough work covertly to give themselves a chance of a passing. As one of the girls we interviewed put it:

'I try to be popular but at same time I'll do my work, but outside school...I'll mess around in school, but as soon as I go home I'll knuckle down and do work but no-one knows I do that.'

# Unit G671

# Topics in socialisation, culture and identity

# Chapter 8

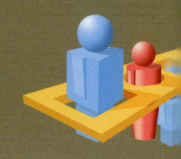

# Sociology of the family

**By the end of this chapter you will be able to:**

➢ identify and define different types of family structure

➢ identify and explain family and household trends over the past 30 years

➢ outline and evaluate functionalist and Marxist views of the role of the family

➢ identify and explain reasons for the range and extent of diversity in contemporary family life

➢ outline and evaluate postmodern and New Right views of family diversity

➢ explore a range of roles, responsibilities and relationships in family life, between men and women and between children and parents

➢ outline and evaluate functionalist, Marxist and feminist (liberal, Marxist, radical and post-feminist) explanations of roles, responsibilities and relationships in family life

➢ identify demographic changes in society and explain their impact on family life

# Key concepts and key trends within the family

### Defining the family

We can look at a number of different ways the family group has been defined, starting with a 'classic' definition from Murdock (1949). He saw the family as a social group characterised by:

➢ common residence

➢ economic cooperation and reproduction

➢ adults of both sexes, at least two of whom maintain a socially approved sexual relationship

➢ one or more children, own or adopted, of the sexually cohabiting adults

Contemporary updates on this theme include Popenoe's (1988) definition, in which:

➤ the 'minimal family composition' is one adult and one dependent person
➤ parents do not have to be of both sexes (they can be of the same sex)
➤ parents do not have to be married.

More recent definitions edge towards defining the family in terms of **kinship**; that is, relationships based on:

➤ **biology** — such as a mother and her child
➤ **affinity** — such as two adults living together (cohabitation)
➤ **law** — marriage being an obvious example

Ambert (2003) defines a family in terms of both **kinship** and **function**. A family involves two or more people, bound over time by ties of mutual consent, who assume responsibility for some of the following:

➤ physical maintenance and care of group members
➤ procreation or adoption
➤ socialisation of children
➤ social control
➤ production, consumption and distribution of goods and services
➤ affective nurturance (love)

Giddens (2006), on the other hand, suggests a very broad definition that simply involves:

➤ people directly linked by kin connections
➤ adult members assuming responsibility for childcare

The above tells us that families involve a complex set of characteristics and relationships — an idea that leads to three observations:

➤ **Qualitative differences**: Families involve different relationships and exist for different purposes from both non-family groups (such as a school class) and family-type groups such as a **household**: a single person, couple or small group (e.g. of students) living together in the same location.
➤ **Essentialism**: It's difficult to identify the essential characteristics of the family; there are conflicts between two types of definition:
  ➤ **Exclusive** definitions (such as Murdock's) focus on the specific characteristics of a family that make it different from other social groups. This has the advantage of being clear about what a family is, but it's difficult to produce a definition that applies to all possible types of family.
  ➤ **Inclusive** definitions (such as that of Giddens) focus on the general relationships, such as kinship or affinity, that make families different. This has the advantage of covering a variety of different family forms, but such a broad definition can include 'family-type' groups significantly different from families.

> **Complexity**: Goldthorpe (1987) argues that we should think about family structures as **networks of related kin**. Rather than seeing the family in terms of a specific set of clearly definable attributes (such as 'common residence' coupled with 'economic cooperation') or relationships (such as 'parents and their children'), we should see it as a **social process** based on relationships involving:
>  > **labels** — such as mother, father, son and daughter
>  > **values** — such as the belief parents should raise their own children
>  > **norms** — such as living together (through marriage or cohabitation)
>  > **functions** — such as primary socialisation

> **?**   Give two examples of how sociologists have defined 'the family'.

## Family structures

Despite arguments over how to specifically define 'families', one way to move the analysis forward is to think about families in terms of **organisational structures**: how different family relationships help to define the form and function of family groups. Rapoport and Rapoport (1982) suggest that organisational diversity refers to broad differences in the organisation of family life based around different family types — nuclear families, extended families and other types, as described below.

### Nuclear families

Nuclear families involve two generations (parents and one or more dependent children). Contacts with wider kin (aunts and cousins, for example) are usually infrequent and more likely to involve impersonal contact (e.g. through telephone or email). In contemporary Britain this type is a self-contained economic unit where family members are expected to support each other socially, economically and psychologically.

### Extended families

Extended families take a number of forms:

> **Vertically extended** family structures involve three or more generations — grandparent(s), parent(s) and child(ren) — living in the same household or close by.
> **Horizontally extended** structures involve extensions to the family that branch within generations — such as aunts and uncles — living with or close to each other.
> **Modified extended** structures, as suggested by Gordon (1972), involve wider family members keeping in touch physically (by visiting or exchanging help and services) and emotionally (through telephone, email and the like). Willmott (1988) suggests three variations on this type:
>  > a **local** type which involves 'two or three nuclear families in separate households' living close together and providing mutual help and assistance
>  > a **dispersed** type, involving less frequent personal contacts between family members
>  > an **attenuated** type — involving, for example, 'young couples before they have children', gradually separating from their original families

### Lone-parent structures

Lone-parent structures involve a single adult plus one or more dependent children. This type is sometimes called a 'broken nuclear' family, because it often — though not always — arises from the break-up of a two-parent family.

### Reconstituted family structures

Reconstituted (or 'step') family structures result from the break-up of one family (through events like death or divorce) and its reconstitution as a new family by remarriage or cohabitation. It may involve children from previous families as well as those from the new family.

### Homosexual families

A homosexual family is a basic nuclear structure that involves adults of the same sex plus children (own or adopted). Gay couples can't legally marry, but since 2005 have been able to form a **civil partnership** that gives each partner legal rights similar to those of married heterosexual couples.

**?** Give examples of two family structures in contemporary British society.

## Households

Household structures take a number of organisational forms: single-person, couple and shared households.

**Single-person households** involve an adult living alone. Historically, death and relationship breakdown have been the main cause, although more people are now choosing to live this way. Self and Zealey (2007) note that there were around 7 million single households in Britain in 2005, compared with 3 million in 1971.

**Couple households** consist of two people living together without children. Hughes and Church (2010) note that around 29% of all households fall into this category — although it does hide a diversity of experiences, including couples who have not yet decided to start a family, whose children have left home or who have chosen to remain childless.

Roseneil (2006) has identified a small but expanding group that muddies the distinction between single and couple households: couples who live apart (described as '**living apart together**' or LATs), for a range of reasons:

➤ **regretfully** — because their different working lives and routines take precedence over living together

➤ **undecidedly** — because they 'had not made an explicit decision about whether to cohabit'

➤ **gladly** — because they want to keep a sense of individual independence and control over their lives

Living apart together

**R** egretfully
**U** ndecidedly
**G** ladly

**Shared households** involve a group of unrelated people living together. This arrangement may be temporary (as when students share a flat) or permanent (families or individuals live together as a **commune**, as with the **kibbutzim** in Israel).

## Key structural trends

We can outline some key structural trends in family and household development in terms of two viewpoints: diversity and convergence.

### Diversity

The argument here is that contemporary family and household structures are now more complex, fragmented and diverse than at any time in our history.

Carlin (2002) argues that the nuclear family structure was dominant in the past. Other structures existed but the main alternative — the extended family — was far less extensive and significant for three reasons:

➤ **Life expectancy**: Average life expectancy was low and parents rarely became grandparents.

➤ **Retirement**: Those (mainly very wealthy) individuals who did survive into old age were expected to retire into households separated from their children.

➤ **Economic factors**: For the majority, earning a family living from small plots of farmed land was difficult. This land could not provide a living for additional families, hence children would move away to secure their livelihood. For the upper classes, children who did not inherit family properly were similarly encouraged to move away (into the clergy, for example) to avoid diluting family wealth.

Contemporary British society is now characterised by the coexistence of a range of different family and household structures (from nuclear and reconstituted, through lone-parent and gay to extended types) where no one type has overall dominance. This 'trend to diversity' has come about because of three main changes:

➤ **Legal changes** have provided relatively easy access to divorce, leading to greater numbers of step-parent (reconstituted) families, lone-parent families and single-person households.

➤ **Lifestyle changes** have meant a greater social acceptance of single-parent and homosexual family structures.

➤ **Increased life expectancy** has given rise to a new grandparenting (where grandparents play an important role in the care of grandchildren).

### Convergence

This view suggests that, when talking about social change, we must avoid contrasting an *idealised past*, where family structures were nuclear, stable, long-term and marriage-based, with an *uncertain present*, where the family is easily seen as an institution 'under threat', battered by changes in society (such as divorce and abortion) and attitudes (a decline in religious weddings and increases in cohabitation and single-parenthood).

Cheal (1999) argues that there has always been a mix of family and household structures in our society. Morgan (1996) argues that the idea of a past where the nuclear family was strong and stable became established for *ideological* reasons: when people believe 'the family' is under threat (from single parents, homosexuals and the like) they look to a 'mythical past' where the nuclear family (a heterosexual, married couple and their legitimate children, sharing a household and operating as an economic unit) was the comforting norm.

In this respect, Neale (2000) argues that families are increasingly 'fluid webs of relationships and practices' and Luscher (2000) suggests that people are becoming increasingly uncertain (ambivalent) about family structures and relationships in the light of social changes: increased divorce has led to the widespread creation of lone-parent and reconstituted families, resulting in a weakening of personal relationships as family members create new social spaces away from their previous family relationships.

One outcome, for Luscher, is families seeking 'geographical distance between different family generations'; in other words, the evolution of a variety of nuclear family types, loosely connected to extended networks. This is a structural convergence based around what Brannen (2003) calls the **beanpole family structure** — a vertically extended family structure with very weak links to people of the same generation.

The beanpole family structure

### Short-term trends

Although there are arguments over the interpretation of long-term structural trends, more recent trends are easier to identify:

➤ **The decline of the classic extended family**: Willmott and Young (1957) argue that this structure was a feature of working-class life in East London (and elsewhere) and included both vertical and horizontal extensions. It has gradually disappeared for a number of reasons:

  ➤ **Economic changes**: The late 1950s was a time of rising living standards and general affluence; younger family members became less economically dependent on their extended family and moved away to form nuclear families of their own.

  ➤ **Education**: Compulsory schooling until the age of 15, introduced by the 1944 Education Act, offered working-class children (boys in particular) increased opportunities for social and geographic mobility.

  ➤ **Welfare state**: The introduction of a universal (available to all) health and welfare system made family members less reliant on each other.

➤ **Parasite singles**: This involves single children who remain in the family home until their late twenties or early thirties. Manacorda and Moretti (2006) estimate that 'In Britain, roughly five out of ten men aged between 18 and 30 live with their parents'.

Curtin (2003) relates this trend to financial factors, such as young people starting work later, interrupting their careers to travel, having more career transitions (and periods of unemployment), and delaying marriage until they are financially secure.

➤ **Boomerang kids**: This involves children first leaving and subsequently returning to the parental home because of a lack of employment opportunities, high levels of personal debt, divorce or lack of affordable housing.

**?** How are parasite and boomerang kids different?

## Extended family networks

Although, as Smallwood and Wilson (2007) argue, 'The once classic extended family is now almost extinct', extended family **networks** have grown in significance for a number of reasons.

**Kinship care** is one reason. Glaser (1997) argues that the growth in the elderly population has resulted in more children returning to the family home to provide both financial and domestic care for their parent(s). Broad et al. (2001) also note that extended family networks provide a popular alternative to state care, whereby 'children and young people are placed with grandparents and other relatives'.

Lee (1999) argues that extended networks develop to provide family members with a range of help and services. These include **childcare** and **financial help**, as discussed by Rake (2009).

Rake argues that we shouldn't see family structures in terms of either nuclear or extended structures, but rather in terms of 'whole family' relationships, with extended family networks becoming increasingly important for **childcare**. Grandparents now provide childcare for 'more than two million British families' with around '200,000 grandparents as sole carers'. As work demands and pressures leave mothers with less time for childcare, **communal parenting** 'will become commonplace in

Grandparents provide childcare for many families

many families'. Rake also estimates that '90% of grandparents now provide some form of financial support for their grandchildren'.

McGlone et al. (1998) identify a range of factors that determine the nature and extent of extended family networks:

➤ **Children**: Parents with dependent children see relatives more frequently.
➤ **Gender**: Women with dependent children see their relatives more frequently than men with dependent children.
➤ **Class**: Manual workers with dependent children are more likely to have frequent contact with relatives.

> **Ethnicity**: Sinha et al. (2006) found that young black Africans and South Asians used extended family networks as a source of help and advice about sex and relationships. Glick (2000) also noted that extended networks provided help and assistance for recent family immigrants.

# Trends in families and households

A **trend** is established by comparing what is happening now with the situation at some point in the past. We can outline a range of short-term family and household trends over the past 30 or so years (longer-term comparisons are sometimes given to illustrate a particular trend).

## Family size trends

Measuring 'average family size' depends on how we calculate family size. If we include **all family members** the picture is distorted if there is an increase in lone-parent families; average family size may decline for *statistical* rather than *demographic* reasons (the result of counting fewer adults now than in the past). If we look instead at **fertility rate** — the average number of children born to women of child-bearing age (roughly 15–44) over their reproductive lifetime — we get a more **reliable** picture of changes in family size (Table 8.1).

Table 8.1    Fertility rate

| Year | Fertility rate |
|------|----------------|
| 1959 | 2.6 |
| 1969 | 2.4 |
| 1979 | 1.8 |
| 1989 | 1.7 |
| 1999 | 1.6 |
| 2000 | 1.65 |
| 2001 | 1.63 |
| 2005 | 1.7 |
| 2008 | 1.97 |
| 2009 | 1.96 |

*Source: Office for National Statistics (2010)*

From this we can identify a range of trends based on fertility rate.

In the longer term, over the past 150 years, the trend has been for a falling average family size:

> In the 1870s, average family size was between 5 and 6 children (Grenham 1995).
> In 1901, the fertility rate was 3.5 children (Diamond 2007).
> In 2009, the fertility rate was under 2.

In the shorter term, we can note that:

➤ From the 1960s onward, a falling fertility rate is reflected in a falling family size. To put this in perspective, Hughes (2010) notes a significant generational change: while women born in 1937 had an average of 2.4 children, their daughters' generation averaged 1.9 children.

➤ The long-term fall in family size peaked around the turn of the twenty-first century, since when the trend has been for a slight rise in fertility rates and average family size (although whether this has peaked is not yet clear).

**?**  Give examples of two trends in family size.

### Explanations

Self and Zealey (2007) suggest that explanations for the long-term decline in family size involve the following factors: changed attitudes, an increase in childlessness, changing female roles, geographic mobility and the availability of family planning.

### *Attitudes*

Social attitudes to very large families have changed (a family with five or more children is now seen as deviant, rather than the norm as it once was) and are influenced by factors like the following:

➤ **Education**: Changes to the education system have meant the 'extension of dependent childhood': in 1972 the school leaving age was raised to 15, while in 2013 children will be required to stay in 'school, training or workplace training' until 18. Whereas in the past children contributed to family income (they were an economic asset), they are now more likely to represent a drain on family resources.

➤ **Cost of children**: As children become more expensive to raise, their numbers fall. As Womack (2006) reports, 'One in five people said they would not be having any more offspring because they could not afford to.'

➤ **Lifestyles**: Rising living costs, Womack (2006) reports, 'have led many people to choose to enjoy the lifestyle they have instead of adding more pressure with the cost of bringing up a child'.

### *Childlessness*

Childlessness is increasingly common among both single females and couples. For the former this can be partly explained by the pursuit of professional careers (especially for middle-class women) and, to a general extent, lifestyle choices. McAllister and Clarke (1998) found that, among couples, reasons given for childlessness varied:

➤ **Choice**: Some couples did not want children.

➤ **Acceptance**: Some had once considered having children but had decided against it.

➤ **Problematic**: For some, the decision to have children had been taken away, through fertility problems or other factors beyond their control.

Childlessness

**C** hoice
**A** cceptance
**P** roblematic
**E** quivocal
**D** elay

➤ **Equivocal**: Some were undecided about whether to have children in the future.

➤ **Delay**: Others were uncertain about wanting children 'at present', but would not discount ever having children.

### Changing female roles

Greater participation in education and work has meant female roles within the family have changed. Where women are giving birth to a first child later (in their early thirties, as opposed to mid-twenties 30 years ago), this reduces the time available for the development of larger families. Later childbirth also means women can establish a career which they can resume after childbirth — which also suggests women are less likely to settle for a traditional 'mother and child-rearing' role.

Finch (2003) also notes that, while younger women have moved towards later childbirth, this has not been offset by older women having more children, something that 'results in a decrease in the average family size'.

### Geographic mobility

Smaller families can be more flexible and mobile than larger families. Improved communications (the ability to stay in close contact with extended family members) also mean geographic mobility may be less disruptive than in the past.

### Family planning

In contrast with even the recent past, the availability of cheap and reliable male and female contraception has given women greater control over their fertility. The 1967 Abortion Act also meant 'unwanted children' could be legally terminated.

> **?** How have sociologists explained falling family size?

## Marriage trends

Marriage trends are complicated by serial monogamy (people can marry, divorce and remarry), which makes simple comparisons between past and present less reliable. However, marriage statistics (Table 8.2) do tell us something about marriage trends.

We can note the following trends:

➤ There is an overall decline for all marriages.

➤ There is a steady decline in first marriages.

➤ Remarriage (second and subsequent marriages) peaked in the 1980s and has since slowly declined. Remarriage, as a percentage of all marriages, has doubled in the past 50 years, peaking around the turn of the twenty-first century and slowly declining over the past 10 years.

➤ Marriage was most popular just after the Second World War and during the 1970s, two events connected by **baby booms** — a greater than usual number of babies born over a relatively short time. The Second World War meant couples delayed starting a family and by the 1950s the average span for family completion (from the births of first to last child) was a historically short 10 years. This compression of family formation produced a population bulge (a rapid, if temporary, increase in the number of children in society) — a demographic change that explains an increase in (i) marriage and childbirth during the 1950s, and (ii) the numbers marrying in the 1970s and 1980s as the 'baby-boom generation' reached adulthood.

Table 8.2   UK marriage patterns

| Year | All marriages (thousands) | First marriage (thousands) | Remarriage (thousands) | Remarriage as % of all marriages |
|------|---------------------------|----------------------------|------------------------|----------------------------------|
| 1970 | 340 | 279 | 61 | 18 |
| 1981 | 352 | 228 | 124 | 35 |
| 1991 | 307 | 192 | 115 | 37 |
| 1996 | 279 | 161 | 118 | 42 |
| 2001 | 249 | 149 | 100 | 40 |
| 2003 | 270 | 160 | 110 | 41 |
| 2004 | 273 | 163 | 110 | 40 |
| 2005 | 247 | 148 | 99 | 40 |
| 2006 | 239 | 146 | 93 | 39 |
| 2007 | 235 | 146 | 89 | 38 |
| 2008 | 236 | 149 | 87 | 37 |
| 2009 | 232 | 151 | 81 | 35 |

Source: adapted from Self and Zealey (2007)/Hughes and Church (2010)

### Explanations

#### Social pressures

There is less stigma attached to having children outside marriage, and social pressures to marry have declined. There is less economic pressure on women to marry for financial security.

#### Alternatives

Although there have always been alternatives to marriage, over the past 30 years a range of alternatives have become more socially acceptable:

➤ **Cohabitation** (see below): This has increased in recent years and, although many cohabiting couples eventually marry, many do not. Self and Zealey (2007) suggest that falling marriage and rising cohabitation are the result of an increase in those choosing to delay marriage until later in life.

➤ **Single-parenthood**: Hughes and Church (2010) note that around 10% of families with dependent children had single (never-married) mothers, compared with 1% in 1971.

➤ **Singletons**: There has been an increase in those choosing to remain single (and childless).

### Secularisation

The influence of religious beliefs in our society has generally declined, leading to changes in the meaning and significance of marriage; it has, in simple terms, become less important and there is less social pressure to marry.

### Lifestyles

Oswald (2002) argues that increased female financial, career and personal independence means marriage has become a 'lifestyle choice'. Women are less likely to enter into a relationship (such as marriage) that restricts their ability to work and develop a career — a lifestyle change reflected in the average age of marriage (Table 8.3).

Table 8.3   Average age at first marriage

| Year | Men | Women |
|------|-----|-------|
| 1971 | 25 | 23 |
| 2001 | 30 | 28 |
| 2007 | 33 | 30 |

### Risk

Beck (1992) argues that people increasingly assess the likely consequences of their actions; the statistical likelihood of divorce, with all its emotional and economic consequences, can lead to the simple step of avoiding risk by not marrying.

**?**  **Give one reason for marriage trends over the past 30 years.**

## Cohabitation

The fact that cohabitation is not legally recorded limits data **reliability**. We know people have always cohabited in our society: Gillis (1985), for example, argues that 'informal marriage' (cohabitation) was extensively practised in the past. However, the past 30 years has seen survey methods produce more reliable estimates for cohabitation. Church and Hughes (2010) note a range of cohabitation trends:

➤ Cohabitation has increased, from 10% of couples in 1986 to 25% in 2006.
➤ The number of young people (aged 25–29) cohabiting has increased, from 18% in the 1990s to 26% by the mid-2000s.
➤ The number of women cohabiting has increased: 1% of those aged 55–59 had cohabited before the age of 25, compared with 21% of those aged 25–29.
➤ The proportion of cohabiting-couple families has increased in the past 10 years (from 9% to 15%).

### Explanations

In a general sense, decisions about cohabitation are related to:
➤ reduced social pressures to marry
➤ lower levels of stigma attached to living with someone of the same or opposite sex
➤ the greater availability of contraception and abortion

Smart and Stevens (2000), however, suggest four reasons that help explain recent upward trends:

➤ **Attitudes to marriage**: They found attitudes to marriage were one reason, ranging from indifference to uncertainty about the suitability for marriage of the person with whom they were cohabiting.

➤ **Assessment**: For some, cohabitation represented a trial for their partner to prove they could settle down, gain and keep paid work and interact successfully with the mother's children. Self and Zealey (2007) suggest that later marriage is a factor here. Prior to marriage, males and females move into and out of **serial cohabitation** (one cohabiting relationship followed by another).

➤ **Legal factors**: Many cohabiting parents were either unwilling to enter into a legal relationship with their partner or they believed it easier to back away from a cohabiting relationship if it didn't work out.

➤ **Opposition to marriage**: Some parents believed cohabitation led to a more equal form of relationship.

> **?** What are the recent trends in cohabitation?

## Divorce

Keeping in mind it's only over the past 60 or so years that divorce has been both a legal and financial possibility for most people in our society, we can begin by looking at a statistical breakdown of divorce (Table 8.4).

Table 8.4   Divorce in the UK

| Year | No. of divorces (thousands) | Average age at divorce | |
|---|---|---|---|
| | | Males | Females |
| 1921 | 3.0 | – | – |
| 1941 | 7.5 | – | – |
| 1947 | 47 | – | – |
| 1951 | 29 | – | – |
| 1961 | 20 | – | – |
| 1971 | 80 | 39 | 37 |
| 1981 | 160 | 38 | 35 |
| 1991 | 180 | 39 | 36 |
| 1999 | 170 | 41 | 39 |
| 2000 | 155 | 39 | 36 |
| 2001 | 157 | 42 | 39 |
| 2005 | 142 | 43 | 40 |

| Year | No. of divorces (thousands) | Average age at divorce | |
|---|---|---|---|
| | | Males | Females |
| 2007 | 129 | 43 | 40 |
| 2008 | 136 | 44 | 41 |
| 2009 | 127 | 44 | 42 |

*Source:* Social Trends *30–40 (Office for National Statistics)*

While data from the early to mid twentieth century are interesting in terms of the relatively small number of divorces, the most interesting data have emerged more recently:

➤ Over the past 40 years, divorce has become more popular.
➤ Over the past 30 years, divorcees have been getting older (reflecting the later average age of marriage).
➤ The past 20 years saw divorce peak in the 1990s, a consequence of the post-war baby boom.
➤ Over the past 10 years, there has been a general slow-down and decline in the numbers divorcing.

There has also, since 1981, been a doubling in 're-divorces' — those going through a further divorce.

Homosexual couples are not immune from break-up; in 2007, 42 civil partnerships (between 28 female and 14 male couples) in England and Wales were legally dissolved. In 2008 this had risen to 166.

While raw numbers of divorces are useful, they're also sensitive to population changes; all other things being equal, the higher the number of marriages, the higher the expected number of divorces. For this reason, it's more reliable to look at divorce *rates*. Table 8.5 shows the rates over the past 30 years (as the number of people divorcing per 1,000 of the married population).

Table 8.5  Divorce rates per 1,000 of the married population in the UK

| Year | Divorce rate |
|---|---|
| 1977 | 10.3 |
| 1999 | 13.9 |
| 2002 | 13.2 |
| 2006 | 12.2 |
| 2007 | 11.9 |
| 2008 | 11.2 |
| 2009 | 10.2 |

*Source: Office for National Statistics*

We can note the following trends from these data:

➢ The general trend is for a fall in the rate of divorce.
➢ Divorce rates peaked at the turn of the twenty-first century and have since gradually declined.
➢ The divorce rate is currently at its lowest since 1977.

### Explanations

Unfortunately, 'all other things' are not equal — and we need to understand how a range of social and individual factors affect divorce trends.

### Social factors

Social factors operate at a society-wide level and reflect structural influences on individual decisions about divorce (just as they influence decisions about marriage and cohabitation). Historically, there are a number of significant **demographic factors** affecting divorce trends, discussed below.

### Legal changes

When major changes in divorce law (Table 8.6) are correlated with trends in the divorce rate, it can be seen that each time divorce is made easier or more affordable, the number divorcing increases.

Table 8.6   Divorce: selected legal changes

| Year and Act | Main change |
|---|---|
| 1857: Matrimonial Causes Act | Available through law courts for first time (but very expensive). 'Fault' had to be proven. Men could divorce because of adultery, women had to show both cruelty and adultery. |
| 1923: Matrimonial Causes Act | Grounds for divorce made the same for men and women. |
| 1937: Herbert Act | New grounds for divorce (desertion, cruelty etc.), and no divorce petition was allowed for the first 3 years of marriage. |
| 1969–1971: Divorce Reform Act | 'Fault' (adultery, etc.) replaced by 'irretrievable breakdown of marriage' as the only requirement. |
| 1985: Matrimonial and Family Proceedings Act | Time limit on divorce reduced from 3 years of marriage to 1 year. |
| 1996–2000: Family Law Act | Introduced range of ideas (counselling, cooling-off period to reflect on application for divorce — not all of which have been applied) to make divorce less confrontational. |

While legal changes are important, we need to note a **reliability** problem with using them to explain divorce trends: changes to the legal definition of divorce mean we're not comparing 'like with like'. For example, we don't know the number of people in 1968 who would have divorced if the post-1969 divorce rules had been applicable.

*Economic changes*
- In 1949 **legal aid** was made available for divorcing couples, making it an option for those other than the rich.
- **Female financial independence** has increased over the past 30 years with greater numbers working outside the home. Where the economic costs of divorce for women have declined, this has made divorce an option.
- With the **welfare state**, the partner (usually, but not necessarily, the wife) who took on sole care of any children after divorce was given a financial safety net.

*Secularisation*
The hold of religious beliefs in our society has gradually loosened. If couples no longer see marriage as a 'sacred institution' then 'breaking the marital bond' is not seen as morally wrong — and there is also less stigma attached to those who divorce.

*Childlessness*
Hughes (2009) notes that around 35% of divorces in 2007 were childless, which makes dissolving a marriage less emotionally and financially complicated.

*Life expectancy*
When people live longer, their marriage also has longer to last. For some couples, this places greater strain on the relationship and increases the chance of divorce.

### Individual factors

A further dimension to understanding divorce trends concerns how individuals perceive their relationships — the 'personal reasons' for both entering and ending a marriage.
Clarke and Berrington (1999) note several relevant factors:
- Young (especially teenage) couples are statistically more likely to divorce.
- Populations with a large proportion of married couples involve higher 'divorce risks'.
- Short courtships are associated with a higher divorce risk. Becker et al. (1977) suggest that stable marriage relationships occur where partners are well-matched — and short courtships don't give couples enough time to ensure this is the case.

**Lifestyle choice** factors are also important. Some couples see marriage in terms of a search for personal happiness, rather than a moral commitment to each other (which may explain the increase in remarriages; divorcees are not unhappy with marriage, just the person they married). This is related to **romantic individualism**. The arguments here are twofold:
- Family relationships have become stripped of all but their personal functions — if people 'fall out of love', there's nothing to hold their marriage together.
- We increasingly have illusions about love, romance and family life — once the reality hits home, people opt for divorce as a way out of an unhappy experience. Becker

et al. (1977), for example, argue that a mismatch between what someone expects to happen in a marriage and what *actually* happens is likely to result in divorce.

**?** | **How can we explain recent divorce trends?**

## Lone- and single-parent families

Although the terms 'lone' and 'single' parent are often used interchangeably, it can sometimes be useful to differentiate (or split) them, so that:

➢ 'lone parent' refers to anyone bringing up children alone, whether widowed, divorced, separated or never married (single)

➢ 'single parent' refers specifically to a parent who has never married

Hughes and Church (2010) note a large increase in the proportion of families headed by a lone mother, as shown in Table 8.7.

Table 8.7    Lone-mother families as a percentage of all families with dependent children in Great Britain: by marital status

| Year | Marital status | | | |
|------|---------|----------|-----------|--------|
|      | Widowed | Divorced | Separated | Single |
| 1971 | 2%      | 2%       | 2%        | 1%     |
| 2007 | –       | 6%       | 4%        | 10%    |

They also note a further trend in the proportion of people living in lone-parent households:

➢ 1961: 3%

➢ 1981: 6%

➢ 2009: 12%

### Explanations

#### Divorce and separation

Around 50% of all lone-parent families are created through divorce or separation. Some are the outcome of female choice, whereas a significant proportion result from the male partner deciding to leave the family group.

#### Economic independence

As more women enter higher education and the workforce, there are increased opportunities to be economically independent of men and lone parenthood is more likely to be the result of **choice**.

Coward (1999) suggests that **economic globalisation** has created a 'seismic shift' in male–female relationships (what Wilkinson (1994) terms a '**genderquake**') because it has created increasing workplace flexibility and more opportunities for female home-working using computer technology. Rowlingson et al. (1999), however, argue that economically independent lone mothers are not the norm in our society; the majority depend on the welfare state for income. In this respect, **choice** and **desertion** by a male partner are equal explanations.

### Morality

There is less **stigma** attached to bearing and raising children as a lone parent, partly as a result of higher levels of divorce (and greater social acceptance of this situation) and partly as a result of changing moral values (a general decline in religious belief, for example).

Lone parents

**D** ivorce
**I** ndependence
**M** orality

> ? What are two recent trends in lone parenthood?

## Single-person households

Since 1961 single-person households have doubled. Darby (2005) further notes how 'the proportion of single-person households has increased steadily over the past 30 years', comprising 22% of all households in 1981 and 30% of all households in 2009. In 2002, this household structure became the most common family or household structure in our society.

### Explanations

Palmer (2006) suggests two reasons for the increase in single-person households:

➤ **Economic changes**: Changing employment patterns (the decline in heavy manufacturing, the rise in short-term contract work in financial services and information technology) have resulted in greater geographic mobility. The single-person household, the most mobile of all family/household structures, fits neatly with the changing (increasingly global) nature of work. Furthermore, many professional career women choose not to marry or cohabit, at least until they have established a career and, increasingly, not at all. McGhie (2009) reports, 'The proportion of single women living alone more than doubled between 1983 (10%) and 2002 (22%).'

➤ **Choice**: This includes those who, while they may be in a relationship, maintain their independence by living alone ('living apart together').

Further explanations include:

➤ **Sexuality**: Urban areas such as Brighton, Manchester and London have large gay communities.

➤ **Divorce**: The splitting of a shared household often results in at least one of the partners (and maybe both if no children are involved) establishing a single household.

➤ **Longer life expectancy**: Women live longer on average than men and since, as Hughes and Church (2010) report, 50% of single householders are above the pensionable age, the death of a partner is a significant factor in the development of this type of household.

**Exam-style questions**

**1** Identify and explain characteristics of the nuclear family. (17 marks)

**2** Identify and explain reasons for the decrease in family size over the past 30 years. (17 marks)

**3** Identify and explain reasons for the decline in marriage over the past 30 years. (17 marks)

# The role of family in society

In this section we examine the role of the family in society from two different viewpoints: functionalism and Marxism.

## Functionalism

**Traditional functionalist** approaches adopt a **consensus approach** to understanding both society and the role of the family, and this involves thinking about two types of cooperation:

➢ **inter-institutional** (between education and work, for example)
➢ **intra-institutional** (between husband and wife, for example)

The functions of the family represent a delicate balance between these two types. We can initially illustrate this using Murdock's (1949) four family functions:

➢ **Sexuality**: The control of sexuality (adult family members only engaged in sexual relations with each other) provided 'stability through exclusivity'; by showing commitment to both each other and their family, adults would focus their efforts on ensuring the survival of their group. By 'looking inward' to the needs of their family, adults would also be 'looking outward' to the needs of the social system.

➢ **Reproduction**: Families 'reproduced society' by creating new members to replace those who die.

➢ **Socialisation**: Children were taught the values and norms of their society.

➢ **Economic provision**: To perform reproductive and socialisation functions, family members had to organise themselves to ensure the group's survival (providing, at the most basic level, food and shelter for the group). To do this they had to develop a particular **division of labour**:

  ➢ **Domestic**: This related to the internal organisation and running of the family group (involving, for example, cooking, cleaning and childcare).

  ➢ **Non-domestic**: In modern societies some form of paid employment was needed to buy the food and services required by the family.

The fact that historically non-domestic work was mainly done by men and domestic work by women creates a problem for functionalists (one that points to an important criticism of this approach). Functionalists argue that institutions always exist for a *purpose* and that purpose can be read from what they *do*. To know the purpose of the family we look at what it does now and then 'think backwards' to discover some underlying explanation about how and why it has reached this stage in its development. This formulation involves two important ideas:

➤ **Evolution**: This is the idea that present family arrangements are always the highest point in any evolutionary scale.

➤ **Design**: Benton (1984) argues that the evolutionary development of the family could not be the product of chance because it is locked into an institutional system of **purpose** and **need**; something exists because it is functional.

While this explains why **social systems** develop, it encounters critical problems when it has to explain very specific functional relationships, such as the division of labour within the family. When functionalists in the 1950s and 1960s looked at the family division of labour, it clearly showed **segregated conjugal roles** — a gendered division of labour whereby men (providers) and women (nurturers) performed very different and clearly separated roles. Since this system had to be functional, functionalists had to identify the 'design principles' that explained segregated conjugal roles — which they did in terms of instrumental and expressive orientations:

➤ **Instrumental orientations**: Outside the family we deal with people in an objective, unemotional way, based on what they can do for us and what we can do for them. An employee, for example, gives their time and labour to an employer and, in return, they receive money. For this arrangement to work the employee and employer do not have to like or love each other (their relationship is not based on affection); if the employer stops paying, the employee won't continue to work 'for love'. Similarly, a lazy, incompetent or thieving employee wouldn't be tolerated by an employer. For men to be successful in their provider role outside the family, they need instrumental orientations.

➤ **Expressive orientations**: Inside the family people deal with each other on the basis of love and affection (in expressive or affective relationships). They do things like childcare not because they expect to get something in return but because it expresses an emotional commitment. The fact that women give birth and nurture children suggests they have expressive rather than instrumental orientations to both their children and their partner and this explains why they are 'better suited' to a domestic labour role within the family.

In the 1950s it was usual for mothers to stay at home to look after their children

### Evaluation

Functionalist explanations of the domestic division of labour suffer from two main problems.

First, if the domestic division of labour changes (as it has over the past 30 years), how can this be explained away? The answer lies in two ideas:

➤ Instrumental and expressive orientations are based on a **biological essentialism**; that is, males and females have fundamentally different biologies that orientate them in different ways. The division between males as providers and females as carers is a natural expression of biological differences.

➤ This is connected to the idea of **dysfunction**; while people can 'go against their nature' (women can reject childcare, men can embrace ironing), this type of family arrangement is not functional for either the family or society.

The second problem is that the emphasis on consensus and harmony, apart from ignoring the 'dark side of family life' (from physical violence to child abuse), ignores power imbalances; traditional domestic divisions of labour suit men (they enjoy a wide range of free family services) and they have the power (physical or economic) to impose this kind of arrangement. Women, from this viewpoint, are domestic labourers not through choice but necessity — they fear male power.

> **?** Give one feature of segregated conjugal roles.

These criticisms aside, Parsons and Bales (1956) suggested that modern families had become increasingly **specialised**. Whereas in the past the family had been multi-functional (performing a wide range of functions), the development of social institutions such as education and medicine or the expansion of existing institutional roles (such as a welfare state) meant the family lost many of its former functions. These changes, for Parsons (1959), were consistent with family evolution because they meant family groups were free to concentrate on two essential functions:

➤ **Primary socialisation**: Families are socialisation 'factories whose product is the development of human personalities'. This function links to social order and system stability as the mechanism through which new family members came to understand and learn the values and norms they would need to play their adult role.

➤ **Stabilisation of adult personalities**: This involved adult family members providing physical and emotional support for each other. Family relationships provided both the motivation for paid work and also the various emotional and sexual comforts that came from the development of relationships based on love and affection.

Weiss (1988) notes how these two ideas can be broken down into a number of specific family functions:

➤ social control of members

➤ consumption and distribution of goods and services

- affective nurturance, whereby children (and adults) are nurtured by people who have bonds of love and affection with them
- maintenance (physical and psychological) and care of family members
- procreation or adoption to add new members

| Family functions | |
|---|---|
| **S** | ocial control |
| **C** | onsumption |
| **A** | ffective |
| **M** | aintenance |
| **P** | rocreation |

Fletcher (1973) drew these functional strands together by arguing that modern families perform core and peripheral functions.

**Core functions** are the things that cannot be performed by either individuals working alone or by any other institution in society:

- **Procreation and child-rearing**: Family groups provide a vital and necessary context for both childbearing (procreation) and child-rearing. Child-rearing involves ensuring the physical and psychological survival of the human infant and its development as a member of a wider society (**primary socialisation**). A child's natural parents are seen as best positioned to carry out this process because they have a 'personal investment' in their child's survival and development.
- **Provision of a home**: The family provides both a 'physical home' (nurture and shelter for the child) and an 'emotional home' in terms of the child's psychological well-being (children feel wanted and loved).
- **Regulation of sexual behaviour**: Norms relating to permissible sexual relationships contribute to social order and stability.

**Peripheral functions** are things that, while still performed by some families at some times, have largely been taken over by other institutions:

- **basic education** — teaching children skills like reading and writing
- **healthcare** (for minor sickness and ailments)
- **recreation** — a function which may still be performed by families in a residual way (through family outings and holidays: 'special events' that serve to bond family members as a group)

### Neo-functionalism

As a structural approach, functionalism looks at how **social structures** (such as families) influence **social actions** (the behavioural choices we make). This influence is important (and desirable) because we have to learn how to behave as part of a group; a society cannot function if its individual members are continually 'doing their own thing' without regard to others.

Neo-functionalist ('neo-' meaning 'new') approaches reflect more recent functionalist thinking about the various processes involved in **linking the individual to society** through family groups. Horwitz (2005), for example, argues that we can understand family functions in the context of the following:

> **A micro–macro bridge**: The family connects the 'micro world' of the individual with the 'macro world' of wider society. The linkage between social structures (the macro world) and social actions (the micro world) explains the relationship between the individual and social structure in terms of, for example, the family's role in the primary socialisation process. As Horwitz argues, 'Families help us to learn the explicit and tacit social rules necessary for functioning in the wider world.'

> **Social relationships**: The family is 'a school for learning social norms'; by initially learning rules of social interaction with family members, children create a template 'for other intimate relationships and the more anonymous relationships' found in wider society.

> **Social order**: Social rules, such as 'instructing children in general concepts of right and wrong and explaining appropriate behaviour', are transmitted to each new generation. Horwitz suggests that 'the family is a superior site for learning these rules of behaviour', for three reasons:

>> **Intimacy**: Rules transmitted and enforced by people who share a deep emotional commitment are more likely to be effectively taught and learnt.

>> **Incentives**: The emotional closeness of families provides incentives to behave in ways that make interaction 'smoother' (cooperation is desirable if people are to avoid too much personal stress and strain). What others think about a child's behaviour (and the parents who raised them) is a further incentive for 'good behaviour'.

>> **Subconscious learning**: Within a family rules can be learned 'subconsciously' by children observing and imitating others' behaviour. A parent 'might be unable to explain the rules that guide her behaviour when interacting with a stranger, but the child can observe and later imitate the behaviour and, in so doing, adopt the implicit rules that are at work'.

### Evaluation

#### Dysfunction

It's difficult to see how the 'dark side' of family life (child abuse and neglect, violence, sexual assaults, family breakdown and divorce) fits into the harmonious and consensual picture painted by functionalists; it's also hard to see how these could be functional for either society or those involved (hence the idea of family *dysfunctions*). There is extensive evidence in our society for a range of **family dysfunctions**:

> **Violence**: Jansson (2007) notes that domestic violence incidents peaked in 1994 at around 1.2 million cases and are currently running at around 275,000 cases a year. Dodd et al. (2004) report that 16% of all violent incidents involve domestic violence.

> **Assault and rape**: Women are most likely to be sexually assaulted by men they know, and 45% of reported rapes were carried out by a current partner.

> **Murder**: In 2000, just over 40% of female murder victims (92 women) were killed by present or former partners. The comparable figure for men was 6%. Rooney and

Devis (2009) report that 'the highest homicide rates are in infants' — the vast majority of which occur within the family.

### Diversity

Family structures and relationships have changed considerably since the middle of the twentieth century. Their contemporary diversity makes it difficult to talk about 'the family' as opposed to a multitude of different types of family arrangements and relationships.

### Conflict theories

Marxist and feminist conflict theories argue that family relationships are based on oppression and exploitation rather than harmonious and functional cooperation.

### Influence outside sociology

Kingsbury and Scanzoni (1993) argue that, while traditional functionalism represents 'a framework that has become virtually obsolete throughout general sociology', it has remained influential outside sociology; many politicians and political parties draw on functionalist ideas when talking about contemporary family life.

Prideaux (2006), for example, argues that 'New Labour, when dealing with welfare, utilises functionalist diagnoses and remedies for the perceived ills within British society'. David Cameron (2011) also echoes functionalist ideas when he argues:

> Strong families are where children learn to become responsible people...you learn how to behave, you learn about give and take. You learn about responsibility and how to live in harmony with others. Strong families are the foundation of a bigger, stronger society.

**?** **What two family functions are now performed by other institutions?**

# Marxism

Marxism also adopts a **systems approach** but, unlike functionalism, it doesn't see society as functioning 'for the benefit of all'; rather, societies operate in the interests of the rich and powerful (the bourgeoisie or 'owners of the means of production'). Capitalism, as we've previously outlined, is a system based around social class, social inequality and social conflicts. The family's general role is, for Marxists, one of supporting the economic system in various ways — a role that has three dimensions: ideological, economic and political.

### Ideological role

The family propagates ideas (an **ideology**) favourable to both capitalism and a ruling class. Althusser (1970), for example, argues that the family is an **ideological state apparatus** (ISA): through primary socialisation the child comes to learn values, such as the importance of competition and the work ethic, and norms, such as work itself, both paid and unpaid, that will eventually allow it to take its place in capitalist society.

Zaretsky (1976) argues that socialisation involves the transmission of a ruling class ideology that encourages largely unquestioning acceptance of 'the capitalist system' and the rights of a ruling class. The family, in this respect, transmits both **ideas**, such as social inequality being necessary and inevitable, and **values**, such as the importance of obeying authority — initially that of the parent and later that of the employer.

### Economic role

The economic role of the family has a number of dimensions.

In terms of **reproduction**, families produce the new members of society that capitalism needs in order to reproduce itself over time. These include those destined to be:

➢ wage workers (who can be exploited for profit)
➢ professionals (doctors etc.)
➢ captains of industry
➢ presidents of global corporations

The family also provides **free services**. The costs of replacing 'dead labour' (both those who literally die and those who become too old or sick to work) are taken on by the family group in terms of the following:

➢ **Production costs**: The major economic costs involved in raising children fall on the family (while employers eventually reap the most economic benefit).
➢ **Consumption costs**: Althusser (1970) argues that the family has moved from being a **unit of production** (family members produced the things they needed to survive) to a unit of **consumption**; it buys most of what it needs. This means, Zaretsky (1976) argues, that families are important targets for advertisers; by encouraging consumption the family has progressively become a major source of **profit**.

The family's role in maintaining social inequality is, for Marxists, illustrated in the following ways:

➢ **Channelling exploitation**: Women — where they still do the bulk of domestic labour tasks (even when in paid employment) — provide 'free services' for men that keep them 'fit and healthy' for their exploitation in the workplace.
➢ **Legitimising exploitation**: If women see domestic labour as an integral part of 'being female' (just as paid labour is an integral part of 'being male'), 'exploitation' — in both the home and the workplace — comes to be seen as 'right, proper and natural'.
➢ **Inheritance**: Social inequality is perpetuated by the rich passing their wealth from parent to child. The family is the vehicle for legitimising this process. Wealthy families are also in a position to 'buy' a start in life for their offspring (private education, university funding, financial assistance with housing and so on). For Marxists, the

idea of marriage as a legal contract is also a means through which wealth can be legitimately passed down the family line.

### Political role

Families are a **stabilising force** in capitalist society because the responsibilities people take on lock them into capitalist economic relationships. Family members have to work to provide both basic necessities — food, clothing and shelter — and the consumer goods that go with modern lifestyles (computers, the family car and so on). The need to take responsibility for family members, both adults and children, also acts as an emotional stabilising force.

Zaretsky (1976) argues for the growth of what Goldthorpe et al. (1968) call the **privatised family**, where family members are focused on the home, the production and care of children, their personal relationships and so forth. This encourages family members to focus on their own private concerns (such as how to pay the mortgage) rather than wider social concerns (such as why some people in our society earn millions of pounds a year while others sleep in shop doorways). By 'seeing the world through a private family lens', political engagement and action against 'the economic system' are discouraged.

In this respect the family becomes a **safety valve** for (male) frustrations. Most men are relatively powerless in the workplace, a condition disguised by allowing them to be powerful figures within their family. This is a safety value which directs frustration away from employers, workplace conditions and social inequality, and on to family members.

It also reflects the **dark side of family life**. Marxists see violence and abuse within the family as the inevitable consequence of the power relationships encouraged by capitalism. While most men are exploited and lack power in the workplace, they can exercise power within the family — and when they meet resistance this can result in domestic violence. Home Office statistics for 2007 show that:

➤ Around 150 people each year are killed by a current or former partner.
➤ One incident of domestic violence is reported to the police every minute (and this is a massively under-reported crime).
➤ 25% of women (and 15% of men) suffer from domestic violence at some point.
➤ 90% of repeat victims are women.

> **?** How does the family group 'help to support the capitalist economic system'?

### Neo-Marxism

A further **cultural** dimension to our understanding of the role of the family in reproducing social inequality is highlighted by contemporary (neo-) Marxists when they suggest some of the specific advantages and disadvantages families give to their children.

**Cultural capital** refers to a variety of non-economic resources that can be 'spent' to give some families advantages over others. Parents, according to Bourdieu (1986), are differently positioned to 'invest' in their children. Middle- and upper-class parents, Silva and Rosalind (2004) argue, are able to equip their children with the knowledge and skills that make their transition to the adult world of work easier. Bourdieu argues that cultural capital operates through the family to give some children a 'head start' in education, in several ways:

> One way concerns the ability of parents to motivate their children by transmitting the **attitudes and knowledge** needed to succeed educationally. Conversely, Willis's (1970) research suggests that a lack of cultural capital consigns working-class children to educational failure and explains 'why working-class kids get working-class jobs'.

Middle-class female emotional labour — such as helping with homework — is an important type of cultural capital

> **Institutional investment** involves the time, money and effort parents put into their child's education; the greater the investment the more likely children are to achieve the qualifications they need for the highest-status universities (which, in turn, ease their route into highly paid employment). Reay et al. (2004) note that middle-class women perform high levels of **emotional labour** in constantly monitoring their child's performance and progress at school — questioning teachers, attending school open evenings and even campaigning to remove 'underperforming' teachers. Their cultural capital provides the resources needed to perform this role successfully.

> Parents invest in cultural **goods and services** — books, computers, extra tuition, getting their child into the 'right school' and the like — that give their children an educational advantage. Sullivan (2001) tested this effect on GCSE performance and concluded that cultural capital was 'transmitted within the home and does have a significant effect on performance'.

**?**  How is cultural capital transmitted from parents to children?

Cultural capital is related to further forms of **family capital**: social and symbolic capital.

**Social capital** refers to people's connections to **social networks** ('who you know') and the value of these connections for what Putnam (2000) calls '**norms of reciprocity**' (what people are able to do for each other). Middle- and upper-class families have greater access to important social networks, in schools or the workplace, that give their children advantages. For example, the current (2011) deputy prime minister, Nick Clegg, gained work with the European Commission because his father 'had a conversation with his neighbour', who just happened to be a former foreign secretary. This social network is not available to very many people.

In this respect, Cohen and Prusak (2001) argue that high levels of social capital involve 'the trust, mutual understanding, shared values and behaviours' that bind wealthy families into social networks that are reinforced by mutual self-interest and cooperation.

**Symbolic capital** relates to upper-class children in particular developing attributes like self-confidence and a strong sense of entitlement and self-worth. This manifests itself in **personal qualities** such as an authoritative manner (directing the efforts of others in the expectation of being obeyed) and personal charisma (used to manipulate others' behaviour).

### Criticisms

➤ **Dark side**: Conflict is overstated and consensus underplayed. While the family clearly has a 'dark side', this involves a minority of men (and women). Most family relationships are neither violent nor abusive.

➤ **Over-determining**: Marxists over-determine the relationship between capitalism, social class and female oppression within the family. Some radical feminists (see below), for example, argue that patriarchy (male domination of women) predates capitalism, having been a feature of all human societies: the 'problem', therefore, is not so much capitalism as men.

➤ **Choice**: Marxism underplays the idea that many women choose to play family roles, such as provider of childcare, because they find them personally fulfilling.

➤ **Sexism**: The emphasis on class relationships ignores (or reduces the significance of) other forms of oppression, such as sexism and racism. For Marxists, capitalism is the root cause of oppression and exploitation within both society and the family — abolish capitalism and you end the exploitation of women. If, as radical feminists argue, men are the problem, then abolishing capitalism can't abolish sexism.

---

**Exam-style questions**

**1** Outline and evaluate functionalist views of the role of the family in society. (33 marks)

**2** Outline and evaluate Marxist views of the role of the family in society. (33 marks)

---

# Family diversity

'The family', according to De Vault (1991), is a 'falsely monolithic' concept. Rather than seeing it as a simple, homogeneous ('all the same') social group, we need to understand family diversity — from **organisational diversity**, based around family structures, to the concept of **life course**, focused around changing family roles and relationships.

## Organisational diversity

Although we've previously outlined a range of well-established family structures, we can further illustrate organisational diversity by outlining three examples of family structures that have seen rapid development over the past 30 years: lone-parent, reconstituted and beanpole structures.

### Lone-parent family structures

Lone-parent structures result from two main causes:

➤ **choice**, involving divorce, adoption, surrogate motherhood or a desire to raise a child independently of its biological father

➤ **unforeseeable circumstances** such as death of a partner, child abuse, abandonment by a biological parent or accidental pregnancy followed by the breakdown of a cohabiting partnership

These reasons for lone-parent family formation can be understood in the context of **social changes**:

➤ In the mid-twentieth century, most lone-parent families resulted from the **death** of a partner.

➤ During the last 30 years, **divorce** became the single most important factor.

➤ Changing social attitudes, such as a decline in the stigma attached to lone parenthood, have also led to an increasingly common form, headed by the **never-married single parent** (usually the mother).

This is not the complete picture, however; lone parenthood is not necessarily a *fixed* family structure. Many lone parents form new long-term relationships as reconstituted families. Bedell (2002), for example, reports: 'The lone-parent stage in a family's life cycle lasts on average 5 years.' Lone parenthood, therefore, is often a **transitional phase** in family development — a prelude to entering further (married or cohabiting) relationships, or the basis for different, more flexible, **alternative** family relationships (such as co-parenting or 'living apart together').

Furthermore, it should not be assumed that lone parents are always socially isolated and in need of state support. While New Right perspectives argue that single parenthood in particular is not as stable or permanent as marriage, a counter-argument is that we are seeing changes to the way some people form family relationships. A proportion of 'lone parents', for example, are actually living in a family arrangement, such as cohabitation, that is not statistically recognised; while an unmarried woman may be classed as heading a 'single-parent family', she may actually be part of a long-term family relationship with a man (or indeed a woman).

To understand the significance of lone-parent families, therefore, we have to move beyond the simple idea that all lone-parent families are exactly the same; as with nuclear families, the reality is that of a complex, ever-changing, highly differentiated group. The children of a divorced couple, for example, are not simply, immediately and automatically cut off from the range of relationships, family and otherwise, formed by their (ex-) parents. Their family situation is very different from that of a young, never-married, teenage girl abandoned by her partner.

## Reconstituted family structures

Reconstituted family structures are formed, according to Hughes and Church (2010), 'when an adult with a child (or children) lives in a partnership with someone who is not the parent of their child (or children)'. For most of the twentieth century the most common reason for family reconstitution was the death of a partner. Over the past 50 or so years, however, divorce has been the main reason for reconstituted families.

We can note the following figures:

➤ 86% of stepfamilies involve a natural mother and a stepfather — a situation that has remained largely unchanged over the past 20 years.
➤ 10% of stepfamilies involve a natural father and stepmother.
➤ 4% are formed by two adults each bringing one or more children to the new relationship.

Reconstituted families, therefore, potentially contain a wide range of relationships, involving:

➤ parents and biological or non-biological children
➤ biological siblings
➤ step-parents
➤ step-siblings
➤ half-siblings

As Juby et al. (2001) note, a significant feature of reconstituted families is their **internal diversity**. We can identify three basic types:

➤ **Step**: This involves a parent and their biological child plus a childless partner.
➤ **Blended**: Both partners bring children into the new family, which creates two subtypes:
  ➤ the union of two lone-parent families
  ➤ biological children from either partner plus children from the new union
➤ **Co-parenting**: This is a situation, as Smart and Wade (2000) note, where children are 'shared' between two (ex-) partners and their new families.

> **?** Give examples of two different reconstituted family structures.

### Advantages

➤ **Continuity** of parenting: children are raised by at least one biological parent. In the case of co-parenting, both natural parents play a part.
➤ **Ties** to family: This type of family produces 'instant siblings' and a large extended family network (since it potentially combines relatives from three or more related families).
➤ **Stability**: Children are raised in a two-parent family which may mean both continuity of parenting and less financial hardship.

### Disadvantages

➢ **Adjustment**: It may be difficult for children to relate to their new step-parent and siblings.
➢ **Financial**: While a reconstituted family may reduce the financial pressures of lone parenthood, a larger family, plus any payments that have to be made to former partners, can place huge financial pressures on the new family.
➢ **Tension**: The mix of new siblings can create petty jealousies within the family group.

## Beanpole families

➢ Traditional representations of the family in our society tend to portray it as a pyramid — much thinner at the top (the elderly generation) and much thicker at the base (the younger generations). However, two observations we've previously outlined question this view:
➢ There is **greater life expectancy**: people are living for much longer into old age.
➢ **Lower and later fertility** have meant a decline in both the number of children being born and average family size.

This '**ageing population**' trend has led Brannen (2003) to argue that the shape of families is also changing in response to demographic changes. Carvel (2003), for example, argues: 'Fewer brothers and sisters in one generation leads to fewer aunts and uncles in the next...instead of a "bushy" family tree with lots of lateral branches, there are longer, thinner patterns of family relationships.'

Brannen studied four-generation families (great-grandparents, grandparents, parents and children) that 'constitute a significant proportion of the population' and found a trend towards a beanpole family — a longer, taller, thinner structure with fewer children and more generations of the elderly. The consequences of this change are felt in terms of both intergenerational and intragenerational contacts.

**Intergenerational contacts** (contacts between generations, or 'up and down' the family tree) are reinforced because:
➢ Grandparents live longer and enjoy greater physical fitness that allows active participation in family life.
➢ Parents and grandchildren offer greater levels of support to their elderly relatives, while grandparents become increasingly involved in the care of grandchildren.

Brannen argues that increasing intergenerational ties provide a range of benefits for family members:
➢ transmission of material assets and values
➢ childcare and elder care
➢ sociability
➢ emotional support

**Intragenerational contacts** (contacts within generations, or 'across' the family tree) are weakened, for two reasons:

> Where relationships are disrupted by divorce, separation and cohabitation breakdown, family members lose contact with each other.
> Families having fewer children has meant a decline in intragenerational numbers — fewer aunts and uncles, for example.

Although this suggests the development of a new and different family structure in our society, Brannen notes an additional dimension of diversity in that **intergenerational** contacts between family members can differ markedly *between* beanpole families. Two factors here are the following:

> **Occupational status**: Families differ in their resources (such as levels of income) and this affects 'the capacity of different generations to provide support, especially material support'. Working-class families are less likely to offer financial support to their children. Changes in occupational status between generations (e.g. grandparents who were low-skill manual workers and grandchildren who've experienced upward social mobility and occupy higher-ranking professional positions) can result in families becoming estranged from one another (e.g. changes in values and lifestyles may mean they have little or nothing in common outside their family connection).
> **Geographical proximity/mobility**: The flexibility of beanpole families means the connections between different generations can be more easily 'lost' when, for example, grandparents retire to another part of the country or parents relocate for work reasons. Although these connections can be virtually maintained (through phone calls, email and the like), the practical help family members can offer each other is limited by geographical mobility.

The structure of beanpole families also creates the idea of a **pivot generation** — sometimes called a 'sandwich generation' or, in Westland's (2008) evocative phrase, 'both-end carers'. In four-generation families, women (mainly) in the 50–70 age group ('the grandmother generation') often take on a pivotal role in the provision of informal family services, looking *upwards* to the care of the elderly and *downwards* to the childcare of grown-up children.

### Evaluation

Grundy and Henretta (2006) argue that a 'sandwich generation' — 'those mid-life adults who simultaneously raise dependent children and care for frail elderly parents' — is very unusual. While a pivot generation exists, its role is not clear-cut: in some instances 'the demands from adult children and from elderly parents compete, with the result that those who provide help to one are less likely to provide help to the other'. Lundholm and Malmberg (2009) also suggest that the role of a pivot generation has been overstated, mainly because 'By the time the parents and parents-in-law of the middle-aged are old and fragile and in need of care, their children have already left the parental home'.

While it's important not to underestimate the significance of beanpole family structures, it's equally important not to overestimate their importance. Although four-generation families have increased over the past 30 years, around 60% of those over 80 are part of three-generation families. In addition, increased childlessness also means we may be talking about very different types of family structure over the next 30 to 50 years.

**?** Briefly define the idea of a 'pivot generation'.

## Household diversity

Under organisational diversity we can also discuss household diversity.

### Single-person households

Single-person households involve an adult living alone. Historically, death of a partner and relationship breakdown (separation in the past and divorce more recently) have been the main reasons for this household structure. However, there's evidence that some in our society are *choosing* to live this way.

Hughes and Church (2010) suggest that 'the increase in the proportion of people living alone…is one of the most noticeable changes in household composition over the past few decades', with numbers increasing as follows:

- ➤ 1961: around 1.7 million
- ➤ 1971: around 3 million
- ➤ 2009: more than 7 million

They also note three points concerning this type of household:

- ➤ **Region**: Single-person households are more likely to be found in urban areas, especially large cities. For example, Eversley and Bonnerjea (1982) note the **'geriatric wards'** located in coastal towns such as Eastbourne which attract large numbers of the retired elderly, living far away from relatives. They also note that **inner-city areas** in London, Manchester and Birmingham attract large numbers of single people (living in cheap private accommodation) likely to be living apart from wider kin (sometimes temporarily in the case of students).
- ➤ **Age**: Of single-person households, 50% involve an adult receiving a state pension. The number of 'single pensioner households' has doubled over the past 50 years (from 7% of all households in 1961 to 14% in 2009) but has stayed roughly the same for the past 30 years. Single households containing people under pensionable age have almost doubled as a proportion of all households over the past 30 years (from 8% in 1981 to 14% in 2009). Since 1961 their proportion has trebled.
- ➤ **Proportion**: One-person households now comprise 30% of all households — double the percentage in 1961 (14%). Over the past 50 years the trend has been upward. Over the last 30 years the rate of increase has slowed (from 22% of all households in 1981), and over the last 20 years growth has all but flattened.

**?** What has been one trend in single-person households over the past 50 years?

### Couple households

Couple households involve two adults living without children. They account for 29% of all households (Hughes and Church, 2010).

In terms of diversity, both single and couple households involve differences in:

➢ **income** — between the employed and unemployed, for example, and between dual- and single-income couples

➢ **age and lifestyle** — with young singles or couples having different lifestyles from older singles or couples

### Shared households

Shared households involve unrelated people living together. Hughes and Church (2010) also note that around 1.5 million people live in a range of 'communal establishments', such as prisons, hospitals, care homes and hotels (live-in staff).

# Other forms of diversity

While organisational diversity is important, there are other significant forms of family diversity. In the following sections we will look at class, cultural and sexual diversity.

## Class diversity

We can look at class differences in family life using a simple distinction between manual (working class) and non-manual (middle class). This rough-and-ready classification has limitations (some skilled manual occupations, for example, have higher income and status than routine non-manual work), but it does let us examine some broad class-based behavioural differences in family life (in addition to those we've noted in earlier sections). Class diversity, in this respect, is manifested in several areas, discussed below.

### Family structures

Single (never-married) parents are, according to O'Neill (2002), more likely to be originally drawn from the working class and to have far lower average incomes than their middle-class peers. They are also more likely to live in poverty than two-parent families of the same class.

Beanpole family structures are less common and long-lived in middle-class than in working-class families (where the age of mothers at first birth is much lower, which means four- or sometimes five-generation families are more likely to develop).

### Adult relationships

**Patriarchal families** are male-dominated and likely to be oppressive and exploitative of women; these relationships are still more common in working-class families where family roles may be **segregated**, with the female partner focused on home and children, the male on paid work. Family roles and relationships are unequal, with the male being the head of the household.

Middle-class families are more likely to be **symmetrical**; symmetrical family relationships, according to Willmott and Young (1973), are characterised by **joint**

**conjugal roles** that demonstrate greater levels of gender equality in terms of both paid and unpaid (domestic) work. Although they suggest that this is an increasingly common family arrangement in contemporary Britain, it is still arguably more characteristic of middle-class families.

### Adult-child relationships

Historically middle-class families have been more **child-centred** (family resources, attention and effort are invested in a child's physical and social development). The decline in average family size across all classes (and within the working class in particular) suggests that working-class families are just as interested in investing in their child's development, but lack the resources (economic and cultural) of their middle-class peers. In terms of **cultural capital**, upper- and middle-class families are better positioned to provide the knowledge, skills and personal motivations to see their children through higher education.

Lareau (2003) also points to differences in the way parents interact with their children:

- **Concerted cultivation** is a style characteristic of middle-class parents who 'actively foster their children's talents, opinions, and skills...The focus is on children's individual development'. This results, she argues, in middle-class children gaining 'an emerging sense of entitlement' they take into their adult life.
- **Natural growth** is an approach to parenting more characteristic of working-class parents: 'Parents care for their children, love them, and set limits for them, but within these boundaries, they allow the children to grow spontaneously...children generally negotiate institutional life, including their day-to-day school experiences, on their own.'

While neither type is 'superior', Lareau argues that middle-class children enter adulthood better equipped to meet the demands of higher education and the workplace — a *cultural* advantage that translates into *economic* advantage.

### Social capital

Kinship networks are important in terms of the help (financial, practical, academic and so on) family members can provide. Working-class families are generally better positioned to offer *practical* forms of help (exchanging services between family members, for example) whereas middle-class families are better positioned to offer both *financial* and *networking* help to their children.

**?** Give examples of two class differences in parent–child relationships.

## Cultural diversity

This is expressed across a range of categories. We will look at attitudes and lifestyles, age, gender and ethnicity.

### Attitudes and lifestyles

Cultural changes here contribute to family and household diversity in terms of **religion**. The decline in organised religion (**secularisation**) among *some* ethnic groups partly accounts for:

➤ increases in cohabitation
➤ a decline in the significance of marriage
➤ increases in divorce
➤ the availability of remarriage after divorce

For other ethnic groups the reverse may be true — their religion puts great emphasis on marriage and disallows divorce.

### Age

Age diversity involves different stages of both individual and family life spans; the family experiences of different **generations** may, for example, be different:

➤ Family members raised during the 1940s had the experience of war, rationing and the like; those raised during the 1990s developed very different attitudes and lifestyles forged through a period of economic expansion.
➤ The family experience of a young couple with infant children is different from that of an elderly couple without children.
➤ Children experience family life differently from adults.

Hughes and Church (2010) note that there are around 13 million dependent children in the UK:

➤ 76% (around 10 million) live in a dual-parent nuclear family (down from 88% in the 1980s).
➤ 22% live with a lone parent (up from 7% in the 1970s). 20% currently live with a lone mother, 2% with a lone father.

### Gender

Gender diversity occurs with regard to paid employment, roles and status.

#### Paid employment

Johnson and Zaidi (2004) note that men are now working fewer, and women more, years than in the past, and that these changes impact on family life and relationships in several ways:

➤ Marriage occurs at a later stage in the life cycle than 30 years ago. Many women delay marriage until they have established a career.
➤ Male and female roles have changed. The family group is less patriarchal and the division of domestic labour is 'less unequal' now — though by no means equal (women still do the majority of domestic work).
➤ Women are less likely to leave paid employment, never to return, once they marry or start a family. In addition retirement — something historically associated with men — is now increasingly associated with women.

### Roles

Matheson and Summerfield (2001) note a significant move away from a 'traditional division of family labour' as more women enter paid work. They also note that 'the proportion of couples with dependent children where only the man is working has decreased'.

The Labour Force Survey (2005) indicates that women with dependent children are less likely to be in paid employment than those without dependent children. In addition, mothers with children under 5 years old are less likely than those with older children to combine childcare with paid work.

### Status

A variety of status differences exist within and between families, focused, for example, around distinctions between:

➤ family types (such as single- and dual-parent types)
➤ individuals (single, married, divorced or cohabiting, for example)
➤ roles (paid employment, domestic employment and combinations of both)

### Ethnicity

Mann (2009) notes that Britain's Asian and black Caribbean populations make up around 70% of the minority ethnic population. Berthoud (2004) has identified some key differences within and between these groups.

**Black Caribbean** families have the following characteristics:

➤ Low marriage rates: Mann (2009) noted that black Caribbean (along with white) families with dependent children 'had the largest proportion of cohabiting couples', while Modood et al. (1997) noted that around 40% of black Caribbean adults under 60 were in formal marriages (compared with 60% of whites).
➤ Division of labour: Dale et al. (2004) found black women more likely to 'remain in full-time employment throughout family formation' than their white or Asian peers.
➤ High rates of separation and divorce.
➤ High rates of single parenthood: Mann (2009) noted that 45% of black Caribbean families were headed by a lone parent, compared with 25% of white families. Hughes (2009) reported around 56% of dependent children living with a lone parent.
➤ Smaller family size (an average of 2.3 people).
➤ Absent fathers (not living within the family home but maintaining family contacts).

**South Asian** (Indian, Pakistani and Bangladeshi) families have the following characteristics:

➤ High marriage rates, with a greater likelihood (especially among Muslims and Sikhs) of arranged marriage. Berthoud (2005) noted that around 75% of Pakistani and 65% of Indian women were in marital relationships by their mid-twenties. Cohabitation, according to Mann (2009), 'is less usual amongst Asian and Chinese populations'.

➢ Low rates of divorce and single parenthood. Self and Zealey (2007) noted that around 10% of Pakistani/Bangladeshi and 5% of Indian families were headed by a lone parent. Hughes (2009) notes that around 15% of all dependent children live with lone parents, the lowest for all ethnic groups.

➢ Larger family size: 'Bangladeshi and Pakistani families tend to be larger than families of any other ethnic group' (Mann 2009).

➢ Power and authority within the family are more likely to reside with men (patriarchy), and are reflected in 'traditional' family roles. A majority of Pakistani and Bangladeshi women, for example, look after home and family full-time. Dale et al. (2004) suggested that Indian women generally opted for part-time paid employment once they had a partner, while both Pakistani and Bangladeshi women were more likely to end paid work once married and producing children.

We can also look at **extended networks** in relation to ethnicity. A number of studies of **white working-class** family life all point to 'the significance of extended kinship networks in the daily life of families' (Mann 2009):

➢ Anderson's (1995) study of Preston in the nineteenth century
➢ Willmott and Young (1957) in East London
➢ Rosser and Harris's (1965) study in Swansea

Two restudies — Dench et al. (2006) in East London and Harris et al. (2008) in Swansea — found that the formerly white areas now included a substantial black minority population for whom extended family networks remained important. The effects of both class and poverty explain why some minority ethnic groups (and sections of the white majority) form extended family networks.

Chahal (2000) argues that minority groups are subject to varying levels of **racist victimisation**, and that extended family networks with traditional family structures and lifestyles can give a sense of group protection in the face of outside aggression.

**Custom and tradition** are further factors influencing family diversity. Chahal (2000) notes that among Pakistani and Bangladeshi ethnicities, older (but not necessarily younger) family members supported cultural traditions involving:

➢ multi-generational households
➢ traditional divisions of labour
➢ arranged marriages

Chahal notes that African-Caribbeans, on the other hand, 'were likely to emphasise individualism, independence and physical and emotional space'.

Two further explanations for cultural diversity — 'individualisation' and 'negotiation' — are explored when we examine postmodern approaches to family diversity.

**?** Suggest two types of family cultural diversity.

## Sexual diversity

While overt stigmatisation may have declined to the point where gay and lesbian families are generally socially accepted, they are still comparatively rare. They do, however, have a part to play in family diversity.

### Family structures

Gay and lesbian families and households include:

➢ singletons
➢ lone parents
➢ cohabiting couples
➢ civil partners
➢ those 'living apart together'

Gay and lesbian families are a small, but important, feature of family diversity

Although some past gay and lesbian relationships have involved children (from a partner coming from a heterosexual relationship), Ryan and Berkowitz (2009) suggest that gay and lesbian couples now have a range of choices about how to have and raise children:

➢ **Surrogacy**: This involves paying someone to carry a baby to term using sperm donated by one of the male partners. A major attraction of this route is that it establishes, as Bergman (2010) argues, a clear biological link between father and child (and some couples take it in turns to father children in this way). A cheaper alternative option is a co-parenting arrangement with either single women or lesbian couples.
➢ **Adoption**: While not always as easy a route as for heterosexual couples, this is increasingly a possibility for those who reject other options. It became illegal for adoption agencies to discriminate against gay and lesbian couples in 2007.
➢ **Instant families**: One or both partners bring children into the (reconstituted) family from previous heterosexual relationships.
➢ **Sperm donation**: Short et al. (2007) argue that a 'lesbian baby boom' (or 'gayby boom') has occurred over the past 30 years. They also note the practice of 'each member of the couple giving birth to one or more children' (similar to the practice of gay men taking it in turns to father children).

### Heteronormativity

Heteronormativity refers to the idea that partners in sexual relationships fall into two distinct and complementary categories; in heterosexual relationships these categories are male and female and are associated with different gender roles and responsibilities.

Homosexual couples, of course, are the same sex so we might expect family roles and relationships to be different.

However, Dalton and Bielby (2000) found that lesbian couples tended to follow conventional notions of motherhood and 'gendered expectations of what it means to be a mother'. Rabun and Oswald (2009) also found many gay families adopting a version of heteronormativity as part of their 'parenting script'; however, a substantial minority did not, and actively questioned the idea that 'good parenting' required one partner to play a 'father' role and the other a 'mother' role.

A further aspect of heteronormativity illustrated by the gay men in Rabun and Oswald's study is that they generally tried to live as a nuclear family, rather than develop a radical alternative. Seidman (2005) argues that this is understandable as a means of both 'gaining cultural acceptance' for gay families and experiencing 'a symbolic feeling of doing family "correctly"'.

> **?** What options are available for gay and lesbian couples to start families?

# Contemporary views of family diversity

Neale (2000) asks the question 'How are we to view the diversity and fluidity of contemporary patterns of partnering, parenting and kinship?' and offers two general options for the answer: 'Should we view these transformations with optimism…or concern?' In this section we can examine each of these options in turn.

## Postmodernism: an optimistic approach to diversity

For postmodernists 'a family' is whatever people want it to be. They reject the idea that we can talk about '*the* family'; rather, what we have is people living out their lives in ways they believe are acceptable and appropriate. Postmodern approaches, therefore, view family groups as **arenas** in which individuals play out their personal narratives, involving two basic forms of individualistic experience:

➤ **Choice**: People are increasingly able to make behavioural decisions that suit their particular needs, desires and circumstances — regardless of what others may think.
➤ **Pluralism**: This is seen as the defining feature of postmodern societies. Societies are now characterised by a plurality of family forms and groups, and each family unit is **exclusive** — every family involves people working out their personal choices and lifestyles in the best ways they can. As Stacey (2002) puts it when discussing same-sex relationships, 'Every family is an alternative family.'

In this respect Elkind (1992) suggests that postmodern society has produced the **permeable family** that 'encompasses many different family forms: traditional or nuclear, two-parent working, single-parent, blended, adopted child, test-tube, surrogate mother, and co-parent families. Each of these is valuable and potentially successful.' Elkind argues that:

> The **modern** family spoke to our need to *belong* at the expense, particularly for women, of the need to *become*.
> The **postmodern** (permeable) family celebrates the need to *become* at the expense of the need to *belong*.

The general argument, therefore, is:
> There is no single, inviolate way to 'be a family' (a position, as we will see, hotly disputed by the New Right).
> If families are simply 'individual organisations', tailored to people's specific needs and desires, it makes no sense to talk about their 'functions' (as in functionalism) or their 'oppressive and exploitative structures' (as in Marxism and feminism).

The 'celebration of difference' is a key attribute of postmodern approaches; diversity should be embraced, either because it points the way towards an optimistic realignment of family roles and relationships or because we are powerless to prevent it. Societies are increasingly global sites of conflict, subject to a range of economic, political and cultural pressures and processes that create ideas (choice, uniqueness, pluralism) that impact forcefully on individual family roles and relationships.

As Zeitlin et al. (1998) argue, postmodern society frees people from the restraints of the past and offers them new ways of thinking, acting and being. There are 'multiple realities, and an exhilarating profusion of world views' that characterise a type of society 'that has lost its faith in absolute truth' so that 'people have to choose what to believe'. A range of ideas about family diversity follow from this characterisation, as discussed below.

**Economic changes** on a global scale, Zeitlin et al. argue, are leading to a breakdown of 'social conformity'. In the past, for example, women generally needed to marry because they were barred from the workplace or consigned to low-paid work which made their survival difficult without male support. Inheritance laws also meant children needed to be produced within marriage. With increasing economic independence and gradual changes in inheritance laws, marriage is no longer an economic necessity for women; they have greater freedom of choice in their relationships. Where choice leads, diversity follows: both **structural diversity** (different family types) and **relational diversity** (marriage, cohabitation, living-apart-together, heterosexual, homosexual). These changes are, postmodernists argue, inevitable and irreversible.

In addition, **exposure to new ideas** (through cultural agencies like the media — television, film, the internet and so on) makes people question traditional ways of thinking and behaving; 'the way things have always been done' no longer holds people in its grip as people start to exercise their increased choices in personal relationships and lifestyles. Diversity follows from different people making different choices, as choices that were once denied (from divorce to homosexuality) become available. Traditional types of family relationship (such as marriage and children) sit alongside newer forms (such as childlessness or living apart while maintaining family relationships).

This leads to **cultural changes**. As exposure to different cultural ideas increases, what was once new and exotic behaviour simply becomes *routine*; people gradually become more accepting of 'single-parents, surrogate-mothers and gay and lesbian families'. In this globalised context, Jagger and Wright (1999) argue that attempts to 'turn back the tide of family diversity' and 'recapture an idealised "nuclear" version of family life where time stands still and traditional values are re-vitalised' is no longer an option.

Neale (2000) summarises the general postmodern position in terms of a '**relational approach**' to understanding diversity that involves:

➤ **Commitment**: Family (and other personal) relationships are increasingly played out in micro-networks; people negotiate their relationships in ways that take greater account of their own personal needs and responsibilities, rather than worrying about what others in the community might think.

➤ **Morality**: In situations where a diversity of family roles, relationships and structures exist, morality-based judgements (that one way of living is better than any other) become weaker and harder to justify. Society in general becomes less judgemental about how others choose to form family relationships.

> **?** Suggest an example to illustrate the idea that 'society is less judgemental about how people choose to form family relationships'.

Picking up on the ideas we noted in relation to ethnic diversity, postmodernists argue that we need to think about family diversity in the context of two processes: individualisation and negotiation.

### Individualisation

Over the past 30 or so years we've become increasingly liberated from the constraints of traditional norms and values, and people have greater levels of choice and control over their personal relationships and sense of self (there are more ways to 'be male or female', 'be a good partner' and so forth than at any time in the past).

Individualisation ('what's right for me') means social norms surrounding marriage, divorce, sexual freedom and the like have changed. This, as Mann (2009) suggests, gives people greater freedom and flexibility in their relationship choices: 'People are far more able to choose the intimate relationships that are important to them, and are more likely to end them if they no longer accord with their personal preferences and objectives.'

To understand ethnic diversity, for example, Berthoud (2005) suggests a scale with two extremes:

➤ 'Old-fashioned values', such as marriage, sexual fidelity and so forth. Pakistani and Bangladeshi ethnicities are closest to this point.

➤ 'Modern individualism', where single parenthood, divorce and the like are openly embraced. Black Caribbean ethnicities are closest to this point (with whites being closer to this point than to 'old-fashioned values').

Differences concerning individualisation, Berthoud suggests, explain why some ethnicities experience higher levels of family breakdown than others.

### Negotiation

Individualisation, Mann (2009) argues, means all types of relationship are open to negotiation. Just as we no longer unquestioningly accept traditional ideas about masculinity and femininity, the same is true of families. We 'need to work at' ideas about who is and who is not 'family', and ideas about relationships between parents and children.

In other words, family relationships are increasingly open to negotiation because there is no longer a 'right' and a 'wrong' way to conduct them. Negotiation, by its very nature, produces change. An example is the role of grandparents, who were once more likely to be seen as a 'burden' on the family, but are now just as likely to be seen as a family resource. Mann, however, notes that negotiation is a two-way process: 'Most grandparents want to help out, but they do not necessarily want to provide child care on a full time basis...Grandparents can no longer be taken as "door mats".'

### Evaluation

#### Individualisation

Postmodernists overstate the extent to which people are disconnected from family and social networks. Although there is greater freedom of choice in contemporary societies, people don't simply exercise those choices in isolation (what's best for me and my immediate social group?). The vast majority live and behave in broadly conventional ways while recognising and tolerating 'unconventional' behaviours. Postmodernists confuse this toleration of 'life at the margins' with the idea that everyone embraces it unquestioningly.

#### Choice

Choice is not unlimited, nor unconnected from wider social processes. People of different classes, genders, ethnicities and age groups, for example, only have the same choices in the sense that such choices exist and can be made; the consequences of making them may have significant, if not dangerous, consequences (which means they may never be made). For example, while the decision to end a marriage may be relatively straightforward and painless for some, Banaz Mahmod was murdered in 2006 by her father and uncle after she left her unhappy arranged marriage and began another relationship.

#### Change

Global economic, political and cultural changes are presented as 'inevitable' and 'beyond our ability to control' — something that seems to actually remove our ability to make choices.

**?** How are postmodern families 'open to negotiation'?

## The New Right: diversity as a cause for concern?

A different take on family diversity comes from a perspective that, while drawing on traditional functionalist approaches, involves more directly political ideas about the significance of families for both the individual and society. In this respect New Right approaches can be characterised in terms of the following distinctive elements:

➤ personalities (politicians such as Thatcher and, arguably, Blair in the UK; Reagan, Bush and the contemporary 'Tea Party' movement in the USA)

➤ theorists (such as Murray, Phillips and Morgan)

➤ practices (issues such as anti-abortion, anti-immigration, anti-Europe and pro-liberal economic policies)

The family here is seen as the cornerstone of any society and the New Right promotes values relating to ideas about 'traditional family relationships'; families should consist of two heterosexual adults, preferably married (to each other) and with clearly defined gender roles and relationships — which normally involve men as 'providers' and women as 'carers' or domestic workers. Neale (2000) characterises this approach in terms of community, commitment and morality:

➤ **Community**: Stable family relationships, created within married, heterosexual, dual-parent nuclear families, provide emotional and psychological benefits to family members that override any possible dysfunctional aspects. Personal and social responsibilities are also created, which benefits society in general; children, for example, are given clear moral and behavioural guidance within traditional family structures — which makes them less likely to engage in deviant behaviour.

➤ **Commitment** to others is encouraged by the sense of moral duty created by stable family relationships. Within the traditional family each adult partner plays a role that involves both personal sacrifice and commitment to others.

➤ **Morality**: The idea that all types of family structure are equal ('moral relativism') is wrong because it challenges the idea of moral commitment to others that sits at the heart of social responsibility. The New Right endorses social policies that encourage 'beneficial' family structures and discourage forms, such as single parenthood, seen as damaging to both individuals and communities.

Single parenthood is seen as being sustained by governments and the welfare state. This encourages a **dependency culture**, both economic and moral: the former because without state support this type of 'family choice' could not exist and the latter because it depends on the moral tolerance of those who eventually pick up the bill for women 'exercising their choice' to have a child outside marriage. In this view, single parenthood is both immoral and unproductive — it produces poorly socialised, dysfunctional children who go on to live adult lives dependent on state benefits, crime or both.

Morgan's (2000) contention that marriage, rather than cohabitation, should be encouraged can be used to illustrate the idea that family diversity is a source of social problems. For Morgan, cohabitation is not just, to paraphrase Leach (1994), 'marriage without a piece of paper'. On the contrary, cohabiting relationships can be described as follows:

➤ **Lightweight**: They 'are always more likely to fracture than marriages entered into at the same time, regardless of age and income'. Cohabiting couples also tend to be more sexually promiscuous than married couples; as Leach puts it, 'Cohabitants behave more like single people than married people' — another reason for instability.

➤ **Fragmentary**: Those (with children) who subsequently marry are statistically more likely to divorce than couples who marry without cohabiting first. Of those who never marry, '50% of the women will be lone unmarried mothers by the time the child is ten'. One reason for this, Morgan argues, is that unlike marriage, cohabitation for women is 'not so much an ideal **lifestyle choice** as the best arrangement they can make at the time'.

➤ **Abusive**: Both women and children are at greater risk of physical and sexual abuse 'than they would be in married relationships'.

Overall, New Right approaches argue that family and relationship diversity is undesirable (and in a sense dysfunctional) because it is confusing to both individuals and society. In the case of individuals, their moral compass becomes disabled, until a situation of 'anything goes' becomes engrained in people's behaviour. In society, a kind of 'moral anarchy' reigns; if no behaviour is undesirable, as postmodernists argue, the New Right response is that some behaviours produce morally undesirable *results* — such as abortion practices that take no account of the 'rights of the unborn'.

In general, therefore, New Right approaches stress the idea of 'family uniformity' in terms of structures and relationships.

In terms of **structures**, the traditional (heterosexual) married nuclear family is seen as being more desirable than other family structures because it provides:

➤ social, economic and psychological stability
➤ family continuity
➤ successful primary socialisation

It is an arena where 'traditional family values' are emphasised and reinforced, thereby creating a sense of individual and social responsibility that forms a barrier against 'rampant, selfish individualism'. Within the traditional family, children and adults learn, as Horwitz (2005) argues, moral values reinforced through their relationship with family members.

**Family relationships** are viewed as a crucial source of both individual happiness and social stability because of a moral core that includes:

➤ caring for family members
➤ taking responsibility for the behaviour of children
➤ economic cooperation and provision
➤ developing successful interpersonal relationships

Traditional family structures, in this view, provide a much stronger moral foundation for the performance of these tasks.

Writers such as Murray and Phillips (2001) equate both structure and relationship diversity with **family breakdown**. This is seen as symptomatic of a social **underclass** characterised by an 'excessive individualism'; where family structures and relationships break down, the individual is forced back on their own resources for survival and, in consequence, develops a disregard for the needs and rights of others.

> **?** In what ways do 'stable family relationships' benefit society?

### Evaluation

The New Right approach is controversial and has attracted a range of criticisms:

➤ This approach is based on an **idealised** view of families and family relationships that takes white, middle-class families as the desirable norm, one to which everyone should aspire. It advocates a 'one size fits all' family in a society no longer characterised by moral and normative consensus and conformity.

➤ It ignores the **darker side** of traditional family life. Making divorce 'harder', for example, may well persuade some to try to make their marriage work — but it also traps others in a spiral of violence and abuse.

➤ This approach confuses rational analysis (what is supposedly best for individuals and society) with a conservative moral desirability; family diversity is seen as **undesirable** because it challenges this conservative worldview.

➤ While this general approach advocates freedom and choice, this doesn't extend to family life. If people 'don't live as they should' they have to be made to follow an approved set of choices. It presumes, according to Finch (2003), 'a standard model of family life' for which governments can legislate.

## Theories and social policies

Finch (2003) argues that family policies are created and enacted within the context of ideological beliefs about the family group, the relationships between its members and its general relationship to wider society. Over the past 30 years Conservative and Labour governments have defined and shaped 'family policies' in ways that attempt to manage behaviour by encouraging some forms and discouraging others; an example of this 'ideological dimension' to family policy was the Conservative government of John Major (1990–97), where a recurring theme was 'traditional family values'.

Barlow and Duncan (2000) argue that for subsequent New Labour governments, family policy was initially underpinned by the desire 'to encourage what are seen as desirable family practices, and to discourage other, less favoured, forms'. This desire was, in turn, based around a combination of two intellectual frameworks (**libertarian** and **communitarian**), the basic beliefs of which have shaped family policy over the past 15 years (Table 8.8).

Table 8.8   Basic libertarian and communitarian beliefs

| | Libertarian | Communitarian |
|---|---|---|
| **Focus** | National: the relationship between the individual and the state. | Local: the relationship between the individual and their community. |
| **Individuals** | Individual: People behave rationally and are driven by self-interest (for both themselves and their families). | Community: People are driven by moral consensus, shared values and a sense of belonging to a wider community. |
| **Politics** | Individual choice, independence from 'state interference', self-reliance and provision for self. | Commitment to welfare of others (not just immediate family) and duty (individuals benefit from community involvement). |
| **Diversity** | Encouraged: People develop family forms and relationships that are 'right for them'. A non-judgemental approach (no type of family is inherently better than any other). | Discouraged: Some types of family are dysfunctional and damaging. A judgemental approach (some forms of family encouraged, others discouraged). |
| **Control** | Family relationships and structures controlled by legal contracts (such as marriage), rights, incentives, sanctions. | Family relationships and structures shaped by 'collective moral prescriptions' (ideas about how people should behave) originating with government. |
| **Welfare** | Restricted to enforcing legal or social obligations (using the law to ensure maintenance payments by an absent parent). Families encouraged to 'provide for themselves' through insurance. | A tool through which social changes can be effected. Welfare systems have a practical dimension (providing help and support for families) and a moral dimension (channelling most support to 'desirable' family types). |

*Source: adapted from Neale (2000)*

Neale (2000) argues that New Labour family policies were confused by combining the most negative aspects of these two frameworks:

➤ **libertarian** assumptions that people are inherently individualist
➤ **communitarian** requirements that they behave in uniform fashion

Family policies over the New Labour period combined, therefore, 'carrot and stick' forms of persuasion with moral prescriptions on how to live the 'good' life.

**Libertarian policies** included the following:

➤ Adoption and Children Act (2002): Unmarried couples were allowed to apply to adopt a child jointly. Single people could also apply for adoption.
➤ Civil partnerships (2005): These gave homosexual couples the same legal rights as heterosexual couples.
➤ Educational Maintenance Allowances (EMAs; 2004): These were weekly payments to encourage students from low-income families to stay in education after reaching 16 years of age (subsequently abolished by the coalition government in 2010).

Family policies
**L** ibertarian
**A** doption
**C** ivil partnerships
**E** MA

**Communitarian policies** included the following:

➤ Children's Act (1999): Finch (2003) notes that this 'redefined parental responsibility to include responsibility towards the child'.

➤ Child Support Agency: This continued the Conservative policy of legally pursuing 'absent fathers' for the maintenance of their children.

➤ Child poverty: New Labour committed itself to introducing a range of financial policies designed to 'end child poverty within twenty years'.

➤ Minister of State for Children (2003): This post was created to 'provide integrated leadership and responsibility for children's services and family'. This led to programmes such as Sure Start, designed to combat early-years disadvantages experienced by the children of low-income families.

➤ Child Trust Fund (2005): Every new child was given between £250 and £500, depending on family income, in an account they could access at 18 years of age. This could be added to (by families) and would be topped up by governments (but was abolished by the coalition government in 2010).

> **?** What differences are there between libertarian and communitarian social policies?

---

**Exam-style questions**

1 Identify and explain two types of family diversity. (17 marks)

2 Identify and explain two reasons for the growth in single-person households in the contemporary UK. (17 marks)

3 Outline and evaluate the view that the family is characterised by diversity in the contemporary UK. (33 marks)

4 Outline and evaluate postmodern views on the diversity of family life. (33 marks)

---

# Roles, responsibilities and relationships within the family

## Men and women

Rather than seeing gender roles one-dimensionally (as a set of things people must do when playing a particular role), an alternative is to see them in terms of **identities** (both social and personal). How individuals interpret and play the 'husband role' is conditioned by their perception of what this role means in general *social* terms (what husbands are expected to do) and in the more specific, *personal* context of the individual's family relationships. If we think about gender roles in this way, we can note two things:

➤ **Change**: In the past, **social identities** were dominant; they provided clear behavioural guidelines for family roles (the mother, for example, worked in the home, raising children). There were few opportunities to develop **personal identities** that differed from the social norm, and the penalties for trying were severe (in terms of male violence against women who tried to reject or renegotiate their role within the family).

➤ **Diversity**: Gender roles within contemporary families, although clearly having some consistency (the role of 'mother' is usually marked out differently from that of 'father'), are not as constrained as they were in even the recent past; people have more **personal freedom** to work out their own particular interpretations of gender roles and identities.

While gender roles and relationships have seen many recent changes, we can examine both continuities and changes in two areas: domestic labour and power relationships.

## Domestic labour

Domestic labour refers to the running of a home and family. It includes cooking, cleaning and shopping, household repairs and chores, as well as care of children, the sick and the elderly. We can note the following points concerning the division of domestic labour:

➤ **Gender beliefs**: Ramos (2003) found that women do more housework in families with 'traditional gender beliefs' than in families where beliefs reflect sexual equality. In households where partners hold conflicting beliefs, men do less domestic work.

Domestic labour

**G** ender beliefs
**R** elativity
**E** mployment
**A** ge
**T** ype

➤ **Relativity**: Gershuny et al. (2006) note that men do less domestic labour each day than women (100 versus 178 minutes), although the trend for both is less domestic labour. The Future Foundation (2001) estimates that:

   ➤ 60% of men do more housework than their father.
   ➤ 75% of women do less housework than their mother.

➤ **Employment status**: Kan (2001) found that, while levels of female housework were marginally reduced by paid employment, retirement or unemployment increased female housework and reduced that of her partner. Ramos (2003), however, noted that where the man is unemployed and his partner works full-time, domestic labour is more likely to be equally distributed.

➤ **Age**: Gershuny et al. (2006) note that female housework increases with age — younger women do less housework than older women.

➤ **Type**: Men and women perform different tasks for different lengths of time; women spend more time on routine domestic tasks, while men spend more time on tasks like repairs and gardening. Where there is no clear **gender association** with particular tasks (such as pet care), these tend to be performed equally.

Gershuny et al. (2006) summarise the general pattern of domestic labour in the contemporary UK as follows:

➢ Women of all ages, ethnicities and classes do more domestic labour than men.
➢ Men, on average, spend more time in the paid workforce than women.
➢ More domestic labour is carried out at weekends than during the week, reflecting the number of women now in paid employment.
➢ 90% of women do some housework each day (compared with 75% of men).
➢ Families with dependent children do more housework than those without (with the main burden of the extra work falling on women).

Trends in domestic labour show both **continuities** and **changes**. Women still do the majority of domestic labour in our society. However, Willmott (2000) argues that there is less reliance on 'traditional roles when dividing up tasks in the home'. Changing family (and wider social) relationships mean domestic labour is 'negotiated by every couple depending on their individual circumstances'. The significant factors in determining 'who does what' in the family are time and inclination, 'not whether they are a man or a woman'.

**?**  **Give some examples of recent trends in domestic labour.**

### Explanations

*Social identities*

Cultural beliefs about male and female abilities and roles are significant in explaining domestic labour differences, an idea initially tied up with notions of **patriarchy**. Gender roles can reflect patriarchal attitudes:

➢ Pleck (1985), for example, noted that the 'more traditional' the views held by couples about gender roles, the greater the level of domestic labour inequality.
➢ Pilcher (1998) found that older people, unlike their younger counterparts, didn't talk about 'equality' but thought instead in traditional ways about gender roles, responsibilities and relationships. This reflected their socialisation and life experiences, where 'Men undertook limited household work, married women had limited involvement in paid work and a marked gendered division of labour was the norm'.

Within this general patriarchal context there are distinct forms of social identity that exert powerful influences on perceptions of male and female identities:

➢ **Femininity**: Although gradually changing, notions of what it means to be a woman are still tied up with ideas about caring and nurture. To 'be a woman' means adopting a certain way of thinking (about the welfare of others) and behaving; as Gershuny et al. (2006) demonstrate, responsibility for childcare within the family still falls mainly on the female partner as an extension of feminine identity.

➤ **Masculinity**: McDowell (2001) noted the 'continued dominance of a "traditional" masculinity' in her study of young working-class men. Notions about how to 'be a man' were bound up in being able to look after the economic well-being of both partner and children.

### Personal identities

Gender roles are interpreted and negotiated according to specific family circumstances.

Callaghan (1998) highlights class, age and educational differences in the creation and performance of gender roles within the family (older working-class men, for example, are more likely to hold 'traditional views' on gender). Dench (1996) suggests that younger men believe 'couples should share or negotiate family roles' and resist conventional ideas that men should be the main breadwinners.

Speakman and Marchington (1999) are more sceptical about changing *attitudes* filtering down to changing *roles*. Some men, they noted, used **learned helplessness** when trying to avoid domestic tasks — their 'inability' to work domestic machinery served to throw domestic tasks back into the hands of their partners. Two further points we could note here involve data **reliability** and **validity**:

➤ **Over-estimations** of male domestic labour: These may occur when (male) subjects are required to self-assess the amount of housework they do.

➤ **Cherry-picking** domestic tasks: Most female domestic labour involves routine and mundane tasks required to keep the family functioning. Men are more likely to do domestic tasks they see as more interesting and personally rewarding; while women are more likely to be involved in washing and dressing their young children, men are more likely to count things like 'playing with their children' as part of their domestic labour.

Do men 'cherry pick' their domestic labour roles?

micromonkey/Fotolia

### Further points

Finally, we can note that the unequal distribution of domestic labour is related to the following:

➤ Social identities involving deep-seated cultural (patriarchal) beliefs about male and female 'natures' that exert a powerful pull, through the gender socialisation process, and lead to the reproduction of traditional gender relationships.

➤ Socio-personal identities involving the way *personal* identities are *pragmatically* ('reasonably') shaped by *social* identities. In a family, for example, where the man is the main income provider, decisions about who will give up work to care for children are pragmatically guided by the reality of differences in earning power.

➤ Personal identities involving specific relationships between family members which may be played out against a background of complex personal and cultural histories. For example, some men may be able to get away with doing little or nothing in terms of domestic labour, even where their partner works full-time; alternatively, a man's personal relationship with his partner may not allow him to shirk his share of family responsibilities.

> **?** **How is the domestic division of labour becoming more equal?**

## Power relationships

Like any social institution, families involve power struggles — relations of domination and subordination between family members. An example we have already discussed is patriarchy (male domination and female subordination). In this section we will look at two very different dimensions of power within the family: physical power (involving domestic violence) and psychological power (involving decision-making).

### Physical power: domestic violence

This covers a range of behaviours (physical and emotional), aimed at aggressively controlling the behaviour of another family member in ways that include:
➤ physical violence (assault)
➤ sexual violence (such as rape)
➤ economic sanctions (denying a family member something they need)

Domestic violence is an **under-reported** crime, which makes it difficult to **reliably** estimate its extent; victims may be reluctant to admit or acknowledge their victimisation to 'outsiders'. Kirkwood (1993) notes that reasons for this include:
➤ low self-esteem of the victim (a belief that they 'deserve it')
➤ dependence on the perpetrator
➤ fear of further consequences (repeat victimisation)

We can, however, identify some significant facts about domestic violence:
➤ 16% of all violent incidents involve domestic violence (Dodd et al. 2004).
➤ 77% of victims are female (Nicholas et al. 2007). This is the only category of violence for which the risks are higher for women than men.

Jansson (2007) notes:
➤ 3% of all women and 2% of all men in Britain had experienced either minor or severe violence at the hands of their partner.
➤ Incidents peaked in 1994 (1.2 million cases) and have slowly returned to 1981 levels (around 275,000 cases each year).
➤ Women are most likely to be sexually assaulted by men they know and 45% of reported rapes were carried out by a current partner.

Coleman et al. (2007) suggest that this is a crime highly prone to **repeat victimisation**:

➤ 40% of victims suffer further victimisation.

➤ 25% suffer prolonged victimisation (three or more attacks).

### Psychological power: decision-making

While we shouldn't downplay the extent of domestic violence, nor should we overplay it — the vast majority of families are not violent spaces. They are, however, places where 'everyday power struggles' are played out; these are non-violent and may involve one or more family members being unaware of their involvement in a power struggle. To understand this, we can outline three 'abilities' identified by Lukes (1990).

#### Ability to make decisions

Although women exercise power within families, it's mainly in areas where they traditionally have greater expertise (the daily management of family resources). Major decisions tend to be made by men, mainly because they control an important 'public domain resource' (family income) that, if removed, would cause acute problems for the remaining family members. Where both partners work, women have more control over decision making (although female power depends on factors like the status of female work, relative level of income, domestic responsibilities and so forth).

#### Ability to prevent others making decisions

This is the 'ability to manipulate any debate over decisions that actually reach the stage of being made'. In terms of gender roles, the personal identities of family members (how each partner sees their role within the family) are important. Gender socialisation is also significant since, if males and females have certain role expectations, the ability to make decisions affecting the family group takes on a 'natural' quality. It appears 'normal' for women to raise children and men to have paid employment, for example. While major decision making *seems* to be made 'with the support and agreement of others', it is men who generally make such decisions because the debate has been manipulated in their favour.

#### Ability to remove decision making from the agenda

This is probably the most powerful form of decision making because those subject to a decision have no idea they were involved in such a process. For example, decisions about who does paid employment, domestic labour and the like are 'removed from the decision-making agenda' (the respective partners don't actually have to make conscious decisions about them) for a variety of reasons: they may share the belief women are better at child-rearing than men. Alternatively, when one partner earns more than the other and has higher career expectations, this partner may remain in work while the other cares for the children.

**?** What does domestic violence tells us about the nature of family relationships?

# Children and parents

We've already noted some aspects of this relationship in areas like:

➤ primary socialisation
➤ grandparents as a childcare resource
➤ parasite kids
➤ boomerang kids

However, we can focus more specifically on the relationship by, initially, noting what Archard (2004) terms 'a dissimilarity in ideas about childhood between past and present'. How parents relate to children has changed, not just over the centuries but more recently too. How we view children determines how we treat them — whether we see them as 'little devils' in need of care and control at one extreme, or 'little angels' to be protected from adult influences at the other.

Fionda (2002) suggests that children in contemporary Britain are variously seen as:

➤ **Objects of concern** (New Labour, for example, focused the majority of its 'family policies' on the parent–child relationship). This mainly involves **protection**, for example from child abuse or from exposure to depictions of violence or sexuality.

➤ **Autonomous possessors of rights** — individuals who should enjoy similar levels of freedom to adults and who should not be denied the rights adults take for granted (such as protection from 'assault').

➤ **Lacking moral consciousness**: Children are exempt from some forms of responsibility (such as the criminal law) to which adults are accountable.

➤ **Accountable for their actions**: If children are to be given adult rights they must take responsibility for their actions.

These ideas reflect a basic uncertainty about how to understand the status of children in contemporary society — as individuals in their own right or as dependent on adults. In the past, writers such as Aries (1962) have argued, the relationship was more clear-cut: children were basically 'little adults' who, from a very early age, were considered an economic asset to the family; they dressed, lived and worked like adults. In the present, however, Robertson (2001) argues that we've reached a stage where children have become 'economically worthless and emotionally priceless' — a significant change in status that has changed the way parents and children interact.

Mann (2009) suggests that contemporary Britain has seen the 'rise of more democratic forms of parent–child relationships...children are taking a greater interest in, and having an input in, decision making'. This relationship is, however, uneasy and at times ambivalent. While parents have legal responsibility for their children and have to assume a certain level of control over their behaviour, children (through the internet) are acquiring ever greater levels of knowledge, if not always understanding, about the adult world and relationships therein.

The 'darker side' of child–parent relationships is, at its most extreme, expressed through **child abuse**. This, Humphreys and Thiara (2002) note, has a strong link to domestic violence (men who are violent towards their partner are also violent and abusive towards children in their care). We can note the following points:

➤ Each year 80 children are killed, mainly by parents and carers. This number has remained constant for almost 30 years.

➤ The most likely abuser is someone known to the child (National Commission of Inquiry into the Prevention of Child Abuse, 1996).

➤ Department of Education figures for 2010 show around 46,000 children on child protection registers or plans.

**?** **How have children become 'economically worthless and emotionally priceless'?**

### Postmodern children

Postman (1985) argues that the development of modern communication systems such as television (which we can extend to include mobile phone and internet technology) casts doubt on the assumption that 'adults' and 'children' are distinct and separate categories. Television and the internet are 'open admission technology' — they cannot differentiate between adults and children. As a result, children are exposed to images of adulthood (sex, violence, the news and so forth).

This, for Postman, diminishes both adult and child abilities to decide where childhood ends and adulthood begins. Children become more like adults in terms of their criminality, sexuality and dress, while adults become more like 'children' in their equation of 'youthfulness' with health, vitality and excitement.

Robertson (2001) argues that child–parent relationships are now less 'adult directed' and more focused on allowing children to find their own general way in life, freed from overt adult direction. This leads to a breakdown of conventional child/adult distinctions (and relationships) in a range of ways:

➤ **Consumption culture**: Children see the world through the eyes of consumers as they're encouraged to buy goods and services formerly the preserve of adults (mobile phones being a recent example). Advertisers target 'children's markets' in ever more sophisticated ways, leading to the development of a 'consumption culture' that encourages children to see their identity in terms of what they consume (which is increasingly 'adult' in nature and tone).

➤ **Autonomy**: Children, as they exercise newly available choices, become more rebellious, sexually precocious and, indeed, active. They become immersed in an adult world that requires they become ever more sophisticated in their outlook.

➤ **Rights**: Where children are seen as 'autonomous individuals' (rather than, as in former times, dependent beings), they acquire 'rights' formerly only extended to adults. The

Child/adult distinctions
**C** onsumption
**A** utonomy
**R** ights
**P** ermissiveness

flip-side here is their treatment as 'adults in miniature' which, in turn, leads to the development of more sophisticated ways of living and behaving.

➢ **Permissiveness**: With autonomy and rights comes a change in the way children are raised; they gain greater control over their own social development but must take responsibility for their mistakes and misconceptions.

### Fathers

In some ways parent–child relationships in postmodernity resemble those of the past (the idea of children as 'little adults'), whereas in others they do not — children are banned from numerous 'adult' experiences (drinking, smoking, sexual activity and so forth).

This '**postmodern ambivalence**' is reflected in changes to parental perceptions of their role. The role of 'father', in particular, is played out against a backdrop of ambivalent understanding (uncertainty about what their role should be). On the one hand, fathers see their primary responsibility to their children as economic provision (which increasingly relates to consumption cultures), while on the other they see their role as providing emotional and psychological comfort and stability. A flavour of the way fathers interpret their role is given by an Equal Opportunities Commission (2002) study of 60 fathers, which identified four main types (with most fathers falling into the middle two categories):

➢ **Enforcer**: Little involvement in childcare; interprets father role in terms of providing clear rules for children's behaviour.

➢ **Entertainer**: Interacts with children regularly, but usually when partner is occupied with more mundane aspects of domestic labour (such as cleaning).

➢ **Useful**: Has greater involvement with children (and domestic labour) but is usually directed by his partner.

➢ **Fully involved**: Plays a role that is interchangeable with his partner's and aims to play as full a role as possible in childcare.

## Sociological explanations

### Functionalism

For traditional functionalist approaches, the historical development of family roles, responsibilities and relationships is seen in evolutionary terms — a gradual move away from **asymmetrical relationships** based around **segregated conjugal roles** with a clear separation between the home (women's work) and the workplace (men's work), towards **joint conjugal roles** involving greater levels of equality in terms of both paid and domestic work.

Family roles start to **converge** through **stratified diffusion**. For Willmott and Young (1973) an initial change in upper-class family roles and relationships gradually 'trickles down' the class structure; joint conjugal relationships are adopted next by middle-class families and finally by the working class. Sullivan et al. (2008) suggest that evidence for convergence can be found in areas like:

➤ an increase in male — and a decrease in female — housework
➤ an increase in the time men devote to childcare
➤ a general acceptance of gender equality
➤ a 'quiet revolution' in family relationships where change occurs 'behind the scenes'

One frequently cited development here is the 'new man' identity we noted in chapter 3.

The Equal Opportunities Commission (2002) also highlighted a range of evidence from fathers suggesting some movement towards role convergence, albeit one juggling work and family responsibilities:

➤ **Support role**: Although most fathers had little involvement with their children during the working week, weekends were 'put aside' for family life.
➤ **Childcare**: Fathers claim to carry out around a third of 'active parental childcare'.
➤ **Income**: Male involvement in childcare increases where their partner has a high income from full-time work.
➤ **Work–life balance**: Fathers balance work and family responsibilities to ensure greater involvement in the latter.

Whatever the reality of this situation (and we always need to be aware of reliability and validity problems with such data — what people say they do may differ from what they actually do), a slightly different recent approach is Swenson's (2004) **neo-functionalist** focus on adults as providers of a stable family environment for primary socialisation. This involves:

➤ roles as both **expressive** and **instrumental**
➤ providing children with a safe, secure environment that gives free range to both expressive and instrumental roles and values

In this respect neo-functionalism suggests parents contribute to the socialisation process by giving their children a knowledge of both expressive and instrumental role relationships. It doesn't particularly matter which partner provides which; all that matters is they do. This means that gender roles in contemporary families can be fluid:

➤ Women can provide instrumental values and men expressive values (or vice versa depending on specific family conditions and relationships).
➤ Same-sex families can perform these roles.
➤ Lone-parent families are not automatically excluded; the parent may successfully combine both roles or they may have help from others (such as extended family) to provide the role content they cannot provide (grandparents could play an expressive role while the parent plays an instrumental role).

Dysfunctional families are not a product of particular family structures; single-parent families are not automatically dysfunctional, just as dual-parent families are not automatically functional. What matters is the *quality* of parental roles; as Swenson

(2004) argues, 'families become dysfunctional when poor parenting produces poor socialization outcomes'. 'Good parenting', therefore, successfully integrates both expressive and instrumental roles and values into the socialisation process.

### Evaluation

#### Family structures

While traditional functionalism is criticised for seeing some forms of family structure as dysfunctional, neo-functionalism argues that the primary role of families — the successful socialisation of children — is related to parental role performance rather than family structures. However, neo-functionalism suggests some family structures are 'more or less optimal' for the performance of primary socialisation. A dual-parent family, for example, may have greater human resources and opportunities than a single-parent family.

#### Child problems

Swenson (2004) argues that the avoidance of 'antisocial behaviour' in children is based around the stability of family roles and relationships. This suggests that, while children can be raised in a variety of family types, 'optimal socialisation' takes place in stable (married) families where husband and wife play complementary roles.

#### Happy families?

All varieties of functionalism generally underplay power imbalances in gender roles and relationships — the idea, for example, that men play instrumental roles inside and outside the family because they have the power to impose their will on others. Ferree (1990) argues, 'male dominance within families as part of a wider system of male power, is neither natural nor inevitable, and occurs at women's cost'.

> **?** What is the main difference between joint and segregated conjugal roles?

## Marxism

We've previously outlined a range of Marxist ideas on family roles and relationships (to which you should refer in this context). We will look here at how Marxist analyses of family life in recent times have focused on conflict and power struggles (not all of which are necessarily and automatically resolved in favour of men) based around **family economies**. Power relationships within families are not always played out in terms of violence or abuse; the vast majority of families experience neither of these things. Morgan (2001) suggests we should consider power relationships in terms of 'three economies': political, moral and emotional.

#### The political economy

The political economy relates to the **economic** aspect of family life which, Pahl (2007) suggests, involves how money is 'received, controlled and managed within the household, before being allocated to spending on collective or personal items'. More specifically, she argues for a **resource theory** where power struggles are an inevitable part of our relationships and 'the greatest power tends to accrue to those who contribute the most resources' (which include money and status, love and affection, or things like 'domestic work, child care or sexual services').

Financial decision-making is a significant indicator of where power lies within a family, since major decisions involve concepts of authority. Pahl and Vogler (1994) found that men made the most important financial decisions.

Other areas of major decision-making in dual-earner families involve paid work and relate to whose work has the greatest priority when, for example, the family is forced to move because of a change in employment. Hardill (2003) found that women were more likely to be the 'trailing spouse' — male occupations had greatest priority.

**Status enhancement**, Coverman (1989) argues, involves 'work done by one partner (typically the woman) to aggrandize the other partner's career' (hosting dinner parties, attending work functions and so forth). In extreme cases, status enhancement takes the form of a 'trophy wife' — a marriage pattern used by some powerful (mainly, but not necessarily, older) men to demonstrate their wealth and power.

### The moral economy

The moral economy relates to the values and norms within a family group concerning the roles and responsibilities of different family members. The female partner can exercise high levels of power through her ability to organise family resources and behaviours even when she earns substantially less than her partner.

### The emotional economy

The emotional economy involves the interpersonal relationships that are almost unique to family life — what Dallos et al. (1997) call '**affective power**'. If someone loves you this gives you power. Pahl (2007) suggests that this 'family power' has a number of aspects:

➤ Who 'loves' the other the most: the partner who 'loves less' can use this to gain power over the one who 'loves more'.
➤ Who 'needs' the other most: the partner who needs the other least is more able to control the relationship (ultimately by threatening to leave).
➤ Who best meets their partner's emotional needs.
➤ Who is most able to resolve conflicts, reduce emotional stress and create emotional well-being within the family.

Finally, the possession and exercise of power within families is not confined to a particular household — just as either partner may draw power from their ability to bring economic resources into a family, the same is true of moral and emotional resources. In extended families, for example, either partner can draw power from their ability to link into a network of power involving wider kin like parents and siblings.

### Evaluation

> **Power**: By seeing families as an extension of the class struggle in wider society, Marxism underplays the genuine feelings of love, affection, intimacy and sacrifice that exist within families.

> **Struggle**: Marxists underestimate the extent to which families are based on shared feelings of mutual cooperation and support rather than power struggles.

> **Choices**: This general view suggests family members have little or no choice over how their roles, relationships and responsibilities are played out (family members are simply one small part of wider class struggles). The evidence from contemporary families suggests relationships involve greater complexity in terms of how and why they allocate different roles.

**?** Give examples of two sources of power used within family relationships.

## Feminism

Feminist sociology has traditionally focused on the role of the family group in the exploitation of women, with attention mainly given to explaining how traditional gender roles are enforced for the benefit of men. The family group is generally seen as patriarchal and oppressive, imprisoning women in a narrow range of service roles and responsibilities, such as domestic labour and childcare.

### Liberal feminism

As we've previously noted, this type of feminism is focused around **equality of opportunity** — gender relationships, roles and responsibilities should be equitable, with men and women being free to choose both their roles and how these are played out in a work or family context. Liberal feminists have traditionally looked to the **legal system** to enforce 'equal gender rights', and to **governments** to carry out **social policies** aimed at dismantling barriers to female emancipation — from equality in political representation, through equal pay and anti-discrimination policies, to protection against domestic violence.

Liberal feminists have, therefore, fought for policies designed to recognise female **dual roles** — as both carers within the family and paid employees. These include the following:

> The development of nursery schooling and childcare facilities that allow women to work and have family responsibilities.

> Maternity and paternity leave: In 2007, New Labour introduced the right of up to two weeks of paternity leave for fathers; maternity leave was extended to a maximum of 52 weeks and consolidated the right for employed women to resume their former job.

> The right to abortion 'on demand'.

> Affirmative action designed to allow more women to break through the 'glass ceiling' in the workplace.

This 'softer' form of feminism promotes 'practical and realistic' ways of creating a gender balance within the family — one that recognises that some women want to focus on family and child-rearing responsibilities, some prefer to focus on a career and others want (or need) to combine family and work responsibilities. Liberal feminists, in this respect, reject:

➢ Marxist feminist claims that family life is simply a reflection of wider economic inequalities
➢ radical feminist notions of patriarchy as an inevitable by-product of male–female relationships

Harriet Harman combines a high-profile career in the Labour Party with her role as wife and mother

### Evaluation

➢ **Status inequality**: Although women have achieved major political and legal changes over the past hundred years, stubborn forms of patriarchal domination are proving resistant to change (despite equal pay legislation, for example, women are still paid on average 20% less than men).
➢ **Family roles**: Men still perform less domestic labour than women, even in situations where both partners work. Despite changes, the private sphere of the family remains wrapped in cultural notions of femininity and the female role.
➢ **Cultural capital**: 'Equality of opportunity' is based on the idea that men and women can, given a legally assured level playing field, compete equally in both the private and public domains. Other forms of feminism argue that male cultural capital (from ingrained patriarchal ideas about 'male and female capabilities' to the fact that men still generally have greater access to important economic and cultural resources) gives them an advantage in both the home and the workplace.

### Marxist feminism

Marxist feminism involves the application of Marxist ideas about wider economic inequalities to an explanation of gender inequalities in family roles, relationships and responsibilities. In specific terms, relationships are based around a range of gendered inequalities:

➢ **Service roles**: Within the family women have the role of 'unpaid servants'. This is sometimes done willingly (women see it as part of the female role) and sometimes unwillingly because their partner is unable or unwilling to take it on.
➢ **Double shift**: Where women are increasingly entering paid work, they often have to perform a double shift. Women are doubly exploited — in the public sphere as paid employees whose labour contributes to ruling-class profits, and in the private sphere as unpaid workers whose labour primarily benefits men.

➤ **Triple shift**: More recently, Duncombe and Marsden (1993) have argued that women perform a triple shift, the third element being emotional labour (investing time and effort in the psychological well-being of family members). Women, rather than men, are expected to make this investment in both their children's and their partner's 'emotional well-being'.

In this respect, Marxist feminists argue, women increasingly suffer from dual forms of exploitation: **patriarchal** exploitation, as domestic labourers, and **capitalist** exploitation, as paid employees.

For Marxist feminists, issues like 'equality of opportunity', in terms of removing legal barriers to female emancipation, are, at best, distractions from the 'real cause of female (and indeed male) oppression' — the capitalist economic system. This follows because capitalism inherently involves relations of domination, subordination and oppression. Female exploitation, therefore, will continue for as long as capitalism exists.

*Evaluation*
➤ **Class**: Both liberal and radical feminists argue that gender is not simply a 'secondary' form of exploitation, but one experienced by all women, regardless of class. Marxist feminism, therefore, pays too little attention to the particular forms of sexist exploitation suffered by women 'simply because they are women'.
➤ **Realism**: Liberal feminists argue that 'real female lives' can be improved on a daily basis through legal and social changes. Marxist feminism simply promises 'freedom tomorrow' once capitalism has somehow been replaced.
➤ **Social change**: Over the past hundred years women's lives have seen radical changes and substantial improvements. It's difficult to see how or why, according to Marxist feminists, these could have occurred; if 'male interests' are served by the exploitation of women it's difficult to see how or why this exploitation should have eased or, in many cases, ceased.

| **?** | Suggest one difference between liberal and Marxist feminism. |
|---|---|

### Radical feminism
For radical feminism, patriarchy is the key source of male domination within the family. We can note several examples of radical feminist solutions to the 'patriarchy problem'.

*Technology*
Firestone (1970) argues that 'a culture of sex discrimination' devolves from **biology** — the fact that women experience pregnancy and childbirth. This is the **essential** difference between men and women from which all other cultural differences flow. If technology can liberate women from childbirth (by enabling children to be born outside the womb), this eliminates an essential sexual (biological) difference and removes male power to discriminate on the basis of biology.

*Femininity*

This strand says women, as a **sex class**, should exploit the 'values of femininity' that derive from their particular **psychology**; these include a sense of community, family, empathy, sharing and so forth that make them different from men, whose patriarchal values are built around aggressiveness, selfishness and greed.

Women should 'embrace the power' that comes from the ability to reproduce since, for Stanworth (1987), 'reproduction is the foundation of women's identity'. She argues that women should reject the 'technologies' embraced by writers like Firestone as being a further source of male power and domination — this time over the one ability (to reproduce) that marks women apart.

*Anti-family stance*

For Frieden (1963) and Millett (1969) the patriarchal structures and practices of the family are the source of female oppression. As Friedan argues, 'A housewife is a parasite' because she is forced to depend on men for her social existence. The solution, therefore, is either the abandonment of the patriarchal family or the development of **matriarchal** family structures that exclude men (through lesbian relationships).

*Evaluation*

- **Motherhood**: This condition is increasingly rejected by a range of women so it becomes difficult to see how and why they would see their identity in these terms. The question, therefore, is whether women who cannot or do not want to reproduce would be considered 'real women'.

Radical feminism

**M** otherhood
**E** ssentialism
**D** estiny
**S** ex class

- **Essentialism**: Butler (1990) argues that men and women do not have fundamentally different natures. Given the high levels of historical and cultural diversity in gender roles and relationships, it seems difficult to sustain the idea that 'men are men, women are women' and there is no way to change their essential natures.
- **Biology is destiny**: If our 'natures' (men as 'aggressive and competitive', women as 'compassionate and nurturing') cannot be changed, it's difficult to see how the gender relationships on which they are built can change.
- **Sex class**: Butler (1990) argues that women are not a sex class. Female histories and experiences are too diverse and fragmented to be seen in these terms.

Post-feminism

For post-feminists the thing missing from other feminist perspectives is the notion of women making **choices** about their lives — to be 'mothers' or childless career women, for example.

The key to understanding family roles, for Butler (1990), is how gender is **performed**, rather than an 'essentialist notion' about what gender *is*. Gender performance inside the family is seen as changing, through a merging of traditional gender roles whereby the rigid separation between 'home' and 'work' is no longer sustainable: just as women move freely into and out of the public domain, so men take the reverse route.

This results in a form of **gender understanding**: family groups form around a range of 'rational choices' about 'who does what' and 'when they do it', with males and females performing a range of different and complementary family roles. These roles can be interchangeable — sometimes the female will look after the children, sometimes the male — such that family roles are no longer the preserve of one particular gender.

According to post-feminists, Marxist and radical feminists ignore significant **changes** in male and female family lives, roles and relationships over the past 50 years.

Women can choose to construct their personal identities in a range of ways. One of these involves 'reclaiming femininity'; they can be both 'feminine' (in terms of seeking and gaining pleasure from the care of others) and 'careerist' (in the sense of wanting economic independence and security).

Overall, post-feminists argue that we should see family roles, relationships and responsibilities in light of how different men and women construct and negotiate their lifestyles and identities. Unlike other feminisms this approach suggests we should neither underestimate female choices (to want a close involvement in the nurture and care of their children, for example) nor disrespect women for making such choices.

### *Evaluation*

➢ **Choice**: Real choice for women may be limited by male power. While women have greater choices now, only a minority enjoy the luxury of 'unlimited choice'. Choice is still tied to economic power controlled mainly by men.

➢ **Change**: Changes in family roles and relationships have been the result of relatively simple political and legal adjustments rather than a radical reappraisal of 'gender as a concept'. These changes have arrived through women collectively (rather than individually) organising and fighting for change. If women cease to see their lives in collective terms they risk losing the rights gained over the past few decades.

 **What differences are there between feminist explanations of family roles and relationships?**

# Demographic changes

In previous sections we've looked at some of the demographic trends which affect families. We can now pull these ideas together in relation to both an ageing population and declining family size (in the context of declining birth rates).

An **ageing population** occurs when the number defined as elderly in a society exceeds the number defined as young. In 2007, for example, the number of people in Britain aged 65 and over exceeded the number aged 16 and under for the first time in our history. Demographically, we can identify two **mega-factors** that cause an ageing population: increased life expectancy and falling birth rates.

## Increased life expectancy

People are, on average, living longer. While there are gender, class and regional differences, during the twentieth century average life expectancy in Britain increased by 30 years (males can now expect to live, on average, 78 years and females 82 years).

Chamberlain and Gill (2005) identify two factors that explain why Britain's population is ageing:

➤ The **death rate** has fallen dramatically, from 16 per 1,000 of the population in 1900 to 10 per 1,000 in 2000.

➤ An '**ageing of the ageing population**': the elderly are 'getting older'; the fastest growing elderly group are now the over-85s.

Increased life expectancy relates to a number of areas: healthcare, public health measures and lifestyle changes.

### Healthcare

Self and Zealey (2007) note a range of factors:

➤ **vaccination** against diseases like polio and diphtheria that steadily reduced their death toll among infants and children

➤ **medicines** (e.g. the development of antibiotics)

➤ **practices**: developments in surgery (such as heart bypass operations)

➤ **prevention**: a fall in **infant mortality rates** — 'one of the major factors contributing to an overall increase in life expectancy' — attributed by Self and Zealey (2007) to three 'areas of improvement':

  ➤ diet and sanitation

  ➤ antenatal, postnatal and medical care

  ➤ vaccines and immunisation programmes

### Public health measures

Arguably of more value in terms of increasing general levels of life expectancy are a raft of improvements in the **physical environment**:

➤ **Housing**: Important steps include slum clearance and the development of cheap, good-quality public ('council') housing after the Second World War.

➤ **Public sanitation**: Steps have been taken to ensure that public exposure to sewage/waste is minimised and that people understand basic sanitation principles (e.g. how disease can be spread).

➤ **Clean water**: The Department of Health (2004) notes that, over the past century, one of the 'most significant contributions to better health has been clean water supplies'.

To this general list we could also add the development of the **welfare state** (post-1944).

### Lifestyle choices and changes

There is now a greater awareness of behaviours contributing to individual health and longevity:

- **Smoking**: Penneck and Lewis (2005) point to the 'dramatic reduction in death from circulatory diseases (in part caused by the decline in smoking)'.
- **Cleaner air**: The Clean Air Acts (1956 and 1993) placed restrictions on smoke emissions (from both private and industrial premises).
- **Health education**: There is a greater awareness of the importance of balanced diets, daily fruit and vegetable intakes, limits on alcohol intake and the like.

> **?** Define the term 'ageing population'.

## Declining birth rates

Declining birth rates involve a range of factors.

### Birth control

Tiffen and Gittins (2004) suggest a couple of specific reasons for a decline in birth rates over the past 40 or so years:
- the increased availability and reliability of **contraception**
- the legalisation of **abortion** in 1967

Although birth control techniques are significant factors, they don't explain why people want to limit **family size** in the first place. To understand this, we need to note a further set of explanations.

### Lifestyle choices and changes

We've seen that increased female participation in the workforce over the past 30 years has led to a delay in the average age of first marriage and a consequent delay in conception and childbirth, but an equally important factor is **childlessness**. Self and Zealey (2007) note a significant rise in childlessness:
- 1985: 11% of women (aged 45+)
- 2005: 18%

McAllister and Clarke (1998) suggest two main reasons for both childlessness and fewer children:
- **Risk**: For single and career women 'parenthood was not considered a viable option'. It was identified with disruption, change and poverty; the childless chose independence over the constraints of childcare, and material security over financial risk.
- **Financial pressures**: The cost of raising children over a lifetime was a factor in either not having children or limiting their number.

Additional factors (Grenham 1995) include:
- less need for children as a protection against old age and illness
- a trade-off between having children and maintaining a higher living standard

Tiffen and Gittins (2004) also suggest that many women have different *aspirations* from both their mothers and grandmothers; they are less likely to accept identities built around the home and motherhood.

## Explanations

The overall relationship between an ageing population, falling fertility rates and the decline in average family size has been explained in several different ways, focusing on demographic transition, wealth flow or optimal investment.

### Demographic transition

Historical development is characterised by Newson et al. (2005) as a progression from high mortality and high fertility to low mortality and low fertility. In other words, demographic transition theory suggests the trends we've identified are part of a general demographic change that occurs in the transition between different types of society — such as, over the past 30 years or so, from a mainly **industrial manufacturing society** (dominated by heavy engineering) to a **post-industrial service society** (characterised by computer technology and financial services).

### Wealth flow theory

The decision to have children (and how many) is sensitive to the specific economic circumstances of a family and a wider sense of economic advantage or disadvantage. Caldwell (1976) suggests children are seen as less of an economic *asset* (through their ability to work) and more as an economic *liability*; where wider economic and social changes turn children from a source of wealth (flowing from the child to the parent) into a drain on family resources (wealth flowing from parents to children), people take the **rational decision** to limit the number of children they produce.

### Optimal investment

Decisions about family size are made on a 'cost/benefit' basis that takes account of both economic and social/psychological factors; these are influenced by the following:

➤ **Psychic income**: For Becker (1991) the psychological pleasures gained from children potentially increase the 'demand' for them (the more children, the greater the psychic income for parents). However, the increased economic costs of children mean parents 'limit their investment' by producing a smaller number in whom they invest a great deal of time, money and effort.

➤ **Consumption choices**: Newson et al. (2005) note that (potential) parents now have a greater range of consumption choices, such that 'They can compare the costs and benefits of a child with those of a new car'.

➤ **Support networks**: Sear et al. (2003) argue that modern families increasingly lack the kin support networks that provide resources — a grandparent looking after children while both parents work, for example — to allow for larger families.

➤ **Status objects**: Parents increasingly view their children as measures of their own status; the success of children in their adult lives reflects back on parents who use this as a means of measuring their own self-worth. Family size is consciously limited to make the greatest possible economic and emotional investment in a small number of children.

**Exam-style questions**

**1** Identify and explain two ways in which relationships between parents and children have changed over the past 30 years. (17 marks)

**2** Identify and explain two ways in which an ageing population affects family life. (17 marks)

**3** Outline and evaluate the view that relationships between parents and children have changed in the last 30 years. (33 marks)

**4** Outline and evaluate feminist views of relationships between men and women in family life. (33 marks)

# Chapter 9
## Sociology of religion

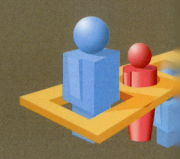

**By the end of this chapter you will be able to:**

➤ understand inclusive and exclusive definitions of religion and be aware of their uses and limitations

➤ examine religious belief, participation and membership as dimensions of religiosity and commitment

➤ compare different types of religious organisations and movements

➤ understand and evaluate functionalist, Marxist, Weberian and postmodern approaches to the role of religion in society

➤ understand and explain the relationship between religiosity and the social categories of class, age, gender and ethnicity

➤ explain the appeal of new religious and New Age movements to different social groups

➤ evaluate arguments for and against the secularisation of society

# Key concepts and the changing nature of religious movements in society

## What is religion?

The question 'How do we define religion?' initially seems quite straightforward. Most of us would probably begin with the idea that religion involves:

➤ a set of beliefs

➤ a set of practices through which belief is expressed

➤ some form of organisation that allows both practices and beliefs to be collectively expressed

An initial problem, however, is that this could apply to many institutions in our society. A school, for example, involves beliefs about what education is, practices (how we 'do education') and organisation (in classrooms and schools).

To put some religious flesh on these bones we need to qualify these ideas:

➤ **Beliefs**: These might include a belief in 'God' (or at least some kind of 'supernatural force or being' that exists over and above human beings).

➤ **Practices**: These might involve things like collective worship and prayer, which could include ceremonies (such as weddings or funerals) and festivals (such as Christmas).

➤ **Organisation**: Here we could point to 'special places' reserved for the expression of religious beliefs and practices (such as a church, mosque or meeting hall) and also people (such as vicars, priests and imams) employed in some capacity (paid or voluntary) by a religious organisation to take services or generally look after the well-being of the religious.

While this gets us closer to answering our initial question — we have identified some features of religion that make it different from institutions like education or the family — this formulation has a number of problems.

In terms of beliefs, some forms of religion are:

➤ **monotheistic** — with a belief in a single God (**Christianity**, **Judaism** and **Islam**, for example)

➤ **polytheistic** — with a belief in many gods (such as **paganism**)

➤ **non-theistic** — they do not involve worshipping a 'god' or 'gods'. The North American Sioux, for example, understood the world in terms of Waken Beings or Powers — the expression of anything they found 'incomprehensible'

For some religions 'god' is:

➤ **external** to the individual (as in Christianity)

➤ **internal** to the individual (the ultimate aim of some religions is to reveal our 'inner spirituality')

In terms of practices, some religions involve:

➤ **personal communication** with God through prayer

➤ **communal worship** (for example, Christianity)

➤ **exorcism** — whereby 'evil spiritual entities' are evicted from a person or place they 'possess' (the Roman Catholic and Eastern Orthodox Churches, for example)

➤ **baptism of the dead** (for example, The Church of Jesus Christ of Latter-day Saints — 'Mormons')

In terms of organisation, some forms of religion are:

➤ **Highly organised**: Catholicism has a highly developed structure with paid workers employed at various levels in a **corporate hierarchy** (with the Pope at its head supported by cardinals). Catholicism also has a strict form of **doctrine** (a set of beliefs and principles to which the practitioner must adhere (for example, contraception is forbidden).

➤ **Loosely organised**: Hinduism is a **religious belief system** involving a multitude of groups, some connected, some not, built around the central idea of a 'universal soul'. It does not recognise a single set of beliefs or practices.

**? What are the features of religion?**

In these respects, religion is characterised by **diversity**. Although it is tempting to see religion as a single (homogeneous) entity, the reality is one of wide variations in beliefs, practices and organisation:

➤ **historically** — in the same society over time
➤ **contemporaneously** — in the same society at the same time
➤ **cross-culturally** — between different societies

These differences help to explain why religion is difficult to define. McGuire (2002) suggests that definitional problems arise because of the 'dual character' of religion:

➤ **Individual**: Religions involve a diversity of beliefs and practices in addition to a variety of ways to 'be religious', some of which involve the communal practice of religious beliefs (such as attending religious ceremonies), others of which do not (it is possible, for example, to be a 'Christian' without ever setting foot inside a church).
➤ **Social**: Religions perform certain **functions** for society:
  ➤ **socialisation** (into a range of moral beliefs and values)
  ➤ **social solidarity** (giving people a sense that they have things in common)
  ➤ **social control** (both direct controls, such as Islamic codes defining what people may wear or eat, and indirect controls — Christian moral values provide a template for how you are expected to lead your life 'in accordance with God')

In this light, Hutchinson (1981) argues, 'Definitions of religion are as numerous as there are students of religion' and they 'illustrate the oriental parable of the blind men describing the elephant, each taking hold of part of the beast and defining the whole in terms of this part. Like the elephant, religion is a large and complex phenomenon'.

**? Why is religion difficult to define?**

If we follow the logic of the elephant analogy, any definition of religion has to avoid focusing too closely on any particular part of religious behaviour (such as beliefs, practices or organisational forms) in isolation from other parts. As a 'large and complex phenomenon', religion has to be defined and understood in terms of how the various parts of the whole both relate to and impact on each other. There are two distinctive approaches to understanding religious behaviour, inclusive and exclusive.

## Inclusive approaches

**Inclusive approaches** see religion in the broadest possible terms by focusing on the **needs** (both social and individual) that they see religious beliefs, practices and organisations as existing to satisfy.

Rather than define religion in terms of 'what it is' (a precise set of beliefs and practices specific to 'religion'), this approach focuses on 'what it does' for both the individual, such as providing answers to the question 'what happens when we die?', and, equally importantly, for society. Durkheim (1912), for example, saw religion as fulfilling two important functions:

- ➢ **Social solidarity**: How religion creates a feeling of 'belonging' to a particular society or social group — by providing individuals with **shared beliefs and values** (they all worship the 'same God', for example) or acting as a source of personal and social identity (by specifying a moral code to follow, such as the Ten Commandments in Christianity).
- ➢ **Social integration**: The specific ways social solidarity is created, through **social mechanisms** like shared practices and experiences such as church services and ceremonies (weddings, christenings and funerals).

Inclusive approaches generally involve a **functional** definition of religion: they focus on what religion does as a way of identifying its general characteristics as a **system of beliefs**.

### System of beliefs

The specific content of someone's beliefs is not important (it does not matter, for example, if they pray to the 'One True God', supernatural forces that control the movement of the planets, a race of hyper-intelligent aliens from the planet Zog or Manchester United Football Club). What is important is that they hold beliefs that influence how and why they behave in particular ways. Worshipping in a Christian church or Muslim mosque is no different from worshipping at the cathedral of Old Trafford. As Cline (2005) puts it: 'If your belief system plays some particular role either in your social life, in your society, or in your psychological life, then it is a religion; otherwise, it's something else.'

Is football the new religion?

TopFoto

Inclusive approaches, therefore, see religion in both:

> **conventional** ways, such as a belief in the existence of God
> **unconventional** ways, in forms people do not normally consider to be 'religious'; political ideologies (such as capitalism or communism) can be included as 'religious-type' belief systems, because their overriding characteristic is **faith**

### Faith

Like conventional forms of religion, political ideologies require their followers to obey certain articles and principles of faith, often in return for some promised goal. For some religions this is a place in heaven (Christianity) or rebirth into a higher social position (Hinduism), whereas in a 'political faith' such as communism the promised goal is a fairer, more equal (*egalitarian*) society.

### Function over form

For inclusive approaches, the way beliefs differ in terms of their specific content is less important than the fact that they function in similar ways. Sharing beliefs — religious or non-religious (**secular**) — promotes the idea of belonging to a community of 'like-minded individuals' bound together by common beliefs, norms and values.

As we have seen, Durkheim suggested that religion functioned in ways that promoted social solidarity and integration (and he took the inclusive approach to what is probably its most extreme position when he argued that 'in worshipping a god' what people are really doing is worshipping the idea of 'society' — an idea to which we will return). In this respect, Haviland et al. (2005) identify examples of two types of religious function:

> **Religious rituals** (such as christenings, marriages and funerals). These 'ritualistic aspects' of social life play a significant role in 'marking important life transitions'. In some forms of Judaism, for example, the bar mitzvah (for boys aged 13) and bat mitzvah (for girls aged 12) symbolise a religious **rite of passage** (a ceremony marking the passing between life stages) from childhood to adulthood.
> **Intensification rites** function to 'mark group occasions' and involve the 'expression and affirmation of common values'. In other words, religious ceremonies or festivals have an integration function, binding people through the beliefs and practices they share.

An extension to this general approach is one that focuses on how people (in different societies and at different times) 'define a situation' as being religious. In other words, rather than a sociologist creating a 'definition of religion' against which to measure the extent to which some forms of behaviour are 'religious', definitions simply develop, according to Blasi (1998), out of how people define their own behaviour. Religion and religious behaviour, from this viewpoint, are effectively whatever people claim them to be. Luckmann (1967), for example, considers any system of belief that explains the nature of the social or natural world to be a form of religion.

Evaluation

*Uses*

➤ **Diversity**: Inclusive approaches overcome the problem of producing a definition that covers all aspects of religious behaviour. We do not have to account for every tiny variation in beliefs and behaviours to develop a workable definition of religion.

➤ **Purpose**: The focus is always on understanding what religion does for the individual and society, rather than simply documenting varieties of belief, behaviour and practice.

➤ **Scope**: By combining a workable definition with an understanding of why societies develop religious beliefs and practices, we have a starting point for the analysis and explanation of why many people are religious.

*Limitations*

➤ **Presence**: Religion is 'everywhere and nowhere'; we can see 'religious-type' behaviour in everything (from football to shopping to church attendance) yet not be able to identify precisely those aspects of behaviour that are uniquely religious.

➤ **Secularisation**: We have no way of telling whether society is becoming less religious or more religious (resacrilisation).

➤ **Measurement**: Religion effectively becomes whatever people say it is, which again impacts on our ability to measure religious behaviour (**religiosity** — see below) in any meaningful way.

## Exclusive approaches

**Exclusive approaches** consider religion in a narrower way, usually in terms of beliefs (god or the supernatural) and behaviours (praying, collective worship) that we would conventionally see as 'religious'. They exclude 'quasi-religious' behaviour that might serve a similar purpose or function to religion but which is not actually religious in the strict sense of the term.

For example, the worshipful behaviour we see in a church and at Old Trafford when Manchester United are playing Liverpool might look similar: both congregations are paying homage to beings ('God' on the one hand, Wayne Rooney on the other) seen as special and worthy of veneration — but the similarity is superficial. If we dig deeper into this behaviour we get at the essence of religion — the idea that religious beliefs are *qualitatively* different from other forms of belief.

Exclusive approaches involve a **substantive definition** focused on the content (or substance) of religion — the things (beliefs, ceremonies and the like) that are distinctively religious behaviours and which, in turn, mark religious behaviour as different from other behaviours. In this respect, Beckford (1980) characterises exclusive approaches as 'restricting the term "religion" to phenomena displaying definite properties which do not occur together in other phenomena'.

Substantive definitions hold that religion has essential characteristics. Eliade (1987), for example, argues that religion involves:

➤ the **sacred** (or special — what Maguire (2001) defines as 'that which is utterly and mysteriously precious in our experience') and the **profane** (or everyday), seen as important religious distinctions
➤ **codes of values** with a sacred origin (such as the Ten Commandments given to Moses by God)
➤ **communication** with the supernatural (through mechanisms such as prayer)

Luckmann (1967) argues that region is a unique **belief system** (an **ideology** or way of explaining something) because it:

➤ explains the individual's place in the world
➤ provides a sense of moral and political order
➤ explains 'why we are here' (and what happens when we die)

Durkheim (1912), in addition to the distinction between the sacred and profane, noted how religion involves:

➤ **symbols** invoking feelings of reverence or awe linked to rituals or ceremonies practised by a community of believers
➤ **collective ceremonies** that occur in special places, such as churches, temples or grounds, that have been religiously dedicated

### Evaluation

#### Uses

Exclusive approaches key into what people conventionally think about 'religion' in the sense of seeing it as behaviour that is both special and different.

Where we can substantively define religious behaviour, we are able to measure levels of religious behaviour in a society — to test whether society is becoming secularised or resacrilised.

#### Limitations

The question is whether religion does have unique and exclusive features. As we have just seen, there doesn't seem to be a great deal of agreement over what they might be.

Exclusive approaches simply adopt a definition of religion that fits mainstream world religions (such as Christianity or Islam). 'Religion' is defined as whatever these religions say it is in terms of their beliefs, practices and organisation. This creates two problems:

➤ Such organisations have a vested interest in ensuring the product they are 'selling' (religious experience) is both unique and has limited competition.
➤ To identify the 'unique characteristics' of religion the definition is drawn so narrowly it not only excludes behaviours not conventionally seen as religious but also behaviour that has some characteristics of mainstream religion. Scientology, for example, makes no distinction between the 'sacred' and the 'profane' and has

no concept of 'God' as understood by Christianity. It does, however, focus on ideas about spirituality that are religious in nature.

**?** What differences can you find between inclusive and exclusive approaches to religion?

# Religiosity

One reason for defining religion is to help us gain some idea about levels of religious belief and behaviour in a society (**religiosity**), and to do this we need to identify **indicators** of religiosity that can be measured. Following McGuire's (2002) notion of the 'dual character' of religion, these need to be:

> **individual** indicators, such as whether someone holds religious beliefs and whether these are orthodox (believing in a single all-powerful deity, for example) or unorthodox, such as believing in witchcraft

> **social** indicators that measure things like religious participation (attendance at religious services) and membership

While there are many different indicators, Cornwall et al. (1986) identify three broad dimensions of religiosity that, taken as a whole, represent an overall level of religious **commitment**:

> **knowing** (or **cognition**) — the '**belief dimension**' to commitment

> **feeling** (or **affect**) — a specific measure of commitment to both an individual's beliefs and any religious organisation they identify with

> **doing** (or **behaviour**) — a measure of religious **participation/ membership** as an indicator of commitment

**?** Define the concept of religiosity.

We can examine each of these dimensions of religiosity and commitment in turn:

## Religious belief

When measuring religiosity we have to take into account the fact that it's possible, as Davie (1994) has argued, to:

> **Believe without belonging**: People can hold religious beliefs while showing little or no commitment to religious organisations or practices. Millions of people in our society quite happily believe in 'God' without ever attending a religious service.

> **Belong without believing**: People can attend religious services without necessarily having any strongly developed religious belief; religious practice may have **secular functions**, with people attending services for reasons of friendship, social status, tradition and so forth.

While uncovering religious beliefs involves **reliability** problems (for example, do 'religious beliefs' mean the same thing to everyone?), one good indicator we can use, as Hughes and Church (2010) note, is whether people believe in a 'higher being':

➤ If they do, this indicates that they hold some form of religious belief.
➤ If they don't, this suggests they are unlikely to hold further beliefs we could classify as religious.

YouGov (2007) reported that for adults aged 18 and over:
➤ 26% 'believe in "something" but I'm not sure what'
➤ 16% agreed they were atheist ('The whole notion of a supernatural God is nonsense')
➤ 22% 'believe in a personal God who created the world and hears my prayers'
➤ 6% 'believe in a God who created everything but then left us to get on with it'
➤ 30% 'didn't know', envied 'those who did believe' or were agnostic (they 'don't think it is possible to know if there is a God or not').

Overall, 54% expressed a belief in some kind of 'higher being'.

The British Social Attitudes Survey (2008), on the other hand, found that 47% agreed 'religion played a somewhat, very or extremely important part' in their life:
➤ 32% somewhat important
➤ 10% very important
➤ 5% extremely important

Over 50% of respondents, therefore, did not feel religion played any kind of role in their life, while only 15% felt religion played a significant part in their life.

The evidence suggests, therefore, that while religion does play a part in some people's lives — and 'most people' seem to have a concept of some kind of 'God' or 'force' — these beliefs are neither particularly strong nor based on a particular set of religious convictions (such Christianity or Islam).

## Religious participation (attendance and membership)

The idea of 'belonging' to a particular religion can be expressed in terms of the extent to which people participate in religious activities through **attendance** and **membership**.

### Attendance

Knowledge of attendance at religious services/meetings relies on data supplied by religious organisations, such as counting people who attend services or meetings. Hewitt (2010), for example, argues that comparative rates of religious attendance for mainstream religious organisations in Britain show: 'The church in this country is no longer in decline. The latest statistics...clearly show stability in church attendance and even signs of growth'. Hewitt notes:
➤ Church of England monthly attendance in 2008 was 1.67 million compared with 1.71 million in 2001.
➤ Catholic Church weekly Mass attendance in England and Wales was 919,000 in 2008 (a slight rise from 915,000 in 2007).
➤ Baptist Church attendance rose from 149,000 per week in 2002 to 154,000 in 2008.

### Reliability

Although this type of data is useful, it cannot simply be taken at face value. It hides a range of methodological problems relating to both how it is created and how we interpret its meaning and significance.

### Definitions

Counting religious attendance is not straightforward. There are many different religious organisations in Britain — the 2001 census identified around 170 distinct religions, ranging in size from 42 million Christians to 99 Voodoo practitioners, and they frequently use different ways of defining and counting attendance.

Some definitions use weekly and/or monthly attendance figures (some of which are simply estimates which, as Bates (2005) notes, have been compiled by 'accepting a vicar's assessments or headcounts on a particular day'). They may also involve counting regular attendees repeatedly, rather than 'unique attenders'.

Others use an 'average attendance' figure based on the number attending throughout the year. Such figures can be inflated by higher attendances at Easter and Christmas, for example.

Samples are frequently used to generalise monthly or yearly averages; they are a snapshot of attendance rather than a precise and accurate count of all attendances.

Hewitt argues that there is evidence to suggest 'unconventional' forms of attendance (such as meetings attended by evangelical groups within mainstream religions) are not accurately counted.

### Comparisons

The lack of a standard way to count attendance means that it is difficult to track changes over time, even for the same organisation, which makes estimates of changing religious attendance unreliable.

An alternative way of estimating attendance is through social surveys — asking people about their attendance. This should give us a picture of attendance that has greater validity for two reasons:

➤ Questions can be **standardised** and this increased level of reliability gives us greater confidence that attendance figures measure what they claim to measure.
➤ Attendance can be **objectively** measured; people simply have to record whether they attended a religious service or meeting.

In terms of 'attendance at church services or meetings' (excluding 'special occasions' such as weddings, funerals and baptisms), Hughes and Church (2010) note that 57% 'never or practically never' attend. Of the 43% who do participate:

➤ 20% attend regularly (at least once a month)
➤ 17% attend irregularly (at least once or twice a year)
➤ 6% attend 'less often than once a year'

Other surveys broadly support some of these figures. Tearfund (2007), a Christian research agency, found:

➤ 59% 'never or practically never go to church'
➤ 10% of the UK adult population go to church at least weekly (which could be in line with Hughes and Church's analysis)

### Evaluation

Surveys are not without their problems. Hadaway and Marler (1998) note that American opinion poll data about 'religious attendance' showed significant discrepancies between the numbers 'claiming to attend services' and those who actually attended.

In Britain, the National Secular Society (2010) noted, 'people tend to "over-claim" when asked about virtuous behaviour'; around 1.3 million Catholic respondents claimed to attend church services at least once a month — compared with a figure of around 840,000 calculated by Christian research (Hewitt, 2010). Furlong (2002) has also noted: 'people questioned about how much they go to church, give figures which, if true, would add up to twice those given by the churches'.

In this respect, it is interesting to note that the Tearfund survey also found:

➤ 15% attend church at least monthly
➤ 26% attend church at least yearly

These figures are significantly different from those reported by Hughes and Church, which suggests that while data for those who attend frequently or not at all are broadly reliable, they become less so for those who attend infrequently.

> **?** **What might be one problem with using religious beliefs as a measure of religious commitment?**

### Membership

Membership figures should be a more *reliable* and *valid* measurement of participation because they count those who actually join a religious organisation. However, these figures are complicated by different interpretations of the 'meaning of membership'.

The 2001 census, for example, suggests that around 72% (41 million) of the British population self-identify as 'Christian'; the figure for 'Muslim' is 1.5 million and for 'Jewish' 270,000. The **methodological** problem here is that 'membership' is confused by **cultural factors** — such as identifying 'religious membership' with **ethnic identity**. In the case of Christian identification, people are likely to self-identify as belonging to this religion on the basis that 'Christianity' is equated with 'being British' or 'British identity'. When questioned about religious identity outside this particular context, the British Social Attitudes Survey (Crabtree, 2009) found that around 50% of the population say they have 'no religion'. It's important, therefore, to distinguish between active members and those simply counted as 'members' on the basis of being born in a country where a particular church is the official (state or established) religion.

Membership figures are further complicated by:

➤ **Size**: Smaller religious organisations are more difficult to research (there are many, with relatively small, but active, memberships).

➤ **Organisation**: Some religious organisations do not hold services or enrol members. They may, instead, have:

  ➤ clients — people who buy a particular course of teaching

  ➤ customers who purchase a particular product or service from time to time

While we may not define these as mainstream religions, they nevertheless claim to be religious organisations whose 'membership' we can only estimate or take on trust.

➤ **Secrecy**: Smaller religious organisations are more reluctant to divulge their membership numbers to 'outside researchers' (where such figures are available they have to be 'taken on trust').

Religious membership

**S** ize
**O** rganisation
**S** ecrecy

> **?** What might be one problem with using religious membership as a measure of religious commitment?

## Religious commitment

The indicators of commitment we have outlined are subject to such a range of qualifications that to gain a valid understanding of religiosity in our society we need to look further at the substance of 'belief and belonging', in terms of specific indicators of religious commitment ('feeling') — the extent to which people feel they belong to a particular religion.

One way to do this is through a **commitment scale**, an example of which is provided by Abrams et al. (1985) when they suggest we can measure commitment in terms of four key variables (Table 9.1).

Additional indicators of commitment could include:

➤ **Charitable giving**: Jones (2001), for example, argues: 'Giving is highly responsive to religious commitment as measured by either the frequency of attendance at religious services, the perception of being "very religious" or membership in religious groups.'

➤ **Religious styles**, such as the Muslim hijab (a style of female clothing) or Sikh turban. We should, however, keep in mind that this type of indicator may, for some groups, owe more to *cultural practices* (including notions of patriarchy and social control) and *ethnic identity* than religious commitment.

Table 9.1   Measuring religious commitment

| 1 Disposition | ✓ | 2 Orthodox belief | ✓ |
|---|---|---|---|
| Do you: | | I believe in: | |
| ...often think about the meaning of life? | | ...God. | |
| ...think life is meaningless? | | ...sin. | |
| ...often think about death? | | ...soul. | |
| ...often regret doing wrong? | | ...heaven. | |
| ...need moments of prayer, etc.? | | ...life after death. | |
| ...see yourself as a religious person? | | ...a spirit or life force. | |
| ...draw comfort/strength from religion? | | ...the devil. | |
| ...think God is important in your life? | | I accept commandments demanding: | |
| ...have spiritual experiences? | | ...no other gods. | |
| ...have superstitions? | | ...reverence of God's name. | |
| ...believe in predestination? | | ...the holy Sabbath. | |
| **3 Moral values** | ✓ | **4 Institutional attachment** | ✓ |
| Absolute guidelines on good and evil exist. | | I have great confidence in the church/synagogue/temple/mosque. | |
| I accept commandments against: | | The church/synagogue/temple/mosque answers my: | |
| ...killing. | | ...moral problems. | |
| ...adultery. | | ...family problems. | |
| ...stealing. | | ...spiritual needs. | |
| ...lying. | | I attend a religious service at least monthly. | |
| Terrorism may be justified. | | I identify with a particular religion. | |
| The following acts are never justified: | | I believe religion: | |
| ...claiming benefits illegally. | | ...is important for my society. | |
| ...accepting a bribe. | | ...will be more important in the future. | |
| ...taking illegal drugs. | | ...will be less important in the future. | |
| ...homosexuality. | | I believe in one true religion. | |
| ...euthanasia. | | Religious faith is an important value to develop in children. | |
| I always respect those in authority. | | People should marry only in a religious setting. | |
| Capital punishment is wrong. | | Religion has a political role in society. | |

*Source: Abrams et al. (1985)*

# Different types of religious institution and movements

In this section we can identify differences within religions in terms of their general organisation and purpose.

## Church

This type, examples of which include the Church of England, Roman Catholicism and Islam, can be differentiated from other types in the following ways.

### Size

A church is large in terms of membership and attendance. Barrett et al. (2001) note that Christian churches worldwide have around 2 billion adherents (around 30% of the world's population), although we need to qualify these statistics in terms of **validity**: they make no real distinction between *active participants* and those simply counted as adherents on the basis of a particular church being the official religion in a country.

### Capacity

Capacity refers to the church's ability to influence governments and other religious organisations. Bruce (1995) argues that churches have traditionally tried to *dominate all areas of society*, from the way people dress, through how they worship, to the beliefs they hold. Historically in Britain Christian churches were the only religious organisations recognised and allowed by government. Bruce suggests the church's secular influence has generally declined (although there are exceptions, such as Islam in countries like Iran or Saudi Arabia). The gradual separation between church and state has meant a refocusing — away from trying to influence government and back to strictly religious matters.

### Organisation

As befits large (national and transnational) organisations, churches are characterised by:
- a **formal** internal structure based around paid officials (who may or may not have a religious function), organised in terms of their different **statuses**; the Roman Catholic Church, for example, has a hierarchical structure based around the Pope, the authority of cardinals, and so forth
- a **centralised** organisation that specifies things like the dates of religious services, the timing of ceremonies and the collection of 'taxes' (or donations) from congregations

### Membership

Membership is **inclusive**. Churches generally allow anyone to join and membership is often assumed rather than necessarily being the result of a conscious choice. Inclusion is encouraged by:
- **ceremonies** such as baptism and confirmation (in Christian churches)
- **conversions** from one religion to another; these are normally welcomed, if not always actively

Membership of a church can be an assumption rather than a conscious choice

pursued (ex-Prime Minister Tony Blair, for example, converted to Roman Catholicism from the Church of England in 2010)
➤ no membership **tests** or **entry qualifications**

## Social capital

Social capital refers to how people are connected to (or disconnected from) **social networks** and the implications these connections have for what Putnam (2000) calls 'norms of reciprocity' (what people are willing to do for each other). Contemporary churches use social capital to build:

➤ **Bridges** between the church and other religious and secular organisations. They strive, in other words, for inclusiveness — something that involves organisational cooperation and trust. Zmerli (2003) suggests this makes contemporary churches:
  ➤ outward-looking — not just concerned with religious matters
  ➤ heterogeneous — they tolerate a range of different beliefs and religious groups; Staples (1998) argues that the Protestant Church is characterised by **pluriformity** — different groups, with varying degrees of freedom, existing within the same general church organisation
  Examples of these networks include civil rights movements and ecumenical (cross-church) religious organisations.
➤ **Bonds** between their members. This is a more **exclusive** form of social capital because its main objective is to bind members of a particular organisation together.

## Ideology

Churches tend to be in tune with the secular values of society (they are well **integrated** into secular society). Churches are generally **accommodating** to secular values and authorities. Historically, this has meant aligning themselves with ruling secular powers by offering their support to the political and economic objectives of ruling elites.

> **?** Give examples of two features of church organisations.

## Denomination

Denominations are normally well established in a society and share many of the features of churches. This is not surprising given that, in many cases, churches are also denominations:

➤ Roman Catholicism and Protestantism are denominations of Christianity
➤ Presbyterians, Baptists and Methodists are denominations within the Protestant Church
➤ Sunni and Shia are denominations of Islam

A denomination can be broadly characterised as a subgroup within a religion usually created through **schism** — a split between different factions within a church, developing out of:

> ideological differences — such as how religious beliefs should be interpreted
> political differences — such as how a church should be organised
> geographic isolation and separation from the main church that leads to differences in beliefs and practices
> **Scope**: Denominations are generally loose-knit groups that may, for example, unite geographically dispersed congregations of people who generally share similar beliefs and practices. They rarely claim a monopoly of religious truth and tend to be more tolerant of alternative religious organisations, beliefs and practices.
> **Inclusiveness**: People may choose to join or they may be born into a denomination (through their parents' membership). As with churches, there are no membership tests; all that is generally required is commitment to the organisation (which may be as little as a 'belief in God').
> **Organisation**: Although there are variations in the organisation of power and authority (individual Baptist congregations, for example, are generally allowed to develop different beliefs and practices within the overall structure of the denomination), denominations normally develop a **professional clergy** with responsibility for tending to their members. They also tend to be more democratic than other types of religious organisation, although again variation exists; some allow all members to contribute to discussion about denomination affairs, others do not.

**?** What is the difference between a denomination and a church?

## Sect

Although sects and denominations share some general organisational features (Cody (1988) notes that Methodism began as a sect before evolving into a denomination), we should not overstate the similarities between the two.

### Development

Glock and Stark (1965) argue that sects normally develop around:

> **Religious dissent**, which involves things like dissatisfaction (disenchantment) with the prevailing religious orthodoxy or a belief that the 'purity' of a religious organisation's ideals are compromised through contacts with secular authorities.
> **Social dissent**, relating to feelings of individual **deprivation**. Glock and Stark suggest various types of deprivation that lead people to form or join sects:
>   > social — membership can provide status, prestige and power
>   > economic — looking for monetary benefits from membership
>   > ethical — where the values of the individual are not compatible with those of the group or society in which they live, a sect can provide a community of 'like-minded individuals'
>   > psychic — people 'searching for meaning and direction' in their lives find it in the sect's strict religious teachings

Deprivation

**S** ocial
**E** conomic
**E** thical
**P** sychic

Wilson (1982) relates sect development to rapid **social changes** that disrupt traditional norms and create feelings of confusion and despair for some individuals and groups. Sects offer a 'solution' to these problems by giving people something 'solid and lasting' in which to believe (an idea we'll examine further in terms of religious **fundamentalism**).

## Organisation

Organisation tends to be less formal than with churches/denominations. Sects place more emphasis on the following:

- **Leaders** (who may claim **divine authority**) rather than a professional clergy.
- **Regulation** — members' behaviour tends to be highly regulated, usually through strict rules enforced by sect members on each other. Depending on sect size, a leader and his (they are normally men) trusted followers may also take responsibility for rule enforcement.

## Size

Sects are small compared with churches or denominations, although size can be difficult to measure reliably:

- **Attendance**: Many sects don't hold the types of services common to churches and denominations — something that makes counting members or attendees difficult.
- **Membership**: For a variety of reasons sects may decline to disclose their membership numbers. Where they do provide such information we have to take its accuracy on trust.

## Exclusivity

Sects are exclusive organisations with membership characterised by:

- **choice** rather than birth
- **commitment** shown to the values and goals of the sect

Full membership is normally granted after a:

- probationary period
- testing of commitment

Scientology, for example, initially invites people ('preclears') to join, but continued membership is dependent on moving through various 'levels of knowledge'. Students (including Hollywood celebrities John Travolta and Tom Cruise) buy courses of instruction and submit to tests ('audits') before being allowed to pass to the next level.

## Ideology

Sects often claim special religious knowledge (such as the 'one true way to salvation') denied to non-members. For Scientology, this special knowledge is knowledge of oneself — how the problems of an individual's 'past lives' have created problems in their current life that need to be identified ('audited') and removed ('cleared'). Familiar ideological themes include:

> **salvation** for the 'chosen' (Jehovah's Witnesses, Heaven's Gate)
> **catastrophe**, usually involving an 'end-of-the-world' scenario (The People's Temple)
> **millenarianism**, involving ideas such as a belief in a return to a spiritual homeland (Rastafarians)

### Types

Although sects are many and varied, Yinger's (1957) typology classifies them in terms of how they see and react to the secular world (Table 9.2).

Table 9.2   Sects as reaction to the secular world

| Type | 'Problem' and its resolution |
|---|---|
| **Acceptance**<br>Example:Christian Science | Members are largely middle class and life has been personally good. The 'key problems' they face are personal and philosophical — such as searching for 'the meaning of life'. The resolution of social problems involves individual and collective faith, self-help and so forth. |
| **Opposition ('aggression')**<br>Example: Branch Davidian (Seventh Day Adventists) | Develop as a radical reaction to problems of poverty and powerlessness; membership is usually drawn from the lower social classes. They both oppose secular society and adopt a generally antagonistic attitude towards it. |
| **Avoidance**<br>Example: Exclusive Brethren | The significance of members' present life is downgraded by projecting their hopes onto the supernatural world; problems are addressed by appealing to a 'higher social order'. They avoid direct contact with secular society. |

Source: Yinger (1957)

Marczewska-Rytko (2003) offers a more contemporary take on sects (Table 9.3) by classifying them as **interest groups** — goal-orientated groups that offer incentives or benefits for members. Such groups try to 'share' these benefits with the rest of society, sometimes benevolently (Jehovah's Witnesses, for example, are tasked with giving everyone the opportunity to be saved from damnation) and sometimes more aggressively.

This relates to Stark and Bainbridge's (1987) **rational choice theory** of religious groups; they argue that sect members weigh up the likely *costs and benefits* of membership:
> Costs might include separation from former friends and family.
> Benefits might involve feelings of superiority through access to 'hidden knowledge' or the feeling of belonging to a strong, supportive, moral community.

**?**   How are a sect and a church different?

Table 9.3   Sects as interest groups

| Type | Sect orientation |
|------|------------------|
| **Reformative**<br>Example: transcendental meditation (TM) | The objective is to change people (in terms of their spiritual awareness) and, by so doing, 'reform the secular world'. The main focus is to convert as many as possible to the sect's world view. |
| **Revolutionary**<br>Example: Aum Shinrikyo (Japan) | The objective is to change a condemned social order, usually by awaiting some form of 'divine intervention' (usually an apocalyptic 'end of the world'). While some are happy to await Armageddon (Jehovah's Witnesses, for example), others are equally happy to try to help things along — members of the Aum Shinrikyo sect released sarin nerve gas in the Tokyo underground in 1995, killing 12 and injuring around 5,000. |
| **Introvert**<br>Example: Scientology | This type looks 'inward' to the spiritual well-being and welfare of members, who derive strength from feelings of moral superiority over the outside world. The focus is on personal development as members strive for spiritual enlightenment. |
| **Manipulative**<br>Example: neo-paganism | This focuses on the manipulation of things like the occult (magic, for example) for the benefit of practitioners. |

*Source: Marczewska-Rytko (2003)*

## New religious movements

Although the term 'new religious movement' (NRM) has been questioned (some 'new' religious movements simply involve a reworking of traditional religious ideas and practices and represent a new label for 'sects' or 'cults'), Barker (1999) argues that the label is justified because NRMs can be:

> ...defined as groups which have become visible in their present form since the Second World War, and which are religious in so far as they offer an answer to some of the ultimate questions traditionally addressed by mainstream religions: Is there a God? What is the purpose of life? What happens to us after death?

However we choose to label them, NRMs have a range of distinctive features:
- **Converts**: Many recruits will be first-generation converts; they were neither born into the religion nor have a family history of involvement. 'Early adopters' tend to be:
  - highly committed
  - highly enthusiastic
  - proselytising — keen to convert others to their faith; groups like Scientology and Hare Krishna use a variety of techniques to spread the word, from street selling to mail drops
- **Membership**: Recent (post-1970) NRMs attract more *young, middle-class* recruits than other religious organisations. This is partly because the young are more open to and desirous of new experiences and partly because this group is more likely to be targeted for recruitment.

➤ **Influence**: Many NRMs are led by a founder with the **charisma** to attract initial followers ('charisma' is the force of personality which enables someone to exert power over others — people want to obey charismatic individuals because they see them as attractive, forceful, exciting and so forth). This often gives such movements an **autocratic** structure involving an all-powerful leader who may directly control all or some of the day-to-day life of converts. A particular form of 'truth' is promoted that is less open to questioning by converts than the 'truths' promoted by churches and denominations.

➤ **Total institution** (arising from an autocratic structure): Goffman (1961) defines this as 'a place of residence and work where a large number of like-situated individuals, cut off from the wider society for an appreciable period of time, together lead an enclosed, formally administered round of life'.

➤ **Voluntarism** (how people make choices about their behaviour): Unlike in some other total institutions (prisons, for example), converts may consciously choose to become part of a total institution, for various reasons. For example, one of Cimino and Lattin's (2002) respondents in *Shopping for Faith* states: 'I want something that is going to change my finances, my sex life, the way I work, the way I keep my house and the way I fix my yard.'

➤ **Identity**: A sharp distinction is invariably made between 'Us' (the movement's members) and 'Them' (non-members or unbelievers).

➤ **Suspicion** (and antagonism) between NRMs, secular society and other religious organisations. Antagonism towards non-members can be an important way for an NRM to:

   ➤ carve out a clear identity in an increasingly crowded 'religious marketplace'
   ➤ maintain a strong sense of self once a niche has been created, by 'demonising the competition'

Wallis (1984) classifies NRMs in terms of their relationship to the secular world (Table 9.4).

Table 9.4   Typology of NRMs

| Type | Orientation to and relationship with the outside world |
| --- | --- |
| **World-rejecting**<br>Example: Heaven's Gate | Critical of the secular world and withdraw, as far as possible, from contact with it — usually in some form of communal living. |
| **World-accommodating**<br>Example: Jehovah's Witnesses | Although this type draws a distinction between the spiritual and the secular spheres, they neither reject nor promote the secular world. |
| **World-affirming**<br>Example: Scientology | This type claims to unlock people's 'hidden potential', spiritual or psychological. They see no need to withdraw from or reject the world (in some cases, quite the opposite — the objective is to achieve material success through spiritual means). |

*Source: Wallis (1984)*

**?**   **Give examples of features of new religious movements.**

## Explanations

We can outline a selection of explanations for the development of NRMs, many of which focus on how various types of **social change** promote their development:

➤ **Technological change**: Wuthnow (1986) argues that the development of scientific ideas and technological changes in society challenge the hegemonic or leadership role of religion and force changes to the way mainstream religious organisations interpret their relationship to the secular world; this results in established religions becoming increasingly liberal in their interpretation of religious scriptures as they try to reach out to and retain members. These changes within religious organisations produce **schisms** ('counter movements') as those opposed to liberalisation split from established religions, leading to an increase in NRMs.

➤ **Globalisation**: Rapid forms of political, economic and cultural change at the end of the twentieth century have created, according to Baudrillard (2001), a situation of 'postmodern uncertainty' that has led some to seek certainties in the teachings and moralities of both traditional (especially fundamentalist) and non-traditional religions — a situation that has arguably led to a **revitalisation** of NRMs in the 'postmodern age'.

➤ **Economic change**: Arjomand (1986) considered the impact of social change on non-Christian religions (such as Islam) and identified processes that both 'strengthen orthodox religiosity' and give rise to new religious movements within Islam:

   ➤ **Cultural integration**: As Islamic societies become integrated into the international economic system they face increasing competition from Western secular and religious ideas and philosophies. The response, among some groups, is a hardening of attitudes toward the West, expressed through radical Islamic movements.

   ➤ **Deprivation**: Urbanisation creates pressure for change where people react to worsening economic situations by developing new responses — which include both NRMs and a reinvigoration/reinterpretation of traditional religious movements.

   ➤ **Education**: As populations become more literate and formally educated they are exposed to a range of ideas that promote the development of new ways of interpreting the world.

➤ **Social unrest**: Eyre (1996) suggests that, particularly in America, NRM growth during the 1960s resulted from **disillusionment**, especially among the young, with both involvement in the Vietnam War and a general questioning of the materialistic values of society. One aspect of this 'rebellion' was to explore alternative lifestyles and beliefs.

➤ **Immigration**: The movement of people across different cultures and the introduction of new ideas into the host culture challenges religious **orthodoxy** ('the things people have always believed') and leads to the development of new religions through a process of **cultural hybridisation**. In the 1960s, for example, Eyre notes how a range of Eastern 'faiths and philosophies' met Western faiths and resulted in hybrid philosophies that subsequently developed into NRMs.

> **?** What reasons are there for the development of NRMs?

### Evaluation

Social change/social unrest explanations have been criticised because the major period of NRM growth occurred in the 1950s, a time of relative political and economic stability. More importantly, perhaps, we can question the extent to which NRM 'growth' is actually a **statistical illusion**: Beckford and Levasseur (1986) argue that recent improvements in the means of communicating ideas allowed NRMs to reach a mass audience. This meant the overall *visibility* of NRMs was increased, without there necessarily being an increase in their number. The development of internet technologies — websites, email and social networking in particular — may have accelerated or amplified this process.

They argue that there hasn't been a 'sudden, significant, explosion of NRMs' that needs to be explained. Rather, NRMs were simply following a 'traditional path' of emergence and growth; their apparent development can be explained by the fact they were able to get their message across to a larger audience. The traditional audience for NRMs (the urban young) are both those most affected by technological/social change and those most receptive to 'new' ideas about the nature of the world. Bruce (2002) argues that NRM membership was and remains relatively:

➤ small
➤ transient (people move into and out of these groups with great frequency)

This suggests that a more useful question is not *why* people are attracted to NRMs, but rather why so many people are *not* attracted to the 'solutions' they offer.

## New Age movements

New Age movements (NAMs) are an interesting and relatively recent development (Melton (2001), for example, argues: 'the term New Age refers to a wave of religious enthusiasm that emerged in the 1970s...only to subside at the end of the 1980s'). They illustrate two ideas:

➤ The '**new religiosity**': NAMs represent new ways of 'doing and being' religious, with the focus on finding solutions to problems through 'personal transformations' (which may or may not lead to wider social transformation). Brown (2004) suggests the range of New Age movements includes, for example:
   ➤ astrology
   ➤ channelling (direct communication with spirits)
   ➤ work with one's 'inner child'
   ➤ unconventional healing techniques

- ➢ **Spiritual consumption**: the idea that rather than being 'members' or 'believers' people 'shop for spirituality' — a search for personal salvation expressed, Cowan (2003) argues, through various individual preoccupations and concerns:
  - ➢ peace of mind
  - ➢ positive self-image
  - ➢ physical health
  - ➢ personal empowerment
  - ➢ enlightenment/insight

NAMs focus on '**transformations**', meaning ways of improving your life through personal changes. Langone (1993) identifies four main 'streams' within NAMs that involve different ways to 'transform the self' (Table 9.5).

Table 9.5   Streams of transformation

| 'Stream' | Transformation |
|---|---|
| **Transformational training** | Transforming personal life through a range of techniques and practices. |
| **Intellectualism** | Personal transformations through the exploration of 'alternative beliefs' rather than the practice of such beliefs. |
| **Lifestyle** | The transformation of society through behavioural changes (such as anti-globalisation movements or environmentalism). |
| **Occult** | Personal transformations through beliefs and practices such as witchcraft ('Wicca') and areas such as astrology, palmistry and crystal healing. |

*Source: Langone (1993)*

NAMs (and possibly NRMs) reflect changes within religious organisations characteristic of postmodern societies:

- ➢ **Fragmentation**: There are wide diversities both within and between different NAMs based around concepts of choice. 'Spiritual shoppers' are looking to buy solutions to problems and willing to consider whatever movement takes their fancy. Choice exists in terms of different 'ready-made' solutions and

a 'pick-and-mix' approach; 'consumers' pick bits they like from different NAMS (meditation, channelling, ear candling, etc.) and mix them to create something new and personal.
- ➢ **Individualism**: Sedgwick (2004) sees NAMS as a reflection of the individualistic tendencies of postmodern society — people 'want the feel-good factor, but not the cost of commitment. Putting it bluntly it is essentially selfish religion'.
- ➢ **Narratives**: NAMs do not 'speak with one voice' beyond a general belief in 'personal transformation'. The individualistic nature of NAMs makes the idea of a 'New Age **metanarrative**' difficult to pin down. All we have are a wide range of personal religious narratives.

> **?**   In what ways do an NAM and a church differ?

### Evaluation

A major question is whether NAMs are 'religions' in the conventional sense. Although there is a general concern with 'spirituality' (in a very wide and loose way), they have little or nothing in common with traditional forms of religious belief, experience and practice. The problem here, therefore, is whether we classify and explain them as something other than religion, or expand how we define 'religion' in postmodern society to include NAMs.

Perhaps they are 'disorganised religions'. Rather than seeing NAMs as organised religions, Sedgwick (2004) suggests we see them as 'private religions' that people can practise 'with minimal interruption to their normal routine and without having to bother about burdensome responsibilities'.

## Religious fundamentalism

'Fundamentalism' refers to any religious groups with 'fundamental religious beliefs' based on **literal** interpretations of religious texts. Sahgal and Yuval-Davis (1992) suggest fundamentalist religious movements have three common features:

➤ **Truth**: They claim their version of religion to be 'the only true one'.
➤ **Fear**: The movement feels threatened by alternative (secular and religious) views of the world. **Christian fundamentalism**, for example, sees both 'atheists' and 'Islam' as enemies.
➤ **Control** over members and non-members:
  ➤ ideological — over what members believe
  ➤ internal — over how members behave
  ➤ external — how people in secular society should behave

Fundamentalist movements 'reach outward' from their pool of believers to change the behaviour of non-believers (sometimes violently, sometimes peacefully). This control feature leads Sahgal and Yuval-Davis to make an interesting distinction:

➤ **Traditional religions** focus on the spiritual message which may or may not 'filter out' to secular society and lead to political changes. They are *religious movements with a political message*.
➤ **Fundamentalist religions** try to impose political changes on secular society using a variety of religious ideas. They are *political movements with a religious message*. Fundamentalist movements, the authors argue, are 'modern political movements which use religion as a basis for their attempt to win or consolidate power and extend social control'.

Giroux (2004) also sees Christian fundamentalism in America as closely aligned to the '**religious right**' (involving loose-knit groups such as the Moral Majority and, more recently (2010), the Tea Party movement). This alignment attempts to legitimise a particular political ideology (intolerant of difference, authoritarian and anti-democratic) with specific and selective forms of 'religious correctness'. The two meet in areas like:

➤ teaching creationism in schools

➤ bans on sex education

➤ subordinating scientific ideas (such as evolution or global warming) to religious dogma

Giroux explains the contemporary development of fundamentalist religious movements, Christian and Islamic, in terms of **globalisation**. Global economic and cultural processes expose people to different views and belief systems. This sometimes leads to a feeling of moral relativism, where nothing is wholly good and nothing wholly bad.

Without moral certainties the world appears a more frightening and dangerous place that leaves some people feeling 'alone, vulnerable and largely unconnected with those around them'. In this situation, 'fundamentalism taps...into very real individual and collective needs' by providing moral certainties 'given by God'.

Berer and Ravindran (1996) argue that fundamentalist religions appeal to 'supreme authorities, moral codes or philosophies that cannot be questioned'. They exist to impose a sense of order and stability on a world that, to some, has become disorderly, unstable and confusing. In postmodern societies, therefore, fundamentalist religions of all types provide believers with a sense of:

➤ **Identity**, based on literal interpretation of religious texts as expressions of 'God's will'.

➤ **Community**: What Castells (1997) calls a 'collective identity' based on a set of fundamental and unchanging moral certainties shared by believers and imposed on non-believers. As Bauman (1992) puts it, fundamentalist religions draw their strength from the ability to provide certainties in an uncertain world — from a belief in the principles laid down in the Old Testament of Christianity (an 'eye for an eye', for example) to the clear specification of how men and women should dress and behave in Islam.

---

**Exam-style questions**

**1** Identify and explain two characteristics of religious fundamentalism.　　(17 marks)

**2** Identify and explain two difficulties in measuring religious belief.　　(17 marks)

**3** Identify and explain two characteristics of new religious movements.　　(17 marks)

**4** Outline and evaluate the view that the rise of religious fundamentalism is a sign of religious revival.　　(33 marks)

---

# The role of religion in society

In this section we explore a range of structural and action perspectives on the role of religion in society.

## Functionalism

Traditional **functionalist** theories focus on understanding how religion contributes to the maintenance of social order. In this view religion functions as a **cultural institution** charged with the creation, promotion and maintenance of **cultural values**.

These values provide a **moral basis** for **social order**. Cultural institutions, which in contemporary societies include education and the mass media, help to create and maintain order and continuity in society by promoting the **collective conscience** — a set of meanings (beliefs and values, for example) that help people make sense of the social world. One function of religion, therefore, is to encourage people to believe they belong to that collective group we call 'society'.

To do this religion promotes **social solidarity** — the idea we're connected into a larger network of people who share certain beliefs, identities and commitments. For such feelings of solidarity to develop, however, societies must create mechanisms of **social integration** — the precise ways people gain a sense of belonging to something larger than the individual. Collective ceremonies and services, for example, serve this purpose.

On the basis of the above, Alpert (1939) suggests religion serves four major functions.

### Discipline

Shared beliefs and values are created by following a set of religious moral rules and codes. These 'common values' connect the individual to a greater whole — 'society'.

### Organisation

Religious ceremonies bring people together in situations where they put into practice their shared norms, values and experiences, thereby cementing and reinforcing social solidarity.

Ceremonies such as marriages and funerals also involve **symbols** with shared meanings. Ricoeur (1974) argues that symbols are important because 'by expressing one meaning directly' (a wedding ring, for example, directly symbolises marriage) they 'express another indirectly' (such as a moral commitment to a partner).

For Durkheim (1912), religious symbols reflected a significant distinction between the **sacred** (or special) and the **profane** (or everyday). The actual form of sacred symbols was unimportant. They could be:
- things (such as a book or an animal)
- ceremonies (like a wedding)
- places (such as the home of a prophet)

Their function was simply to help develop shared values — the fundamental things on which people could agree and, in so doing, be drawn closer together as a society.

### Vitalisation

Common values and beliefs are essential (or vital — hence 'vitalisation') dimensions of culture, socialisation and social control (also a function of religion). People use the 'ideas binding them together' as sources of:

➤ **identity** ('vitalisation') — we 'understand who we are' through membership of religious groups

➤ **revitalisation** — a common culture is transmitted from one generation to the next, thereby providing social continuities through things like religious traditions and customs

### Euphony (harmony)

There are times of pain and crisis in our lives that require individual or collective efforts to re-establish normality. Religion's euphonic function is expressed in:

➤ **Tension management**: Parsons (1937) argued that the religious rituals surrounding death serve to manage this traumatic situation by providing a social structure (the funeral) that permits and encourages certain forms of social action (such as grieving for a certain length of time). Farley (1990) also notes that religion provides psychological support in times of personal crisis.

➤ **Meaning**: In his study of the Trobriand Islanders, Malinowski (1926) noted how religion provided 'explanations for the inexplicable' (such as what happens when we die). Thompson (1986) suggests 'Religion offers an explanation of the events for which other frameworks could not account.'

Euphonic functions

**D** iscipline
**O** rganisation
**V** italisation
**E** uphony

Funerals provide emotional support by giving private grief a social structure

**?** **What are two functions traditionally performed by religions?**

## Neo-functionalism

Although many of the ideas we have just noted still have currency in contemporary British society, one obvious problem is that the majority of the population is not particularly 'religious'. Relatively few people, for example, actively participate in collective ceremonies and services outside of 'life events' such as marriages and funerals.

Neo-functionalists, therefore, have explored how religion has evolved in **postmodern** society to focus, as Luhmann (1977) argues, on very specific functions — such as to 'explain that which is not currently known or understood'.

### Diversity

Religion is seen as functional for some individuals and groups rather than 'society as a whole'. This follows because postmodern societies are characterised by cultural **diversity** and, in consequence, the social significance of organised religion (such as the Christian Church) has declined.

### Identity

For Kung (1990) the functions of religion have similarly evolved to focus on questions of **identity**. Gans (1971) argues that in culturally diverse societies 'few phenomena are functional or dysfunctional for society as a whole and most result in benefits to some groups and costs to others'. Membership of a religious organisation can confer certain benefits to individuals — by defining who they are, promoting clear moral guidelines and satisfying psychological, social and spiritual needs, for example. Such things, as Perry and Perry (1973) note, are 'particularly important in times of rapid social change, in which problems of identity are critical'.

### Dysfunctions

In this respect, neo-functionalism places much greater emphasis on **dysfunctions**. Merton (1957) argues that religion is not automatically and inevitably functional. In a culturally diverse society it can be dysfunctional when it creates conflict — some American Christian fundamentalist groups, for example, are violently opposed to abortion. As Bruce (1995) observes:

> Social scientists have long been aware of the role of religion as social cement; shared rituals and shared beliefs that bind people together... What is not so often noted is the idea religion often divides one group from another.

### Social change

The greater emphasis on small-scale functionality is expressed in terms of **social change**: religion can be a mechanism for change, as membership of a religious organisation may provide oppressed people with the solidarity and sense of purpose they need to challenge unjust laws. The black civil rights movement in 1960s America, for example, was organised and articulated through Christian church membership.

**?** Suggest one difference between functionalist and neo-functionalist perspectives on religion.

### Evaluation

#### Methodology

Methodologically, an important question is how to test or measure ('operationalise') the concept of function. How, for example, do we know whether something like religion is actually functional (and do these functions outweigh any dysfunctions)?

In addition, Durkheim (1912) argues that by worshipping an 'all-powerful' and 'all-seeing' (but stubbornly invisible) deity, what people are really doing is worshipping *society* (something that has similar properties). Religion, from this perspective, becomes 'the worship of society' — which is an interesting idea, but one that cannot be proved or disproved.

#### Inclusive theory

Functionalist theories focus more on what religion *does* (its functions) than on what it *is*, and this means *any* social institution can be considered 'a religion' if it performs the required functions. This idea is *convenient* because it allows functionalists to explain seemingly contradictory or mutually exclusive observations by using **functional alternatives**. For example:

➤ If religious observance and practice is widespread in a society, this is evidence for the function of religion.

➤ If religious practices decline (Christian church attendance has fallen steeply in Britain over the past century), the theory can be saved by reference to functional alternatives to religion that take over the role it previously performed. An example here is something like **football** performing a **social solidarity function** (large numbers of people sharing and showing their support for the national team).

#### Conflict

While neo-functionalism recognises that religious conflicts can be dysfunctional for both individuals and societies, we cannot separate functional from dysfunctional behaviour in a culturally diverse society. For example:

➤ Is religion functional or dysfunctional to atheists?

➤ Are Islamic beliefs functional or dysfunctional for Christianity?

> **?**  Give an example of a functional alternative to religion in our society.

# Marxism

The Marxist approach is based on the idea of **conflict** — that capitalist societies, for example, involve conflicts of economic interest between the bourgeoisie (or ruling class) and proletariat (or subject class). The role of religion in such societies is to promote a consensus that ultimately benefits a ruling class.

To understand how and why this happens we can begin by noting that **traditional Marxism** takes an **exclusive view** of religion: the focus is on the particular qualities of religion that make it *qualitatively* different from other forms of belief and practice.

In specific terms, traditional Marxists have explored the role of religion in promoting consensus through its status as a **belief system** — something capable of explaining 'everything about everything' (what postmodernists call a **metanarrative**). Religion shapes the way people see the world, and its role is to 'represent the world' in a way that reflects and supports the existing social order. In other words, it maintains the political and economic status quo (it keeps things as they are).

For Marx (1844), religion was an **oppressive force** in society — it worked to make people 'feel happy' about themselves and the world, even under conditions (as in England in the nineteenth century) that were grim for all but a small minority. The abject poverty and misery of the working class was a potential source of conflict with the ruling class (those who 'had everything'), and religious ideas and teaching were seen as a way to control the behaviour of the 'dangerous classes'.

For Marx, therefore, religion was a source of **social control** — its message was that everyone, rich and poor alike, should accept the world 'as it is'. Traditional Marxism saw the purpose of religion as to stifle conflict — to stop people questioning why poverty existed in a rich society. Religion was an efficient form of control because a 'belief in God' helped to:

- **Uphold the status quo**: The social world could be portrayed as 'god-given' and beyond the power of anyone to change.
- **Legitimise economic exploitation**: If God made the world, it was not people's place to question why some were rich and most poor.
- **Justify poverty**: Religion portrayed poverty as a virtue — something to be endured in an uncomplaining fashion. It was a means of achieving spiritual riches in heaven (once the individual was conveniently dead).

Marx (1884) called religion 'the opium of the people' because, like a painkilling drug, it 'dulled the pain of oppression' with its promise of eternal life (Christianity) or reincarnation into a higher social caste (Hinduism) for those who did their religious duty.

He also argued it was a form of **false consciousness** because by embracing religious ideas people failed to understand the real causes of their misery and oppression — an all-too-real man-made economic exploitation rather than an invisible 'God'.

### Evaluation

One problem with this approach is that Britain in the twenty-first century is a very different place from Britain in the nineteenth century — an observation that leads to major criticisms of traditional Marxist approaches.

### *False consciousness*

There are a couple of problems with this idea:

> **Historical**: Turner (1983) argues that if we measure religious conviction by church attendance, involvement in and membership of religious groups and the like, the working classes have never been particularly religious.
> **Contemporary**: Religion arguably has even less influence now than in the past. For most people it plays a relatively minor public role — restricted, in many instances, to 'hatching, matching and dispatching' (christenings, weddings and funerals).

These ideas cast doubt on religion as a significant form of social control.

### Conservative force

If religion supports the status quo and prevents social change, it can be difficult to explain its pivotal role in some secular conflicts:

> The **Iranian Revolution** of 1979 involved the overthrow of the (secular) regime of the Shah of Persia.
> **Liberation theology**: Boff and Boff (1987) note the involvement of Roman Catholic priests in revolutionary political movements in parts of South America from the 1960s onwards.
> The **civil rights movement**: In the USA, from the 1960s onwards, social change was promoted and supported by black religious activists and leaders (such as Martin Luther King).

The Reverend Martin Luther King's 'I have a dream' speech in 1963 was inspirational in the American civil rights movement

## Neo-Marxism

Partly as a result of social changes (Britain is a more culturally diverse society now than in the past) and partly because of weaknesses in the idea of false consciousness, neo-Marxism has embraced the idea of **hegemony** to explain the role of religion in contemporary society. Originally put forward by Gramsci (1934) and developed by Poulantzas (1974), hegemony involves the idea that beliefs about the world that benefit a ruling class are not simply imposed by religious organisations.

Rather, as Strinati (1995) suggests, ruling groups maintain their dominant position through the 'consent' of those lower down the social scale, something 'manufactured' by **cultural institutions** such as religion, education and the media (what Althusser (1972) calls '**Ideological State Apparatuses**'); all these, in their different ways, transmit messages supporting the status quo. For example, one common message is the idea that there are legitimate ways to express dissent and discontent — like voting for a change of government or marching to protest against particular social policies — that don't directly challenge the status quo (and the hegemony of the ruling class).

Hegemony makes it possible for 'religious ideas' to be seen as influential in contemporary societies without the majority of people necessarily either believing or supporting them. Strinati, for example, suggests the lower classes 'accept the ideas, values and leadership of the dominant group not because they are physically or mentally induced to do so, nor because they are ideologically indoctrinated'; rather, they do so because they are powerless to challenge or change them.

Rather than seeing the lower classes 'indoctrinated' by religion into ideas that benefit the ruling class, Turner (1983) argues that neo-Marxists see religion as a **cohesive force for a ruling class**. Religion represents one way the various elements of a ruling class come to see themselves as a 'class apart' that has political and economic interests to pursue. Religion provides a set of moral guidelines for ruling-class behaviour in relation to things like marriage and the inheritance of property (Christianity, for example, laid down the rules for legitimate relationships and hence for the inheritance of property).

> **?** How does religion support the status quo in society?

# Weberianism

Weberian approaches focus less on what religion *does* (its functions or ideological purpose) and more on what it *means*, for:

➤ **Individuals**: This involves studying, for example, the motivations, behaviours and beliefs of those who classify themselves as religious.

➤ **Society**: This looks at 'collective religious beliefs' existing in a particular society and how these influence the development of **cultural identities**, legal systems or, in Weber's case, a complete economic system (capitalism) — an example we can use to both introduce Weberian ideas and demonstrate Weber's argument that religion can be a force for **social change**.

Weber (1905) wanted to understand why capitalism had developed in some societies but not others, even though they had reached similar levels of economic and technological development.

He argued it was religion (or a particular form of Protestant religion called Calvinism) that provided the 'final push', allowing Britain to change, in the late sixteenth century, from a relatively poor, agriculture-based, **pre-modern** society into an immensely rich, modern, **industrial society**. It was Calvinism, Weber argued, that provided the 'spirit of capitalism' — a unique set of ideas, beliefs and practices — that promoted a strong and lasting social transformation.

The basis of this 'spirit' was the idea of **predestination**: Calvinists believed God would know before someone was born whether they were destined to achieve salvation — and nothing they could do would change this situation. However, since God was not going to allow people who sinned into heaven, the way to prove (to yourself and others) you were one of those destined for heaven — the 'Chosen' or 'Elect' — would be, as

Bental (2004) notes, to 'associate morality and Godliness with hard work, thriftiness, and the reinvestment of money'. In basic terms, those destined for salvation had to be:

➢ successful (throughout life)
➢ hard-working
➢ moral
➢ thrifty (prudent in how they spent their money)
➢ modest

Weber argued that these were just the kinds of attribute required to develop capitalism — an economic system based around creating and reinvesting profits to ensure long-term business success.

> **?** Briefly explain the meaning of predestination.

### Evaluation

Evaluations of Weber's analysis focus on:

➢ **Meaning**: The analysis is a good example of how meaning can be shown to influence social action. Calvinism involved a belief in predestination, which meant believers developed norms and values resulting in a specific form of behaviour.
➢ **Methodology**: The argument that Calvinism was a 'cause of capitalism' has been questioned. Tawney (1926), for example, argued that capitalism came into being through technological developments that revolutionised the way goods could be produced and distributed. Fanfani (2003) suggests capitalism developed in some areas of Europe where Calvinism was not a religious force.
➢ **Calvinism**: Viner (1978) argues that where Calvinism was the dominant religion in a society it acted as a conservative force that put a brake on economic development and change. Calvinist Scotland, for example, developed capitalism much later than England.

Although there are arguments over the role of religion in the development of capitalism, one obvious question is: 'why should events 300-odd years ago concern us here?' The answer, perhaps, is that of trying to establish evidence for a general **principle**: while structural theory suggests religion is always a conservative force, action theories generally argue that there is no reason why religion should not be a force for change.

In this respect, contemporary Weberian analyses look at the various ways religion can be a **focus for dissent** — a channel through which discontent can be expressed. Examples here include:

➢ **Liberation theology**: Bruneau and Hewitt (1992), for example, argue that in Brazil the Catholic Church became a 'vehicle for working with the poor' as a way of promoting social and economic changes.

> **Arab Spring**: In 2011 many Arabic countries experienced pro-democracy protests on a huge scale. In Egypt, for example, religious organisations such as the Muslim Brotherhood played a role in organising and channelling dissent.

## Neo-Weberian ('interactionist') theories

Contemporary Weberian (or 'interactionist') theories have focused on how 'collective religious beliefs' function as **belief systems** — ways, for Berger (1973), of organising knowledge about the world. Before the development of scientific explanations, for example, religion provided a way to explain events in a seemingly chaotic and threatening world. Religious beliefs, he argues, impose a sense of meaning and order on a world threatened by things like death, disaster and disease that cannot be explained in any other way.

By its ability to 'explain the inexplicable', religion encourages certainty — there is nothing religion cannot explain — an idea that links into religious fundamentalism. It also links to explanations for the role and persistence of religion in contemporary societies through **culture mapping**: religious beliefs are part of the 'mental maps' that help us to navigate our way through increasingly complex cultural formations (the problems we face, for example, in making sense of our place in a diverse, multicultural society). Religion helps to guide our understanding by:

> explaining our experiences
> interpreting their meaning and significance
> creating common cultural meanings

| ? | How does religion produce 'common cultural meanings'? |

Whether or not we're 'personally religious' is not particularly important because the way we look at and understand the social world is shaped by religious beliefs, behaviours and practices. We can be:

> **Strongly influenced**: Some groups live their lives in accordance with strict moral teachings derived from their religion.
> **Weakly influenced**: While other groups may, at times, make reference to 'Christian', 'Islamic' or whatever values, they have no strong allegiance to a particular religion.

The relationship between belief systems and cultural mapping is significant because it helps us understand how and why religious ideas change and persist throughout the history of a society. It also explains why some groups hold very strong religious beliefs while others have weak or indeed no religious attachment.

This view involves an **inclusive approach** to religion: Neo-Weberian sociology explores how religious ideologies provide an organising structure to our lives. The specific content of religious beliefs is, consequently, of no real importance — what matters is that they are believed because they 'plausibly explain something'. If religious beliefs cease to be **plausible explanations** they are discarded or replaced with more plausible explanations. Luckmann (1967), for example, suggests this 'plausibility test' explains why religious practice is less in contemporary societies. Although people still seem to hold relatively high levels of individual belief, there are different areas of plausibility:

➤ **The public**, where religions 'compete for plausibility' with other belief systems (such as science) that may have greater plausibility.

➤ **The private** — the realm of individual beliefs where questions of identity, what happens when you die and so forth are reduced to private, personal concerns to which religion may provide plausible answers (sometimes in the absence of any other sort of answer).

### Evaluation

#### Structure and action

Weberian sociology overplays the significance of action and underplays the importance of social structures in explaining religious behaviour. Wuthnow (1992), for example, argues that this perspective neglects to examine how and why social conditions influence our beliefs: 'When research finds Christian friendships reinforce Christian convictions, the question still remains why some people choose Christian friends and others do not.' The suggestion is that religious beliefs and behaviours persist because they serve important and significant functions for both the individual and society.

#### Inclusiveness

One of the problems with an inclusive view of religion is that just about anything can be considered 'religious' if it seems to perform a particular role in supporting a belief system. This also applies to beliefs and behaviours that are only nominally religious. New Age religions (involving things like crystal healing and an emphasis on 'spirituality') have little or nothing in common with conventional religions aside from their general classification as 'religions'. In this respect it is very difficult to evaluate the influence of 'religious beliefs' in contemporary societies when it's impossible to define what is meant by this idea.

# Postmodern approaches

Grassie (1997) suggests postmodernism 'represents a great range of viewpoints' that are frequently difficult to group into a coherent and unified perspective. Taylor (1987), for example, observes that 'postmodernist' approaches to religion include those who argue:

➤ 'God is dead' and religion is disappearing
➤ we are seeing a 'return of traditional faith' (**resacrilisation**)
➤ religion is evolving and taking new and different forms

While it is difficult to reconcile these different views under the banner of a 'postmodern perspective', it's possible to identify a range of general concepts that can be applied to a 'postmodern understanding' of religion, based around the concepts of narrative and metanarrative:

➤ **Narrative**: Knowledge about the world consists of stories that compete to explain something. From this position, religion represents just another form of narrative.

➤ **Metanarrative** (or 'Big Story'): Metanarratives are all-encompassing stories that seek to explain 'everything about something' (or, as Vaillancourt-Rosenau (1992) suggests in the case of both religious and scientific metanarratives, 'everything about everything'). Religious metanarratives represent a general framework around which individual beliefs, practices and experiences can be orientated and ordered. It follows that metanarratives invariably involve a claim to **exclusive truth** about whatever it is they're explaining.

For Lyotard (1979), postmodernism involves an 'incredulity toward metanarratives'; that is, in postmodern society there is a denial that any single set of beliefs — religious, scientific or whatever — has a monopoly of truth. This also means, as Ritzer (1992) notes, that postmodern approaches reject the idea of social structures and perspectives (such as functionalism and Marxism) that are based on this kind of approach.

Scepticism about religious metanarratives as plausible explanations of the world means two things:

➤ a decline in the ability of religion to exert significant power and control over people's lives

➤ a gradual retreat into 'local narratives' — small stories about people's situations and circumstances

## Identity

Where religion continues to exert influence, however, is in terms of individual identities. In postmodern society people are exposed to a wide (globalised) variety of sources of information and ideas, both religious and secular, that compete for attention, and this involves a range of choices. This encourages:

➤ **Scepticism towards metanarratives**: For every 'big story' there are a multitude of 'alternative stories'.

➤ **Hybrids**: Postmodern society encourages the development of *new* ways of thinking and acting out of the combination of *old* ways of thinking and behaving. This includes new forms of religious belief and experience.

## Consumption

In postmodern society identity is related to patterns of consumption ('I shop therefore I am') and religion becomes just one more choice in the consumer market place — if Catholicism isn't to your taste or doesn't suit your lifestyle then when not try Kabbalah?

In the global marketplace:

➤ Religious **symbols** lose much of their original meaning and power as they are adopted into the everyday (profane) world of fashion and display — an example being the way Rastafarian religious symbols (such as dreadlocks) have been co-opted into some parts of mainstream fashion.

➤ Religious **practice**, in the sense of attending church services, no longer holds a central place in people's everyday lives or identities (we're too busy or too preoccupied with other aspects of life and leisure). Instead, it lives on as a set of adornments to the construction of identity — something that occurs not only in the world of objects (rings and pendants, for example), but also in the world of beliefs.

New forms of religious belief develop not as metanarratives but as part of individual narratives. These, as with the objects that accompany them, are 'picked up, worn for a time and then discarded', much as one might wear a fashionable coat until it becomes unfashionable.

A good example of the way some forms of religion have become 'identity statements' might be Kabbalah. Graham (2004) describes how:

> Shopping for Kabbalah is the newest new age mantra of anyone who wants to attach themselves to the craze, but doesn't necessarily want to invest years in earnest study. While most of us will never fully appreciate the intimacies of the ancient mystical Jewish religion, enthusiastic consumers often argue that the ritual and the ecstasy of shopping is nothing short of a religious experience.

Kabbalah, in common with other forms of New Age religion, fits the postmodern condition perfectly. It involves little:

➤ Commitment: All you need are 'Unconditional Love' dog-tags.
➤ Practice: Just wear a red string on your wrist to 'ward off evil'.
➤ Difficult belief: Just wear the T-shirt proclaiming 'Listen to your soul'.

## Contradictory beliefs

Postmodernism reflects (or encourages) a contradictory set of beliefs about the significance of religious ideas, practices and organisations in both the past and the present. At one and the same time, for example, we see discussion about:

➤ **Religious decline**: Organised religions lose their ability to control and influence events in the secular (non-religious) world.

➤ **Religious development**: Religious beliefs and practices shift and change, reflecting perhaps basic beliefs in 'supernatural phenomena', but expressed in ways far removed from organised religious services. In this respect, 'religions' are seen as being constantly reinvented to reflect the ways people choose and discard different forms of personal identity (Kabbalah being a case in point). This idea leads to a further observation:

➤ **Resacrilisation**: One of the odd things about religion in postmodernity, McLeod (1997) suggests, is that it becomes:

> less important in terms of practice (fewer people joining or attending church, for example)
> more important as a source of personal and social identity

Thus the very (globalising) processes that cause people to lose faith in the power of metanarratives also mean that in a world that appears increasingly confusing, unstable, risky and dangerous, religions become beacons of order and stability by their ability to produce moral certainties.

This is reflected in ideas like the **privatisation** and **deprivatisation** of religion. Although there are clear signs of a move towards privatised forms of religious belief (religion as something practised in the private rather than the public sphere), organised religion stubbornly refuses to disappear. On the contrary, there is evidence (with some forms of Islam and Christianity in particular) of a process of organised religion re-emerging as a significant aspect of public life.

| **?** | Why should we see religion as a metanarrative? |
|---|---|

### Evaluation

> **Metanarratives**: Callinicos (1991) argues that postmodernism itself is a form of the 'metanarrative thinking' postmodernists claim to dismiss as being unsustainable.
> **Inclusiveness**: Rtizer (2008) argues that it is a mistake to consider different types of belief (such as science and religion) as being more or less the same simply because they are both metanarratives. Theories of evolution, for example, are backed up with logical, empirical evidence; creationism (or 'intelligent design', a belief about how the Earth was created based on a literal interpretation of the Christian Bible) is based on little more than faith in biblical texts and a lot of wishful interpretation.

---

**Exam-style questions**

**1** Outline and evaluate the functionalist view of the role of religion in society.  (33 marks)

**2** Outline and evaluate Marxist views of the role of religion in society.  (33 marks)

**3** Outline and evaluate the view that religion promotes social change.  (33 marks)

---

# Religion and social position

This section explores the relationship between religiosity and social position considered in terms of four variables: class, age, gender and ethnicity.

Much of the information we have about the relationship between social position and religiosity is based on survey material from sources such as:

> **government departments** — e.g. the Home Office's citizenship survey and the ten-yearly census

➤ **private polling organisations** — e.g. YouGov, the internet-based polling organisation

➤ **religious organisations**, some of which produce attendance and membership figures

As we have previously noted when looking at beliefs and participation, we need to keep questions of data **reliability** and **validity** in mind here. Data about sects, and new religious and New Age movements in particular tend to be patchy and partial. This means anything we say about the relationship between religion and social position must be considered in the light of the methodological difficulties in collecting reliable and valid data.

**?** How can we gather data about religion and social position?

## Social class

We can outline a range of associations between class and religiosity.

### Belief

There is little significant class difference in beliefs surrounding ideas such as:

➤ **Religious affiliation**: The working classes are slightly more likely to describe themselves as Protestant or Roman Catholic, whereas the middle classes are slightly more likely to describe themselves as 'other Christian' (Jews, however, are three times more likely to be middle class than working class).

➤ **Prayer**: Slightly more middle-class people believe in praying.

➤ **General beliefs**: There seems to be no significant class difference in terms of belief in things like heaven, God, life after death, the devil and hell.

### Practice

In terms of attendance at religious services:

➤ **Regular attendees** (weekly or monthly): Around three times more of the middle classes classify themselves in this way.

➤ **Occasional attendees**: Little significant class difference.

➤ **Never attend** (apart from ceremonies such as weddings and funerals): The working classes are slightly more likely to 'never attend'.

### Characteristics

O'Beirne (2004) suggests there are general social **characteristics** of different faith groups involving:

➤ **Occupation**: Christians were more likely than any other faith to be employed in middle-class occupations.

➤ **Civic participation** (such as membership of voluntary groups): With the exception of 'Christian respondents of black or mixed race ethnicity', an important indication of the way social class combines with other statuses, in this case ethnicity, religious affiliation made no difference to participation levels.

➤ **Education**: General levels of education were higher among those with no religious affiliation. Among faith groups:

   ➤ Jews and Hindus were more likely to have higher-level qualifications (such as a university degree).

   ➤ Christian and Muslim faiths had the 'smallest proportions with the highest educational qualifications' and were most likely, of all faith groups, to have no formal educational qualifications.

If we change the focus slightly, O'Beirne notes that those 'affiliated to particular faiths share certain socioeconomic experiences and characteristics' in terms of:

➤ **Status**: In the past, religion was a source of status for both the upper and middle classes — the former in terms of their positions within powerful religious institutions and the latter in terms of using things like church attendance as a way to demonstrate 'respectability'.

➤ **Group identity**: It is arguable whether, in contemporary Britain, religion functions as a source of group identity in quite the same way (if at all) as in the past. Colls (2005), for example, argues that in postmodern society the relationship between 'religion and respectability' that was once a feature of class identity markers (to be middle class meant attending church) no longer holds true.

➤ **Individual identity**: O'Beirne found little evidence of religious belief/practice forming a significant part of self-identity; only 20% of 'Christians' considered religion 'an important part of their personal description' (and even then religion came somewhere down the scale after family, age and work). For some minority faith communities (such as Muslims and Hindus) religion was more likely to be seen as a significant part of their identity — but this was true for all social classes within the community.

➤ **Class cohesion**: We noted earlier the neo-Marxist argument that religion serves as a cohesive force for a ruling class in capitalist society, rather than as a means of keeping the lower classes in their place. O'Beirne found the highest levels of religious affiliation amongst respondents with the lowest levels of social deprivation, except for one significant exception: Muslim faith was associated with high levels of deprivation — a finding that suggests the relationship between ethnicity and class is perhaps more significant than social class alone.

> ? How is religion related to social class?

### Explanations

In general, there seems to be no *strong* relationship between class and religiosity in contemporary British society. We can examine a number of explanations for this. One argument is that in relation to **identities**, postmodern societies are different from those of the past in two ways:

➢ **Individuals**: People are less likely to define themselves in terms of class. Religious belief and behaviour is, consequently, less likely to have a strong association with individual class identities.

➢ **Institutions**: Finke and Stark (2004) argue that **religious pluralism** is a feature of contemporary societies: the 'religious consumer' enjoys a wide range of choice between and within religions. They argue that religious affiliation now relates to 'individual, personal identities' rather than the 'collective, social identities' of the past. The weakening of 'traditional class associations', coupled with increased consumer choice, explains why social class no longer correlates very closely with affiliation. As Bruce (2001) notes, the logic of this argument is that 'competitive free markets [in religion] are better at meeting not only material but also spiritual needs'.

## Age

The relationship between religiosity and age is methodologically more straightforward because we can reliably measure age.

In terms of what people say they believe, identification with religious beliefs, practices and organisations varies **intergenerationally**. Christian affiliation (Table 9.6) has a distinctive age profile.

Table 9.6   Christian affiliation by age from 2001 census

| Age group | % of Christians |
|-----------|-----------------|
| 0–15 | 18 |
| 16–34 | 22 |
| 35–64 | 41 |
| 65 and over | 19 |

Source: Census 2001 (Office for National Statistics, 2003)

O'Beirne (2004) found that all major UK faith communities (Muslim, Hindu, Jewish, Sikh and Buddhist) show increasing affiliation with age. She also found those affiliated to a religion to be older on average than those who were not.

In relation to **beliefs**, YouGov (2007) found:

➢ Belief in God was highest in the 55+ age group.

➢ It was lowest among the young (18–34).

➢ The reverse was true for non-belief.

➢ Nearly twice as many elderly as young respondents expressed a belief in prayer.

➢ In terms of 'basic Christian beliefs' there was little appreciable age difference.

One of the most striking features of 'belief' is that a significant and consistent majority of young people have expressed no positive religious belief or affiliation:

➤ 60+% in YouGov (2007)
➤ 60+% in British Social Attitudes Survey (2000)
➤ 65% in Park et al. (2004)

Park et al. also note the trend of an increasing number of adults with no religious affiliation.

In relation to **practice**, Brierley (1999) concludes that not only are churchgoers 'considerably older than non-churchgoers', but the age gap has widened over the past 25 years — a trend consistent across all major Christian faiths. One explanation, Bruce (2001) argues, is the inability of the established church to **socialise** young people into religious belief and behaviour. The decline in Sunday school membership, for example — from 55% of the population in 1900 to 4% in 2000 — is indicative of the inability of established churches to capture and keep young adherents.

### Explanations

#### Generation gap

The '**generation gap**' refers to age-related differences in attitudes and behaviour; and when it comes to religiosity there's a widening gap between the religious behaviour of different generations. As Jowell and Park (1998) put it, 'All the differences between age groups...are minor in comparison with those on religion. The fact is the young are overwhelmingly less religious than their elders.' There are various possible reasons for this.

#### Lifestyle

Traditional forms of belief and practice appeal less to the young than to the elderly, which may reflect lifestyle situations and choices. O'Beirne argues that the young have less time available to commit to religious practice. Religion has to compete for time with many more alternative activities than in the past; watching popular professional sports like football, for example, is now as likely to take place on a Sunday as the traditional Saturday.

While traditional forms of religion have declining appeal to the young, the same is not necessarily true, as Bader (2003) notes, of **NRMs** or **evangelical missions** (which have a strong resemblance to some NRMS) within established churches. These offer, as Cooke (2003) notes, nightclub-style services, complete with flashing lights and rock music, overseen by a 'worship director'.

#### Anti-fundamentalism

Although religious certainties can be attractive for some, the reverse may also be true; prescriptive moral codes (such as the anti-abortion, anti-contraception and anti-gay teachings of some religions) may be, in the words of one of Robins et al.'s (2002) young respondents, 'a big turn-off'. Where organised religions no longer have a 'monopoly of knowledge', they have consequently lost some of their ability to control how people think about the world.

Stark and Bainbridge (1987) found evidence of **NAMs** being popular among older age groups, while Francis and Robbins (2004) found evidence among young (13–15-year-old) males of **implicit religion**: the idea of 'believing without belonging' is an increasingly significant trend in contemporary societies among the young.

### Disengagement

As people get older they progressively 'retreat' from a society that, in turn, disengages from them. The ageing process, for Cumming and Henry (1961), involves a (functional) 'coming to terms' with death, the ultimate disengagement; religious belief (if not necessarily practice) increases as a way of coping with death psychologically. A decline in religious practice in our society among the 65+ age group can be explained in terms of **reduced physical mobility**. While this may be true for believers (religiosity increases with age), Hunsberger (1985) argues that there is little evidence that 'young nonbelievers' become 'elderly believers'.

Age and religiosity

**G** ap
**L** ifestyle
**A** nti
**D** isengagement

> **?**  How is religion related to age?

## Gender

Walter and Davie (1998) argue that 'women are more religious than men on virtually every measure', including:

➤ **Affiliation**: O'Beirne (2004) notes that across the major UK religions more women than men claimed some form of affiliation. Of those classed as non-religious, 60% were men.
  ➤ British Social Attitudes Surveys (1983–99) showed men are less religious than women and their affiliation is rapidly declining.
  ➤ Census 2001 showed women have greater levels of involvement in non-traditional religions such as spiritualism and Wicca (both nearly 70% female), with some variations — Rastafarianism, for example, was 70% male.
➤ **Belief**: The British Social Attitudes Survey (2008) found that women demonstrate higher levels of belief in:
  ➤ God
  ➤ prayer
  ➤ life after death, heaven, the devil
  Men were also more likely to be atheist and agnostic.
➤ **Participation**: In terms of Christian religions:
  ➤ Crockett and Voas (2004) suggested young women were more likely to attend services.
  ➤ O'Beirne found women slightly more likely than men to participate 'in groups or clubs with a religious link'.

Only Muslim men showed higher participation levels and one reason for this may be cultural norms relating to gender — women not being allowed to participate independently of men in religious activities.

In relation to **power and authority**, Malmgreen (1987) points out: 'In nearly every sect and denomination of Christianity, though men monopolized the positions of authority, women had the superior numbers.'

### Explanations

#### Gender socialisation

One explanation for greater levels of female religiosity involves the idea that men and women develop different cultural identities. This has been used by feminists in particular to explain participation differences based on **patriarchy**. Christianity, Steggerda (1993) notes, promotes concepts of love and care that are more attractive to women, and Daly (1973) argues that in a 'male-dominated world' religions provide women with a sense of:

➤ shelter (a 'home and haven')
➤ safety in a threatening world
➤ belonging (a sense of personal identity)

The price women pay for these benefits, she argues, is submission to patriarchal control.

**Fundamentalist** sects and denominations generally emphasise an exaggerated form of 'traditional' gender roles and relationships. Bartkowski (2000), for example, notes the driving theme behind the American-based Promise Keepers sect is the 'rejuvenation of godly manhood'.

#### Feminisation

Swatos (1998) argues that many contemporary religions are undergoing fundamental changes that make them more 'female friendly'. God, for example, is portrayed as loving and consoling rather than as authoritarian and judgemental, and clergy are seen as 'helping professionals' rather than as 'representatives of God's justice'.

### Evaluation

Miller and Stark (2002) argue that there is little hard evidence to support the idea that 'gender differences in religiousness are a product of differential socialization'.

In terms of **evolutionary psychology**, Kanazawa and Still (2000) link a lack of religiosity in men to their predisposition towards 'risky behaviours' (such as not believing in God); as Stark (2002) notes, 'in every country and culture men were less religious than women'.

Lizardo and Collett (2005), however, argue that although there are differences in 'risk-taking behaviour' between men and women, there are also differences between different groups of men and different groups of women. They suggest 'gender differences in risk preference are closely related to class based differences in the socialization of children; women raised in patriarchal families are more likely to be risk-averse than men raised in the same type of households and women raised in more egalitarian households'.

**?** How can religion be related to gender?

## Ethnicity

Although we need to keep in mind Cooke's (2003) warning that 'Collecting data on ethnicity is difficult because...there is no consensus on what constitutes an 'ethnic group', Table 9.7 outlines religious affiliation in Britain by selected ethnic groups (very small percentages of some faiths are not included: around 0.5% of white British are Jewish, for example).

Table 9.7   Ethnicity and religious affiliation from 2001 census

| Ethnic group | Percentage of each ethnic population | | | | | |
|---|---|---|---|---|---|---|
| | Christian | Hindu | Muslim | Sikh | Buddhist | None/unstated |
| White British | 76 | | | | | 23 |
| Black Caribbean | 74 | | | | | 24 |
| Indian | 5 | 45 | 13 | 29 | | 6 |
| Pakistani | | | 92 | | | 7 |
| Bangladeshi | | | 92 | | | 7 |
| Chinese | 21 | | | | 16 | 62 |

Source: Census 2001 (Office for National Statistics, 2004)

Although these data don't tell us a great deal about beliefs or affiliation strength (the 76% of 'Christian white British' are unlikely to share similar levels of affiliation), there are some useful points we can note.

Our society has a range of ethnicities and religious affiliations, considered not just in terms of different ethnic groups associated with different religions, but also in terms of the **diversity** of affiliation *within* some ethnic groups (Indian, for example).

When comparing two apparently similar ethnic groups (such as Indian and Pakistani, often grouped as 'South Asians'), wide disparities of affiliation exist. The different forms of affiliation found among Indian respondents (Hindu, Muslim and Sikh, for example) suggest a higher level of ethnic *fragmentation* among this group than among Pakistanis.

How significant this might be, in terms of study and behaviour, is related to questions of **identity**. Just as we would avoid claiming that all 'white Christians' share similar norms, values and beliefs, we should be wary of attributing this to ethnic minority groups. O'Beirne (2004), however, has noted that religion is a relevant factor 'in a person's self-description, particularly for people from the Indian subcontinent', mainly because immigrant groups use religion as a way of hanging on to a sense of cultural and ethnic identity when moving to a different country. In the 2001 census, for example:

> White British ranked religion as the tenth most important aspect of their identity; Asians ranked it second.
> Christians ranked religion the seventh most important aspect of their identity; Muslims, Sikhs and Hindus ranked it second.

The optional nature of the census question means it's impossible to know exactly how many of those not stating a religion did so because they considered it a private matter, didn't know how to classify themselves or whatever. However, there were wide ethnic differences in **non-religious affiliation**: a relatively high number in some ethnic groups (British and Chinese, for example) and a relatively low number in others (such as Pakistani).

We need to note a problem of **validity**. Those self-classifying as belonging to various new religious movements/sects may not see their beliefs in the 'conventional religious terms' defined by Census 2001; they may also have used the 'not stated' category as a way of recording their beliefs.

### Explanations

As we've seen, the highest levels of religious affiliation are found among Pakistani (92%) and Bangladeshi (92%) minorities, and Berthoud (1998) notes that these groups are among the very poorest in Britain.

**Deprivation** alone is not, however, a sufficient explanation for higher levels of religiosity since, as we've seen, the highest levels of Christian affiliation are found in the higher social classes. Crockett and Voas (2004) also note that, regardless of class, 'All major ethnic minority populations are more religious than British-born whites.' The question, therefore, is: 'Why do some ethnic groups but not others display high levels of religiosity under similar economic circumstances?'

The answer can be found by returning to the idea of **identity** — and, in particular, the idea that minority ethnic groups (especially those of recent origin in Britain) are more likely to use religion as an important component of identity. Bruce (1995) explains the reasoning behind this association in terms of the idea that in contemporary secular societies a distinction arises between two spheres of behaviour and practice involving different values and norms:

> The **public** sphere is governed by ideas of science, instrumental relationships and, most importantly, universal values and norms (as he argues, 'Supermarkets do not vary prices according to the religion, gender or age of the customer'). This sphere is that of the **community** — a space where people meet, greet and interact according to a set of shared ideas and beliefs.
> The **private** sphere is characterised by ideas of expression and affection. It is also a space where the individual is set apart from the communal, public sphere.

Bruce argues that Christianity has evolved to **accommodate** itself to secular changes in the public sphere (such as secular politics, globalisation and cultural diversity) and, by so doing, has slowly retreated from the public sphere of religious practice into the private sphere of religious belief. The church has been forced to come to terms with the idea that, for the ethnic majority, the role and function of organised religion has changed. Religion is no longer needed to perform functions like:

➢ communality (bringing people together)
➢ social solidarity
➢ identity

As the Christian church loses its public functions, attendance and practice also decline — but religion doesn't necessarily disappear from people's lives; rather, Christianity has, Bruce argues, been reworked into the **private sphere**. It has become a largely private matter, even though there are times when, as Davie (2001) argues, religious practice is important, usually in terms of **life events** (e.g. marriages and funerals) that require both private and public acknowledgement.

For minority groups, Bruce argues, the situation is different; they have moved from a situation in which 'their religion was dominant and all-pervasive to an environment in which they form a small, deviant minority, radically at odds with the world around them'. Recent immigrant groups frequently find themselves in, at best, an indifferent world and, at worst, one that's hostile and uninviting — and they look to the traditions, customs, values and norms that are familiar and certain in their lives. These need to be affirmed and reaffirmed through public religious practices because they relate to the solidarity and identity of social groups rather than individuals.

Similarly, religions such as Islam, Davie suggests, are articulated in the **public sphere** and create **belonging** — not just in the sense of 'belonging to a religion or organisation', but also of belonging to a specific, definable **group**, membership of which is affirmed through public practices. Religiosity performs significant services and functions for ethnic minority groups:

➢ **Social identity** provides a sense of homogeneity, shared purpose, history and permanence. This involves both a sense of **group self** ('who we are') and, by definition, a sense of the **Other** ('who we are not').
➢ **Emotion** involves a psychosocial sense of belonging and well-being created by membership of a particular religion. For some minority groups the emotional aspect of religious belief and practice is valued in a world that appears hostile and dangerous.
➢ **Power**: For politically and economically marginalised minorities, belonging to a group in which you are valued confers a sense of power with which to face the world.

**?** How is religion related to ethnicity?

# The appeal of modern movements to different groups

## New religious movements

When considering the appeal of new religious movements to different social groups we can note two **methodological problems**:

➤ **Reliability**: Our knowledge of NRM affiliation is limited by the fact that some organisations are **secretive** about their memberships; many of those that are not, Miller (2003) suggests, 'exaggerate their numbers, sometimes wildly'. This makes precise statements about the appeal of NRMs difficult, because our knowledge of adherents is limited.

➤ **Diversity**: Miller argues: 'Counting NRMs and their members precisely is impossible. Groups come and go steadily, as do their members.' This again makes it difficult to identify their appeal to specific social groups.

While these problems are important, they are not insurmountable. We can, for example, broadly group NRMs around a number of **key themes** (what Daschke and Ashcraft (2005) call 'interrelated pathways'), which, in turn, give us a general indication of their appeal to adherents.

### Perception movements

Perception movements appeal to those searching for a **new way** of looking at the 'problem of existence and understanding'. Their focus is on philosophical questions ('the meaning of life') and they are particularly attractive to **young and middle-aged**, **middle-class males** — mainly because they allow individuals to separate their secular existence (work and leisure routines, for example) from their spiritual.

This pathway is similar to Wallis's (1984) **world-affirming** category in which he argues that this type provides:

➤ **spirituality** for those disillusioned by or questioning the secular world

➤ **techniques** that can be used to increase personal happiness and become more successful in life

➤ **opportunities** for people to work on their 'inner selves'

### Identity movements

Identity movements focus on human potential and the development of new **personal identities**. They appeal most to those seeking personal **enlightenment** through the mastery of techniques and practices designed to release their 'inner spirituality'. Saliba (2003) suggests this type appeals to **young** people looking for a spiritual grounding to their life because it provides a:

➤ **safe haven** from the pressures of mainstream society

➤ **sense of self** — a way of taking time out to reflect on identity and future plans

The appeal of identity movements to the young is also explained by their **moral certainties** — something especially attractive to those occupying the borderlands between childhood and adulthood.

### Community ('family') movements

Community movements focus on the **social solidarity** aspect of religious practice by offering a sense of community and well-being through the development of close personal relationships with like-minded individuals. The appeal is to those who want to explore 'alternative' ways of living and working (especially, but not exclusively, **women**), usually by distancing themselves, as a group, from wider society.

The Unification Church ('Moonies'), studied extensively by Barker (1984), is an example of a family NRM that has particular appeal to **young**, **middle-class** adherents (university students in particular), partly because they are targeted for recruitment (Barker refutes the idea they are 'brainwashed'). The young are more open to new experiences, and having no dependents makes it easier to live 'as a family'. The Moonie philosophy is, for the ordinary member at least, 'anti-materialist', and young, middle-class converts are more likely to be economically active than older or retired adults — a significant consideration where income is given to 'the family'.

Family NRMs are also attractive to the young because their message of friendship, companionship and communality is more likely to appeal to those searching for an identity as they move out of their personal family group into the wider world. Westley (1978), however, argues that the roots of the NRM appeal to the young go deeper than a simple quest for community.

Where social upheavals (such as those in 1960s Britain and America) bring an increased sense of liberty and freedom, religious movements can 'fill the void' left by the retreat of traditional ideas and values; religious communality, in other words, provides a sense of order and values attractive to some young people.

### Society movements

Society movements focus group solidarity *outwards*. Their major appeal is the possibility of changing society to align it more closely with the (spiritual) beliefs of the group. This involves transforming social institutions (such as work, school and the family) through the application of a particular moral code or spiritual design for living. NRMs such as Black Muslims or Nation of Islam (particularly in America) draw their membership predominantly from the **black working class**, mainly because:

> Their leadership is antagonistic to the white bourgeoisie.
> Working-class blacks have least to lose and most to gain from social changes that place them at the centre of a new social order.

### Earth movements

The goal of Earth movements is to transform the whole world. Some of these NRMs focus on:

- **Planet transformation**: Usually through belief in an **apocalyptic** end to the Earth and the creation of a new 'golden age' (through supernatural or human intervention).
- **Group transformation**: A characteristic of some 'exit-orientated' movements is the idea that the group itself is the centre of any transformation. Members of Heaven's Gate (which fits Wallis's 'world-rejecting' category), for example, believed themselves to be 'extraterrestrials' whose task was to study the human race. In 1997, the appearance of the Hale-Bopp comet was taken as a sign that their mother ship had returned to transport them to a new planet and their earthly forms were duly 'discarded' in the mass suicide of 39 members.

**?** | **Why do NRMs appeal to young people?**

### Explanations

To put the appeal of NRMs into context, Beckford and Levasseur (1986) suggest their membership is tiny compared with both old religious movements (ORMs) and the number of people who subscribe to neither. While we should, perhaps, be asking why their appeal is not greater, for those who do subscribe (mainly the **young**, **white**, **female middle classes**), NRM appeal is based around what Chryssides (2000) suggests is the search for the satisfaction of different needs:

- **meanings**: providing answers to fundamental questions (such as the meaning of life)
- **life strategies** that address 'problems of existence' rather than simply personal life issues
- **ethical codes** that set out how to live your life

This, however, begs the question of why traditional religious organisations (which address much the same needs) are not attractive to those who choose NRMs.

One answer might be **deprivation**: some NRMs make a deliberate appeal to the 'dispossessed' — those who have experienced both social and economic deprivation. Wuthnow (1976), however, argues that NRMs actually appeal to very few older, working-class and ethnic-minority adherents (the kinds of groups we would expect to be most attracted by religious organisations offering a 'spiritual solution' to deprivation).

Further, NRMs in Britain have a relative lack of appeal to ethnic minorities (many of whom are among the most deprived groups in society). Szerszynski (1992), for example, notes: 'Only the Rastafarian movement has recruited mainly from ethnic minorities in Britain.'

Another suggested answer is **relative deprivation**. This argues that adherents are those who, while not objectively deprived (such as the poor), experience 'feelings of deprivation' when compared with other social groups (a sense of **subjective deprivation**). Relative deprivation can be both physical and, more importantly, spiritual. Japp (1984), however, casts doubt on this type of explanation when he notes: 'grievances are everywhere, movements are not'. The problem, here, therefore, is why only a very small minority of 'relatively deprived' people seek solutions in NRMs.

More contemporary explanations focus on **postmodern societies**. The general argument here is that ORMs represent the kinds of top-down, inflexible organisation that are no longer a successful feature of postmodern societies. Postmodern organisations are increasingly open, flexible and more responsive to individual needs, and NRMs fit this model more neatly because they offer greater levels of choice.

Wallis (1984) suggests NRMs appeal to those who seek new ideas and solutions tailored to their individual circumstances (rather than the 'one-size-fits-all' approach of ORMs). In this respect, ORMs are **producer-led** — believers must accept whatever the organisation is offering in terms of beliefs and practices.

Many NRMs, on the other hand, are **consumer-led** — they offer, for example, mix-and-match opportunities, whereby spiritual beliefs can be tailored to individual needs. Instead of the 'One True Way' to spiritual enlightenment offered by ORMs, there are many paths to truth in postmodern society — and the concept of spirituality is sufficiently loose and ill-defined to accommodate each and every path the individual wants to explore.

Wallis also suggests two further reasons for the fit between NRMs and postmodernity:

➤ **Pluralism**: Where choice is not only tolerated but *demanded*, a diverse range of ways to 'enlightenment' open up. Where the idea of 'truth' is questioned in postmodernity, this can be easily turned to mean that any interpretation of 'truth' is as valid as any other.

➤ **Uncertainty**: Where societies no longer provide clear guidance on 'right' and 'wrong' ways to achieve desired goals, NRMs 'fill the moral vacuum' by providing not only 'something to believe in', but a something that can mean whatever the practising individual wants it to mean.

**?** How are NRMs 'consumer-led'?

## New Age movements

Understanding the appeal of NAMs to different social groups also involves **methodological problems** in terms of:

➤ **Organisation**: Many NAMs do not have conventional organisational structures or members, which makes it difficult to identify the groups to which these movements appeal. As Chryssides (2000) suggests: 'The New Age Movement is nebulous, with little formal organization or membership.'

➤ **Spirituality**: This covers a huge range of ideas, the majority of which are not conventionally religious (which, for Chryssides, is an important part of their appeal). Some could arguably be more properly classified as *leisure activities* — yoga, for example (which despite claims for its 'ancient philosophical origins' is probably a relatively modern practice) is something people practice rather than join.

> **Diversity**: Although NAMs are many and varied, which makes them difficult to classify, Miller (1989) suggests each movement is 'a loosely structured network of organizations and individuals' bound by common:
>    > values — based around things like mysticism or magic
>    > vision — ranging from near-religious beliefs in the coming of a 'New Age' of peace/enlightenment to simple self-improvement

On this basis, van Leen (2004) suggests a **typology** of NAMS based on three types.

### Explicitly religious movements

This type is probably the closest to an NRM. Movements such as Hare Krishna and the Divine Light Mission are well organised, often highly centralised and have a particular philosophy to 'sell' (often literally). The appeal is to:

> the spiritual/religious — this type tends to be **syncretic**: picking and mixing elements of different, frequently Eastern, philosophies to create something new
> those looking for a 'family type' experience.

Zimbardo (1997) suggests these groups appeal on a number of levels:

> Imagine being part of a group in which you will find instant friendship, a caring family, respect for your contributions, an identity, safety, security, simplicity, and an organized daily agenda. You will learn new skills, have a respected position, gain personal insight, improve your personality and intelligence. There is no crime or violence and your healthy lifestyle means there is no illness... Who would fall for such appeals? Most of us, if they were made by someone we trusted, in a setting that was familiar, and especially if we had unfulfilled needs.

### Human potential movements

These movements help individuals 'fulfil their potential' by realising their 'inner spirituality' and are generally what Stark and Bainbridge (1987) call **client movements** because they focus on providing a 'service' to members/practitioners based around a 'provider–client' relationship. The individual can, for example, achieve spiritual enlightenment by following a set of teachings and practices (transcendental meditation being a good example).

Human potential movements work on three related levels:

> **Individual**: Lasch (1979) suggests these are based on the idea that 'the individual will

Practitioners of transcendental meditation see it as a path to both individual spirituality and social transformation

is all powerful and totally determines one's fate'; by following a set of teachings and practices, individuals experience improvements in their personal life and circumstances.

➢ **Social**: The NAM claims that if enough people follow its principles, society itself will be transformed. Transcendental meditation, for example, claims collective meditation produces changes that 'radiate into society and affect all aspects of society for the better'.

➢ **Appeal to organisations**: A recent development has been a move into 'applications for organisations', with some movements expanding their interests into the idea of transforming organisations. The Lausanne Movement, for example, offers 'transformational business' courses that hold out the promise of creating 'profitable businesses' through a transformation at three combined levels, of individual, organisation and wider society — at a price, of course.

Szerszynski (1992) argues that the appeal of this type is based on the idea that 'sacred power comes from within the individual'. Its application is in everyday life: clients learn techniques designed to realise their human potential, with an assumption along the lines of 'success at work is indicative of spiritual development'. This type is particularly attractive to a **young**, **middle-class** clientele; as Szerszynski argues: 'the pressure and competitiveness of the middle-class career' becomes the vehicle for spiritual development 'modelled along the same lines as career development in modern societies; courses, seminars, training, management, the learning of techniques'.

Explanations for the appeal of this type of movement are, therefore, focused around the workplace:

➢ Bruce (1995), for example, argues that their appeal is to 'university-educated middle classes working in the "expressive professions"...whose education and work cause them to have an articulate interest in human potential'.

➢ Yankelovich et al. (1983), on the other hand, see the appeal as more individualistic; despite the evidence of their current social role, people believe they have 'more to offer' — something that can be realised through the release of an 'inner, real, self'.

### New Age/mystical movements

The third type reflects what Stark and Bainbridge call an '**audience**' approach to spirituality. These movements rarely have a central organisational structure but instead represent a *range of interests* (astrology or tarot reading being good examples). Their audience can be serviced by providing/selling teachings, practices and paraphernalia designed to help the individual achieve greater levels of expertise and hence understanding.

These are again 'spiritual' movements, embodying beliefs that can be picked up, modified and discarded almost at will, with ideas drawn from a mix of 'ancient' religious, secular and philosophical teachings. One appeal is that involvement can be as superficial as the individual desires — hence the idea of audience or 'leisure' movements;

they don't involve deep commitments and can be practised in ways that don't interfere with everyday life and responsibilities. As Szerszynski suggests, 'they tend to separate off their spiritual activities into a private realm, distinct from their working life'.

### Explanations

There are clear differences between various New Age movements, mainly expressed in terms of what people are supposed to do with the knowledge they gain (**client** movements, for example, focus on secular success whereas **leisure** movements focus on 'self-understanding'). However, they have a number of themes in common that unite them as a different kind of movement from both NRMs and ORMs.

### Clients

Anyone, regardless of age, class, gender or ethnicity (although not many ethnic groups seem interested) can join — and, just as easily, leave. In this respect members can be seen more as **practitioners** who subscribe to particular beliefs and perform certain practices — from tantric sex through witchcraft or the ever-popular ear-candling. As Szerszynski puts it: 'Membership is typically part-time, voluntary, and revocable.'

While women have a greater involvement in religious behaviour than men, their involvement in NAMs is greater still. As König (2000) suggests, women — and middle-class women in particular — are over-represented in New Age movements, for three main reasons:

➤ **Organisational**: Where they generally lack the solid, centralised structure of ORMs and NRMs there are few, if any, positions of male power that exclude women.
➤ **Ideological**: Whittier (1995) suggests many of the ideas propagated by NAMs are 'female friendly' (they don't, for example, involve sexist language or male deities).
➤ **Practical**: Commitment levels can be as involved or superficial as the individual desires (which is important when trying to juggle family, work and spiritual commitments).

More generally, Heelas (1996) argues that the appeal of NAMs is rooted in:

➤ **Postmodern individualism**: A situation in which individuals place themselves at the centre of all interaction: the world revolves around them and their 'needs' and the solution to all problems is found by 'changing the person' rather than the system that produces the person — a situation Marin (1975) has called the 'new narcissism'. This aversion to collective organisation is part of the postmodern condition.
➤ **Spirituality shopping**: Postmodern individualism lends itself to what Fraser (2005) calls 'spirituality shopping'. NAMs 'offer a language for the divine that dispenses with all the off-putting paraphernalia of priests and church...it's not about believing in anything too specific, other than some nebulous sense of otherness or presence. It offers God without dogma.'

NAM adherents resemble consumers encouraged to buy into whatever form of 'spiritual enlightenment' is being offered. The appeal here is that if the individual perceives no benefit they simply move on to the next movement.

Similarly, the long-term appeal of NAMs is limited by **knowledge**: once someone has learnt the basics required to do something (how to relax using transcendental meditation or yoga, for example), they may have little reason for continued involvement.

This aspect of NAMs defines both their general and, paradoxically, short-term, appeal in the sense that they involve **meaning without motivation**. Middle-class, disillusioned and middle-aged people may turn to NAMs that promise to help them live more harmoniously or successfully in a world that seems to largely pass them by, their 'talents' variously undervalued and unfulfilled. While NAMs offer meaning to life, without the need to make any great break with routine or personal sacrifice, this is both a strength and a weakness:

➤ If individuals feel their involvement produces benefits, they will consume more of what's on offer (buying into 'new and deeper levels of enlightenment', for example).

➤ For the majority there is likely to be no great life change — which produces **consumer disenchantment** and a desire to move on to the next product in the shop.

Finally Bruce (1995) describes the general appeal of NAMs to the middle classes in the following terms:

> Spiritual growth appeals mainly to those whose more pressing material needs have been satisfied. Unmarried mothers raising children on welfare tend to be too concerned with finding food, heat and light to be overly troubled by their inner lights and when they do look for release from their troubles they prefer the bright outer lights of bars and discotheques.

**Exam-style questions**

1 Identify and explain two reasons for the appeal of New Age movements in the contemporary UK. (17 marks)

2 Identify and explain two ways in which religiosity is influenced by ethnicity. (17 marks)

3 Identify and explain two ways in which religion may be seen as patriarchal. (17 marks)

# The strength of religion in society

**Secularisation** refers to the decline of the influence of religion in contemporary societies. While this may seem a relatively straightforward idea to test — a simple comparison between levels of religious behaviour past and present — the situation is complicated by three ideas:

- **Definitions** of religion will affect evidence for and against secularisation: **inclusive definitions** are more likely to support theories of **anti-secularisation** because they give greater scope for finding evidence of religious behaviour in ways that are not conventionally religious.
- **Dimensions** of secularisation: There are different areas of religious activity we could examine, each of which provides different evidence for and against secularisation. For example:
  - **Institutional**: This dimension looks at the role played by religious organisations in the general governance of (secular) society; its focus is on the power wielded by these organisations.
  - **Practical**: This looks at the extent to which people practise their religious beliefs through things like attendance and membership.
  - **Ideological**: This is the extent to which people hold religious beliefs that may involve no actual practice (Davie's (1994) concept of 'believing without belonging').
- **Operationalisation**: Definitions and dimensions come together in terms of how we operationalise secularisation. Does, for example, evidence of decline have to be found across all three dimensions, two out of three or just one?

Bruce (2002) argues that we can only really measure secularisation across two types of decline:

- **institutional** — reflected in a reduced role for religious organisations in areas such as government and the economy
- **organisational** — reflected in a general questioning of the plausibility of religious ideas (religious explanations of the world, for example, losing their influence) and practices (such as a decline in religious commitment)

Although 'personal religious beliefs' can be measured after a fashion, we have no reliable data from the past against which to compare them. As Hadden (1987) notes, 'Public opinion polling has only existed for about sixty years.'

Marshall (1994), on the other hand, argues that the focus should be on **beliefs**, since the extent of people's beliefs lies at the very heart of religion, and hence of secularisation. He argues that to understand secularisation we must take account of possible changes to the nature of religious belief. We need to focus, therefore, on the 'privatisation of belief' rather than the influence of organisations or public religious practice; the focus here is on measuring people's 'core beliefs' as expressed through:

➤ the importance of religion in any society
➤ how seriously people take it
➤ the number of people who take it seriously

While beliefs are likely to be the most valid indicator of secularisation, the problem is not just objectively measuring these ideas but also the fact we have no data from the past against which to compare them.

Although these methodological qualifications are clearly important, we can outline a range of evidence for and against secularisation.

**?** **What are the problems involved in the study of secularisation?**

# Evidence indicating the secularisation of society

**Pro-secularisation** arguments are based on the claim that religion has declined in significance from dominating all aspects of political, economic and cultural life, to its influence being marginal to the first two and increasingly marginal to the third. The general theoretical justification underpinning secularisation arguments is **social change**: Crockett and Voas (2004) argue that as societies change, 'the social significance of religion, and religious participation, declines'. This is because:

➤ People are exposed to **knowledge** (such as scientific explanations) and ideas (such as different cultural beliefs) that challenge religious ideas and, in so doing, weaken their power.
➤ **Ideas and organisations** that once had a strong hold over people's lives are weakened in large-scale, complex societies.
➤ **Religious pluralism**: As people develop a more individualistic outlook, their choices of behaviour and belief are reflected in different forms of religious and non-religious belief.

Secularisation
**S** ocial change
**K** nowledge
**I** deas
**P** luralism

**Religious diversity** undermines the 'plausibility of any single religion', leading to a general decline in religious influence. It means religious organisations can no longer present a 'united ideological front' to the world; their ability to impose religious discipline and sanctions, influence social and economic policies or challenge scientific ideas is, therefore, seriously weakened.

While, in the sixteenth century, the Catholic Church could suppress Galileo's argument that the Earth moved around the Sun (the Church taught that the Sun moved around the Earth), it's unlikely that any religious organisation has similar levels of power in contemporary Western societies.

Hadden (2001) suggests we can best understand secularisation by thinking in terms of its impact on three dimensions of **behaviour**, where the influence of religion is either weakened or in decline:

> **Cognitive**: This focuses on how information and beliefs are organised. People in postmodern society think very differently from people in the past about the nature of God, the social and natural worlds and the like — and the *plausibility* of religious explanations declines.
> **Institutional**: Many of the functions once performed by religion have been taken over by secular institutions.
> **Behavioural**: Religious behaviour retreats from the public to the private sphere. Religion becomes a private matter.

## The evidence

For pro-secularisation theorists, religious decline is evidenced in terms of the three areas we noted previously: institutional, practical and ideological.

### Institutional

Institutional decline involves ideas like:

> **Privatised beliefs**: Religion is relegated to personal beliefs about 'God' or the supernatural that have little or no meaning outside 'personal crises' (such as illness and ill health — we look to religious beliefs 'as a last resort' when all else fails).
> **Expendable functions**, such as losing the ability to provide social cohesion or the monopoly of knowledge in society.

Bruce (2001) suggests further evidence includes:

> **Clergy**: Over the past 100 years in Britain the number of full-time professional clergy has declined by 25% (despite a hugely rising population).
> **Rites of passage**: The trend for baptisms, confirmations and weddings is one of decline. As Bruce argues, 'In the nineteenth century almost all weddings were religious ceremonies.' Comparable recent figures are:
>> 1971: 60%
>> 2000: 31%

### Practical

Practical decline involves:

> **Relevance**: Only a small minority (around 10%) of the population are members of the main Christian church in Britain.
> **Engagement**: Dobbelaere and Jagodzinski (1995) argue for a long-term decline in attendance since the nineteenth century (with a particularly sharp decline since the 1950s).
> **Compensators**: NRMs are often cited as evidence of religious:
>> transformation — people expressing their religiosity in non-traditional ways
>> revitalisation — a growth area in terms of numbers

However, Bruce (2001) argues that if NRMs were 'religious compensators' we should have seen 'some signs of vigorous religious growth'. This, he argues, has not happened.

### Ideological

Although 'believing without belonging' is often seen as evidence against secularisation, Bruce argues that the evidence for a general decline in religious beliefs is strong — it simply 'lags behind' the decline in religious practice.

Gill et al.'s (1998) analysis of British **survey data** over the past 70 years 'shows an increase in scepticism about the existence of God, the related erosion of dominant, traditional Christian beliefs, and the persistence of non-traditional beliefs'.

In explanation, Wilson (1982) argues that an important individual dimension of secularisation is the extent to which people's understanding of the natural and social world has changed; as a society, for example, we have moved away from a magical (spells and charms) or religious (prayer) understanding to one based on secular, scientific explanations. The things we once explained by reference to religion are now explained by science.

> **?** What arguments are there in favour of secularisation?

# Evidence against the secularisation of society

**Anti-secularisation** theorists have offered their own interpretations of the evidence put forward by their pro-secularisation counterparts, based around the following ideas:

➤ **Overstatement**: Stark (1999) argues that the influence of religious organisations and beliefs in the past has been *overstated* and the contribution made by religion to contemporary societies *understated*.

➤ **Religious influence** in modern societies is still strong. It provides, for example, the basic rationale for moral codes underpinning political life and takes the lead in arguing for **ethical** practices to inform economic life. There is also a strong undercurrent of individual religious belief, even in secular societies.

➤ **Evolution**: Religion has changed, rather than 'declined' in influence. People are, for example, less likely to follow religious practices because these served functions either no longer needed or performed by other institutions. Religious organisations, for example, served a **leisure function** in the past when there were few, if any, other sources of leisure. A religious festival, for example, was a day spent not working. In the contemporary world we're surrounded by leisure services, so religion no longer serves this function. This is not evidence of secularisation, but simply an evolution of the role of religion.

Although Hadden (2001) notes that 'secularization theory was the dominant theoretical view of religion for most of the twentieth century', over the past 30 years a number of writers (especially, but not exclusively, in America) have challenged the notion of secularisation itself, in terms of both evidence and interpretation.

## The evidence

### Is decline only European?

Berger (1999) argues that declining congregations are a phenomenon seen in western Europe that has not been replicated in America. The idea that secularisation, if it is occurring, does not have worldwide causes is important, because it refutes the argument that religious decline is an inevitable feature of contemporary societies.

### Accommodations

Kelley (1972) suggests that secularisation, where it occurred, was related to particular forms of religious organisation — those that try to accommodate to the secular world — rather than to religion itself. Religious practice *declined* only in organisations that were:

➤ image conscious — appealing to the widest range of people
➤ democratic in their internal affairs
➤ responsive to people's needs (by changing to accommodate particular audiences)
➤ relativistic in terms of their teaching and morality

Religious *growth*, on the other hand, occurred in organisations offering a set of basic ideas and principles that were:

➤ traditional
➤ autocratic
➤ patriarchal
➤ morally absolute

The argument here, therefore, is that religious organisations that evolve into **consumer religions**, responsive to a range of individual needs, actually end up losing adherents. They neither attract those looking for something different in their spiritual life (NRMs and NAMS could offer far more) nor can they keep those who are looking for the 'traditional' features of a religion.

### Religious economy theory

The idea that people will 'buy into' religious/spiritual experiences they find attractive and useful opened the door to a different way of approaching the secularisation debate. Traditionally religion is seen simply as a **cultural institution** to be studied and evaluated in terms of its success or otherwise in propagating particular values. This is fine in culturally *homogeneous* societies where ORMs have little or no competition. In culturally *diverse* societies where spiritual competition is all around, the argument is that we should see religions as **economic organisations** actively engaged in 'selling religion'. In this way the argument is that we should study religion in a similar way to the study of non-religious business organisations.

**Religious economy theory**, according to proponents like Iannaccone (1994) and Stark and Finke (2000), argues that the standard view of secularisation is too limited a way of explaining developments in postmodern societies, for a range of reasons.

One reason is to do with **monopolies**. In Britain, Christianity, in the form of the Catholic Church and the Church of England, were historically able to establish a 'monopoly of belief' that not only discouraged competition but actively destroyed it (through the idea of **heresy**, for example — anything other than the beliefs held by the monopoly religion were not tolerated).

While this made established religions powerful, it also made them 'lazy' — they took their customers for granted. This is not a problem when the secular order supports religious monopolies (believers have nowhere else to go). However, when societies change and the established order is challenged we start to see **religious pluralism** — the development of different religious organisations (from ORMs, through NRMs to NAMs) that are forced to compete for a limited pool of believers. In economic terms, therefore, organisations must compete for 'customers' in the religious marketplace if they are to survive.

Monopoly religions have often not tolerated alternative forms of belief; the 'Oxford Martyrs' Latimer and Ridley were burned at the stake for heresy in 1555

**Competition** encourages:

➤ innovation — religious organisations have to find new ways to attract customers
➤ invigoration — organisations must listen and be responsive to their customers, otherwise they may decide to shop elsewhere
➤ reinvigoration — organisations continually reinvent both themselves and their services as a way of 'keeping ahead of the competition'

Where established religions are slow to change in the face of increased competition, as their congregations decline they focus their efforts on retaining their monopoly position rather than finding new ways to attract adherents.

> **?** What arguments are there against the secularisation of society?

### Summary

On one level, therefore, anti-secularisation theorists concede that a form of secularisation occurs among the old, established religions — they lose members and attendance at services declines, as does their influence over secular matters.

However, just because **established religions** go into decline (secularisation), this doesn't necessarily mean the decline of **religion itself**. It simply evolves, into new religious movements that compete with established religions — and their success is measured in terms of their ability to offer alternative:

➤ forms of religious beliefs
➤ ways to express those beliefs

In other words, they develop innovative methods of providing people with religious services (which also serve as testing grounds for ideas that can subsequently be exploited by mainstream religions — as with evangelical movements within the Church of England). To put these ideas into a contemporary economic context:

➤ If Tesco were the only supermarket chain in Britain, everyone would have to buy their food from them.

➤ If other supermarket chains are allowed into the marketplace then Tesco will lose customers (their economic position will gradually decline).

However, the bigger picture here is that people still shop for food — and it doesn't really matter if they shop at Tesco, Aldi or the corner shop — they are still buying food. As with supermarkets, so too with religion.

The anti-secularisation argument, therefore, is not that religious belief itself has necessarily declined but that the nature and shape of religious organisations have changed. As Crockett and Voas (2004) note, this theory involves the use of two significant ideas:

➤ **Supply and demand**: Religious organisations, if they are to survive and prosper, have to meet the (changing) demands of their actual and potential customers.

➤ **Rational choice**: People are attracted to (or turned off by) religious organisations on a **cost/benefit** basis. If the benefits outweigh the costs, individuals will join; if they don't, they won't. The task of religious organisations, therefore, is to make the benefits of membership more attractive than the costs — and this is something NRMs and NAMs are very good at doing.

In the contemporary religious marketplace, therefore, people have more choice, so they 'shop for religion' in different places. These places are many, varied and difficult to measure — but difficulty in measuring something doesn't mean, as pro-secularisation theorists implicitly argue, that these kinds of religious expression are irrelevant. Rather than see religious development as *either* flourishing *or* declining, the argument here is that like any business, religions are subject to **cycles of expansion and contraction** — sometimes they flourish, at other times they contract.

Just as when a large business goes bust or a particular sector of the economy goes into decline we don't talk about the 'end of capitalism', the same is true of religion. When some religions 'go bust' or spin into terminal decline, the 'underlying religious economy' still exists — people want to buy and spend **spiritual capital** — they just choose to do it in ways that are difficult to:

➤ measure

➤ fit into conventional notions of religion

Anti-secularisation theorists such as Stark (1999) don't, however, simply question secularisation. Rather, they argue that religious changes — the decline in some forms, the rise in others — are evidence of a **resacrilisation** of society. That is, people are actually becoming more, rather than less, religious:

➤ In the *past* they had no choice but to 'be religious' (sometimes on pain of death). While this meant there were a lot of apparently religious people, we don't know about their actual religious commitment — did they attend church services because they were, as Turner (1983) has argued, coerced in various ways into attending?

➤ In the *present* people *choose* their religion — and by so doing they are actually showing greater religious commitment. Having fewer but more committed believers demonstrates resacrilisation.

### Evaluation

Resacrilisation has caused a great deal of controversy and argument:

➤ **Proponents** suggest it explains things like the growth of fundamentalist religious movements (Christian and Islamic, for example), as well as the fact that, as Greeley and Jagodzinski (1997) note, in many countries around the world religious beliefs and practices are, at worst, not declining and, at best, flourishing. **Antagonists**, however, point to a number of problems:

   ➤ Crockett and Voas (2004) note that in the UK 'British religious markets have become more competitive' through the influence of ethnic groups, but there has been little or no corresponding rise in overall religious practice or belief.

   ➤ Norris and Inglehart's (2004) research goes further to argue that, in Europe, countries with the closest links between church and state have the highest levels of practice (contrary to religious economy theories).

On a wider level, the debate appears *inconclusive*; whether secularisation is a feature of contemporary societies depends to a large extent on how different 'pro' and 'anti' positions interpret the problems we identified earlier — definitions, dimensions and operationalisations. For these reasons, ideas about the significance of religious behaviour have moved beyond a simple 'pro' and 'anti' secularisation debate to 'post-secularisation'.

# Post-secularisation

Contemporary approaches to this debate cover a range of positions, a number of which acknowledge both:

➤ pro-secularisation in the sense of a decline in the influence of religion in some areas of social life (such as government and economic activity)

➤ anti-secularisation in that religion still makes significant contributions to other areas, such as culture, personal morality and beliefs

Yip (2002) characterises this general position as being one where religion is 'in a constant state of transformation (and persistence)', an idea from which we can draw two conclusions:

➤ **Non-linearity**: Secularisation is not a simple, linear process from 'the religious' to 'the secular'.

➤ **Dimensions**: The institutional, organisational and individual dimensions of religion are interconnected:

   ➤ **Pro-secularisation** theory takes a 'top down' approach, whereby institutions become secularised, followed by organisational practices and, eventually, individual beliefs.

   ➤ **Anti-secularisation** theory reverses this process, with individuals seen as being 'prone to religion'; religion is a **cultural universal** serving some form of human need. Maslow (1943), for example, sees the 'safety' people derive from religion as a significant psychological need.

**Post-secularisation** theory attempts to resolve this argument by redefining secularisation.

### Differentiation

Phillips (2004) argues that secularisation can be redefined using the idea of **differentiation**. Institutions once heavily under the influence of — or controlled by — religious organisations and ideas become secularised, so that a separation between religious and non-religious institutions occurs in contemporary societies. However, the general thrust and extent of secularising tendencies is limited to institutions and practices. In other words, post-secularisation theory argues that differentiation also involves a **separation** between social structures and social actions.

This makes it possible to chart the secularisation of *two* dimensions of religiosity (institutions and religious practice) by arguing that a *third* dimension (individual beliefs) should be left out of the equation.

### Social actions

The question of whether, in an institutionally secularised society, people hold religious-type beliefs is unimportant. These beliefs are significant only if they inform general social actions; in other words, it is not the fact of people saying they believe in ideas like 'God' that's significant; rather, it's what they do — or fail to do — on the basis of such beliefs.

➤ If, for example, religious beliefs are so strongly held they become the basis for **social action** — such as the creation of, and active involvement in, political parties that advocate religious laws — then this becomes a matter that must be addressed by secularisation theory.

➤ If, however, religious beliefs are simply matters of **personal preference** that have little or no impact on social structures, then for post-secularisation theory they are irrelevant.

Casanova (1994) notes that secularisation, under these terms, involves the liberation of secular spheres (politics, economics, etc.) from the influence of religious organisations, values and norms, but it does not necessarily involve the disappearance of personal religious beliefs (as traditional pro-secularisation theory generally argues).

Similarly, Tschannen (1991) suggests that, for post-secularisation theory, the main object of study is the changing position of religion as an institution in society. Whether or not people believe religious ideas on a personal basis is conceptually unimportant. As Sommerville (1998) argues, **institutional differentiation** is not something that 'leads to secularisation. It *is* secularisation.'

## Social capital

We can develop this idea further in relation to **social capital**: Putnam (2000) reworks the idea of 'believing without belonging' by arguing that social capital refers to the extent to which individuals are **connected**. In other words, it represents the idea of:

> social networks
> participation in social/communal activities and the extent to which people trust each other

Social capital, therefore, is the 'social glue' that binds people as a *society* (rather than as a collection of isolated individuals) — the roles, values, norms and so forth developed to facilitate communal living. It relates, as Cohen and Prusak (2001) suggest, 'to the stock of active connections among people: the trust, mutual understanding and shared values and behaviours that bind the members of human networks and communities and make cooperative action possible'.

In this respect, any decline in religious participation is linked to wider questions of participation across all social groups (such as trade unions, political parties and the like). The **secularisation of participation**, therefore, is not simply a question of religious transformation, but one of a **general social transformation**.

In other words, we can explain the relative decline in religious participation in terms of a general 'process of withdrawal from the public sphere' in contemporary societies — hence Putnam's use of the *Bowliwling Alone* metaphor to describe how the traditionally social activity of ten-pin bowling in America has been transformed into an individual activity. This metaphor has been challenged however; Crockett and Voas (2004) note that 'unlike bowling, people are not "praying alone"'.

The implication of this idea (one shared by Davie, 2001) is that post-secularisation theorists don't need to account for any increase or decline in religious practice/participation in religious terms (the activities of religious organisations, the influence of secular ideas and so forth). Rather it can be explained in terms of **social capital** and a decline in general **social cohesion** (measured in various ways, such as participation rates in voluntary work).

**?** Briefly explain the concept of post-secularisation.

## Evaluation

### Social capital

Wuthnow (2002) has questioned the extent to which social capital in America has declined. He argues that while there has been some decline in social capital, this has not been to 'drastically low levels' — and certainly not enough to fully explain changes in religious participation. While Putnam's thesis suggests lower levels of social capital should result in a decline in religious participation, many religions in America have witnessed a recent revival.

### Beyond secularisation

A wider form of evaluation is to move beyond a narrow debate about whether religion is declining or reviving since, as Harper and LeBeau (1999) note, 'The evidence is pervasive and clear; religion has disappeared nowhere but changed everywhere.'

Spickard (2003) rejects the idea that we can see secularisation as something that can be operationalised and objectively tested; instead, he argues, we should view it as one competing **narrative** among many in postmodern society.

This follows because the same 'secularisation data' can have different meanings, depending on the observer's interpretation:

> The membership declines of American mainline Protestant denominations can be interpreted as the result of growing secularisation or increased fundamentalism… or as a sign of growing religious individualism, or as the result of these denominations' failure to deliver a religious product that appeals to American consumers. Or, it can be all of these…

Rather than attempt to resolve an insoluble problem, going 'beyond secularisation' means we should, according to Spickard, simply see religiosity in terms of six main **competing narratives in postmodern societies**:

- **Secularisation**: The 'decline and loss of influence' story, backed up to some extent by evidence relating to 'European religion (and its decline), the relative decline of American mainline churches, and a loss of religiosity on the part of many intellectuals'.
- **Fundamentalisms**: The idea, mainly perpetuated through the media, that religion is becoming 'increasingly Fundamentalist. A resurgent Islam certainly makes this story plausible. So does the intrusion of American rightwing religion into national politics.'
- **Reorganisation**: the shape of religious organisations is changing, rather than declining or becoming more fundamentalist. The phenomenon of 'cell churches' (where people meet in small groups in each other's houses rather than in a church) is an example here.
- **Individualisation** sees religion as increasingly 'a matter of personal choice' — not only in terms of things like worship and practice, but also of a 'pick-and-mix' approach to religions (combining various ideas and philosophies to create personalised forms

of belief). Such individualisation evolves to satisfy religious yearnings in situations where individuals 'can no longer rely on social institutions'.

➢ **Religious markets**: This story, as we've seen, relates to an anti-secularisation message that involves a plurality of organisations servicing a range of religious needs.

➢ **Globalisation**: In a sense, a catch-all story that sees the ease of communication coupled with economic and cultural globalisation contributing to the rise (and decline) of religious organisations, fundamentalism and the like around the globe.

**Exam-style questions**

1 Outline and evaluate the view that religion has lost its importance in the contemporary UK. (33 marks)

2 Outline and evaluate the view that the rise of new religious movements shows that religion is still strong in the contemporary UK. (33 marks)

3 Outline and evaluate the view that secularisation is taking place in the contemporary UK. (33 marks)

# Chapter 10

## Sociology of youth

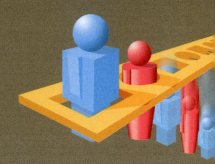

**By the end of this chapter you will be able to:**

➢ understand the key concepts of youth, youth culture, youth subcultures and peer groups

➢ identify and explain a range of spectacular youth subcultures

➢ understand how a range of agencies (the media, schools and the economy) and processes (consumption, demography and globalisation) contribute to the social construction of youth

➢ outline and evaluate functionalist, Marxist, feminist and postmodernist explanations of the role of youth culture/subcultures in society

➢ outline and evaluate post-feminist perspectives on the relationship between gender and subculture

➢ examine issues relating to ethnic involvement in subcultures (racism, ethnocentrism, resistance and hybridity)

➢ identify and explain key patterns and trends in youth deviance

➢ outline and evaluate functionalist, Marxist and labelling explanations for key patterns and trends in youth deviance

➢ explore the experience of schooling in relation to class, gender and ethnicity

➢ identify and explain patterns and trends in subject choice

➢ explore a range of pro- and anti-school/education subcultures

# Key concepts and the social construction of youth

## Youth

Although there have always been 'young people' in our society (people of a certain biological age), there haven't always been 'youths'. This follows because 'youth' is the *meaning* societies give to a particular biological age group. Pearson (1983), for example, suggests that youth (as opposed to 'young people') first appeared in Britain in the late nineteenth century (with newspaper references to 'rowdy youths' around 1898).

Until the early twentieth century, most societies seemed to distinguish merely between 'childhood' and 'adulthood'. One reason for this was that since the lives of young adults were not significantly different from their older adult counterparts, there was little reason to distinguish between them.

## Youth as a social construction

The fact that we do now distinguish between youth and adulthood suggests that youth is a **social construction** rather than a biological given. This follows because the meaning of 'youth' has changed — and continues to change:

➤ **historically** — in our society over time
➤ **cross-culturally** — different societies define 'youth' in different ways

### Labelling

In this respect, one way to start to explore youth is to see it as a **labelling process**. This age group is not only given a name but also a set of characteristics — social and psychological — associated with the label — something we can illustrate using the term '**teenager**'. At midnight on their thirteenth birthday, children acquire this **social identity** and, in so doing, are somehow changed in the eyes of the people around them. They have suddenly acquired a new **status** — one with characteristics that are both:

➤ positive — the former child receives privileges reserved for 'teenagers'
➤ negative — adults associate things like moodiness and rebellion with teenagers

There is, of course, nothing different about the individual — the child has not been magically transformed overnight. What has changed is how people *react* to the new status — and this is significant for our understanding of not just 'teenagers' but youth in general.

### Boundaries

**Boundaries** are a further aspect of contemporary youth that points to its social construction. At what age does youth begin and end? There are various age markers we can use to help us decide when youth begins:

➤ the age of criminal responsibility (10 years old)
➤ the start of teenage years (13)
➤ the school-leaving age (16)

Similarly, there are markers for when it ends:

➤ **rites of passage** (21 used to be the age at which 'adulthood' began; now it's 18)
➤ the end of teenage years (20)
➤ the end of formal education (21 or 22 for some)

**?** What problems do sociologists face when defining youth?

## Peer groups

If youth were simply a biological category, marking its beginning and end would be relatively straightforward. There doesn't, however, seem to be much agreement about which markers we should use to define youth — and this confusion reflects a general ambivalence in our society about youth that we can start to examine in terms of **peer groups** (people of a similar age).

If we consider youth a time of **ambivalence**, peer groups are significant in two ways:

➤ **Status**: Youth is a part of neither childhood nor adulthood — both of which are relatively **centred identities**. Children, for example, are generally told how to dress, talk, behave and so forth; while adulthood is centred around a range of rights (some of which are shared with youth) and responsibilities (the majority of which are not).

➤ **Situation**: Youth exists in the margins between childhood and adulthood. This is reflected in a kind of sliding scale of age-related rights — from what you can watch in the cinema, to things you can or cannot do until the appropriate age (legally smoke, drink alcohol, join the army, get married).

Youth, therefore, is largely a **decentred identity** — there are few, if any, hard and fast guidelines about 'how to be a youth'; Fine (2001), for example, argues that young people 'engage in both adult and childish activities simultaneously'.

While young people are given freedom to develop their own ideas about the meaning of youth, freedom and choice lead to **uncertainty** — there can be no guarantees you're 'doing youth correctly' and this makes youth an increasingly **risky** status. As Furlong and Cartmel (1997) argue, 'young people in contemporary industrial societies have to negotiate a set of risks which were largely unknown to their parents'.

Peers, therefore, play an important role as a **reference group** whose behaviour can be monitored, copied, modified and so forth in a way that allows young people to retain a sense of individuality, freedom and choice while simultaneously being part of a much wider group of similar-minded individuals. Peer groups operate on two levels in this respect:

➤ **Primary peer groups** generally involve a few close friends whose help and advice are strongly valued. As Ellis and Zarbatany (2007) found, these people tend to be important influences on our behaviour (as we, of course, are similarly influential), to the extent that primary peer group members adopted similar forms of behaviour, partly under the influence of **peer pressure** to conform to group norms.

➤ **Secondary peer groups** involve a much wider network of relationships, some of which are face-to-face (such as being connected to other peer groups through shared friends), but also include relationships derived from secondary groups such as the media.

One of the most significant influences of secondary peer groups is in terms of **consumption patterns** relating to the development of particular youth fashions and behavioural styles. While the precise role played by the media is much debated, their general role seems to be one of picking up and amplifying styles that originate within particular youth groups. Punk, for example, originally began within a very specific and highly localised group of young people in a small area of London. The media picked up and amplified this style by bringing it to the attention of a much wider youth audience.

The significance of the peer group also suggests youth is a **negotiated process**. In the absence of clear guidelines about how young people are supposed to behave (on the one hand youth is celebrated as a time of choice and freedom from responsibility while on the other young people who exercise these choices and freedoms too vigorously are demonised as being 'out of control', 'feral youth' and so forth), they are, in some respects, left to their own devices. They are relatively free to construct youth in whatever way they see as fit or appropriate — options that frequently bring them into conflict with adult values and norms.

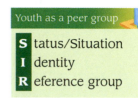

Youth as a peer group

**S** tatus/Situation
**I** dentity
**R** eference group

> **?** How is youth a decentred identity?

# Youth culture

Although, as we have suggested, the idea of 'youth' has been around for some time in our society, it wasn't until the 1950s that the idea of 'youth culture' as something in need of explanation really began to develop — Hine (2000), for example, argues that 'teenagers' didn't make much of an appearance in Britain 'until the mid-to-late 1950s'.

A significant reason for this was the development of compulsory universal **education** (at least in Britain) following the 1944 Education Act. By setting a school leaving age of 15, the Act created a '**period of dependency**' for all young people (while middle- and upper-class boys had historically been educated into their mid to late teens, this wasn't true of youth as a whole). This led to the idea of youth being 'qualitatively different' from adulthood or childhood.

### Youth culture as transition

**Youth culture** refers to a 'shared way of life' among young people. The emergence of this new and distinctive social grouping was initially explained by **traditional functionalist sociology** in terms of its being functional for both the individual and society. Specifically it was argued that 'youth' developed as a way to 'manage the **transition**' between:

> childhood, governed by **affective relationships** within the family group, and
> adulthood, governed by **instrumental relationships** in the workplace and wider society

Since 'all youth', regardless of class, gender or ethnicity, faced the same general problem of making this transition successfully, it followed that they must develop a common culture designed to help them manage and cope with it — hence the idea of a 'youth culture'.

There are, however, two initial problems we can note with this idea:

➤ **Definitions**: If it's difficult to define 'youth' precisely, then it will be equally difficult to see what this particular group has in common by ways of values, beliefs, norms and behaviours.

➤ **Transition routes**: Even if we accept the idea that all youth face much the same general problem — how to manage the transition to adulthood — it doesn't necessarily follow that they all manage it in the same way. Middle-class youth, for example, take a very different route into adulthood from working-class youth — and where the transition routes are different it makes more sense to analyse the particular ways different groups handle the transition.

### The generation gap

While the idea of a clear and distinctive form of youth culture gradually fell out of favour, a more recent revival of the concept focused on the idea of a **generation gap**. Although popular versions of this idea focus on simple age divisions between youth and adulthood, Mannheim (1936) focused on the idea of **cultural generations** — groups born around the same time characterised by common cultural experiences and, latterly, distinctive consumption patterns.

Although this idea is similar to youth culture, generational differences arise not from 'problems of transition to adulthood' but from fundamentally different experiences linked to major and rapid **social changes**. The generational experiences of those entering their teenage years in the late 1950s, for example — a time of general and increasing affluence — were very different from their children's. For the younger generation affluence, plentiful jobs and a general feeling of social progress and optimism were replaced by the realities of widespread unemployment, falling living standards and a general pessimism about the future. In America, for example, Kitwana (2002) has argued that the hip-hop generation of black youth developed cultural forms based around music, art (graffiti), dance, fashion and style that marked it apart as distinctive from previous generations of black youth and hence adults.

# Youth subcultures

Although the concept of **subculture** is linked to culture, theories of youth subculture are different from notions of youth culture for three main reasons:

➤ **Fragmentation**: 'Youth' is not a **homogeneous** category; young people are not 'all much the same' in terms of their values, beliefs and norms. As with the general population, they can be differentiated by categories like class, gender and ethnicity — each with their own particular problems and outlooks (the experiences of white, male, middle-class youth, for example, are qualitatively different from those of black, male, working-class youth).

> **Generations**: Youth subcultures are not linked to generations in the way that theories of youth culture suggest. Rather than seeing their development as specifically related to 'general problems of cultural transition', we can trace their development to the particular circumstances of distinctive groups of young people, in terms of things like:
>
>> - **economic** problems — punk subcultures, for example, developing as a reaction to high levels of youth unemployment in the mid-1970s
>> - **political** problems — the 1960s hippie movement developing, initially in America, as a reaction to the Vietnam War
>> - **cultural** problems — in the sense of each new subcultural wave developing in opposition to the norms and values of previous subcultures (punks, for example, being particularly opposed to the hippie philosophy of 'peace and love' or the racism and homophobia of skinhead subcultures)
>
> **Adulthood**: Brannen (2002) argues that theories of youth culture (and, in a slightly different way, subculture) focusing on the 'problems of youth' in relation to the transition to adulthood assume 'adulthood' in contemporary societies to be unproblematic, something fixed, stable and clearly defined. While youth is seen as a *decentred* identity, adulthood is seen as *centred*. For Brannen, however, 'the problem for youth', is not so much finding ways to manage a clearly defined transition between youth and adulthood, as having little or no clear idea of what adulthood actually means. As she argues, 'rapid economic changes have created uncertain job markets' where 'traditional notions of male adulthood are increasingly redundant, while new notions of female adulthood are still emerging'.

## Ordinary youth?

Before we look at some examples of youth subcultures and explanations for their development, we need to note a criticism of youth subcultural theory (and also, in a slightly different way, cultural theories of youth). This is the idea that most young people are not involved in youth subcultures (and only a small minority are involved in the spectacular variety we'll examine in a moment). Since part of the rationale for cultural/ subcultural theories of youth is that they develop in response to various problems faced by young people, it seems surprising that more youth are not involved in these behaviours. Contemporary responses to this argument focus on two ideas:

> **Submerged subcultures**: Subcultural behaviour is more widespread than the simple 'ordinary youth/subcultural youth' split might suggest. The argument here is that young people have always developed a wide variety of relatively small, highly localised, subcultural groups, the vast majority of which have not attracted wider attention. This is particularly the case, as we'll see, with more recent subcultural activity influenced by globalisation processes.

> **Normalised deviance**: A second response is that while in the past we could establish a relatively clear distinction between 'ordinary' and 'subcultural' youth

on the basis of things like how they dressed, the culture they consumed, how they behaved and so forth, this is made more difficult in contemporary societies because behaviour that was once 'different and deviant' has become — for many young people — normal and everyday. Gourley (2004), for example, notes that the kind of recreational drug use associated with youth subcultures in the past has become 'normalised' in the sense of 'the emergence of widespread recreational drug use amongst relatively large numbers of ordinary youth'.

**?**    **What is the difference between youth culture and youth subculture?**

## Spectacular youth subcultures

Cohen and Young (1981) used the term '**spectacular**' to describe a range of youth subcultures (Table 10.1) notable for their high social visibility. These were the subcultures (mods, skins, punks) that burned most brightly in the cultural firmament and, by so doing, captured the interest and attention of the media and public alike.

Table 10.1  Timeline of spectacular UK youth subcultures

| Name | Main appearance | Basic composition | Style |
|------|------|------|------|
| Teddy boys | Mid-1950s | Male, working-class, white | Drape coats, crepe shoes, quiffs, rock 'n' roll |
| Rockers ('greasers') | Late 1950s/ early 1960s | Male, working-class, white | Leathers, motorcycles, tight T-shirts, slicked hair |
| Mods | Early 1960s | Male, working-class, white | Parkas, mopeds, soul music |
| Hippies | Mid-/late 1960s | Male and female, middle-class, white | Kaftans, long hair, flared trousers, 'flower power', 'peace and love', psychedelic rock |
| Skinheads | Early 1970s | Male, working-class, white | Crombie overcoats, Ben Sherman shirts, braces, Doc Marten 'bovver' boots, cropped hair, ska music |
| Glam | Early 1970s | Male and female, working-class, white | Androgyny, glam rock |
| Punk | Mid-1970s | Male and female, working-class, black and white | Ripped and torn 'DIY' clothing, zips and safety pins, mohicans, punk rock, reggae |
| Goth | Late 1970s | Female, working-class, white | Black clothing, heavy coats, big boots, black makeup, goth rock |
| Rave/ acid house | Early 1980s | Male and female, working- and middle-class, white | Dance music, raves |
| Hip-hop | Late 1980s | Male, working-class, black | Sampling, beatbox, bling, emceeing, graffiti, break-dance, hip-hop, rap, urban music |

Although this list is by no means exhaustive (groups such as New Romantics in the early 1980s, for example, have been excluded) and only lists subcultural developments as they appeared in the UK (hip-hop, for example, made its initial appearance in America around the mid-1970s), it does tell us something about spectacular subcultures:

Mods and rockers in the early 1960s — fighting against social change?

➤ **Social change**: They cover a period of around 30 years, from the mid-1950s to the mid-1980s, since when (unless we include subcultures such as Emo, an offshoot of goth) they have all but disappeared from the cultural landscape. This timescale reflects a period of rapid and widespread economic, political and cultural changes (from the appearance of Teddy boys in the immediate aftermath of the Second World War, through punk appearing at a time of severe economic problems, to the advent of postmodern society). This suggests explanations for spectacular youth subcultures are tied in to wider social changes.

➤ **Class**: With one or two exceptions (hippies, for example, originated among middle-class American students at a time of widespread disillusion with involvement in the Vietnam war), spectacular youth subcultures overwhelmingly originated in the working class. This once again suggests a relationship between subculture and social change — working class youth are most likely to feel the negative impact of economic changes.

➤ **Age**: Although youth subcultures clearly involve 'young people' the problem, as we've previously suggested, is how to define 'youth'. This is significant for two reasons:

  ➤ While most spectacular subcultures appeal to relatively young people (around the 15–18 axis), this is not always the case. Hippies were older (university students) and eventually embraced a significant range of adults (in their mid to late twenties, for example). Skinhead groups also seem to expand beyond the simple constituency of 'youth' as, arguably, does hip-hop.

  ➤ Explanations that focus on youth subcultures as a reaction against 'adult society' are difficult to sustain if adults are involved.

➤ **Gender**: One feature of early spectacular subcultures is the general lack of female involvement (an exception being hippies — partly explained by any movement preaching 'free love' and 'equality' being unlikely to exclude women). While women did feature in these subcultures, their participation was generally **marginal**; as peripheral roles played out through their attachment (as girlfriends, for example) to male members. Later subcultural groups, such as punk, goth and rave, seem to have reversed this situation to some extent, with women playing similar roles to their male counterparts.

One explanation here is changing social attitudes; by the latter part of the twentieth century women were less likely to be seen as subservient to men. The sexist nature of some aspects of hip-hop (with women reduced to 'bitches') points to both the validity of this argument and the fact there has been a (male) reaction to changing female statuses.

➢ **Ethnicity**: Most participants in early spectacular subcultures were white — something that reflected both the ethnic composition of Britain (in the 1950s and early 1960s there were far fewer black minority young people) and the lack of cultural mixing between black and white youth. Later subcultures, such as punk, began to see not only greater black involvement but also the development of predominantly black youth subcultural groups.

Spectacular subcultures

**C** lass
**A** ge
**G** ender
**E** thnicity
**S** ocial change

## Explanations

### Affluence

At various times some groups of youth find themselves with increased spending power that they can use to consume various products and styles (clothing and music in particular) that marks them apart from other youth. Teddy boys, for example, appeared at a time of increased youth affluence, as arguably did rave culture.

Other youth groups arise as an explicit **rejection of consumerism**, for ideological reasons in the case of hippies and political reasons in the case of punk. The latter's 'do it yourself' attitude to style (illustrated by plastic bin-liner clothing) was seen as a reaction to the lack of jobs and opportunities for some working-class youth in the mid-1970s.

### Socialisation

Explanations based on socialisation take a range of forms, mainly focusing on a failure by parents to properly socialise and control their offspring, leading to the development of deviant subcultural behaviour. This concept is also occasionally used to explain gender differences in subcultural behaviour. While young males are given more freedom in the public sphere (to hang around in groups 'on the streets' for example), female behaviour is more tightly controlled. Girls are given less 'freedom of association' in the public sphere and therefore less opportunity to form or participate in youth subcultures.

### Extension of education

This argues that youth subcultures developed once young people were forced to stay in education for longer — something that created a clear break between dependent childhood and independent adulthood. Youth started to be seen as 'different' in the sense of going through a 'special phase' in their development. Commercial interests saw youth as a new and developing market and so started to create products aimed at young people — which led to the development of various different and unique youth styles.

### Globalisation

Initially this explanation focused on the way cultural ideas, products and styles (mainly from America) were imported and adapted by youth groups to create their own sense of style and difference. More recently it has been applied to the way the internet has 'internationalised' cultural ideas and styles; people in one country are quickly able to see, pick up and purchase a range of cultural styles developed in one country and subsequently exported to others around the globe.

In this latter sense of 'globalised youth', the multiplicity, **fragmentation** and disappearance of large, spectacular subcultural styles is explained by the highly specialised nature of cultural exchanges. Young people are exposed to such a wide and rapidly changing cultural landscape that spectacular styles have little time to develop before youth move on to the next style.

### *Mass media*

One version of this idea is that youth subcultures are simply 'creations of the media'. A more sophisticated argument, however, is one noted by Thornton (1995) when she argues, 'there is a continual and shifting exchange between subcultural authenticity and media manufacture'. This observation reflects Cohen and Young's (1981) argument that while spectacular youth subcultures begin authentically, with a group of young people developing a new and different form of behaviour, this is then picked up and amplified by the **mass media**. Two consequences follow from this:

➢ The publicity given to a relatively small group attracts more and more 'followers' — the vast majority of whom simply pick up on the *style* rather than the *substance* of the behaviour being copied. Hippies, for example, originally developed around a very specific set of ideas and issues that were important to a relatively small group of American students. By the time hippies appeared in Britain the attraction was a set of new and exciting styles (of behaviour, clothing and music); the experiences that produced the original, authentic subculture had little or no interest or meaning to the 'new hippies'. Punk followed a similar trajectory: originating in a small, specific area of London, its style was rapidly adopted across the country.

➢ A shape, structure and meaning to youth behaviour is created through media reporting and commentary (in postmodern terms, a '**subcultural narrative**' was created that explained, for those who had merely picked up on a style, the 'meaning' of 'punk' or 'rave', for example). Young people who have little or nothing in common except a desire to party are manufactured by the media into some form of social collective with common interests, aims and beliefs.

> **?** How are youth subcultures related to class?

## Unspectacular youth identities

This type of argument also goes some way towards explaining the decline in spectacular youth subcultures over the past 25 years. In the past, terrestrial media (newspapers, magazines and television) had both a **captive audience** (there were no real competitors) and one that included large numbers of young people (to the extent that a wide range of magazines aimed specifically at youth existed in a way that is no longer the case). When a particular aspect of youth behaviour was highlighted there was, therefore, a ready-made captive market for the style on offer.

While a huge range of youth identities/subcultures currently exist across the globe (Wikipedia (2011), for example, lists a very conservative 78 examples, but it's probable the actual number runs into the low hundreds), very few, if any, have developed spectacular identities in recent years. The argument here is that mainstream media's hold on the audience has diminished through competition from the internet. While young people are increasingly exposed to a range of styles — which some pick up, play with and then discard — there is no coherent narrative coming from mainstream media to a youth audience about the meaning and content of these identities. They consequently appeal to a select audience of followers/adopters rather than the mass audience of spectacular subcultures.

# The social construction of youth

'Youth' is a socially constructed category, whereby the biological ageing process (together with 'phases of social development' based around different age groups) is associated with a range of characteristics. In this section, therefore, we can examine the contribution made by a range of agencies and processes to this social construction: the media, consumption, schooling, demographic trends, the economy and globalisation.

## The media

The role of the media in the social construction of youth can be outlined on two levels.

### Role performance

The media are used by young people to understand and monitor how they 'perform youth'. Through **role performance**, media (from style magazines to music videos) aimed specifically at the youth market help young people understand the:

➤ **meaning** of youth: What 'young people' are supposed to be like, how to play the role of youth and so forth.
➤ **correct** ('cool') and **incorrect** ('uncool') styles and behaviours: This not only monitors fashion and style developments (what's hot and what's not) but also covers general beliefs about youth styles (60-year-old punks are probably not cool).

### Contexts

Contexts are aimed at adults rather than young people (although youth will, of course, consume at least part of the general message) and relate to a media **discourse** on youth. This, according to Foucault (1980), is always exclusive; contexts are constructed to convey a one-sided message designed to influence how an audience sees and understands 'youth'. The dominant media discourse for much of the past 50 years has centred around **problem youth** — expressed in a range of **narratives** (stories that support the discourse) portraying youth as:

➤ an individual problem — the various forms of risky behaviour (from drug-taking to binge-drinking) that 'self-harm'
➤ a social problem — youth subcultures are simply one more example of how the behaviour of young people is 'a problem' (one that, as Pearson (1983) has demonstrated, has recurred over the past century or so)

**Youth narratives** within the overall 'problem discourse' focus on different specific problems related to areas like class:

➤ **Working-class narratives**, for example, frame 'the problem' in areas like:
  ➤ sexuality and reproduction — not just teenage pregnancy and irresponsible fathers but wider problems of single parenthood and 'benefit dependency'
  ➤ 'feral youth' — 'out of control' and a serious threat to social order
  ➤ crime and delinquency
  ➤ drug-taking and hedonism
  ➤ unemployment — normally framed in terms of the 'unwillingness' of working-class youth to take jobs 'in plentiful supply'
  ➤ help and advice — how 'middle-class professionals' in particular can help working-class youth
➤ **Middle-class narratives** frame 'the problem' differently — in terms of how to successfully make the transition from youth to adulthood, through:
  ➤ education — how to ensure 'high achievers' are not excluded from the 'best' universities
  ➤ work — the problems associated with gaining employment that matches their abilities
  ➤ housing — problems with 'getting on the housing ladder' at a time of high house prices

By constructing youth in this way the media frame the overall debate in terms of **social control**: although all young people are held to require adult supervision and control (as Lesko (1996) argues, 'adolescence becomes defined as problematic, out of control and needing to be constrained by adults'), this is framed in different ways:

➤ Working-class youth require strong, frequently punitive, controls to save them from both their own risky behaviours (the individual dimension) and the social problems these behaviours create.
➤ Middle-class youth require softer controls — ones designed to ease their way into a 'successful adulthood' by preventing them 'going off the rails'.

**?** How are working-class youth constructed differently from middle-class youth?

## Consumption

Featherstone (1990) argues that in postmodern society consumption shapes identity: we use what we buy to make statements about who we are. In this respect, the lives of young people in particular are shaped by considerations of style and identity and by the forms of consumption used to support and enhance them.

The 'youth market' has been a social space mapped out by commercial enterprises and advertisers from the emergence of teenagers in the 1950s. Teenagers then were defined in terms of their consumption of styles in music, fashion, language and behaviour that were not only different from those of adults but in some ways opposed and threatening. The sense of self and style of contemporary youth is wrapped up in mobiles and connected networks.

Consumption of style in the **past** had two main features:

➤ **Gender**: Different media focused on different genders (young women, for example, were the target for style magazines built around fashion and relationships; young men were targeted for things like sport, music and technology).
➤ **Production**: In the main, youth were **passive** consumers of mass-produced, ready-made products.

**Contemporary** consumption — while still having these elements — has also seen the idea of youth as **active** consumers; emerging technologies (such as social networks) provide tools that allow youth to define their own social spaces and relationships.

Although they are clearly significant, we need to avoid over-determining consumption and style as integral features of all youth experiences. Just as young people are not 'all the same', there are wide-ranging differences, as Jones and Martin (1997) note, in consumption patterns among different categories of youth — not only in terms of the idea that any 'transition to adulthood involves costs' (finding a place to live, for example) but also in terms of the idea that 'spending on style and leisure may mask, or be a response to, material or social deprivation'.

## Schooling

Education contributes to the social construction of youth in two main ways.

### Extension of schooling

As we've noted, compulsory secondary education, with a school-leaving age set at 15 (raised to 16 in 1972 and projected at the time of writing to rise to 18), created a category that came to be defined as youth. Advertisers began to cater for this new market of teens with money and freedom from mundane adult responsibilities (children, mortgage or a need to earn a living). This new status was reinforced through peer group interactions, and new identities emerged around new styles and consumption patterns.

### School experience

A second aspect to education is the reinforcement of youth identity not only through the experience of being in school (as opposed to work) but more importantly through the age-grading system used. As young people increased in school seniority simply by getting older, age differences became associated with identity differences; the world of a 15-year-old became very different from that of a 12-year-old. This association represents a significant step in the social construction of youth because it anchors rapidly changing youth identities around age.

Besley (2002) also points out how schools contribute to general ideas about youth being a **deficit state**: young people are seen as both incomplete and involved in a process of 'becoming' that will culminate with their arrival and acceptance into 'adulthood'.

> Education and the social
> construction of youth
>
> **S** chooling
> **E** xtension
> **E** xperience

## Demographic trends

The most significant demographic trend was the post-Second World War 'baby boom' that created a 'bulge' of young people in the general population (described in the chapter on Family). This had two consequences:

➤ Young people, as a significant segment of the population, became far more visible as a distinctive social group.

➤ The greater number of young people, helpfully if inadvertently age-graded through education, drew the attention of media and advertisers to this new and economically untapped grouping.

## The economy

Economic factors contribute to the social construction of youth in various ways.

Economic behaviour reinforces ideas about **age distinctions** in terms of a rough-and-ready set of age-graded divisions:

➤ children — no paid work

➤ youth — part-time work leading into full-time work paid at lower levels than adults

➤ adult — full-time work

In addition, while youth work is generally low-paid, low-skill and low-status (burger flipping being an obvious example), it does signify the ability to **participate** in part-time work while still living in the family home, where there may be few, if any, general household expenses. This creates a pool of personal spending power that, for some young people, is focused on creating and cultivating youth identities (through the consumption of various cultural products).

Participation is, in turn, a significant **cultural marker**. Things like leaving school and entry into full-time work can be an important marker for the transition into adulthood. While this is perhaps not as clear-cut now as in even the recent past, it still represents a significant change in status for many young people.

## Globalisation

Global cultural processes have played a significant role in the social construction of youth in a number of ways.

➤ **Cultural imports**: In the 1950s the import of American cultural styles and products (music in particular) influenced the early development of British youth styles and subcultures (such as Teddy boys); later groupings such as mods and hippies were similarly influenced by musical forms and styles. More recently, various global products from T-shirts and jeans to baseball caps and beyond have been incorporated into youth styles. Large commercial interests (global companies like Nike, Coca-Cola and McDonald's) have also created products that have been incorporated into various youth identities. As Besley (2002) suggests, 'Now, more than ever, kids find their identities and values in the marketplace, rather than in traditional sources such as the family, church and school.'

➤ **Cultural exports**: Similarly, various forms of specifically British youth subcultures have been exported across the globe, from Beatlemania in the early 1960s to punk in the mid-1970s.

➤ **Cultural hybrids**: The 'globalisation of youth' has seen different cultural products and styles incorporated and adapted by youth. Both Teddy boy and mod culture, for example, illustrate early cultural hybrids: global cultural products (such as rock and roll/soul music) incorporated into a more localised form of youth identity that was both new and very different.

➤ '**World-kids**': More recently, Besley argues that the notion of world kids refers to 'a globalised sense of youth'. Youth, in this respect, has now become big business, a social space where multinational companies not only compete to sell things 'to kids' but do so on a global scale. This involves the construction of a 'globalised youth' that consume much the same global products, differentiated only by localised variations in the meaning of those products.

---

**Exam-style questions**

**1** Identify and explain two features of spectacular youth subcultures. (17 marks)

**2** Identify and explain two ways the media contribute to the social construction of youth. (17 marks)

**3** Outline and evaluate the view that youth is socially constructed. (33 marks)

---

# The role of youth culture/ subcultures in society

In this section we examine how different sociological perspectives have analysed and explained youth culture and subcultures.

# Functionalism

Traditional functionalist explanations focused on what Parsons (1964) termed the role of youth culture in 'easing the difficult process of adjustment from childhood emotional dependency to full maturity'. The general logic of this **systems approach**, therefore, was to explain how modern industrial societies developed ways to 'manage the transition' between the two relatively fixed cultures of **childhood**, centred around *affective relationships*, and **adulthood**, centred around *instrumental relationships*.

For writers such as Eisenstadt (1956), the extension of education coupled with an increase in general spending power among the young (something Abrams (1959) characterised as 'affluence without responsibility') led to a situation where youth increasingly straddled an uneasy gap between childhood and adulthood cultures. The ambivalent status of youth left them open to **anomie**: young people experienced confusion and uncertainty about the behaviour expected of them by society. In essence, they found themselves 'in limbo' between childhood and adulthood.

Since all young people were faced with a common problem — how to successfully manage the transition from full childhood to complete adulthood — it was assumed they developed a 'common response', a form of cultural adaptation specific to youth. Coleman (1961), for example, found that the behaviour of young people was influenced more by their peers than by their families or by wider social values and norms. They developed a culture that was both separate from, and in many ways opposed to, adult culture.

Although this is sometimes taken to mean youth developed a common culture notable only for its **homogeneity** — the idea that all young people basically shared much the same norms and values — this is not what functionalists were arguing. Eisenstadt, for example, expressed the need for a 'common response' to a 'common problem' (anomie and the transition to adulthood).

Young people could and did respond to this general problem in a range of ways, the most notable being in terms of **gender**. Male and female youth responded in different ways precisely because they were positioned differently within the social structure. Cohen (1955), for example, argued that some young working-class males experienced **status deprivation/frustration** and joined subcultural groups that would allow them to achieve the status/respect denied to them by wider society.

The female route to adulthood was seen to be very different. Their status would come from starting their own family, which meant they rapidly moved from one private sphere governed by affective values (their parents' family) to another private sphere (their own family). Since there was no real disunity of values in their lives (young women did not, for example, have to develop strong instrumental values and orientations), their cultural response was very different.

Eisenstadt argued that particular forms and variations within youth culture are unimportant. If some youth find their way to adulthood as Teddy boys, mods or rockers, while others take the educational route of school and university, it makes no real difference; all that's important is that they find their way through to adulthood.

While the overall **function** of youth culture was to manage the transition between the family (childhood) and work (adulthood), we can identity some of the specific functions involved.

### Social solidarity

In a society undergoing rapid social and economic changes, such as Britain in the 1950s, strains and tensions develop that must be successfully managed if the system is to continue to function. Where a gap develops between the private and public spheres (through the extension of education, for example) societies have to find ways to integrate a category of young people who are no longer children but not quite adults.

### Integration

Youth culture provided norms, values and statuses that created the sense of belonging and common purpose required to help young people negotiate the stresses and strains of a potentially difficult experience — leaving the comfort and security of the family home to make their own way in the world.

Youth culture resolved the problem of anomie and ensured young people would be successfully **integrated** into adult society. This was marked by **rites of passage**: youth was 'a necessary phase' through which everyone had to pass — a transitory phase marked in different ways by different societies (in the 1950s it was common to celebrate the 21st birthday as the symbolic entry point into adulthood).

### Tension management

Eisenstadt noted that the break from the family is a stressful period, especially for young people who may not have the emotional capabilities to deal successfully with such a split if it is sudden and clear-cut. Youth culture, therefore, was seen as a way of reducing tensions by gradually allowing young people to turn away from the family towards the peer group — people in a similar position who had personal experience of the problems involved. The group could, consequently, help each other navigate the choppy waters towards adulthood.

The function of youth culture

**F** unction
**I** ntegration
**S** olidarity
**T** ension

> **?** Give two functions of youth culture.

## Evaluation
### Homogeneity

Although functionalists don't see youth as a homogeneous category, there is a general assumption that categories such as adulthood are unproblematic. However, the idea that adulthood represents a clear, homogeneous category which youth simply have to reach can no longer be sustained (if indeed it ever could). For example, Mitterauer (1993) suggests four 'markers of adulthood' that have stayed fairly stable over time:

➤ leaving the parental home
➤ finding employment
➤ setting up a new home
➤ marriage

The problem here is that although these markers would, up until the last 30 years, have been fairly unremarkable, it's debatable as to whether they are useful in contemporary societies — not least because:

➤ Fewer people marry, and when they do it's later (in their early thirties) than in the past.
➤ Young people find it much harder to leave the family home.

In the 1960s marriage and setting up home together were markers of adulthood — is this still true today?

➤ 'Leaving home' is not necessarily a simple, clean break any more. Manacorda and Moretti (2006) estimate, for example, that: 'In Britain, roughly five out of ten men aged between 18 and 30 live with their parents.'

### Stages

Functionalist theories assume 'youth' is an age category that has associated physiological and psychological **characteristics** that mark it apart from other categories; 'youth' is simply a developmental stage through which everyone must pass. This, however, raises the question of why 'youth' is so difficult to define precisely; if it is a fixed and functional life stage it should be relatively easy to categorise.

The fact that it is not suggests that definitions of youth and youth culture are more complicated than might at first seem to be the case. White and Wyn (1997), for example, suggest that youth is a **relational concept**: it changes over time, and how we define it depends on a range of social and cultural factors and practices (such as how we define the school-leaving age or, more radically, whether we have schools at all).

### Consensus

While functionalism sees youth cultures and subcultures as essential and ultimately supportive of social order, Marxist approaches argue that youth subcultures are indicative of something more threatening (and so have to be discouraged and demonised by those in power).

**?** **Give one criticism of functionalist explanations of youth culture.**

# Marxism

Although Marxist perspectives are also based on a structural, systems approach to understanding society, their explanations for youth subcultures are substantially different. The focus here is on **conflict** — specifically that arising in capitalist societies between social classes. It is no great surprise that most spectacular youth subcultures have their origins in working-class youth. Marxists have carved out a unique take on youth subcultures by focusing on two ideas, hegemony and relative autonomy.

### Hegemony

'Hegemony' means how a ruling class exercises its leadership and control over other social classes through cultural values. People buy (literally) into consumption values; they buy the idea that happiness is found through desirable products, or that these products are **status symbols** (things used to demonstrate an individual's standing within a group or society that also serve as significant sources of personal identity).

### Relative autonomy

People enjoy a level of freedom (autonomy) to make decisions about their behaviour, albeit heavily influenced by structural factors (wealth, power and so forth). Although the vast majority choose broadly **conformist** behaviour (partly because they're 'locked in' to capitalist society through family and work responsibilities), others (mainly young, working-class males) are in a position to resist 'bourgeois (ruling class) hegemony'. Their cultural position, as neither children subject to direct adult supervision, nor adults with the weight of social responsibilities that inhibit their ability to break free of ruling-class control, gives young people a unique (if perhaps fleeting) sense of freedom and opportunity.

The focus here, therefore, is on youth subcultures as **forms of resistance**: as groups in capitalist society whose behaviour is seen as:

➤ **threatening** to the social order (youth subcultures have traditionally been labelled as 'deviant youth')

➤ **resistant** to dominant values and norms — they frequently put forward values and behave in ways that present a challenge to the 'normal way' of thinking and behaving in capitalist society

The resistance of subcultural groups to conventional norms and values is seen by Marxists as indicative of two 'solutions', real and symbolic, to the problems some young people face in capitalist society.

### *Real solutions*

This approach is characterised by the **Centre for Contemporary Cultural Studies (CCCS)**, with research focused on how working-class subcultures develop as a response to, and attempt to resist, economic and political change. For example, we can note how youth subcultures developed as a reaction to changes in areas like **social space**. This refers to both:

> **Literal space**: This is the 'loss of community' idea put forward by writers such as Cohen (1972a), according to which urban renewal in working-class communities created a subcultural reaction (frequently violent and ill-directed) among young, working-class males (mods).

> **Symbolic space**: Subcultural groups develop as a way of establishing and developing a 'sense of identity' in a rapidly changing world. Cohen, for example, argues that skinhead subculture, with its violent response to the loss of a traditional 'British' identity (with anger directed towards immigrants in 'Paki-bashing' and 'deviant sexualities' in 'queer-bashing') — is indicative of this type of resistance to change.

Subcultural behaviour, therefore, represents a **collective attempt** to deal with a sense of loss and, in some respects, reclaim spaces through the fear and revulsion of 'normal society'. Hall et al. (1978) linked youth subcultures to tensions and upheavals in capitalist society by suggesting that increases in deviant behaviour (real or imaginary) were linked to periodic 'crises in capitalism' (high levels of unemployment, poverty and social unrest, for example).

While spectacular subcultures have attracted a lot of attention, writers such as Willis (1977) and Corrigan (1979) transfer the subcultural focus away from the streets and into the classroom to examine less spectacular, but equally significant, forms of cultural resistance. Young (2001) notes how, for Willis, subcultural development among lower-stream, lower-class 'lads' was an attempt to 'solve the problem of educational failure' by 'playing up in the classroom, rejecting the teacher's discipline' and giving 'high status to manliness and physical toughness'.

### Symbolic solutions

Although all forms of subcultural behaviour had symbolic elements (the skinhead 'uniform' of cropped hair, bovver boots and braces imitates 'respectable' working-class work styles), the emphasis was shifted further into the cultural realm by focusing on how subcultures represent symbolic forms of resistance to ruling-class hegemony. Hall and Jefferson (1976) and Hebdige (1979) characterised youth subcultures as **magical** (or ritualistic) attempts at resistance by consciously adopting behaviour that appeared threatening to the 'establishment', thereby giving the powerless a feeling of power. This behaviour doesn't, however, address or resolve the problems that bring subcultures into existence — hence its characterisation as symbolic resistance.

Finally, the decline and disappearance of spectacular subcultures is explained by their being **taken over** or incorporated into the dominant culture. Rebellion and revolt — especially when restricted to relatively harmless symbolic gestures (attending gigs or wearing the T-shirt) — is attractive to many young people who use it to distance themselves from both their peers and adults. Clark (2003) suggests part of the attraction of spectacular subcultures was their ability to *shock*; but images of 'rebellion' are also attractive to business interests and as subcultures become commercialised they become normalised; when 'everyone's involved', the exclusivity, power and status of a subculture loses its appeal.

> **?**   What are the key Marxist concepts in relation to youth subcultures?

## Evaluation

➤ **Spectacular subcultures**: Clark argues that 'with the death of punk, classical subcultures died'; if subcultures are symptomatic of 'structural problems' in society (such as mass youth unemployment), why have they disappeared over the past 30 or so years?

➤ **Symbolism**: Ideas like 'symbolic resistance' lack supporting evidence; one interpretation of 'symbolic' is no more and no less valid than any other. When Hebdige, for example, writes about 'the meaning of style', the problem is that it's *his* meaning filtered through *his* perception. As Young (2001) points out, Hebdige's assertion that some punks wore Nazi swastikas in an 'ironic way' is unsupported by any evidence (not least from those who wore them).

➤ **Identities**: The focus on class neglects a range of other possible factors — gender and ethnicity in particular. The majority of subcultural studies, both functionalist and Marxist, focus on the behaviour of white, working-class men.

➤ **Manufacture**: Cohen (1972b), from a **social action** perspective, argues that what is significant about youth subcultures is that they are created by the mass media. Cohen argues that youth subcultures are not coherent social groupings arising 'spontaneously' as a reaction to social forces. Rather, he questions whether youth subcultures are really subcultures at all.

The media manufacture youth subcultures by focusing attention on disparate, possibly unconnected, forms of behaviour and giving them a shape or structure. Media **labelling** (mods, punks, goths, etc.) gives 'meaning' to these behaviours by assigning certain stereotypical characteristics (hippies = 'peace and love', punks = 'anarchy' and so forth). By applying a meaningful label, the media create something out of very little in that they provide young people with a framework in which to locate their behaviour (and live up to manufactured media myths concerning that behaviour).

➤ **The Other**: Marxist subcultural theory sets up 'the subculture' in opposition to some real or imagined outside group or agency (the school, media, 'ruling class hegemony', etc.). The problem, for Stahl (1999), is that this ignores the idea that subcultures may simply be a reflection of how they are seen by such agencies — as social constructions of the media, for example. Grossberg (1997) also argues that 'oppositional influences' (such as the 'loss of community' explanation underpinning

Cohen's (1972a) analysis of mods), against which subcultures supposedly develop, are little more than unsubstantiated attempts to give substance to a particular and partial view of subcultural development.

# Feminism

Traditional feminist views on youth subcultures have largely been dominated by **Marxist feminism** (we will outline **post-feminist** views when we look at 'gender interests'), and analyses focus on two main areas, patriarchy and invisibility.

## Patriarchy

While most spectacular subcultures involve women — either as full participants (Teddy girls, female skinheads) or in peripheral roles (wives and girlfriends on the margins of subcultural behaviour) — the focus has largely been on the lives and problems of men. One reason for this is that working-class youth subcultures reflected the everyday patriarchal sexism and practices of working-class life (especially, but not exclusively, in the 1950s and 1960s). Just as women didn't participate to any great extent in other public spheres, they were similarly excluded from subcultures.

## Invisibility

A second strand focuses less on the content of youth subcultures and more on a **'male-stream bias'** among sociologists, expressed in two ways:

➤ McRobbie and Garber (1976), although part of the general CCCS school, argued that women in youth subcultures were invisible as a result of:
  ➤ **stereotypes**: 'When women do appear, it is either in ways which uncritically reinforce the stereotypical image of women…or they are fleetingly and marginally presented.'
  ➤ **the male gaze**: We invariably view female involvement and participation through the eyes of men — both male researchers and respondents (in Willis's (1978) study of biker subculture, for example, women are seen through male eyes and experiences).
➤ **Neglected female cultures**: McRobbie and Garber argue that the preoccupation with *public sphere* activity (from which women were largely excluded) meant a significant aspect of young people's experience, the *private sphere* of the home and the family, was ignored — and this sphere, they argue, was precisely the one in which *unspectacular* female youth subcultures developed around what they called **bedroom culture**.

### Bedroom culture

In common with their male CCCS counterparts, McRobbie and Garber were concerned with understanding how youth negotiated and colonised social spaces:

➤ **Physical spaces**: Whereas male subcultures looked outwards, to the public sphere of streets, pubs and clubs, female subcultures looked inwards, to the home. This was because for most of the twentieth century female involvement in the public sphere was marginal. Girls' behaviour was subject to far stricter social and parental controls and, as Valentine et al. (1998) note, girls 'were often unable to engage in spectacular leisure activities which were dirty, dangerous or hedonistic, such as motorcycle riding or hanging around the urban streets'.

> **Cultural spaces**: The restricted activity of girls explains how males and females developed different individual and cultural identities. Whereas male teenage resistance to dominant cultural norms (ruling-class hegemony) was expressed through subcultural groups that took spectacular public forms, female resistance was restricted by the sexist norms and assumptions surrounding 'femininity' that prevailed until the end of the twentieth century. In other words, females expressed their, largely **symbolic**, cultural resistance in the one arena where they were relatively free to express their identities — the bedroom.

Teenage female subcultures thus developed around a 'bought-in', pre-packaged and highly manufactured 'pop culture' of fashion, style and music which they nevertheless sought to adapt to their own particular subcultural **lifestyles**.

Although 'bedroom culture' is frequently dismissed as a commercialised, packaged and compromised form of subculture, Carter (1984) argues that this misses the point. Consumerism itself wasn't particularly relevant; it was what girls did with what they bought that was of real significance. They didn't consume manufactured cultural products uncritically. On the contrary, Carter argues that female subcultures deconstructed and reconstructed conventional consumer cultural products (such as manufactured 'teenybopper boy bands' like the Osmonds) in ways that allowed them to break free from conventional cultural norms surrounding female sexuality and desire.

> **?** How do feminist explanations of youth subcultures differ from Marxist or functionalist explanations?

### Evaluation

> **Gender**: The focus on gender, while understandable and interesting, has tended to neglect analysis based around categories such as class and ethnicity — particularly where they relate to women.
> **Interpretations**: As with criticism of CCCS writers such as Hebdige (1979), part of the problem with these kinds of analysis is that they over-interpret the ability of young women to 'break free' from conventional ideas and behaviours — as evidenced, perhaps, by the simple fact they were restricted to a bedroom-based culture.
> **Identities**: The move towards looking at youth in terms of lifestyles and identities in many ways marked a move away from 'subcultural theories of youth'; this, coupled with rapid and far-reaching economic and cultural global changes, led to a significant change of emphasis in the analysis of the role of youth cultures in society.

# Postmodernism

For postmodernists the world has moved on — which means we need to rethink the way we theorise the behaviour of youth in the light of societies that are:

➤ **Global not national**: Exposure to and interaction with other cultures, ideas and forms broadens our horizons; our eyes are opened not just to new ideas but also new opportunities — ways to adapt and develop cultural forms into different ways of looking and behaving.

➤ **Connected not isolated**: Whereas, in the past, youth subcultures could develop, grow and disappear in local or national isolation, this is no longer true. New styles flash around the globe in an instant — to be picked up, played with and discarded in rapid time.

➤ **Individual not collective**: The emphasis is on the 'individualistic development of self' in postmodern society. People work on their own individual sense of style and are consequently less likely to see their identity in collective, group terms as members of a distinctive subculture. This is a significant idea in the sense that, as Marx (Groucho as opposed to Karl) once said, 'I don't want to belong to any club that will accept people like me as a member'. In other words, we need to understand youth in terms of a **tension** between the **search for identity** and the **individualisation of choice**.

### Identity and individualisation

While 'identity' by definition involves being part of a group — we can only know 'who we are' in the context of people who are 'like me' and, of course, people who are 'not like me' — group membership involves a loss of individuality.

Individualism, on the other hand, involves being different, standing apart from others. However, to be 'wholly individual' means we lose a sense of 'who we are'; we cannot sustain a sense of identity.

Malone (2002) captures this conundrum when she notes: 'Hip Hop as a cultural product and marketed commodity of youth culture has emerged as having a significant influence on young people seeking to explicitly celebrate and support ethnic diversity, individualism and collective communities — simultaneously!'

While, in the past, this circle of identity was squared by trading individualism for group (subcultural) membership, postmodernists argue that the reverse is now the case: group membership is traded for individualism — and this means we must replace 'subculture' with a concept that captures the changed relationship between young people and society.

Maffesoli (1996) suggests we should see youth behaviour as **tribal**. Rather than a 'way of life', it involves dynamic, loosely bound and constantly changing groups with a range of different, fleeting identities and relationships centring around **lifestyles**. Behaviours formerly conceptualised as subcultures (punks, goths, etc.) could more easily and consistently be explained in terms of young people gathering around a set of **totems** — clothing, music, language and so forth that could be adopted, shaped and moulded into various styles.

### Neo-tribes

Bennett (1999) developed this tribal idea as '**neo-tribes**' — a descriptive term for contemporary youth behaviours. Neo-tribes reflect a wide range of styles and identities, adopted by what Luke (2000) calls '**hybridised world-kids**' — youngsters with a 'globalised sense of youth' connected:

➤ **Physically**: Some styles and identities common to very loose groups of youth are reinforced by personal, face-to-face contact and interaction.
➤ **Virtually**, through social networks and messaging. Such contacts create a sense of identity, belonging and community, even though these individuals will never be in the same physical space.

World-kids adopt a range of global — and globalised — styles, fashioning them into a range of unique (hybrid) identities. Some of these may be picked up and adopted by large numbers of youth and others only have meaning for relatively tiny numbers.

The concept of neo-tribes replaces the idea of relatively permanent and physically tangible subcultures with that of:

➤ loose-knit, fluid, unstable associations
➤ interactions that shift and change
➤ temporal associations — the product of a particular time, place and set of circumstances
➤ lifestyles that favour appearance and form

Neo-tribal development is facilitated by technology. The development of the internet, for example, has led to what Polhemus (1994) calls **supermarkets of style**. Just as with traditional forms of consumption supermarkets opened up a massive range of consumer choice, the global arena — opened up by new communication systems — is now a supermarket for the sale and consumption of style. This has important consequences for postmodern youth identities:

➤ **Appearance equals identity**: In a complex, fragmented and anonymous world, how we choose to look becomes 'a calling card signalling who we are and where we are at'.
➤ **Brands** are more than just status symbols and displays of conspicuous consumption (expensive brand = 'I am very wealthy'). They are **lifestyle statements**, an immediate, visual, shorthand way of signalling the 'values and beliefs of potential consumers'. Branding, under this interpretation, becomes an identity statement. (There are, of course, alternative interpretations: that branding simply represents the power of global corporations to embed their identity into individual cultural relationships, for example.)

> **Style** refers to how youth tribes mark out their boundaries, in terms of similarities within and differences between tribal groupings. Polhemus argues that traditional social categories such as class or age 'have become increasingly irrelevant to personal identity'. The latter is now based around:
>   > **'people like us'**: those who share the same sense of taste and identity
>   > **styles-r-us**: style 'has emerged as the key defining feature of social life'; those who share a style also share an identity

Neo-tribalism is sometimes seen as an example of **post-subcultural theory**, replacing subculture as an explanation for youth behaviour. Thornton (1996), however, suggests subculture is still a useful concept, albeit in a modified form. Her study of **club cultures** suggests youth tribes are not necessarily as fluid and free-forming as writers such as Polhemus suggest; some youth behaviours have strong subcultural elements (such as divisions in terms of **status**, **power** and **identity**).

Thornton uses the concept of **subcultural capital** to reference the ability of individuals to establish their identity within a particular group through things like different types of knowledge:

> **insider**: knowing how a particular 'scene' (such as a club) works in terms of organisation; who you know, your relationship to 'prime movers' and so forth; being, in other words 'in the know'
> **cultural**: understanding the history and development of a style, for example
> **consumption**: knowing what to buy and what to reject
> **style**: knowing what to wear and how to wear it

**?** | What is one postmodernist criticism of the concept of youth subculture?

## Evaluation

### Style

The differences between 'old-style' youth subcultures and 'nu-style' tribal cultures is overstated — a difference in terminology rather than substance. Thornton's work suggests similar internal processes of status, power, style and identity are at work whichever concept is used to describe them.

### Classless styles

Post-subcultural theorists argue that postmodern youth identities transcend categories such as class; it no longer matters *who* you are, just *what* you are. This argument can, however, be questioned in two ways:

> **Consumption** is still related to categories such as class, age, gender and ethnicity. Jones (2011), for example, has noted the contemporary 'demonization of working class youth' in the form of 'Chavs'. By daring to appropriate the symbols and images of British upper-class culture — Burberry clothing, flashy jewellery ('bling') that imitates 'the real thing' — working-class youth crossed a class divide and brought into sharp relief underlying notions of class and difference in our society.

➤ **Social divisions**: Shildrick and MacDonald (2006) argue that subcultural theories (such as those of the CCCS) are more convincing explanations of the relationship between youth and style than neo-tribal explanations would suggest. They argue that 'youth cultural identities and practices' in contemporary societies are still shaped by notions of class, gender, age and ethnicity.

# Issues relating to gender

### Feminist and postmodern views

**Post-feminists** have pointed to significant **social changes** over the past 30 or so years that have altered how we think about gender and female involvement in youth subcultures.

➤ **Economic**: Women have greater involvement in the public sphere and, in consequence, have gained greater access to a significant form of **power** (economic independence).

➤ **Political**: Perceptions of women have similarly changed as they take on new social roles equal to men in many areas of social life. A range of **stereotypes** (such as women as natural mothers) and **stigmas** (surrounding divorce, lone parenthood, childlessness, work and so forth) have also gradually disappeared.

➤ **Cultural**: The patriarchal attitudes and assumptions that relegated women to a peripheral role in male-dominated youth subcultures or to a 'bedroom culture' that looked inward to the home (centred around commercially manufactured and packaged 'youth icons' and concerns about 'love and relationships with boys') are no longer as strong as they were. Young women, in particular, have a new freedom to develop and express their identities in postmodern culture.

These changes are expressed in terms of:

➤ **Choice**: Women have greater freedom to construct gender identities in a range of ways (from conventional notions of femininity to new notions based around masculinity and self-expression).

➤ **Exchange**: Behaviours once considered 'masculine' may now be incorporated into female identities (and vice versa). Traditional ideas about masculinity and femininity are questioned and women have greater access to behaviours — such as youth subcultures and styles — that were once the preserve of men.

### Girl subcultures

One consequence of these changes has been the development of both greater female involvement in 'youth culture' (such as the rave scene) and female subcultures. McRobbie (1994), for example, explored a shift away from the relatively *passive* consumption of culture noted in her earlier analysis of **bedroom culture** to one where young women have become more *actively* involved in the creation of female styles and identities, which we can outline as follows.

### Bedroom culture revisited

Harris (2001) argues that computer technologies have transformed how young women use space. Where 'the bedroom' was once a physical space into which various consumer products (such as magazines and music) were brought, 'The days of girls gazing longingly at posters on their bedroom walls and hoping to gain status by attaching themselves to popular boys seem long past.'

This private-sphere space has been transformed by the ability to link into wider global networks. This has resulted in the development of a range of 'female voices' being heard by young women. Harris argues that this new form of bedroom culture is one some women have chosen as a way of challenging conventional notions of 'girlhood' and of creating new forms of female participation.

Hodkinson and Lincoln (2008), for example, investigated young female use of 'online journals' (such as personal blogs and social networks) as **private social spaces** which they used both to 'exhibit and develop' a sense of personal identity and to engage in a variety of virtual social interactions with a wide circle of friends and acquaintances.

This use of bedroom culture suggests a need to rethink our understanding of female subcultures, participation and identity in the light of technological developments that allow global participation in virtual spaces focused on private physical spaces.

Hodkinson (2003), however, argues that while post-feminists have theorised the potential for young women to participate in a variety of different cultural groups 'from the comfort of their homes', the reality is somewhat different. While social networks clearly expand the possibilities for young women to engage in wider cultural activities, Hodkinson argues that they are used not to explore fluid and rapidly changing identities and styles but rather to solidify conventional behaviours and concerns. In this respect, he argues, contemporary societies are not inevitably '**post-subcultural**'.

### Grrrl power

This represents an alternative development that examines female participation in the public sphere through the formation of various female subcultures/tribes.

➤ **Riot grrrl**, for example, was an early form of female subculture based around punk bands, fanzines and some forms of political action focused on ideas about female identities and exclusion.

➤ **Girl gangs** might be a more conventional subcultural form (especially in America). Although juvenile male gangs of the kind described by Venkatesh (2008) are far more common, female gangs such as the Playgirls (an off-shoot of the male Playboys) are not unknown. An interesting feature of these gangs, documented by writers such as Chesney-Lind and Hagedorn (1999), is how they develop hierarchical structures allied to ways of introducing and socialising new members into the gang structure.

**?** What significant changes have there been in female lives over the past 30 years?

# Issues relating to ethnicity

## Ethnocentrism

A feature of many **spectacular** subcultures is the relative absence of minority ethnic groups. One reason for this is that researchers have generally taken an **ethnocentric** view of subcultures, considering them mainly in a British context focused around **class** (the CCCS approach) and **gender** (Marxist feminism). As Böse (2003) puts it: 'The racism of white working class youth was not always at the top of the subculturalist's agenda.'

Although many of the early spectacular subcultures developed among white working-class boys in the relative absence of substantial numbers of minority ethnic youth in the population, there was also a tendency to downplay the significance of **black youth subcultures** (Jamaican Rudeboys, for example, in the late 1950s) and cultural influences. Punk, for example, was heavily influenced by reggae and Rastafarian political ideas. While Rastafarianism could be considered a form of black youth subculture, this characterisation is slightly misleading; it is, first and foremost, a *religious movement* with an appeal across all age groups. While many black youths identified with Rastafarian ideals and objectives, it was never a specifically youth subculture.

More recent analyses have drawn attention to minority ethnic involvement in a range of styles:

➤ **Historical**: Some aspects of punk drew heavily on black Jamaican influences (the incorporation of reggae music for example), styles of dress and language, and symbols ('red, green and gold', for example, the colour of the Ethiopian flag, Ethiopia being the spiritual homeland of Rastafarians).

➤ **Contemporary**: Examples here range from the development of hip-hop and rap subcultures, initially in black urban America and subsequently around the globe, to Asian Desi subcultures ('Desi' being the self-given name for those originating in the Indian subcontinent). One commonly discussed is 'Big Bhangra' (the fusing of rock music with Indian Bhangra folk music).

**Post-subcultural theory** has arguably been less **ethnocentric** (something that reflects both the increasing **globalisation** of youth behaviours and the move away from analyses based on categories like **class** and **gender**). Huq (2003), for example, analyses the popularity of 'new

Poster in a British street advertising Indian and Pakistani music

Asian dance music' in Britain and the appeal of French rap music in the context of the development of 'transnational European identities' — identities that reach across national borders.

However, analyses of ethnic involvement in youth subcultures are present in something like the CCCS work we outlined earlier. Perhaps the best-known of these, Hall et al.'s (1978) analysis of the 'black mugging' media panic in the early 1970s, drew on ideas about racism and black cultural history but nevertheless focused mainly on how black youth were targeted and scapegoated as a symbol of political and economic problems in Britain at the time.

Post-subcultural theory and ethnicity

**P** ost-subculture
**E** thnocentric
**G** lobalisation

## Racism

Analysis of early youth subcultures (from Teds to skinheads) generally shows a lack of ethnic minority involvement. Two possible reasons are:

➤ **Racism**: These subcultures reflected the racism of British society at this time (the 'No Irish, No Blacks, No Dogs' mentality that prevailed through the 1950s and 1960s). In other words, youth subcultures, largely constructed around white, working-class youth, both reflected these racist mentalities and, in some cases, were openly antagonistic to non-whites (skinheads being a classic example). Although this may explain ethnic minority exclusion from 'white' youth cultures, it doesn't explain why minority youth didn't develop subcultures based around their own ethnicity.

➤ **Demography**: Ethnic minority subcultures might not have developed because of the demographic make-up of minority populations. Large-scale ('first-generation') immigration to Britain began in the 1950s and it took time for second-generation immigrants to become sufficiently numerous to form youth subcultures. Greater black involvement in the subcultures of the 1970s and 1980s suggests this may partly explain the relative absence of minority participation in earlier subcultures.

The development of 'Big Bhangra' among young (second- and third-generation) British Asians, for example, represents a youth subcultural style that did develop, as a unique (hybrid) cultural identity, embodying elements of white British and Asian music, dress, language and style. Its development arguably represented a search for a positive self-identity — among young minority males in particular — in a situation where they faced both racism and a sense of alienation from mainstream white and Asian culture.

**Post-racial** youth styles (the idea that contemporary youth tribes are largely unsegregated and 'race blind') have been highlighted by post-subcultural theories, but Moore (2010) argues that this is largely wishful thinking. The dominant figures in the majority of American style movements are, as in the subcultural past, largely white males: 'strong, individualistic characters navigating a world in which white male hegemony is crumbling amid globalization'. These 'new cultural groupings', he argues, 'replicate and support traditional roles and power in white, patriarchal American society'.

**Retro-subcultures** (the revival of **older** forms of swing, ska and rockabilly for example) are not post-subcultural but merely attempts to recreate times when 'men were the makers of their own fortunes'.

> **?**  Define ethnocentrism.

## Resistance

One of the main themes of Marxist and feminist subcultural theories ('resistance' to dominant economic and/or cultural norms and values) is largely absent in the analysis of minority youth behaviour. This, however, may owe more to how we define both youth subcultures and 'resistance'.

One suggestion here is that ethnic minority resistance is directed **inwards** rather than being expressed in **outward** forms of opposition. The idea is that minority youth identities involve resistance in areas like:

> **Self-description**: Minorities label their own behaviour (a recent example being Desi styles), as opposed to being labelled by a dominant culture. This is a significant aspect of minority youth identity. On occasions, self-descriptions can resist cultural stereotypes by actually employing racist labels designed to stigmatise a minority group (an example being the self-labelling of 'paki-culture').
> **Ascription**: Identities and styles are also shaped through resistance to dominant cultural labelling. The negative media stereotyping of young blacks, for example, led to the adoption of ironic references (such as 'gangsta') that resisted this type of labelling.

## Hybrid subcultures

True cultural hybridity — a fusion between elements of different cultural traditions to produce something new and culturally distinct — is actually quite rare. It's difficult to identify many youth subcultures that fit the bill (one of the closest is probably Big Bhangra, but even here the hybrid element is largely focused on musical development).

We can, therefore, more usefully think about hybrid subcultures in two ways.

### Hybrid elements

Many youth subcultures have hybrid **elements** — from hippies co-opting military uniforms, insignia (such as dog tags) and symbols in the name of 'peace', to skinheads taking working class styles to exaggerated levels (bovver boots, belts and braces). As Luke and Luke (2000) argue, 'hybridity is not new, nor an invention of postmodernism and globalization'.

### Glocal subcultures

**Glocal subcultures**, Malone (2002) suggests, are a more recent form of hybridity in contemporary societies. Glocal involves **global** styles and identities filtered through **local** subcultural groups (hence 'glocal'). Styles existing on a global scale are given a unique local interpretation and twist through their incorporation by different cultural groups.

As Malone suggests, hip-hop exists as a **global youth culture** based around a particular style and identity. However, the meaning of this style is interpreted differently by youth in different countries, depending in part on their own local cultural background and traditions, so it is also glocal.

**Glocalised youth subcultures** are, by definition, hybrids since they involve mixing and matching a variety of different cultural traditions in the context of a global youth style. They have obvious advantages for their members: they are able to key into a global (virtual) community of youth who all have a common understanding of this style (reflecting Thornton's (1996) concept of **subcultural capital**), while simultaneously being part of a local subcultural community that allows hip-hop styles, for example, to be adapted to particular individual tastes.

---

**Exam-style questions**

**1** Identify and explain two features of girl subcultures. (17 marks)

**2** Identify and explain two reasons for the absence of ethnic minority groups in the sociological study of subcultures (17 marks)

**3** Outline and evaluate Marxist views of the role of youth subcultures in society. (33 marks)

**4** Outline and evaluate the view that the role of youth culture is to assist in the transition from childhood to adulthood. (33 marks)

---

# Youth and deviance

In this section we explore the idea of 'problem youth' in more detail by looking at the extent to which young people engage in deviant/criminal behaviour and at various sociological explanations for that involvement.

## Key concepts

### Deviance

All societies develop **rules** (norms) to guide the behaviour of their members, and 'deviance' refers to any and all behaviours that 'break the rules'. Deviance, therefore, is behaviour that deviates from the norm:

➤ **Criminal deviance** involves breaking **formal**, legal rules (**laws** or **formal norms**).
➤ **Non-criminal deviance** involves breaking **informal** non-legal rules (**informal norms**).

This distinction is important because it reflects a **qualitative difference** between deviance and crime:

➤ **deviance** — rule-breaking behaviour of *any kind*
➤ **crime** — rule-breaking related to legal norms; while crime is always deviant, not all deviance is criminal

While everyone 'breaks the rules' at some point in their life, not everyone engages in criminal rule-breaking and, for this reason, it would be interesting to know how and why some people and groups engage in higher levels of crime than others.

## Crime

Crime, as we have suggested, is a particular form of deviant behaviour. Not only is it considered more serious than, say, forgetting to send a friend a card on their birthday (it might be embarrassing but you're not going to be sent to prison); it is also much easier to measure. This follows because we have an **objective standard** (the law) against which to compare behaviour.

For example, if you stand on a street corner and start shouting abuse at anyone who passes by, you're committing a crime and will probably be arrested. A failure to remember a friend's birthday may have certain personal consequences, but these are unlikely to include arrest and imprisonment. While both are technically deviant, how people **react** to them will be very different.

**?** **Give one difference between crime and deviance.**

For these reasons — because crime is a more **serious** form of deviance and easier to **measure** — we are going to focus on the relationship between youth and crime, rather than youth and deviance. Young (2001) suggests four ways to measure crime in our society.

➤ **Official crime statistics**: these record crimes **reported** to the police.
➤ **Victim surveys**: these record crimes people have experienced, but not necessarily reported; they include both sociological surveys (such as the **Islington Crime Surveys** (Young et al. (1986, 1990)) and official government surveys such as the **British Crime Survey**.
➤ **Self-report surveys**: these ask people to admit to crimes they have committed.
➤ **Agency surveys**: Maguire (2002), for example, notes that we can collect 'systematic information about unreported crime' by studying things like hospital admission and treatment records.

Although these sources give us a good idea about the nature and extent of crime, they are by no means perfect indicators, for the following reasons.

### Crime and criminals

Not everyone who breaks the law is a criminal; the latter is a label given to someone convicted of a crime. While two people can commit exactly the same crime (such as stealing a car), if one is never convicted he or she does not appear in the official crime statistics and, as far as anyone knows, is not a criminal. This creates problems if we are interested in studying the social and psychological characteristics of 'young criminals'.

### Defining youth

This is a problem because to understand the relationship between youth and crime we need to have a standard definition of youth — and, as we've already seen, there are a number of different definitions. Legally, for example, the lower limit for criminal responsibility in England is 10 years old. Normally, we would probably classify someone this age as a child rather than a youth. In Belgium, for example, the age of criminal responsibility is 18.

The upper limit is normally taken to be 18 (all under 18 are classified as 'minors' or 'juveniles'), but this again could perhaps be too low (since some definitions of youth set the upper limit around 25).

> **?** Why is it easier to measure crime than deviance?

## Delinquency

This concept is frequently used to refer to relatively minor forms of criminal behaviour (something that, in recent years, has come to be seen as 'anti-social behaviour', although it does, of course, include actual criminal behaviour) committed by 'young people'.

**Juvenile delinquents** are generally taken to mean those under 18 convicted (or suspected) of committing criminal or 'anti-social' acts. Legally, however, the **Police and Criminal Evidence Act** (1984) defines a 'juvenile' as anyone aged between 10 and 16. The fuzziness of definitions (both legal and sociological) is something we need to keep in mind when analysing the relationship between youth and criminal deviance.

### Social construction

Problems of definition notwithstanding, a wider issue we need to consider is the idea that concepts of crime and deviance are **socially constructed**. As Becker (1963) suggests, societies not only 'create deviance' by making the rules governing criminal behaviour (without rules there can be no deviance); they do so in different ways at different times:

➤ **Historical**: Homosexuality was a criminal offence in England until 1967.
➤ **Cross-cultural**: Drinking alcohol in a bar is legal at 18 in England; in Saudi Arabia it's a criminal offence.
➤ **Context**: The same behaviour can be interpreted differently depending on who does it and why they do it. A soldier killing an enemy in war is not deviant; the same soldier killing a civilian is a criminal.

These differences led Becker to argue that deviance (including crime) is:

➤ **not** a quality of what you do
➤ a quality of how someone **reacts** to what you do

### Labelling

This means we need to think about crime, in particular, as **labelling** — a concept that has two main qualities:

➤ **Name**: We need ways to identify what we see (such as 'youth' as opposed to 'child').

➤ **Characteristics** attached to the label: When we think about a label we also think about a range of things that describe it.

The characteristics associated with the label 'youth' are significant in terms of:

➤ **Social identities**: How you think about 'youth' will affect how you behave towards 'young people'. If you see them, for example, as 'sullen, thuggish, violent criminals' then you're probably going to avoid them whenever possible — unless you're a police officer, in which case we may see the development of a self-fulfilling prophecy.

➤ **Self-fulfilling prophecy**: A prediction about behaviour (prophecy) that itself brings about the predicted behaviour (self-fulfilling). For example, if you 'know' who is more likely to commit crime in our society (because crime statistics tell you it's young people rather than the elderly), then you're more likely to watch youth behaviour more closely. The closer you watch, the more likely you are to uncover evidence of crime — which confirms your original belief because more young people are arrested and convicted. Campbell et al. (2000), for example, found that nearly 70% of persistent young offenders were already known to the police.

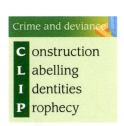

Crime and deviance

**C** onstruction
**L** abelling
**I** dentities
**P** rophecy

A further aspect to labelling is that some labels have more power than others. Becker, for example, argues that **master labels** are important because, once attached, everything about an individual is interpreted in the light of the label. Someone publicly labelled a 'paedophile', for example, is likely to have all of their behaviour interpreted in the light of this label (hence the idea of a 'master status' — one that defines everything about you).

> **?** How can youth sometimes be considered a 'master status'?

## Moral panics

A combination of master labelling and self-fulfilling prophecies can help to create what Cohen (1972) has called **moral panics** — a situation where an individual or group is:

➤ **labelled** by the media

➤ **defined** (in a '**moral crusade**') as 'a threat to society's values'

➤ **presented** in a 'stereotypical fashion'

➤ **made the target of** 'demands for action' from the authorities (a '**moral clampdown**')

In relation to youth and deviance:

➤ **Labelling**: The behaviours of young people are frequently defined and publicised in the media as a 'social problem'.

➤ **Self-fulfilling prophecies** develop when the media look closely at these behaviours.
➤ **Moral panics** occur when the 'behaviour of youth' seems to be spiralling out of control (as judged by sensational media reporting). What Cohen calls 'folk devils' are created — people whose behaviour causes public panic and alarm and who should, in consequence, be severely punished.

Examples of periodic moral panics relating to youth are not difficult to find. See for example:

➤ Cohen's (1972) analysis of mods and rockers 'fighting in seaside towns' in the early 1960s (a good example of a self-fulfilling prophecy: the media 'predicted trouble' between these 'mortal enemies' and both groups duly turned up looking for where the action was supposed to be)
➤ Critcher's (2000) analysis of 'rave culture' and the panic that developed around the use of Ecstasy
➤ Young's (1971) analysis of drug takers in Notting Hill: an example of both the way illegal drug taking is consistently associated with youth and, more significantly, the idea of deviancy amplification

**Deviancy amplification** is Wilkins's (1964) argument that an over-reaction (by the police, public and politicians) can lead ultimately to the criminalisation of large numbers of people for behaviour that was originally mildly deviant.

We should, however, note that the concept of moral panic is not without its critics:

➤ McRobbie (1994) argues that it has been over-used, especially by the media, to describe behaviour that is not immoral and does not justify a panic.
➤ McRobbie and Thornton (1995) also argue that the media have become so sophisticated in their understanding of how amplification and moral panics work that 'moral panics, once the unintended outcome of journalistic practice, seem to have become a goal' — a way of whipping up public excitement to sell more newspapers.

# Pattern and trends in youth deviance according to social class, gender and ethnicity

## Age

A consistent finding of statistical and survey methods is the **correlation** between age and deviant behaviour. Youth (the 10–25 age group) have far greater involvement in crime than their older counterparts — a relationship Hirschi and Gottfredson (1983) argue is constant both historically and across different societies. It can, however, be qualified in relation to categories like:

➤ **Class**: Working-class males have higher rates of offending.
➤ **Ethnicity**: Black males have higher rates of conviction.
➤ **Gender**: Males have consistently higher rates of offending.

Kanazawa and Still (2000) suggest 'crime and other risk-taking behaviour' peaks 'in late adolescence and early adulthood' (Table 10.2).

Table 10.2   Offenders by age (England and Wales) in 000s

| Age group | 2003 | 2004 | 2005 | 2006 | 2007 | 2008 |
|---|---|---|---|---|---|---|
| 10–19 | 156 (32%) | 160 (34%) | 169 (34%) | 175 (34%) | 179 (34%) | 152 (31%) |
| 10–29 | 330 (68%) | 320 (68%) | 331 (66%) | 341 (67%) | 349 (67%) | 323 (65%) |
| 30–60+ | 155 | 153 | 159 | 165 | 170 | 175 |
| All | 485 | 473 | 490 | 506 | 519 | 498 |

*Source: Hughes and Church (2010)*

Hales et al. (2009) found, over a 4-year period, that a small minority of young offenders (4% of 10–25-year-olds) were disproportionately responsible for around one third (32%) of all offences committed by this age group.

Looking more specifically at the most serious (**indictable**) offences, in 2005:
➤ 15% were committed by those aged 10–17.
➤ 12% were committed by those aged 18–20.

In terms of less serious 'anti-social behaviour', 40% of Anti-Social Behaviour Orders (ASBOs) issued in 2007 were to those under 18.

**?**   What is one pattern and one trend in age-related crime?

### Explanations
Some explanations focus on the idea that there is something unique about 'youth' that makes them more criminal:

#### Socialisation and social control
Maruna (1997) notes that young people have fewer social responsibilities and ties; **informal social controls** are consequently less effective and there is a greater likelihood of **risk-taking behaviour** (such as crime).

#### Social distance theory
Conversely to the above, Maruna argues that certain activities and responsibilities *distance* (mainly) older people from (public) situations in which opportunistic criminality occurs. These include:
➤ finding employment
➤ staying in education
➤ getting married
➤ starting a family

*Peer-group pressure*

Criminal behaviour may confer the status that many youths lack through education, the workplace and the like. FitzGerald et al. (2003) suggest two peer-related factors in youth criminal activity:

➤ **Cultural**: 'Image-conscious' youth need to maintain and constantly update a sense of image and style (clothes, mobiles and so forth).

➤ **Economic** (the need for money to finance their image): They found that where family financial support was absent, crime was a source of funding.

*Lifestyle factors*

Young people are more likely to:

➤ be involved in activities in the public domain (such as pubs and clubs) that bring conflict with other youths, the police and so forth. Campbell et al. (2000), for example, found 'Boys who hung around in public places were more likely to be offenders'

➤ have a lifestyle conducive to opportunistic (unplanned) crimes

*Other explanations*

Other explanations focus less on youth itself and more on how those in authority *react* to youth behaviours:

➤ **Spatial targeting**: The police focus on groups (young people) and places (clubs, pubs, etc.) where large numbers of youth meet.

➤ **Social visibility**: Young people, especially those under the influence of drink and drugs, are more likely to commit crimes where witnesses are present.

## Social class

Where **official crime statistics** don't distinguish between classes, it's harder to disentangle the relationship between class and youth crime. However, one way we can do this is to look at **risk factors**: those most closely **correlated** with crime relate more to working-class than middle-class youth.

McAra and McVie's (2009) 10-year longitudinal **Edinburgh study** found a strong correlation between criminal convictions and:

➤ leaving school at the earliest opportunity

➤ exclusion from school at 14

The Youth Justice Board (2005) identified four areas and risk factors most closely correlated with those young people convicted of crimes:

1 **Family**

➤ deprived households

➤ absconding from home

➤ inconsistent adult supervision and boundary setting

➤ significant adults involved in criminal activity

**2 Education**
- underachievement
- lack of attachment to school/own education

**3 Community**
- associating with predominantly pro-criminal peers

**4 Personal**
- offending to obtain money for substances
- lacking understanding of the effect of behaviour on victims

Pitts (2008), however, argues that youth involvement in **serious crime** is most closely related to living in disadvantaged neighbourhoods, rather than to the individual, family or educational characteristics of the children who live there.

**?** | **What explanations are there for trends in youth crime?**

### Explanations

Risk factors relate to **convicted** youth and we need to consider the **dark figure of crime**: most crime in our society (with notable exceptions such as murder and car theft) goes unreported — reported crime is, therefore, just the tip of the iceberg. This means explanations based around the social and individual characteristics of convicted youth may not necessarily apply to those who commit crimes but are never caught.

### *Lifestyles*

**Working-class** youth are more likely to experience:
- **socialisation** problems within the family (inconsistent adult supervision and boundary setting)
- **encouragement** to commit crimes through both greater parental involvement in crime and peer pressure through association with criminal peers
- **poverty and disadvantage** in home and neighbourhood life (including high levels of unemployment); Smith (2006) suggests poverty has negative impacts on family life and educational achievement and makes working-class youth more open to criminal behaviour

**Middle-class** youth are less likely to be involved in 'lifestyle offending' (various forms of street and opportunistic crimes), for reasons of:
- **status** — a criminal record is likely to affect potential career opportunities
- **education** — they stay in education longer and have greater career development opportunities
- **economics** — they are less likely to turn to crime for income to support their lifestyle

### Spatial targeting

Police resources are focused on areas and individuals where crime is highest — working-class spaces such as clubs, pubs, estates or designated 'crime hotspots' — something that contributes to a **self-fulfilling prophecy**.

### Social visibility

Working-class youth 'street' crime has a high visibility — clear victims, witnesses and little attempt to hide criminal behaviour; detection and conviction rates are consequently higher.

### Status deviance

Many crimes are not committed for economic reasons alone; some relate to power and prestige within a social group and involve a combination of **risk-taking** and the idea of 'thumbing your nose' at authority. Smith et al. (2005) suggest working-class youth contact with the police is more likely to be **adversarial** (conflict-based) and hence more likely to involve arrest (rather than cautions or warnings).

## Gender

While young males and females commit much the same *types* of crime (theft, drug offences and assault being the main categories), Maguire (2002) notes that higher **male** involvement is a feature of all societies, past and present.

Campbell et al. (2000) note the following:

➤ For **women**:
  ➤ **Under 16**: The most common offences are criminal damage, shoplifting, buying stolen goods and fighting.
  ➤ **Over 16**: There is less criminal damage and shoplifting, and more fraud and buying stolen goods.
  ➤ **Over 21**: There is a fall in all types of offending (fraud or buying stolen goods were the most common offences).
➤ For **men**:
  ➤ **Under 16**: Around 12% of boys admitted to fighting, buying stolen goods, theft and criminal damage.
  ➤ **16–17**: There is a similar pattern of offending, but more than one third of offences involved fighting.
  ➤ **18–21**: Here is the highest level of offending, with increased fighting but a decline in shoplifting and criminal damage. Entry into work brings new opportunities for fraud and theft.

Although the overall **trend** in both male and female crime over the past 15 years is **downwards** (with one or two exceptions — male violence has increased), the average male and female prison population has steadily increased over the past 30 years (Table 10.3).

Table 10.3   The average prison population in England and Wales

| Year | Males | Females |
|------|-------|---------|
| 1978 | 40,409 | 1,387 |
| 1988 | 47,113 | 1,759 |
| 1998 | 62,194 | 3,105 |
| 2008 | 78,158 | 4,414 |

*Source: Hughes and Church (2010)*

Nacro (2009) argues that although there has been a rise in both detected female criminality and female imprisonment in recent years, this doesn't necessarily mean young women are engaging in higher levels of crime. Changes to the way the police handle female deviance (a reduction in the use of informal measures when responding to girls' misbehaviour and a greater readiness to arrest young women) are more likely to explain this increase.

Overall, the peak offending years for youth are:
➢ female: 14–15
➢ male: 16–19

Both male and female offending declines gradually with age. Smith (2006) notes that girls stop offending at an earlier age and the decline in their offending is also more rapid than for boys.

With regard to **Anti-Social Behaviour Orders**, Hughes and Church (2010) note that males were ten times more likely than females to receive an ASBO in 2007.

**?**   What differences are there between trends in young male and female criminality?

### Explanations

➢ **Masculinity and identity formation**: Davies relates risk-taking to ideas about masculinity and femininity — risky behaviour, such as street crime, is associated with 'being male'. McIvor (1998) argues that young male criminality is linked to a range of risk-taking behaviours 'associated with the search for masculine identity in the transition from adolescence to adulthood'.

➢ **Opportunity structures** reflect different forms of participation in the *public* and *private* domains. Davies (1997), for example, notes how young men have fewer home and family responsibilities and consequently greater opportunities for crime. Where young men and women have *similar* opportunity structures (such as McMillan (2004) notes for shoplifting) they commit similar levels of crime. The effect of changing opportunity structures is also significant — older youth are more likely to be in work and so commit offences (fraud and theft) that reflect this new status.

➤ **Risk**: Males and females have different attitudes to risk-taking. Lyng (2004), for example, uses the concept of **'edgework'** to refer to various forms of 'voluntary risk-taking' — young males in particular engage in behaviour that continually pushes at behavioural boundaries ('exploring the edges') in dangerous, sometimes life-threatening, ways. This includes crimes committed for the 'thrill' and 'danger' as much as the economic reward.

Gender and crime

**M** asculinity
**O** pportunity
**R** isk
**E** dgework
**S** ocialisation

➤ **Socialisation and control**: Young males have greater levels of freedom of movement and association than females and they spend more time in the public domain — places where crimes are more likely to occur.

> **?** Why are there lower levels of female criminality in our society?

## Ethnicity

The Commission for Racial Equality (2004) suggests **ethnic minorities** are more likely to be:

➤ **victims** of household, car and racially motivated crimes
➤ **arrested** for notifiable offences

Nacro (2009) found that minority ethnic youth were more likely to be:

➤ **remanded** in prison (refused bail)
➤ **over-represented** in the prison population

### Imprisonment

The Youth Justice Board (2009) found that while black youth made up 3% of the general population aged 10–17, they accounted for:

➤ 7% of those brought to the attention of the youth justice system
➤ 14% of those receiving a custodial sentence
➤ 33% of those given long-term detention

### Offending rates

There is little difference between ethnic minority young people in terms of overall offending. Young black males are, however, at greater risk of gun crime/murder (as both victims and offenders).

### Victims

Asians have a higher risk of being victims of household crime, whereas black minorities are at greater risk of personal crimes such as assault.

### Explanations

➤ **Demographics**: Ethnic minority groups have two significant characteristics:
  ➤ **Social class**: They are more likely to be working class.
  ➤ **Age**: They have a younger age profile than both the white majority and the UK population as a whole.

These characteristics are significant because of the relationship we have noted between class, age and crime.

➤ **Social control**: The relatively low levels of female Asian offending can be partly explained by higher levels of family surveillance and social control. Similarly, black minority youth are more likely to be raised in single-parent families than their white peers, and this type of family profile is statistically associated with higher rates of juvenile offending.

➤ **Over-representation**: One set of explanations for black over-representation in prison focuses on what Young and Mooney (1999) argue is **institutional police racism** (a belief running through the police service in greater levels of minority criminality). Black youth have far greater chances of being:

  ➤ **Targeted** by the police as potential/actual offenders: Clancy et al. (2001) note that when all demographic factors are controlled for, 'being young, male and black increased a person's likelihood of being stopped and searched'.

  ➤ **Arrested and prosecuted**: Urban areas (such as London and Manchester) had a lower ratio of black/white arrest rates than rural areas (such as Norfolk, where blacks were eight times more likely to be arrested than whites). Significantly perhaps, black suspects were also more likely to be acquitted in both magistrate and Crown courts.

# Sociological explanations of the patterns and trends

We can look briefly at how different sociological perspectives have explained the patterns and trends in youth crime and deviance.

## Functionalism

When we looked at functionalist perspectives on the role of youth culture we identified two ideas that we can develop to help explain the relationship between youth and crime:

➤ **Transition**: Youth is seen as a period of transition between childhood and adulthood.

➤ **Anomie**: According to Merton (1938), this is '**normative confusion**' — not knowing, or being unable to follow, the norms expected of different statuses. In other words, youth is a status where young people are potentially confused about how they're supposed to behave because they exist 'between childhood and adulthood'. Without clear normative guidance from various **reference groups** — parents, teachers, peers, the media and so forth — young people are likely to become deviant (as we've seen with the 'risk factors' associated with youth crime).

For Merton the relationship between youth and anomie related to the ability of societies to provide routes not just into adulthood but, most importantly, into the *successful* performance of adult roles. 'Success' could be measured in a range of ways:

➤ **economic** — getting a good, well-paid, high-status job

➤ **psychological** — surviving youth unscathed by a criminal record

➤ **cultural** — successfully achieving a desired role (such as motherhood)

What mattered, therefore, was the ability of societies to provide the **means** by which young people could successfully achieve adult **ends** (or goals) — one of the most significant being the desire for **status**:

➤ **Middle-class youth**, for example, were less likely to be deviant because their future was mapped out in terms of success at school, going to university and then into a well-paid, high-status, professional career.

➤ **Girls** were less likely to turn to crime because their future adult roles were also partially mapped out in terms of movement from their parents' family (where they were subject to more rigorous forms of social control) to a family of their own. Status could, therefore, be successfully achieved via this route.

➤ **Working-class boys**, on the other hand, experienced greater problems in their search for status — their relatively low educational achievement, for example, meant the 'middle-class route' to status was effectively blocked. They were also less likely to see status success in terms of family roles because concepts of successful masculinity stressed being able to provide for a partner and children.

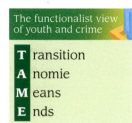

The functionalist view of youth and crime

**T**ransition
**A**nomie
**M**eans
**E**nds

A range of theories developed to explain the relationship between male working-class youth and deviant behaviour:

### Status frustration

Cohen (1955) argued that youth subcultures enabled some young males to achieve status (or 'respect') among their peers. Hargreaves (1967), for example, showed how boys who were denied status in school developed **oppositional subcultures** through which they gained peer status by rejecting the behaviours valued by the school (being attentive and respectful to teachers, working hard, regular attendance and so forth).

### Opportunity structures

Cloward and Ohlin (1960) gave a wider picture of the search for status. Where young working-class boys were denied a route to status through 'legitimate opportunity structures' such as work, they developed alternative ways of finding it through different kinds of subculture:

➤ **Criminal**: These subcultures developed in stable communities with successful criminal **role models** ('crime pays') and a **career structure** for aspiring criminals.

➤ **Conflict**: Without community support, **gang cultures** developed by providing 'services' such as prostitution and drug dealing.

➤ **Retreatist**: Boys unable to join criminal or conflict subcultures (they failed in both legitimate and illegitimate job markets) retreated into 'individualistic' subcultures based on drug abuse, alcoholism and petty crime.

### Focal concerns

While the explanations above focus on how some young people react to **status denial**, another way of looking at the problem can be found in Miller's (1958) argument that some working-class youth developed a 'route into adulthood' that brought them into conflict with the values of wider society through **focal concerns** that emerged from the realities of working-class life 'at the bottom of society'. These led some male youth to develop values, norms, identities and lifestyles that brought them into conflict with wider society. The focal concerns Miller identified are:

➤ **Trouble**: Working-class life is tough, occasionally violent, and young males quickly learn to identify 'trouble' and how to handle it — abilities that confer status on the individual.

➤ **Toughness**: The ability to handle 'trouble' (to see violence as a means of resolving problems) involves being able to 'take care' of both yourself and your mates. Once again, toughness is an important source of status.

➤ **Excitement**: Working-class boys were denied self-expression in places like school (something to be tolerated) and work (invariably dull, menial and boring). Lack of employment also meant 'fun' couldn't be easily bought. However, excitement could be created in a variety of ways — such as through the 'edgework' of crime.

➤ **Smartness**: If status was just about being tough, most young men would fail the test, but it could be gained in other ways. Being clever or witty, capable of telling a good joke, making a funny comment or defusing 'trouble' without losing face were seen as valuable attributes.

➤ **Fate**: Working-class boys were fatalistic ('whatever will be, will be'), mainly because their lives lacked power or the ability to influence what happened to them. This, in turn, produced a fatalistic attitude to risky behaviours — whatever happened to them was going to happen regardless.

➤ **Autonomy**: A feeling of control over their lives was expressed through their behaviour towards 'middle-class' authority figures (teachers, social workers, government officials, police officers, etc.). By refusing to cooperate, working-class youth gained a (fleeting) sense of freedom.

These ideas come together in something like Parker's (1974) study of youth gangs in Liverpool, where the significant point to focal concerns is that they involve behaviours highly likely to bring them into contact and conflict with authority.

> **?** Briefly explain the concept of 'status frustration'.

## Marxism

We can illustrate Marxist approaches by looking at two general ways they have focused on and explained youth behaviour: deviance and crime.

### Deviance

The CCCS approach, as we have already outlined, has focused on the two general themes of loss and resistance.

### Loss

This theme is based around the idea that youth deviance — especially among working-class males — is a **response** to something being taken away or 'lost'. Cohen (1972), for example, argued that the break-up of working-class communal life created a 'cultural vacuum' in the lives of young men in particular — a sense of loss they attempted to rectify by adopting a range of communal styles and behaviours (from mods and rockers to skinheads) that brought them into conflict with wider society.

### Resistance

Resistance is the second key theme in the CCCS approach. Some youth more than others experience the impact of rapid **social and technological changes** in ways that are disruptive and disturbing. These include things like:

➢ unemployment
➢ low wages
➢ deskilling (the idea that what was once skilled manual work has been reduced to mundane and repetitive tasks controlling the machines that do the work)
➢ high-rise housing estates that lack any facilities for young people

Some young men at the sharp end of social changes who, because of their position at the bottom of society, lack the power to do anything more than protest about these changes, develop forms of **cultural resistance** through subcultural groups. As the CCCS literature suggests, these represent **symbolic** or **magical** attempts to resist the changes impacting on their lives. The cultural styles and deviant identities they create are conscious and meaningful alternatives to the way those in positions of power would like them to behave.

For **middle-class youth**, resistance to social changes tends to take more tangible forms, sometimes expressed in terms of a **counter-culture** such as living in a style that rejects 'capitalist consumer values', participating in environmental groups (resisting road building, for example, or the destruction of natural habitats for houses and out-of-town shopping malls) and peace camps (resisting the militarisation of society). Middle-class deviance has tended to take a more directly **political** form (such as the demonstrations against increased university tuition fees in 2010). Brake (1977) has also suggested that middle-class youth subcultures (such as hippies) tend to be reasonably well organised around a particular 'philosophy of self' — one that stresses individual development, 'doing your own thing' and so forth and that brings them into conflict with dominant cultural norms.

### Crime

A more recent approach is Lea and Young's (1984) **left realist** argument that crime and deviance are more likely to occur when each of three conditions is met:

➢ **Relative deprivation**: Poverty in itself is not a cause of crime; what is significant is how deprived people *feel* compared with others. Young, working-class males are likely to see themselves as relatively deprived when they look at their middle-class peers.

➢ **Marginalisation** relating to social status: Young, working-class men are frequently 'pushed to the margins of society' through educational failure and low-pay, low-status work. Politically, the authorities are not interested in listening to their problems or grievances (the response of the powerful is more likely to involve tougher policing and increased surveillance). Where young men see themselves as having nothing to lose, crime becomes an option.

➢ **Subculture** (although **neo-tribes** would probably fit just as neatly): the ability to form groups is a **collective response** to a particular social situation. In this instance, the form of the subcultural group is determined by feelings of **relative deprivation** and **marginalisation**. Specific subcultural values are not independent of the culture in which they arise and, for Lea and Young, it is precisely because working-class youths *accept* the general values of capitalist society that they indulge in criminal behaviour — the pursuit of desired ends by illegitimate means.

## Labelling

Labelling theory approaches youth deviance from a different direction. Rather than thinking in terms of individuals or groups having particular **qualities** that lead to deviant/criminal behaviour, labelling theories focus, as Becker (1963) argues, on how the powerful **react** to the behaviour of young people. To understand youth deviance, therefore, we need to look at:

➢ how and why some groups in society are **negatively labelled** (as social problems, for example)
➢ the effect of negative labelling on those labelled

As we've seen, the behaviour of young people is more likely to be negatively labelled (youth subcultures and styles, for example, invariably break conventional social norms) — although negative labelling is more likely to be applied to some youth rather than others:

➢ **Gender**: males rather than females.
➢ **Class**: working-class rather than middle-class.
➢ **Ethnicity**: black youth rather than white. As Cashmore and McLaughlin (1991) put it when referring to police labelling: 'Young blacks over the past twenty-odd years have been officially defined as a social problem and given special treatment.' A similar, if more recent, process has, Kundnani (2004) argues, occurred among young Asians since the 9/11 terrorist attacks, with 'racial profiling' being used to target particular groups.

The general idea, therefore, is that **powerful** groups (such as the police, media and politicians) shape our perception of **powerless** groups (such as young, black, working-class males) through a **labelling process** that justifies whatever action (from increased imprisonment to a range of quasi-judicial actions — ASBOs, curfews, dispersal zones) the authorities want to take against 'deviants'.

This can lead to what Wilkins (1964) described as a **deviancy amplification spiral**: the behaviour of some individuals or groups (**primary deviation**) is singled out for attention, condemnation and action, which leads to **secondary deviation** (increased deviant behaviour as the targeted group reacts to the initial labelling process). This, in turn, justifies further action against 'deviants' — such as widespread arrests, new laws to deal with 'the problem' and so forth — that leads ultimately to the criminalisation of behaviour that may initially have been only mildly deviant.

One (unintended) outcome of this negative labelling process is, Becker (1963) argues, a **deviant career**. The successful application of a label 'confirms the individual' as deviant, both to themselves and others around them (teachers, employers and the like). This can block participation in normal society (a youth with a criminal record, for example, may be unable to find work), which, in turn, means the deviant seeks out the company of similar deviants, resulting in increased involvement in deviant behaviour.

---

**Exam-style questions**

**1** Identify and explain two characteristics of moral panics involving young people. (17 marks)

**2** Identify and explain two ways in which youth deviance is influenced by social class. (17 marks)

**3** Outline and evaluate interactionist explanations of youth and deviance. (33 marks)

---

# The experience of youth in education

## The experience of schooling

Education is a form of secondary socialisation involving two related processes that constitute the experience of schooling, the formal and informal curriculum.

### The formal curriculum

The **formal curriculum** is the material schools exist to teach (maths, physics, history and so forth). Gaining qualifications in these subjects is a significant part of the educational experience for many young people.

### The hidden curriculum

The **hidden curriculum**, as Jackson (1968) argues, involves the things we learn from the experience of attending school. Skelton (1997) suggests it involves 'messages relating to knowledge, values, norms of behaviour and attitudes that learners experience in and through educational processes'. The messages teachers give to students in the course of their teaching include:

➤ status messages (such as whether boys are more valued than girls)
➤ beliefs about ability (who has it and who doesn't)

Some aspects of the hidden curriculum are taught to all pupils:

➤ respect for authority
➤ punctuality
➤ time-keeping

Many, however, are taught in different ways to different pupil categories, according to social class, gender and ethnicity.

## Social class

### Formal curriculum

If we measure the quality of an individual's educational experience in terms of qualifications, it rapidly becomes apparent that, for working-class pupils especially, that experience is not particularly pleasant:

➤ **Key Stages 1–4**: The figures for those claiming free school meals (FSM) is a broadly reliable guide to social class (FSM children are generally working-class). The statistics show FSM children do consistently worse than non-FSM children at all Key Stages.
➤ **GCSE**: Table 10.4 demonstrates how those with parents at the top of the class system (higher professional) are more than twice as successful in GCSEs as those with parents at the bottom.

Table 10.4   Five or more GCSE grades A* to C or equivalent at age 16 (%)

|  | 2008 | 2002 | 2000 | 1989 |
|---|---|---|---|---|
| Higher professional | 81 | 77 | 74 | 52 |
| Lower professional | 75 |  |  |  |
| Intermediate/skilled manual | 61 | 52 | 45 | 21 |
| Lower supervisory | 47 |  |  |  |
| Routine manual | 43 |  |  |  |
| Other/not classified | 37 | 32 | 26 | 12 |

Source: Hughes and Church (2010)

### Hidden curriculum

This involves a range of ideas and experiences.

#### *Type of school*

This has an impact on educational experience. A working-class pupil attending an inner-city school (such as Lilian Baylis Technology School) has a different educational experience from an upper-/middle-class child who attends a top private school such as Wellington College.

Wellington College

Table 10.5   Wellington College and Lilian Baylis Technology School compared

|  | **Wellington College** | **Lilian Baylis** |
|---|---|---|
| **Size** | 1,000+ | 624 |
| **Location** | 400 acres of Berkshire countryside | Inner-city location next to busy road |
| **Type** | Independent fee-paying | Technology school |
| **Pupils** | Majority from upper/middle class<br>A small number of means-tested bursaries and scholarships available | Majority from deprived or disrupted backgrounds<br>75% on free school meals<br>20% pupils are refugees or asylum seekers<br>50% pupils with learning difficulty or disability<br>50+ languages spoken in students' homes |
| **Extra-curricular** | 8 rugby pitches, 2 floodlit Astroturf pitches, state-of-the-art sports hall, 22 hard tennis courts, 12 cricket pitches, athletics track, 2 lacrosse pitches, 6 netball courts, shooting range, 9-hole golf course | Purpose built sports hall, 3 basketball/netball courts, floodlit Astroturf pitch<br>Use of local swimming pools |
| **Facilities** | 6 art studios, professional recording studio, several concert venues, own theatre and TV crew | Careers events<br>Study trips for all Y10 students to a European capital<br>Residential study conferences |
| **Curriculum** | Small classes<br>Sets own curriculum, plus International Baccalaureate, GCSE and A-level | Large classes<br>National Curriculum<br>No sixth form |
| **Cost** | £30,000 per year | Free |

### Class sizes

Private (fee-paying) schools dominate school **League Tables**, and one explanation for this is that teachers give more time to individual students because of smaller class sizes. Figures from the Department for Education and Skills (2010) show average class sizes as:

➤ state-funded secondary schools: 20.5
➤ private schools: 10

### Exclusion

Self and Zealey (2007) note that around 9,400 pupils were permanently excluded in 2005. The vast majority were working class. Around 55,000 pupils each day take unauthorised absence from school; again, the majority are working class. Babb et al. (2006) notes that persistent truants are 15 times more likely than those who never truant to leave school at 16 with no qualifications.

**Ability grouping** (a general label for practices such as **streaming**, **setting** and **banding**) is a more subtle form of exclusion. Hallam et al. (2001) noted how lower set pupils were **stigmatised** as 'thick' through the association between lower sets and unemployment, higher sets and good exam grades. Teachers also gave 'more creative work and privileges to higher set students while restricting lower sets to tedious, routine tasks'.

Power et al. (2003) noted how successful middle-class students labelled themselves as failures for their inability to match the achievements of some of their high-flying peers.

### Teacher labelling

Gazeley and Dunne (2005) suggest 'teachers and trainee teachers often hold stereotypical ideas about pupils and parents according to their social class'. The 'class expectations' some teachers hold (working-class pupils as low achievers, middle-class pupils as high achievers) translated into classroom practices that 'located the source of a pupil's underachievement within the pupil or the home'.

Some teachers held **fatalistic** views about the ability of working-class children who were 'destined to fail' because of their class and family backgrounds, regardless of the teacher's efforts. Not all teachers held these views, however. As one put it, 'I believe there is a danger in setting low expectations of a child. If a child already does not expect to do well the last thing a teacher should be doing is reinforcing that view'.

Gazeley and Dunne also found 'middle class pupils and parents were viewed more positively' and 'Teachers had higher expectations and aspirations for the future for middle class pupils than for working class pupils' — ideas that are particularly interesting in the context of the observation that 'pupils identified positive relationships with teachers as crucial to their learning'.

**?** **How does the hidden curriculum relate to social class?**

### Perspectives on schooling

#### *Functionalist perspectives*

These locate the experience of schooling within an overall context of the **purpose** and **nature** of education systems in contemporary societies:

➤ **Purpose**: To sift, sort and grade children (the '**coordination of human resources**') as preparation for adult roles — especially those relating to work. Testing and measurement is, therefore, a necessary part of the school experience; children have to be **differentiated** on the basis of their abilities (not their social or class background). Ability measurement must be **objective**: tested against known competence standards (such as GCSE or A-level).

➤ **Nature**: The education system has to be **meritocratic**. All pupils, regardless of class, gender, ethnicity, sexuality or whatever must have an **equal opportunity** to achieve national standards. In this way, educational 'success' or 'failure' is down to individual levels of effort, motivation and so forth.

As we have just seen, one problem with this idea is that schools are not necessarily meritocratic in practice; not all pupils have an equal opportunity to succeed. Hattersley and Francis (2004) also point to a further problem — as some *whole schools* become labelled as 'failing', their pupils are labelled 'failures' as soon as they start school.

#### *Marxist perspectives*

Marxist perspectives take a different approach, focusing on how the education system is biased in favour of those with the **economic and cultural capital** to make the system work to their advantage:

➤ **Class reproduction**: The underlying purpose of education is to ensure the continued hegemony of a ruling class; while Willis (1977) talks about how working-class kids get working-class jobs, the opposite is also true: upper-class kids are destined to get upper-class jobs. Mac an Ghaill (1996), for example, argues that social class origins remain the single best predictor of educational success or failure. Demack et al. (1998) also note: 'social class differences are still the largest differences of all and the children of professional parents have the largest advantage of all'. For middle-class pupils, educational success does come with a price — their experience of education is conditioned by a need to succeed — and parents invest heavily in their children (such as buying a private school education).

➤ **Emotional labour**: Middle-class parents also invest in non-economic ways. Reay (2000) suggests middle- and upper-class parents are better positioned to draw on **emotional capital** — the ability to decisively influence the focus and direction of a child's education. Middle-class mothers, for example, invest a lot of time and effort (emotional labour) in their children's education. This includes not just the ability to help with things like homework but, more importantly perhaps, a willingness to ensure the school is providing what the parents believe are appropriate levels of support, teaching, testing and so forth — and to act swiftly and decisively if they are not.

➤ **Correspondence theory** is a particular strand of Marxist thinking. Bowles and Gintis (1976 and 2002) argue that education is a proving ground in which the organisation of the workplace is reflected in the organisation of schools. Education, therefore, becomes a test of control and conformity — those who conform are allowed into the higher areas of education (and, by extension, work) whereas those who do not are excluded (or even self-excluded — they leave school at the earliest opportunity).

The *unstated* role of education, therefore, is cultural reproduction: the inequalities of the workplace are reproduced in the organisation of schooling. The distinction between academic education and vocational training reflects the education–workplace correspondence; academic education is the preserve of those (largely upper- and middle-class) students destined for professional employment, while working-class students (in the main) are encouraged to pursue various forms of vocational training that will prepare and qualify them for (lower-paid and lower-status) employment.

| ? | Give one argument for and one argument against the idea that the education system is meritocratic. |
|---|---|

## Gender

### Formal curriculum

Measuring the quality of educational experiences in terms of qualifications, the general pattern, as Hughes and Church (2010) report, is that girls outperformed boys at every **Key Stage** in 2009 bar one (Key Stage 2 Maths, where levels of achievement were the same), a pattern unchanged for the past 10 years, including Key Stage 4 (Table 10.6).

Table 10.6　Five or more GCSE grades A* to C or equivalent by gender (%)

|      | Male | Female |
|------|------|--------|
| 1996 | 40.6 | 50.5 |
| 1997 | 41.4 | 51.3 |
| 1998 | 42.3 | 52.8 |
| 2006 | 54.3 | 63.9 |
| 2007 | 56.9 | 65.8 |
| 2008 | 60.0 | 69.0 |

*Source: Hughes and Church (2010)*

At **A-level** the pattern of relative achievement between the sexes is maintained, with 45% of women and 35% of men achieving two or more passes in 2006. In terms of grading, the gender gap has stayed roughly constant over the past 15 years (at around one percentage point): in 2011 the pass rate was 97% for boys and 98.1% for girls.

Although these data suggest gender, in itself, is related to achievement, we need to be careful about drawing this conclusion — not *all* girls do better than *all* boys.

➤ *Within* social classes: girls generally experience higher achievement.

➤ *Between* social classes: upper- and middle-class boys achieve more than working-class girls.

In other words, although there's 'something about gender' that is very significant when comparing experiences within the *same* class, it's not that significant when comparing *different* classes.

We should also note that achievement is relative: it is not simply a case of girls over-achieving and boys underachieving; at GCSE, for example, boys gain 50% more passes than they did 10 years ago. In addition, female underachievement (among working-class and minority ethnic group girls, for example), is frequently ignored.

## Hidden curriculum

### Feminisation

In recent times, one set of explanations for changing male and female educational experiences has focused around the **feminisation of school and work**. Epstein et al. (1998) argue that wider changes in the workplace and female behaviour have resulted in young males losing control of their unique identities and their lives — with some boys seeing education as irrelevant to their future as a result of changing:

➤ **Opportunities**: Females have more opportunities to express a range of different 'femininities' — including ones that involve a career rather than just part-time work and family responsibilities.

➤ **Workplace changes**: These reflect back onto family socialisation processes. Parents, for example, change their perception of their children's future adult roles and, consequently, the relative importance they place on male and female educational experiences.

### Educational initiatives

More specifically, recent changes within education have resulted in changes to the way males and females experience education:

➤ **National Curriculum**: Introduced into schools in 1990, this made subjects such as maths and science compulsory up to GCSE level and encouraged the breakdown of gendered subject choices.

➤ **Coursework**: The expansion of this option, mainly through the introduction of GCSE, benefits girls because it demands steady, consistent work over time (something which is supposedly more suited to the way girls work). 'Concerns' about male underachievement have led to a marked reduction in this option.

➤ **Curriculum initiatives** such as **Girls into Science and Technology** (GIST): these encouraged the breakdown of barriers around traditionally male subjects, while work experience initiatives introduced girls to the possibility of full-time work at an early age (although, as Mackenzie (1997) has demonstrated, there are arguments about whether girls and boys are still encouraged to follow 'traditional' employment options). Evidence from vocational qualifications (Department for Education and Skills, 2006) suggests they are. In 2005, for example, 'Nearly all vocational qualifications awarded for construction, planning and the built environment were to men...around 90 per cent of vocational qualifications for health, public services and care were awarded to women.'

Francis (2000) argues that changes within the school and wider society have altered the way girls construct femininity (they no longer see it mainly in terms of the home) whereas concepts of masculinity have remained largely unchanged. Walker (1996) similarly identifies changing conceptions of masculinity, in terms of 'finding a role in a fast-changing world', as a challenge many young men are unable to resolve in the education system.

### *Stereotyping*

**Labelling** and **stereotyping** suggest educational experiences have changed, with a reversal of traditional forms of gender labelling; girls are increasingly positively labelled (as high achievers who work hard and have least behavioural problems). Boys, on the other hand, are increasingly negatively labelled in terms of underachievement, laziness and behavioural problems.

### *Hypermasculinity*

In this respect, **hypermasculinity** is an exaggerated form of masculinity ('laddishness') that emphasises and values things like physical strength and sexual virility — ideas that are at odds with educational achievement.

| Hidden curriculum |
|---|
| **F** eminisation |
| **I** nitiatives |
| **S** tereotyping |
| **H** ypermasculinity |

> **?** What are the gender trends in educational achievement?

## Ethnicity

### Formal curriculum

Different ethnic groups have different educational experiences when measured in terms of achievement:

➤ **Key Stages 1–3**: Department for Education and Skills (2005) figures, for example, show attainment by ethnicity (in descending order):

➤ Chinese

➤ Indian

➤ white British

➤ mixed ethnicity

➤ Bangladeshi

➤ black Caribbean

➤ black African

➤ Pakistani

> **GCSE**: The Key Stage pattern is largely reproduced, the main exception being the relative underachievement of black Caribbean children (Table 10.7). Although their performance has improved significantly over the past 15 years, they still achieve worst at GCSE.

Table 10.7    Five or more GCSE grades A* to C by ethnicity (%)

|             | 1989 | 1992 | 1996 | 1998 | 2000 | 2002 | 2004 |
|-------------|------|------|------|------|------|------|------|
| **Indian**      | n/a  | 38   | 48   | 54   | 60   | 60   | 72   |
| **White**       | 30   | 37   | 45   | 47   | 50   | 52   | 54   |
| **Bangladeshi** | n/a  | 25   | 25   | 33   | 29   | 41   | 46   |
| **Pakistani**   | n/a  | 23   | 23   | 29   | 29   | 40   | 37   |
| **Black**       | 18   | 23   | 23   | 29   | 39   | 36   | 35   |

*Source: Babb et al. (2006)*

When we include **gender**, girls outperform boys in all ethnic groups. Similarly, for all ethnic groups boys are more likely to leave school with no A*–C passes at GCSE.

## Participation

Post-16 **participation** rates for black youth (especially in Further Education colleges), rank second only to Indian youth. This suggests that black parents and children value education but have problems with schools.

Blair et al. (2003) suggest colleges 'provide a space where young black men are supported by a community of black students, an opportunity to study a curriculum that celebrates black cultures and histories and to develop positive relationships with tutors'. Mirza (1992) additionally notes one reason for higher black participation is the number of black women staying in education post-16.

## Hidden curriculum

The hidden curriculum impacts on the experience of education for ethnic minority groups in a range of ways.

## Racism

Post-16 participation rates suggest racism plays some part in the black experience of schooling.

### Overt racism

Aymer and Okitikpi (2001) argue that black Caribbean boys are more likely to report negative abuse and harassment from their peers. Kerr et al. ( 2002), for example, found British students had less positive attitudes towards 'immigrants' than students of many other countries. This, they argued, shaped peer group interaction and black experiences of education.

Mirza (1997) sees the development of 'Saturday schools' (supplementary teaching involving parents and teachers) as indicative of a general dissatisfaction among black parents and children with 'white institutions' that seem to regularly fail them.

*Cultural racism*

**Cultural racism (ethnocentrism)** is a more subtle form, expressed in areas like:

➤ **The curriculum**: This may involve, according to Blair et al., teaching practices and expectations based on cultural norms, histories and general cultural references unfamiliar to many ethnic minority pupils.

➤ **Role models**: Blair et al. also point to a lack of role models within the school for ethnic minority pupils. Ross (2001) estimates that 5% of teachers are currently drawn from ethnic minorities (around 15% of English school pupils have an ethnic minority background).

*Teacher–pupil interactions*

The Runnymede Trust (1998) argues that a range of hidden processes occur within schools that 'deny equal opportunities'. Ethnic minority students, for example, reported:

➤ high levels of control and criticism from teachers

➤ stereotypes of cultural differences, communities and speech that betrayed negative and patronising attitudes

*Identity*

One feature of the educational experience of black Caribbean boys is that as they move through school, achievement seems to fall (until, at GCSE, they have the worst academic performance of all children). Reasons here include:

➤ **Masculinity**: This is sometimes defined in terms of rebellion against 'white' schooling. Foster et al. (1996) suggest the over-representation of black Caribbean boys in low status sets and bands within the school is the result of 'unacceptable behaviour'.

➤ **Discipline**: Diane Abbott (a black Labour MP) has argued (Hinsliff, 2002) that 'a failure to challenge disruptive behaviour leads to an escalating situation which results in black boys being *excluded* from school' (black Caribbean boys are more frequently excluded than any other ethnic group).

➤ **Family structure**: Children from single-parent families generally have the worst educational experiences across all ethnic groups; black Caribbean families have the highest rates of single parenthood and the lowest rates of educational achievement.

*Labelling*

If we leave open the question of whether schools are **institutionally racist** (the idea that racist attitudes and practices go unchallenged — or are covertly encouraged — at all levels of the school), various forms of subtle labelling and stereotyping, intentional or otherwise, do seem to impact on ethnic-minority experiences of education.

Generally positive teacher attitudes to Indian pupils (based on knowledge of their high levels of attainment) may be offset by negative beliefs about black Caribbean pupils. Gillborn (2002) argues that schools *are* institutionally racist, especially in the light of curriculum developments 'based on approaches known to disadvantage black pupils':

➤ selection in schools by setting
➤ schemes for 'gifted and talented' pupils
➤ vocational schemes for 'non-academic' pupils

Teachers, Gillborn argues, 'generally underrate the abilities of black youngsters', which results in their assignment to low-ability groups, a restricted curriculum and entry for lower-level exams. The Pupil Level Annual School Census (2002), for example, shows black pupils are more likely to be classified in terms of Special Educational Needs (SEN):

➤ 28% of black Caribbean secondary pupils
➤ 18% of white pupils

### Stereotyping

Figueroa (1991) suggested teachers frequently limit ethnic minority opportunities through the use of culturally biased forms of assessment (the way students are expected to speak and write, for example) and by consigning pupils to lower bands and sets on the basis of teacher assessment. Teachers also have lower opinions of the abilities of some ethnic minority groups, which results in a **self-fulfilling prophecy** of underachievement.

> **?** How does the hidden curriculum impact on minority ethnic groups?

# Patterns and trends in subject choice

This section examines patterns and trends in subject choice across two variables — the conventional one of **gender** and the less conventional one of **social class**.

## Gender and subject choice

### Institutional choices

Some choices are made for students by the schools they attend — the most obvious examples here being **types of school**. Before the general introduction of comprehensive schools, pupils were allocated to one of two types of secondary school based on their performance in IQ tests (the 11+):

➤ **Grammar schools**, for those pursuing a mainly academic education (there were more grammar schools available for boys, which meant they had a greater chance of being selected). The intake was also mainly white and middle-class (although not exclusively so).
➤ **Secondary modern schools**, where the curriculum was split between vocational training and academic subjects (with a bias towards the former). The majority of pupils were working-class, with much higher levels of ethnic minority representation. The vocational bias of these schools frequently meant boys and girls followed

different educational paths. They were encouraged to follow traditional masculine and feminine routes into adulthood — the former in terms of practical skills such as bricklaying, car mechanics, metalwork, woodwork and sciences, the latter in terms of subjects and skills designed to prepare them for both their role within the family (child care, cooking and needlework) and traditional female occupations (nursing and secretarial work).

The introduction of **comprehensive schooling** changed this situation, although there was still evidence of **subject differentiation** within, rather than between, schools (with more males opting for subjects based around maths, science and technology and more females opting for humanities subjects).

The **National Curriculum** (introduced in 1988) made selected subjects (English, maths, a modern foreign language and so forth) **compulsory** up to GCSE. This development meant fewer subject options were available and consequently fewer subject choices were made on the basis of gender.

### Individual choices

Although subject choice does exist in secondary schooling (such as the choice of academic or vocational GCSEs), the main evidence for curriculum gendering now comes post-16, at **A-level** (Table 10.8). When given the opportunity, males and females make different subject choices.

Table 10.8  UK A-level or equivalent entries for young people

| Subject | Males (%) | Females (%) |
|---|---|---|
| Physics | 76 | 24 |
| Computer studies | 73 | 27 |
| Economics | 70 | 30 |
| Design and technology | 65 | 35 |
| Mathematics | 60 | 40 |
| Biology | 38 | 62 |
| English literature | 30 | 70 |
| Social studies | 30 | 70 |
| Modern languages | 30 | 70 |
| Drama | 30 | 70 |
| Art and design | 30 | 70 |
| Home economics | 6 | 94 |

Source: Babb et al. (2006)

The Department for Education and Skills (2007) suggests: 'Gender differences in subject choice become more accentuated post-16: girls' most popular subject is English, while boys' is Maths. Psychology, Art and Design, Sociology and Media/Film/Television

Studies are amongst the 10 most popular choices for girls, while Physics, Business Studies, Geography and Physical Education are in the top 10 for boys.'

**?** **What are the trends in male and female subject choice?**

## Explanations

### Socialisation

Eichler (1980) highlighted how the different socialisation experiences and social expectations of males and females help to construct different gender identities and adult role expectations. In the past, for example, the education system contributed to the way women saw their primary adult role in the *private sphere* of the family (as mother and housewife, for example). Although female horizons have widened over the past 25 years, feminists argue that traditional assumptions about masculinity and femininity continue to influence both family and work relationships. Educationally we can note:

> **Textbooks and gender stereotyping**: Males appear more frequently and are more likely to be shown in *active* roles ('doing and demonstrating') rather than *passive* ones. Best (1992), for example, demonstrated how pre-school texts designed to develop reading skills remain populated by sexist assumptions and stereotypes. Gillborn (1992) also notes how the hidden curriculum impacts on ethnic (as well as gender and class) identities through citizenship teaching, where the content of the subject teaching (democracy, racial equality, etc.) frequently clashes with the 'learned experiences' of black pupils.

> **Subject hierarchy**: Both teachers and pupils quickly appreciate that some subjects are more important than others — both *within* the school curriculum (English, maths and science have a special status in terms of the time and testing given over to them) and *outside* the curriculum — subjects that are not considered worthy of inclusion and hence knowing (sociology, psychology, politics and media studies, for example). The argument here is that gender hierarchies reflect these subject hierarchies, with males opting for special status subjects in far greater numbers.

### Teachers

Norman et al. (1988) argue that **teacher expectations**, especially in early-years schooling, emphasise female roles related to the mother/carer axis. While this may no longer *automatically* translate into women seeing their primary role in terms of caring for their family, work roles continue to be framed around the idea of different male and female (mental and physical) capabilities.

Thirty years ago Stanworth (1981) found that both male and female A-level pupils underestimated girls' academic performance and teachers saw female futures in terms of marriage, childrearing and domestic work (while future careers were stereotyped into 'caring' work such as secretarial and nursing). The question we have to consider is the extent to which, for all the changes in male and female educational performance, the general picture is *still broadly similar* in terms of the adult roles performed by men and women in our society.

### Identity

Feminist research in the recent past focused on ideas like the gendering of the school curriculum, in terms of how pupils saw different subjects as 'masculine' or 'feminine'. Such gendered perception, Woods (1976) argued, helped to explain things like lower levels of female participation and general achievement in science subjects. Similarly, social policy initiatives, such as **Girls Into Science and Technology** (GIST), explored why girls were under-represented in science subjects:

➤ Sciences were seen as both difficult and demanding (and hence more suited to male aptitudes).

➤ The image of 'scientists' was seen by girls to be both unflattering and unfeminine.

### Academic hierarchies

Abbot and Wallace (1996) point out that feminist research has shown how concepts of masculinity and femininity are influenced by factors such as **academic hierarchies** — how the school is **vertically stratified** in occupational terms (men at the top being the norm). Mahony (1985) argued that staffing structures reflected male importance in the workplace (the highest status teaching jobs were — and remain — occupied by men). Mirza et al. (2005) note: 'Women make up 53% of the secondary teaching population, but are still under-represented in secondary school senior management positions, particularly headships' (around 30% of secondary heads are women). In the nursery/primary sector, although only 16% of teachers are male, 34% of head teachers are male.

> **?**    **What explanations can you give for the trends in male and female subject choice?**

## Social class and subject choice

This is a significant, if less widely researched, relationship considered in relation to choices.

### Institutional choices

As we have seen with gender, before the development of comprehensive schooling subject choices for working-class pupils were largely limited by their over-representation in secondary modern schools, whose technical curriculum was geared towards **vocational education** rather than the academic curriculum of grammar schools. Both subject choice and the level to which subjects were examined were conditioned by the *type of school* attended (grammar school pupils mainly took O-levels, secondary modern pupils mainly CSEs — a top grade in the latter equated to the lowest grade in the former).

Contemporary examples focus mainly on differences between private, fee-paying schools (which do not have to follow the National Curriculum) and state-maintained schools (which do). The main difference here is that pupils in the former generally have a wider range of curriculum (in terms of things like modern and ancient languages, for example) and extra-curricular choices. (Wellington College, for example, offers 'wellbeing' as a core subject and options in philosophy and religion, Mandarin, Latin, Greek and classical civilisation.)

### Individual choices

Sullivan et al. (2003) found that subject choice was influenced by things like **parents' social position and interests**:

➤ Middle-class children were likely to choose the prestigious university subjects of medicine and law, independent of ability.
➤ Children were more likely to choose subjects that corresponded to their parents' interests.
➤ Children of the 'economic elite' were more likely to choose subjects related to commercial and financial skills.
➤ Children whose parents had high levels of cultural resources were more likely to focus on 'cultural' subjects (such as social sciences or literature) that have less direct economic value.
➤ Working-class children were more likely to choose technical subjects that reflected their parents' manual job experiences and because these had more secure job market prospects.

# Pro- and anti-school subcultures

A range of writers have explored the idea that the experience of many young people in education is shaped by a range of **school processes** (such as positive and negative teacher labelling, racism or the denial of status) that, in turn, lead to a variety of pro- and anti-school subcultural responses (the focus, in other words, is mainly on the development of **reactive subcultures** based around the way different groups adapt to the school situation).

Woods (1979), for example, argued for a range of **subcultural responses** ('adaptations') to school culture:

➤ **ingratiators** at one extreme — pupils who tried to earn the favour of teachers (the most positive adaptation)
➤ **rebels** at the other extreme — those who explicitly *rejected* the culture of the school

The subcultural responses in Mac an Ghaill's (1994) study, on the other hand, were a more subtle outcome of a complex interplay of class, race and sexuality:

➤ **Macho lads**, for example, were similar to 'the lads' in Willis's (1977) study. While both were 'anti-school', Willis's lads could eagerly look forward to leaving school at the earliest opportunity and entering paid work; for the macho lads this type of work had all but disappeared (creating what Mac an Ghaill called a 'crisis of masculinity'). All they had left to cling to was an outdated mode of masculinity focused around traditional forms of manual waged labour that no longer existed — and they frequently employed racist explanations ('the blacks have taken our jobs') to explain/rationalise this situation.

➤ **Academic achievers**, by contrast, were the *pro-school* youth, similar to Willis's conformist 'earoles' — pupils who had a strong schoolwork ethic and looked to academic qualifications as a route to social mobility.

➤ **New enterprisers**, also *pro-school*, had bought into the 'new vocationalism' and rejected the academic route to mobility. They focused instead on developing practical skills (business and IT in particular) that they hoped would be beneficial in the changing labour market.

Blackman (1995) also captured how tensions within the school contribute to subcultural development. He noted:

➤ **Boffin boys** were generally conformist and *pro-school*, with a group identity based on working hard and aspiring to social mobility.

➤ **Boffin girls** were the female equivalent. They worked hard and were *pro-school*, although their conformity was sometimes *instrumental* rather than committed: if school practices (such as poor teaching) clashed with their academic aspirations, for example, the latter took priority.

➤ **New Wave girls** were more ambivalent in their attitude to the school and shared Boffin girls' instrumental approach. While Boffin girls 'specialised in academic superiority', New Wave girls had wider interests and tastes. On the one hand they generally conformed academically but, unlike Boffin girls, they were sexually active and more confident in their ability to challenge ideas and practices (particularly those they saw as patriarchal and sexist).

➤ **Mod boys**, the male counterparts of New Wave girls, were similarly ambivalent, walking a fine line between deviance and conformity. These boys were generally *anti-school* but *pro-education* — they wanted academic qualifications but didn't particularly value their schooling.

Sewell (2000) examined how black youth adapted to the experience of schooling in terms of four main responses:

➤ **Passive accepters**: those African-Caribbean boys who passively (unconsciously) accepted the white cultural values of the school. They accepted the conventional wisdom that it was 'black kids' who gave the school a bad name and were generally *pro-school*.

➤ **Active accepters**: those who 'acted white' in the school. Sewell found this to be the most common *pro-school* strategic response.

➤ **Passive resisters**: those who developed 'innovative' ways of maintaining a delicate balancing act between satisfying the demands of their peer group (through relatively minor acts of deviance) while simultaneously avoiding direct and open confrontation with teachers. Sewell argues that this type was particularly characteristic of black girls and was neither particularly *pro- nor anti-school*.

> **Active resisters** — those pupils who recognised the racist assumptions of the school and worked in ways that actively rebelled against their teachers and the school.

Shain (2003), on the other hand, examined the subcultural responses of Asian girls:

> **The Gang** were generally *anti-school*. They adopted an 'Us and Them' approach that involved a positive assertion of Asian identity. They generally opposed the dominant culture of the school, which they saw as white and racist.

> **The Survivors** were *pro-education* and *pro-school*. They were generally seen as 'ideal pupils' who worked hard to achieve success, avoided confrontation and were labelled by teachers as 'nice girls' and 'good workers'. This group played up to the stereotype of Asian girls as shy and timid while being actively engaged in a strategy of self-advancement through education.

> **The Rebels** who, despite the name, were generally *pro-school*. Their rebellion was against their cultural background: they adopted Western modes of dress and distanced themselves from other Asian girl groups. Their survival strategy was one of academic success, and school was equated with positive experiences not found in their home life.

> **Faith girls** whose identity was based around religion rather than ethnicity. Although this group fostered positive relations with staff and students and pursued academic success (they were *pro-education* in this respect), they were aware of racism as a major source of oppression in the school (which in some instances made them *anti-school*).

The various studies we have outlined generally share a preoccupation with the behaviours of 'extraordinary youth' (Blackman, for example, clearly found the New Wave girls far more exotic and interesting than their Boffin counterparts).

Brown (1987) noted the existence of subcultural groups:

> **Rems** — pupils generally seen as not very bright ('remedials')
> **Swots** — the most academically able (and despised) kids

He was, however, more interested in examining the '**ordinary kids**' whose lives are generally ignored by teachers and sociologists alike. He was interested in how economic changes — a rapid increase in youth unemployment during the time these pupils were in secondary school — impacted on their passage towards adulthood and their understanding of their working-class backgrounds.

Ordinary kids, Brown argued, entered into a tacit agreement with the school (and society): in return for conformity and working towards qualifications, they would get 'tidy jobs', jobs that had some status, were relatively secure and reasonably well paid. While this agreement held, ordinary kids would be pro-education and not anti-school (it's often difficult to see them as pro-school). However, Brown argued, if this agreement broke down — the 'tidy jobs' disappeared, as they have done in the 25 years since the study — the ordinary kids would become both anti-school and anti-education.

> **?** Give one difference (other than being pro- or anti-school) between pro- and anti-school subcultures.

## Pro- and anti-education subcultures

While school subcultures focus on orientations to schools as **institutions**, education subcultures develop around orientations to the idea of education itself. Lees (1993), for example, noted:

➤ **Pro-school girls**, who valued school as an enjoyable place for socialising with friends, but who were generally *anti-education*; qualifications were not particularly important.

➤ **Pro-education girls** — some who *intrinsically* valued education (as enjoyable and worthwhile), and others who took a more *extrinsic* or *instrumental* approach to their studies, seeing qualifications as a necessary means towards a desired end (they did not value school 'for its own sake').

➤ **Anti-education girls**, who were *anti-school* and *anti-education*; school was a pointless waste of time, a disagreeable and uncomfortable period in their life that they had to get through before escaping into the adult world of work and family.

A number of studies have found youth who are *pro-education but anti-school*. Mac an Ghaill (1994), for example, identified **Real Englishmen** — a group of middle-class pupils who aspired to university and the professional careers enjoyed by their parents. This group played an elaborate game of ridiculing school values while simultaneously working hard (mainly in private) to achieve success, which they saw as being gained on their own terms.

Similarly, Fuller (1984) found the black girls she studied were strongly *pro-education but anti-school*. They valued qualifications but resented the negative labelling by some teachers (a combination that made them work harder to 'disprove the label').

In terms of more explicitly *anti-school, anti-education* subcultures:

➤ For Willis (1977), 'the lads' generally saw school as a place to be tolerated (a place to 'have a laugh' with your mates) while waiting to leave.

➤ Johnson (1999) described schools in Northern Ireland where some pupil subcultures were marked by 'hostility and indifference' to learning, which correlated with high levels of absence and lower levels of achievement.

➤ Power et al. (2003), as we have seen, examined how some groups of middle-class children who found themselves situated in lower sets and streams were pro-education while not valuing their school experience.

> **?** How do pro-education subcultures differ from pro-school subcultures?

# Alternative education

A slightly different take is to consider a range of **social movements** (or **educational subcultures**) that, while stridently **pro-education**, are **anti-conventional** forms of schooling.

## Supplementary schooling

**Supplementary schooling** refers to what Strand (2002) defines as 'extra schooling organised by and for particular ethnic groups outside of mainstream provision. These schools are organised mainly on Saturdays, hence are also sometimes called Saturday schools'. This type of school, as Mirza et al. (2005) note, is particularly popular with black Caribbean parents and pupils. The aim is to provide a setting where:

➢ black rather than white is the norm
➢ parents are included rather than excluded
➢ the curriculum is negotiated between teachers, parents and pupils

The pro-education nature of these schools is suggested by Mirza (1997) when she argues: 'The image of mainstream schooling is that these children don't want to learn, that they are not interested in education. But that is not true — these schools would not exist if it were. There is a desire and motivation to learn.'

## Non-conventional schooling

A different form of pro-education alternative is evidenced through schools such as **Summerhill**, a private, fee-paying school established by **A. S. Neill** in 1921 to reflect his educational philosophy that placed the happiness and personal freedom of the child at its centre. At Summerhill the pupils decide whether they will attend formal lessons or take exams, and the school is run democratically with regular school meetings held to decide and enforce rules. The basic aim is to develop self-discipline rather than external control.

**Steiner** schools reflect Rudolf Steiner's philosophy that education involves children developing a 'love of learning' and 'enthusiasm for the school' with an emphasis on the development of 'the imagination as integral to learning'. This approach is based on children learning at their own pace in a creative environment rather than being forced to learn specific things at specific times (as in conventional state schools). Such schools are pro-education while rejecting the ideas on which conventional schooling is based.

## Home tutoring

A final form of alternative schooling is the idea of **home tutoring** — a movement that is much larger in America than in the UK. As the name suggests, children are educated outside mainstream education (by parents or private tutors). Again, the general philosophy here is pro-education but anti-conventional schooling.

**Exam-style questions**

**1** Identify and explain two ways in which ethnicity may affect a pupil's experience of education. (17 marks)

**2** Outline and evaluate the view that school subcultures are a product of the social class background of the young people involved. (33 marks)

**3** Outline and evaluate the view that pupils' experience of school is related to their gender. (33 marks)

**4** Outline and evaluate the view that pupils' experience of school is related to their ethnicity. (33 marks)

in other words, is simply the absence of illness. This definition has some significant **advantages**:

➢ **Measurement**: A disease or condition (such as a heart attack) can be measured and quantified in terms of its severity (unlike health or wellness).

➢ **Objectivity**: Health is not a subjective interpretation or state of mind. It can be objectively established (as the absence of illness) through scientific testing.

➢ **Detection**: Detection relies less on patient reporting (based on an awareness that something is wrong) and more on the ability of medical professionals to diagnose health problems.

➢ **Scaling**: While the positive model sees health as an 'either/ or' condition (either you're healthy or you're not), the negative model allows for grades of illness (such as chronic, life-threatening or temporary). This, in turn, suggests a sliding scale of health.

Advantages of negative state models

**M** easurement
**O** bjectivity
**D** etection
**S** caling

**?** What is the difference between positive and negative state definitions of health?

However we define health, the idea of being unwell looms large in any definition. We can consider this in terms of three related ideas: disorder, disease and disability.

**Disorder** refers to anything that upsets the normal functioning of the human body, for example through disease.

**Disease** is an *abnormal* condition that can be medically diagnosed (different diseases are associated with different symptoms and signs). Medically, diseases can have an *external* cause, such as a virus, or an *internal* cause, such as some kind of body malfunction. More generally, 'disease' refers to any medical condition involving pain, discomfort, distress or even death.

**Disability** is a specific form of 'disorder', physical or mental, explored in more detail in a later section.

# Illness

We tend to see disease and illness as being much the same thing. However, Morris (2000) argues that while disease is an *objective* disorder (something you *have*), illness is more *subjective* (something you *feel*). Illness, in this respect, can be defined in a range of ways.

First, illness can be defined as the actual experience of pain, treatment and so forth. An individual with an infectious disease, for example, has very different experiences from someone without the disease.

Second, illness can be defined in terms of how different people respond to it. Someone can, for example, be objectively ill (for example, having a disease with no outward symptoms), but show no signs of illness (they live their 'normal' life). On the other hand, someone can be ill without being diseased, through **hypochondria** (a belief you are ill without having any definable medical condition) or the belief that a perfectly normal experience is a symptom of a wider illness.

Third, illness can be defined in terms of the ways others react to an individual's sense of illness. Our reaction to someone vomiting will be different depending on the social context of their behaviour.

For example, someone who drinks 10 pints of lager and vomits the next morning is not considered ill. Similarly, pregnant women frequently display symptoms and signs we normally associate with illness (vomiting, loss of appetite, skin changes and so forth) without being considered ill. On the other hand, someone who contracts food poisoning (even after drinking 10 pints of lager) is considered ill.

We should also note that concepts of illness are related to different **historical and cultural contexts**. Ideas about the causes of physical and mental illness in contemporary Britain, for example, are very different from those of 500 years ago. An example of cross-cultural contrast is **obesity**: this is considered a disease in contemporary Britain, whereas in some societies it is a symbol of wealth — of having more than enough food to eat.

## Sickness

If disease is what you *have* and illness is what you *feel* about what you have, then sickness is what you *are* — it reflects people's expectations about how to behave when 'sick'. If health is defined as 'normal', illness is seen as 'abnormal' and, more importantly, **deviant**.

However, this is a special kind of **non-culpable deviance** — something for which the sick can't be blamed. It needs to be managed differently from culpable forms of deviance (such as theft, where the deviant is to blame and for which they can expect punishment). This is achieved, according to Parsons (1951), through the **sick role** — 'a temporary, medically sanctioned form of deviance'.

In this functionalist explanation, the person playing the 'sick role':

➤ **manages** their deviant status by cooperating with the people around them (doctor, parent, partner, etc.) to resolve their deviance by being nursed back to health

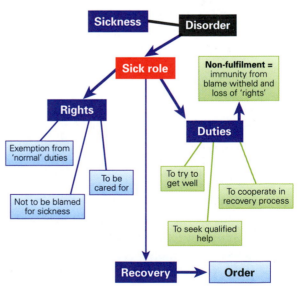

Figure 11.1 The sick role
*Source: Parsons (1951)*

> **negotiates** certain *rights* (such as not having to go to work or school) in return for taking on particular *obligations* (such as resting, taking prescribed medicine and so forth)

As with any other social role, the sick role is **policed** (by doctors or other interested adults, such as parents or partners).

### Evaluation

The idea of a sick role accurately describes a familiar and recognisable process many people experience, in terms of less serious forms of sickness (such as influenza or minor surgery). By defining sickness as 'non-culpable deviance', Parsons highlights the way health is constructed as a normal aspect of social order. The concept does, however, have a number of weaknesses:

> **Stigma**: The patient may reject the sick role, especially in cases where an illness or condition is stigmatised. Some patients may similarly reject the 'illness' label.

> **Blame**: In some situations the patient is held responsible for their illness. Chalfont and Kurtz (1971) argue that, with stigmatised illnesses such as alcoholism, the patient does not qualify for the *rights* normally associated with the sick role.

> **Expectations**: For many forms of **chronic illness** there is no expectation of recovery and, therefore, no possibility of 'restoring order' through the sick role. Such patients are not, however, treated as deviant and do not have their rights removed.

> **Roles**: Although Parsons separates the roles of 'patient' and 'carer', in some instances the roles are confused. For example, in **Munchausen's syndrome by proxy**, the 'carer' deliberately makes their patient ill in order to nurse them. In this case, a mother deliberately making her child ill seems to be playing the carer role (policing deviance) when in fact she is the one who is ill; her child, on the other hand, cannot successfully play the sick role because they can never really 'get better'.

**?** Why should we see 'sickness' as deviance?

# Approaches to health and illness

While the ability to define concepts like health, disease and illness is important, these definitions also reflect different approaches to understanding health and illness. To show this, we will look at two different models: **biomedical** and **social**.

### The biomedical model

Most of us will be reasonably familiar with the biomedical approach because it has been the dominant medical **discourse** in our society for 200 years or more. It has strongly shaped our thinking about **causes** of ill health and **treatment** of illness.

Sociologically, we can outline the model in terms of its underlying **assumptions**, the social **relationships** that devolve from these assumptions, and its general **strengths** and **weaknesses**.

## Assumptions

**Health** is defined as a **negative state** — the absence of disorder (such as disease).

In terms of **causality**, Blaxter (2004) argues that this model is shaped by the 'doctrine of specific aetiology': every disorder has a *single observable cause* that can be identified, isolated and (once we have sufficient scientific knowledge) treated. Ill health is seen as the result of two medical processes:

> **External** processes: The normal, healthy body is 'invaded' by viruses, bacteria and so forth that cause particular types of disorder.

> **Internal** processes: The normal functioning of the body breaks down because of physical changes or because of genetic disorders and predispositions.

As a result, this approach is sometimes characterised as a **mechanical model** of order. Just as a machine like a car has a 'normal state' where the parts work as they should, so too does the body. When a machine breaks down — through normal wear-and-tear or because something has caused it to malfunction — the cause can be established, the problem fixed and normal functionality returned. Similarly, the cause of 'mechanical breakdown' in the body can be established and treated, such that the body returns to its normal, ordered state. Malfunctions, therefore, are **engineering problems** capable of resolution by skilled technicians.

If ill health has clear, definable causes, it follows that a **scientific approach** to understanding causality must be based on **objectivity**. Our understanding and treatment of ill health are based on clear and incontestable *rules of evidence* that have to be followed if treatment is to be successful. The **subjective beliefs** about disease that may be held by those who treat it (such as a doctor) or those who seek treatment (the patient) are largely irrelevant — health cannot be restored on the basis of things like prayer, faith, charms or rituals.

A further aspect of objectivity is the idea that disorders are largely *random events* — disease doesn't strike people because they are 'evil' or 'sinful', or because someone has worked a 'magic spell'.

## Relationships

These assumptions shape the social relationships surrounding health and illness in terms of **roles** and **power**.

### Roles

The *objective* view of disease leads to an *objective* relationship between a doctor (someone medically qualified to diagnose and treat illness) and their patient (the person who is treated). This relationship has the following qualities:

> **Formal**: While the patient's role is to describe their symptoms, the doctor's role is to correctly interpret and treat those symptoms.

> **Distant**: While the doctor–patient relationship can be friendly, how they interact socially is largely irrelevant in terms of diagnosis and treatment. The objective

nature of the process means that a treatment will work regardless of the relationship between those involved.

➤ **Instrumental**: The relationship is based on what each individual needs and can provide in return. The patient needs treatment and expects the doctor to provide it; the doctor needs the patient to cooperate in their diagnosis and, in return, suggests a treatment for their disorder.

### Power

There is a clear power difference between doctor and patient based on differences in knowledge (about the cause of illness) and skills (in treating a disorder). Health, in this respect, is something medical professionals:

➤ define — on the basis of scientific observation

➤ police — to ensure that only those properly qualified can make diagnoses

➤ measure — in order to determine effective treatments

### Evaluation

The biomedical model has a number of strengths and weaknesses.

### Strengths

➤ Health is simple to define and measure.

➤ The model is **evidence-based**. In basic terms, *it works*; it has what Keat and Urry (1975) call **instrumental utility** — it works successfully even though a patient may not know exactly how or why a cure works. **Cause-and-effect** relationships can be **reliably** tested and established — for example, we know that malaria is caused by a parasite passed on to humans through a mosquito bite.

➤ Knowledge of causality leads to knowledge about **prevention**. For example, one of the greatest life-savers of the twentieth century was clean water — and we understood why clean water was important because of our scientific knowledge of deadly bacteria.

### Weaknesses

➤ A simple cause-and-effect analysis, whereby exposure to a particular virus causes a particular disorder, for example, doesn't always hold true. Two people exposed to the same influenza virus don't always both fall ill — which suggests that health and illness sometimes have a **complex causality** which is not simply and easily established.

➤ Modern medicine is centred on **technology** rather than the patient. In other words, it has become focused on finding more and better 'cures' rather than seeking to prevent disease occurring in the first place. While this has made the medical profession powerful and produced huge profits for private transnational pharmaceutical companies, the overall health of the population has not greatly improved beyond a certain minimum level.

➤ The focus on technology (more and better medical machines) and drug-based cures has made medicine increasingly **expensive**. In private health systems even basic forms of medical care have been priced beyond the reach of many citizens; Smith et al. (2011), for example, note that in 2009 around a quarter (26%) of all American citizens 'experienced at least 1 month without health insurance coverage'. In the UK, where the National Health Service is funded from taxation, the cost has increasingly risen each year.

➤ Another issue is **iatrogenesis** — illness caused by the medical profession. According to Illich (1976), there is a general assumption (advanced by an increasingly powerful medical profession) that medicine represents an inevitable progression from ignorance about disease to enlightenment about the nature and causes of illness, but this assumption ignores the fact that people can be 'made ill' by the medical profession in three main ways:

  ➤ **Clinical iatrogenesis** refers to the use of ineffective, toxic and unsafe treatments.

  ➤ **Social iatrogenesis** refers to the way social life is increasingly 'medicalised': a wide range of 'disorders', from children misbehaving to adult criminality, are seen as having a medical cause requiring a medical response (such as the application of new drugs). This process also leads to an increasing rate of 'discovery' of new conditions (especially, but not exclusively, those of the mind) that can be 'cured' using drug-based technology.

  ➤ **Cultural iatrogenesis** refers to the hegemonic (or leadership) role of the medical profession: alternative forms of treatment or ways of dealing with pain, illness and so forth are marginalised or brought under the control and oversight of the medical profession.

Richardson and Peacock (2003) concluded that an increase in the number of doctors resulted in increased mortality rates: 'The hypothesis that iatrogenic effects may more than off-set the direct beneficial effects of additional, and largely unregulated, medical services must be contemplated seriously. Maybe Ivan Illich got it right!'

**?** What is one strength and one weakness of the biomedical model of health?

## The social model

The social model is an **oppositional discourse** on the nature of health and illness — one that challenges the biomedical assumptions concerning the way to promote health (and well-being) and the doctor–patient relationship.

### Assumptions

**Health** is a **positive state** that, for Seedhouse (1988), involves something more than the 'absence of illness': 'health' is given a much wider interpretation, based around the idea of '**human potentials**'. In this view, healthy individuals are those able to fully participate in the groups, communities and societies to which they belong. The (**functional**) emphasis, Wolinsky (1980) notes, is on the individual's ability to perform particular roles and tasks in their everyday life.

Seedhouse argues that health is determined by certain central conditions:

➤ **material conditions** such as food, shelter, warmth and peace — the basic **prerequisites** for health

➤ **non-material conditions** that include access to information about health and disease and the ability to understand and use such information to promote a healthy lifestyle

### Relationships

The social model assumes that health and illness have *multiple causalities*, ranging from individual factors (such as age and genetic inheritance) through group factors (such as lifestyles) to wider community factors (such as the quality of water and air supplies). It also assumes that health involves a combination of individual and wider social relationships.

Healthcare is a matter not simply for individuals, based around a doctor–patient relationship, but for societies as a whole. A range of individual, social and environmental factors and relationships combine to create healthy or unhealthy individuals. As an extreme example, people living in a war-zone without access to clean water, food and shelter will have demonstrably worse health than people living peacefully with access to the basic necessities.

The focus of this model, therefore, is not professionals and their patients (although these roles may be part of the overall health equation) but rather **demographic factors** — how, in basic terms, individuals and groups interact with their natural and social environment.

The biomedical model sees health as primarily a **private** concern — the health of the individual normally plays no part in the health of the community (except in the case of highly contagious diseases). In contrast, the social model sees health as mainly a **public** concern — the health of the community goes a long way towards determining the health of the individual.

Dahlgren and Whitehead (1991) represent the relationship between the individual, their social environment and health in terms of **layers of influence** (Figure 11.2). These layers capture the relationship between two types of asset: **fixed** and **modifiable**. At the bottom of the diagram are the fixed assets: those that can't be changed, including personal factors such as age and genetics. (Consider, for example, the greater vulnerability to illness of the very young and the very old, and the effect of hereditary diseases.) Above the fixed assets, the diagram shows several levels of modifiable assets. These are assets that can be changed and include the following:

➤ **lifestyle choices** (such as heavy alcohol use) that impact directly on the health of the individual

➤ **social and community influences** determining the levels of mutual support that contribute to, or minimise the likelihood of, ill health

➤ **living and working conditions** (e.g. the condition of people's housing and the nature of their work environments)

➤ **general social and economic conditions** which affect a whole society (e.g. the wealth or poverty of a society, whether it is peaceful or war-torn, levels of medical knowledge)

Figure 11.2  The social model

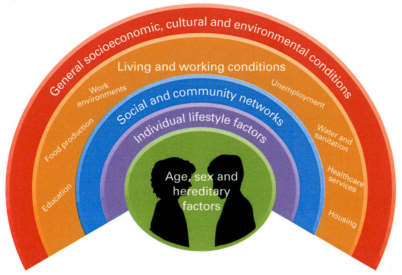

Source: Dahlgren and Whitehead (1991)

## Evaluation

The social model has a number of strengths and weaknesses.

### Strengths

➤ **Responsibility**: The responsibility for a population's health is shared throughout a community; illness is a 'collective problem' related to a range of social and economic conditions, some of which are the individual's responsibility (such as smoking and drinking), while others relate to community responsibilities (such as waste disposal, safe working conditions and the like). The model also highlights how large-scale **social inequalities** (such as extremes of wealth and poverty) contribute to individual health problems.

➤ **Community**: Government behaviour impacts on individual health. The provision of proper sanitation or adequate housing are factors beyond individual control that have significant impacts on individual health. Governments also have a role in ensuring that drugs and medical services known to injure health are controlled.

➤ **Diminishing costs**: The general health of a population improves as social and economic conditions improve (e.g. through the provision of clean water and air, or the banning of unsafe working conditions). Health is not based on constant technological developments in medicine.

> **Causality**: This approach focuses on the *'causes of the causes'* of ill health: the social conditions (poverty, malnutrition, unsanitary conditions and so forth) that *cause* disease which, in turn, *causes* individual ill health.

*Weaknesses*

> **Responsibilities**: Where health is seen as a collective problem, the question arises as to who is ultimately responsible for ill health — the individual? the community? some combination of both? It's not clear from the model where responsibility ultimately lies.

> **Entrenched interests**: Where a medical system is based on private profit, there is little incentive for health prevention because profits mainly lie in curing illness (through expensive individual treatments).

> **Victim blaming**: Where health is conceptualised as a community problem, it ironically becomes easier — once certain 'community responsibilities' have been met, such as the provision of clean water — to attribute ill health to the individual and their personal lifestyle choices.

**?** Give one strength and one weakness of the social model of health.

# Morbidity and mortality rates

Whatever the actual model of healthcare in any society, we need some way of measuring its general effectiveness and we can do this using rates of **morbidity** (ill health) and **mortality** (death). For the moment we can simply define these concepts and note some general problems with them, as preparation for examining patterns and explanations for ill health in a later section.

## Morbidity rates

These focus on the proportion of a population (such as the number per thousand) suffering ill health over a given period (such as a year) and are usually expressed in two ways:

> **General morbidity rates** provide a comprehensive picture of the health of a population, although they often aggregate a small range of important disorders rather than every form of ill health in a society. (Sweet (2011) notes that the three most common groups of disorder in Britain are cancer, circulatory diseases and respiratory diseases.)

> **Specific morbidity rates** examine the occurrence of specific diseases in a society or particular locality. They can be used to measure the effect of relatively minor illnesses (such as influenza) on a population.

Marshall (1998) notes two main ways in which morbidity data are collected:

> **official statistics** that 'provide data on persons who have had some contact with the health services — so-called "treated" cases'

> **community surveys** that involve asking people to self-report instances of ill health

### Problems

Although official statistics may be consistently produced (all visits to a doctor or hospital, for example, are likely to be accurately recorded), there are a couple of major problems with **reliability**:

➤ One is the **iceberg effect**: the number reporting medical conditions is just the small, visible tip of the morbidity iceberg. Not everyone who develops an illness, for example, reports it to a doctor.

➤ People with the *same* symptoms or illnesses may or may not choose to report these to a doctor, making statistical comparisons difficult.

Marshall (1998) argues that the **validity** of official morbidity statistics is limited by 'illness behaviour'. This is affected by several factors:

➤ One is people's willingness to use health services. They may choose not to do so because they don't see their illness as particularly serious, or because they prefer to self-medicate or even use alternative medical treatments.

➤ Another factor concerns the ease of access to health services. For example, the time and effort involved in accessing services may outweigh any perceived benefits.

**Self-report studies** overcome these **methodological problems** to some extent because they provide information on illnesses unreported to the health service:

➤ They have greater **validity** because they include relatively minor illnesses that go unreported in official statistics.

➤ **Reliability** is more problematic since, as Marshall (1998) argues, the meaning of 'illness' varies from person to person (does 'feeling under the weather' count as ill?) and everyday (or 'lay') definitions of illness are often different from clinical definitions. If an individual 'feels ill' this will be included in self-report statistics even though their 'illness' wouldn't be diagnosed as such by a doctor. This may lead to an over-estimation of 'ill health' in a society.

## Mortality rates

Mortality rates measure the proportion of people in a given population who die during a particular time period (such as yearly). Marshall (1998) suggests that if we know when and why people die, this gives an indication of their 'life-time health'. Mortality data are **reliable** and **valid** — every death in our society must be officially recorded. In addition, **death certificates** contribute to the reliability and validity of other statistics (such as average life expectancy) by recording a range of information about the deceased:

➤ cause of death
➤ age
➤ residence
➤ gender
➤ occupation

Death certificates

**C** ause
**A** ge
**R** esidence
**G** ender
**O** ccupation

**Problems**

➤ **Ageing populations**: These may have higher mortality rates, even though the *general health* of a society may be high because more people live longer.

➤ **Reliability**: It can be difficult to reliably compare mortality rates **historically** and **cross-culturally** because population differences, class, age and gender all affect such rates.

> **?** What is the difference between morbidity and mortality?

# Social construction of health and illness

Social construction, in this context, refers to the way different societies develop different ideas about concepts like health and illness. In other words, these concepts are socially constructed:

➤ There is no fixed, universal, agreement about their meaning.

➤ Their meaning changes over time and between groups.

Conrad and Barker (2010) suggest some ways in which health and illness are socially constructed:

➤ **Health**: There is no general agreement on how health should be defined.

➤ **Illness**: There are differences in what counts as illness and in how this state is seen by others. In some societies obesity is an illness, while in others it demonstrates health.

➤ **Knowledge of medicine**: This changes over time. What was once an accepted medical truth (e.g. smoking isn't bad for you) is often revealed to be mistaken.

➤ **Experience of illness**: People experience illness — even the same disorder — in different ways depending on a range of cultural factors (age, gender, class and so forth).

➤ **Sickness**: Some people conform to the **sick role**, others reject it and those who are chronically ill cannot play it.

Social construction

**H** ealth
**I** llness
**K** nowledge
**E** xperience
**S** ickness

The meanings of concepts like health and illness are, therefore, relative in both time and space; interpretations change over time, across different societies and in different contexts. We can explore these ideas further in the context of cultural relativity and 'lay' definitions.

> **?** How is illness socially constructed?

## Cultural relativity

The meaning of health and illness differs within the **same society** over time. The way we currently perceive mental illness is very different from how our society perceived it

400 years ago. As Foucault (1961) notes, 'the mad' in the seventeenth century were seen as being in touch with 'mysterious forces of cosmic tragedy'.

Similarly, there are arguments about the origin and nature of mental illness. On one side it is seen as having a physical reality that can be treated using medications. On the other, Foucault (1961) sees 'mental illness' as a category with no objective validity — it is whatever the powerful (in this case medical professionals) define it as being.

Meanings also differ **between cultures**, which again points to their social construction:

➤ **Homosexuality**, for example, is probably seen by most people in Britain as something that's socially acceptable, largely unremarkable and part of the normal sexual landscape. However, it has been classified in some cultures as a mental illness (it was listed as a 'mental disorder' by the American Psychiatric Association in 1952, although this classification was quickly revoked). Recent debates have focused around whether homosexuality has a *genetic origin*. Some Christian fundamentalist groups argue that it is a 'disordered state'. Whitehead and Whitehead (1999) argue that homosexuality is 'abnormal, unnatural' and can be changed (or cured) by therapy.

➤ **Symbolism**: Some cultures (in parts of China and India, for example) understand health in terms of the symbolic power of different foods ('hot' and 'cold') — health and illness involve the balance between these two types.

➤ **Prophetic medicine**: In Morocco, Martinson (2011) argues, medicine is based around a range of 'spiritual, psychological and socio-cultural' ideas that, while not totally rejecting biomedical models, see the treatment of patients in holistic terms; they locate health and illness in a context that considers biological, social and spiritual factors (with the latter involving aspects of 'faith healing').

### Lay definitions

While 'official' definitions of health and illness are clearly important, individual or subjective definitions are also significant because they affect the way people react to things like illness. Lay definitions involve explanations of health and illness that are not always consistent with official definitions.

Lay definitions generally focus on **well-being**. Walters (2000) suggests that this is a

> ...broadly defined and positive state...a deliberate statement that the medical model is an inadequate description of health. The presence or absence of health is determined by the subjective assessment of the individual concerned, not by the objective assessment of others.

Walters notes that lay definitions generally involve a wider range of ideas about health and its (self-)assessment, based around notions like fitness, strength, 'energy, vitality and psychosocial wellbeing'. People may 'define themselves as healthy despite having a disease'.

However, we shouldn't assume that lay definitions are somehow 'wrong' or 'ignorant of medical realities'; rather, we need to understand them as part of a complex process whereby people construct concepts of health and illness in ways that draw on different social, psychological and physical experiences. As Blaxter (1990) suggests, lay definitions involve a combination of two dimensions.

First, they involve an understanding of certain **attributes**, such as physical indicators of health and illness based on conventional biological notions. When we catch a cold, for example, there are a range of physical indicators, or biological attributes, that tell us we are 'ill' — a blocked nose, sneezing, headache and so forth.

Second, there is a **relational** dimension to lay definitions, based on how we react to biological attributes. Our perception of illness

Lay definitions of health often focus on vitality and well-being

Warren Goldswain/Fotolia

is conditioned by social factors, such as our class, age and gender. For example, different people react differently to catching a cold: a young woman might carry on with her busy life as if the cold is nothing more than a minor hindrance, while an older man might retire to his bed for a couple of days. To develop this point, we will look at a range of less stereotypical examples of the relational dimension to lay definitions. We will consider age, gender, education and social class.

### Age

Blaxter (1990) argues that our society generally thinks in terms of **health capital** — we are born with certain hereditary health attributes (the most negative being inherited genetic disorders, the most positive being good health) that are progressively modified and diminished by social factors, such as those associated with age.

Blaxter found that the elderly reported more problems with mobility, eyesight and hearing than the young. These were seen as evidence of diminished health capital — as something that was to be expected and part of a **natural process**. The elderly 'lived with' experiences of pain and restriction that, in younger people, were more likely to be interpreted as evidence of disorder or illness. Lay definitions here see health as functioning — if you can look after yourself and carry out routine tasks, you are healthy.

### Gender

The Office for National Statistics (2010) suggests that women are more likely to believe they are in poor health, but less likely to die over the following 5 years. Women are also more likely than men to visit their GP, although this is partly explained by **health routines**: women tend to visit their doctor for routine healthcare (such as gynaecological examinations and pregnancy health checks) and are also more likely to take their children for health checks. Men are more likely to see a visit to the doctor as something non-routine.

### Education

Sen (2002) argues that higher levels of education are associated with higher levels of reported illness. For example, he found a greater willingness to report ill health in America than in India, even though mortality rates were lower and life expectancy higher in America. This finding is partly explained by the idea that greater knowledge of 'health problems' has led to higher levels of reporting.

### Social class

Blaxter (1990) found greater acceptance of ill health among the working class than the middle class. This was partly explained by their differing types of work experience (manual labour, for example, causing more 'natural wear and tear') and partly by their different attitudes to health; the working class showed a greater acceptance of pain and discomfort and a greater reluctance to visit the doctor for 'minor complaints'.

Calnan (1987) found that working-class and upper/middle-class definitions of health differed considerably. While the former defined it in terms of 'getting through the day' and 'never being ill', the latter saw it in terms of 'being active', 'feeling fit and strong', and as a 'state of mind'.

More recently, Beale et al. (2010) found that those in the lowest council tax valuation bands (who are most likely to be working class, although the fit is by no means perfect) were more likely to 'take their children to a doctor for everyday symptoms'. Although this seems to contradict Blaxter's findings, it fits with the idea of **health capital** and class — working-class parents are more likely to take steps to protect initial health capital in light of their experience of how it diminishes over time.

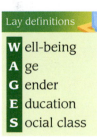

Lay definitions

**W** ell-being
**A** ge
**G** ender
**E** ducation
**S** ocial class

### An overall view

In terms of an overall view of lay definitions, Williams and Popay (1994) argue that they:

➤ do not mimic medical views of health
➤ are logical and coherent assessments of health
➤ are biographical and based on lived experience
➤ are framed by cultural beliefs within different societies

**?** **Suggest one difference between lay and medical definitions of health.**

## The social process of becoming ill

The relationship between 'health' and 'illness' is a complex one that involves a range of *definitions* (both official and lay, positive and negative) and *processes* (from identifying symptoms, through recognising them as 'illness', to having them officially validated as 'illness').

We can think of the social process of becoming ill in terms of a **labelling** process (Figure 11.3). It begins with the individual who recognises and accepts certain symptoms of illness. By so doing, the individual enters into a systematic process involving certain choices and decisions that ultimately lead to an **official classification** of illness. However, as the diagram suggests, the process may be stopped at a number of points for various reasons:

➤ Symptoms disappear and no illness develops.
➤ Symptoms initially interpreted as illness are reinterpreted as 'normal'.
➤ Self-medication (in the form of rest or over-the-counter drugs, for example) proves effective.
➤ The doctor finds no evidence of illness.
➤ Doctor-validated illness proves to be minor and no treatment is required.

The social process involves three forms of validation:

➤ Self-certificated illness simply involves the individual 'feeling unwell'.
➤ Other-validated illness involves the unwell individual convincing (or being convinced by) others, such as family, friends, or work colleagues, that they are ill.
➤ Doctor-validated illness is the stage at which an illness becomes 'officially defined' as such.

Figure 11.3   The social process of becoming ill

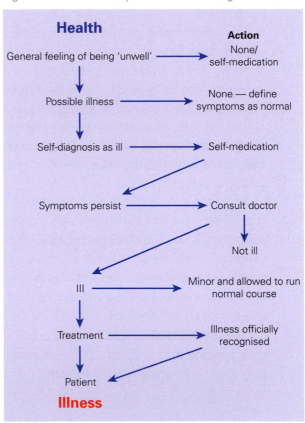

Source: adapted from Lawson et al. (2000)

# Patterns and explanations of ill health in society

Despite the existence of a National Health Service providing free comprehensive healthcare for all, patterns of **health inequality**, as Marshall (1998) argues, remain stubbornly persistent in our society. We can explore this claim by noting a range of **morbidity** and **mortality** patterns associated with **class**, **gender** and **ethnicity** and examining how each, in turn, is explained by artefact, social selection, cultural and structural models.

## Social class

How we define social class is a significant factor in both the identification and explanation of patterns of morbidity and mortality. A major problem is that different sources, both sociological and non-sociological, frequently define class in slightly different ways. While some define class subjectively, for example, others insist it must be defined objectively.

**Subjective definitions** involve people's 'own conceptions of the class structure and their position in it' (Bulmer 1975) — in other words, how people define their own class position. There are problems in using this type of definition for our current purpose, because of the **meanings** people give to social class. They understand 'class' in different ways and consequently define class position using a variety of criteria — from how people speak, to where and how they live, to how much money they earn.

There's also a general tendency to define class in very broad ways, such as working class or middle class. This makes **comparisons** between classes difficult; if there are many different, personal meanings to class it's effectively impossible to compare 'like with like' for statistical purposes.

**Objective definitions** involve identifying class criteria that operate independently of subjective beliefs. The most common form of **objective class indicator** is **occupation**, mainly because the type of work people do correlates with a range of other factors — levels of education, experiences of family life and, most significantly for our purpose, levels of health and illness.

While occupation is a good, general, objective measure of class, there are disagreements about how to classify occupations. Until 1980, the most common official (government) classification was the Registrar General's social class scale (Table 11.1). This divided the population into five basic classes, based on a distinction between non-manual (middle-class) and manual (working-class) work.

Table 11.1   Registrar General's social class scale (1911–80)

|  | Social class | Example occupations |
|---|---|---|
| Non-manual (middle class) | 1 Professional | Accountant, doctor, clergyman, university teacher |
|  | 2 Intermediate | Pilot, farmer, manager, police officer, teacher |
|  | 3N Non-manual skilled | Clerical worker, sales rep., shop assistant |
| Manual (working class) | 3M Manual skilled | Butcher, bus driver, electrician, miner |
|  | 4 Semi-skilled | Bar worker, postal worker, packer |
|  | 5 Unskilled | Labourer, office cleaner, window cleaner |

Since 1980 a range of scales have been developed and used by the UK government:
➢ The Standard Occupational Classification (1990), for example, identified nine class groups, but this was revised (2000) to include slightly different occupational groups.
➢ The National Statistics Socio-Economic Classification (2005) has also been used but, to add to the confusion, it has three different versions based around groupings of eight, five and three classes.

While we need to keep these differences in mind, we can use a relatively simple distinction between manual (working class) and non-manual (middle class) for the purposes of highlighting class-based health inequalities.

We can start with the idea of **health chances** (such as chances of avoiding long-term illness or premature death). These, Knott (2011) observes, are unequally distributed in our society: 'Despite the welfare state and the improvement in health in all sections of societies, this discrepancy remains and it applies to all aspects of health.' An interesting benchmark, in this respect, is The Black Report (1980), which noted that the working class experienced:
➢ higher infant mortality rates
➢ lower life expectancy
➢ higher death rates (over twice as high in the lowest class as compared with the highest)
➢ greater inequalities in the use of medical services

Thirty years later, current morbidity and mortality patterns show a broadly similar trend.

**?** What problems are there with defining social class?

## Morbidity

We can note a range of patterns related to class.

Morbidity rates are higher in those with lower income. Around 40% of adults aged 45–64 on below-average incomes have a limiting long-standing illness or disability — a rate around three times higher than for those on high incomes. There is a similar morbidity relationship for those aged 65–74.

Morbidity rates are higher in those of lower class. Adults aged 45–64 in manual occupations have higher rates of morbidity (limiting long-standing illness or disability) than those in non-manual occupations. There is a similar morbidity relationship for those aged 65 and over.

Smith et al. (2010) found higher rates of **self-reported** limiting long-standing illness or disability for those lower down the class structure. They also found that the highest social classes enjoyed longer life expectancy, and also greater disability-free life expectancy (almost twice as great for a male child born in Kensington as for one born in Manchester). Upper-class males and females could expect (respectively) 12.6 and 11 years longer without a disability than their working-class counterparts.

Those at the bottom of the class structure (the poorest 20% by income) have a greater risk of developing a **mental illness** than their higher-class counterparts. Overall, those in manual occupations have a slightly higher risk of developing a mental illness than their non-manual counterparts.

**Child morbidity** follows a similar pattern. Working-class mothers have a higher risk of producing babies with a low birthweight, and a low birthweight greatly increases the chances of the child developing a life-threatening illness in later life. Working-class children have more dental problems (decayed or filled teeth) than their middle-class peers.

## Mortality

Working-class men aged 25–64 are twice as likely to die prematurely as those from managerial or professional backgrounds. The position is not as bad for working-class women, but sizeable differences remain. These class differences are repeated for all the major causes of death (cancers and circulatory diseases, such as heart disease). Death rates from all major causes for working-class men aged 25–64 are much higher than those for middle-class men.

Working-class children are 35% more likely to die as infants than their middle-class peers and they are more likely to suffer accidental death.

**?** Summarise the relationship between morbidity, mortality and social class.

## Explanations

### Artefact

The apparent relationship between class and morbidity/mortality is not the result of a real and strong correlation but rather an outcome of how such statistics are created and relationships measured. In other words, the relationship we seem to observe is an **artefact** of the **measurement** process.

Defining social class is both difficult and subject to competing interpretations; measuring 'health' (in terms of things like long-term illness or premature death) is similarly problematic. Given these problems, it is argued, we should not assume that any relationship we find between the two is either **reliable** or **valid**.

There are two main problems with making **comparisons**:

➤ **Overgeneralisation**: When studies focus on very broad class categories (such as 'working class'), differences are overgeneralised, because the working class is getting smaller and the middle class larger. This overestimates class differences because a comparison is made between a smaller group who suffer generally poorer health and a larger group who enjoy higher levels of health.

➤ **Undergeneralisation**: Comparisons between those at the top of the class structure and those at the very bottom exaggerate the overall difference in health between the classes, because the two groups being compared are relatively small.

### Evaluation

➤ **Patterns**: Although different studies use different definitions and measurements of class and health, they all show a consistent relationship between poor health and lower social class.

➤ **Mortality**: Even if we assume that morbidity measures are less reliable indicators, the relationship between class and life expectancy remains strong however we measure class (by occupation, household type, income, education or whatever).

➤ **Refinement**: Berkman and Macintyre (1997) argue that, while artefact effects are a particular risk when relating class to health, we should develop a more refined approach to operationalising class, rather than abandon attempts to measure it because of the difficulties. This follows, they argue, because there is clear evidence of a strong statistical relationship between class and health.

### Natural/social selection

The approach explains class differences in health on the basis that those who are seriously unhealthy generally drift down the class structure because they are unable to find employment or are employed in relatively low-paid work. Periods of chronic ill health may mean they are forced to move from job to job rather than focusing on an established career. For this approach, the relationship between health and class, although real, is the reverse of what we might expect.

We might expect that class determines health — that belonging to a lower social class leads to greater morbidity and lower life expectancy. However, in this approach

**health determines class**. When those higher up the class structure experience serious illness, they gradually slip down the class scale (from middle to working class). This means we would naturally expect the working class to be unhealthier than the middle class because this class is continually accepting unhealthy people from higher up the class structure.

The crucial idea here is that **health**, rather than class, is the most important **variable** in the equation; individuals are sifted and sorted into different classes on the basis of their different health statuses.

### Evaluation

There is some statistical evidence of a 'drift' down the class structure for those with very poor health. However, it doesn't necessarily follow that 'health determines class', since there is strong evidence that the class into which children are born plays a significant role in patterns of adult health and illness.

In terms of *physical* health, for example, the General Household Survey (2002) found that children born into *workless* working-class households are twice as likely to develop limiting long-standing illness. More significantly, those living in working-class households are more likely to report a long-standing illness. Since chronic illness tends to develop later in life, when working careers and patterns are already long established, it follows that class must influence health, rather than the reverse.

In addition, if class origin was *not* a significant factor in social mobility, the 'working-class healthy' should experience *upward* social mobility. The evidence suggests this isn't the case.

### Cultural/behavioural factors

This type of explanation focuses on the **individual** and their **health choices**, in terms of behaviour known to be **detrimental** to health (such as smoking, excessive drinking and poor diet) and behaviour known to **promote** good health (such as a healthy, varied diet and regular physical exercise). These choices are related to social class:

➢ **Working classes** generally display riskier and more damaging health behaviours: higher levels of smoking, heavy and regular consumption of alcohol, and diets high in saturated fats and low in fruit and green vegetables.

➢ **Middle classes** generally display healthier and less risky behaviour: varied diet, less smoking, more exercise and so forth.

When we aggregate these individual choices, we find that those at the bottom of the class structure have greater morbidity and on average die younger.

### Evaluation

While there is clear empirical evidence of class differences in lifestyles, risky health behaviours and ill health, how we interpret this evidence is key to understanding the relationship between class and heath.

One interpretation focuses on **individuals**. Lifestyle choices determine health — and the working class clearly make 'poorer' choices than the (healthier) middle classes. Class, therefore, is only related to health in the sense that we can group individual behaviours; there is nothing specific to social class itself that causes ill health. The solution to working-class health problems is, therefore, better health education and the adoption of less risky behaviours.

An alternative interpretation considers why risky health behaviours are rooted in **social class**. Rather than looking at individual behaviours, we need to ask if there is something about 'being working class' that makes people take higher individual health risks. For Spector et al. (2006), the strong relationship between class, ill health, age-related disease and lower life expectancy is explained in terms of 'stress factors'. Ill health results from the strain of being in low-paid, manual work allied to 'the psychological stress of having lots of areas you cannot control in your life'.

In this view, lifestyle choices are related to social class, not the other way around. The working classes smoke, drink and have poorer diets because of the stresses associated with low-paid work; psychological pressures relating to family life, unemployment, a lack of savings for old age and the like mean that the working classes are more likely to associate 'risky health behaviours' with pleasure. These behaviours are 'ways of coping' with a difficult and precarious social status.

Some studies suggest that cultural/behavioural explanations place too much stress on lifestyle choices. Wadsworth et al. (2006) found that 'early social environment' was crucial for many aspects of adult health, including life expectancy, 'independent of the adult life environment'. Lifestyle choices, therefore, played only a relatively minor role in overall adult health across different classes.

Even in 'best case scenarios', such as the relationship between smoking and lung cancer, lifestyle choices do not explain everything. Carroll et al. (1994) found that, among those who had never smoked, there were higher levels of the disease in the working class than the upper class.

### Structural and material factors

This approach focuses on the various ways in which the material conditions of people's lives impact on their health. Higher levels of ill health, life-threatening conditions and infant mortality, and lower average life expectancy are all related to factors such as:

➢ poverty
➢ relative deprivation
➢ substandard and overcrowded housing
➢ lack of material resources
➢ lack of cultural capital (such as knowledge about health)
➢ lower educational achievement
➢ higher-risk occupations

Bartley and Blane (2008), for example, note how 'poverty exposes people to health hazards' such as air pollution and damp housing (the latter being closely associated with higher rates of childhood respiratory disease).

Over the longer term, Self and Zealey (2007) suggest that a range of **public health measures** introduced in Britain over the course of the twentieth century have played a large part in lowering working-class morbidity and mortality rates. These measures include slum housing clearance, improved public and private sanitation and clean water supplies. This argument suggests a strong relationship between class, health and material conditions.

Poor housing contributes to ill health

Marshall (1998) suggests that 'social factors play a major part in generating health and illness', with higher levels of good health among the highest social classes being related to factors such as the following:

➤ **Autonomy and control at work**: The more someone has of these, the less the likelihood of heart disease.
➤ **Effort–reward balance**: Work with high career prospects, excellent job security and high financial rewards is related to lower levels of physical and mental ill health. The reverse holds true: work that is highly demanding but offers limited security, career prospects and financial rewards has a greater association with serious ill health.

In this respect social class is demonstrably related to health; the working classes experience poorer health *because* they are working class — a relationship explained by their lower living standards and the riskier health behaviours that compensate in some way for their poorer material conditions.

### Evaluation

The evidence for the relationship between social class, material conditions and ill health is strong — arguably stronger than the evidence for any other explanation. In addition, a strength of this approach is that it can explain, as we've seen, the relationship between lifestyle choices and health. However, several problems persist:

➤ **Artefact effects**: As we've seen, there are clear problems involved in defining both class and health, and some 'class differences' in health may be questionable — although, as we've also noted, these probably occur more at the margins of the overall analysis.
➤ **Life expectancy**: Women generally enjoy longer life expectancy than men across all cultures; and working-class women live, on average, longer than working-class men.

➤ **Long-term effects**: While the kind of material improvements noted by Self and Zealey have clearly impacted on working-class morbidity and mortality, their long-term effects are more questionable. The working class in the twenty-first century generally live under material conditions which are far superior to those experienced by their counterparts at the beginning of the twentieth century — yet they still suffer relatively worse health than those higher up the class structure. Bartley and Blane (2008) also note that 'In the UK, relatively disadvantaged people receive various kinds of state help (rent, school meals etc.) which, some argue, makes diet or poor housing unlikely to account for all inequalities in health outcomes'.

Structural explanation of patterns of ill health

**A** rtefact
**L** ife expectancy
**L** ong-term effects

> **?** Give examples of two material factors that are more likely to affect working-class health.

# Gender

'Women get sicker, but men die quicker.' This observation is often used as a simple way of summarising the relationship between gender and health. We can demonstrate this by outlining gendered patterns of morbidity and mortality.

## Morbidity

### Physical health

The overall picture is one of greater morbidity in women. Women are more likely to:
➤ visit their doctor more frequently
➤ have regular health checks
➤ be admitted to hospital
➤ suffer conditions such as allergies and headaches

Sweet (2011), however, notes broad similarities between men and women in two areas (Table 11.2): first, the proportion of life spent free from a disability (disability-free life expectancy), and second, the proportion of life spent free from debilitating illness (healthy life expectancy).

Table 11.2   Freedom from disability and debilitating illness by gender

|  | Males | Females |
| --- | --- | --- |
| **Disability-free life expectancy** | 82% | 79% |
| **Healthy life expectancy** | 63% | 64.5% |

*Source: Sweet (2011)*

**Self-reported illness** is a less reliable measure, but the evidence suggests little or no gender difference in self-reported health and sickness (Table 11.3). These differences have remained roughly constant over the past 30 years.

Table 11.3   Self-reported health and sickness

| 2009 | Males | Females |
|------|-------|---------|
| Bad or very bad health | 5% | 5% |
| Long-standing illness or disability | 30% | 31% |
| Limiting long-standing illness or disability | 17% | 19% |
| Restricted activity | 10% | 12% |

*Source: Sweet (2011)*

## Mental health

In terms of common mental disorders (those generally seen as 'lower-level' disorders, such as anxiety and depression), Sweet notes that women are significantly more likely than men (21% versus 14%) to suffer some form of mental health problem. In addition, women have:

➢ higher hospital admission rates for mental illnesses
➢ greater antidepressant drug use
➢ more psychotic, neurotic and depressive disorders
➢ more depressive episodes (and for longer periods)

Men, on the other hand, are more likely to receive treatment for alcohol-related and drug-dependency problems.

## Mortality

Hughes and Church (2010) note that **average life expectancy** for both males and females has risen by around 30 years over the past century. In 2008, men could expect to live on average for 78 years and women for 82 years (a gender difference that holds true across all industrialised nations).

Men suffer **premature death** more frequently than women. Men are more likely to commit suicide or die an accidental death. However, Sweet (2011) notes that cancer is the main cause of death for both sexes.

Men have a higher risk factor for the three main causes of death (circulatory and respiratory diseases and cancers). This trend has been consistent over the past 40 years.

## Explanations

### Artefact

Compared with men, women have greater general morbidity, measured in terms of things like doctor visits, hospital admissions and levels of ill health. However, they have similar levels of chronic illness and higher average life expectancy. This suggests that morbidity levels are a statistical artefact — that higher morbidity is explained by women being more willing to seek medical attention and more likely to visit doctors for routine health checks. As Ashley (2010) reports, 'Women are more likely than men to complain about their health even when they are in better shape'.

Although White et al. (2010) found 'limited evidence' that men delay reporting symptoms of serious *physical* illness such as cancer, they did find that men are more likely to under-report mental health problems. Pilgrim and Rogers (2010) also found that 'women are approximately twice as likely as men to refer themselves on for psychiatric treatment'. One possible reason is the greater **stigma** attached to mental illness in men.

*Evaluation*

An alternative interpretation focuses on women having a greater willingness to:

➢ identify symptoms
➢ act on those symptoms
➢ seek treatment for illness

Pilgrim and Rogers (2010), for example, suggest that a greater willingness to report ill health increases the chances of the early diagnosis of serious illness and, most importantly, *recovery*. Greater morbidity and lower mortality are not, therefore, mutually exclusive but *complementary*.

**Opportunity structures** may be an overlooked factor. We can't take 'medical visits' at face value. Gendered assumptions about the female caring role mean that women are more likely than men to take their children to the doctor for minor conditions — and this gives them greater opportunity to talk about their own health problems. Verbrugge (1985) found evidence of greater female opportunity, both through their children and because their roles as part-time workers or housewives allowed greater flexibility in medical visits. This kind of explanation fits with Macintyre et al.'s (1999) findings of little real evidence that men were less willing to report serious symptoms or seek healthcare.

Natural and social selection

*Morbidity*

Higher female morbidity rates can be partly explained in terms of natural and social selection:

➢ **Natural selection**: Women are more likely to come into contact with the medical profession for reasons of pregnancy and childbirth, especially if complications occur.
➢ **Social selection**: Where women have greater responsibility for childcare, they are more likely to have greater contact with doctors through the needs of their children.

*Mortality*

Explanations for greater female longevity focus on life expectancy as a function of natural and social selection:

➢ **Natural selection**: One of the most striking features of mortality rates, consistent across all industrialised nations, is longer average female life expectancy. One explanation for this is biological — women are 'genetically programmed' to live longer because of greater resistance to serious diseases and so forth.

> **Social selection**: Where men have traditionally had greater involvement in the public sphere, such as the workplace, they are exposed to greater levels of risk. This includes both general risk (e.g. from harder physical labour) and specific risk (coal miners, for example, have far higher rates of respiratory diseases). It is this greater exposure to risk that explains their lower average life expectancy.

*Evaluation*

Social factors play a significant role in rates of male and female mortality. Over the course of the twentieth century, for example, average female life expectancy has risen faster than male life expectancy — mainly because fewer women now die in childbirth (which means that the increase is a **statistical artefact**).

A further qualification is that average life expectancy is influenced by **class**. Table 11.4 (using region as a proxy for social class) demonstrates that longevity is not simply a biological phenomenon, since upper-class males have a higher life expectancy than lower-class females. This suggests that we need to explain gendered mortality rates in some other way.

Table 11.4   Chances of reaching age 75 by gender and region (class)

|  | Males | Females |
|---|---|---|
| **Highest** | 78% [Buckinghamshire] | 86% [Surrey] |
| **Lowest** | 54% [Manchester] | 69% [Manchester] |

*Source: Smith (2011)*

### Cultural/behavioural factors

*Morbidity*

Explanations for gendered morbidity focus on the following factors:
> **Patriarchy**: Female bodies are subjected to higher levels of scrutiny and control (from parents, partners and medical practitioners) which leads to higher morbidity reporting.
> **Risk**: Men are exposed to greater health risks in the workplace (such as accidents and unhealthy working conditions).

*Mortality*

Explanations for gendered mortality focus around the following:
> **Lifestyles**: Men generally tend to have riskier lifestyles in terms of smoking and excessive drinking. Women, therefore, live more healthily and hence longer.
> **Dieting and eating disorders**: These, on the other hand, have greater associations with women and can lead to a wide range of medical problems (some of which, like anorexia, are life-threatening).

> **Social selection**: As previously noted, men have greater risk exposure to serious work-related diseases, which makes them more prone to chronic illnesses.

*Evaluation*

> **Self-fulfilling prophecy**: Greater public and private scrutiny of female bodies leads to higher morbidity: the greater the scrutiny, the more likely illness will be discovered. In other words, women may not necessarily have higher morbidity, just a higher *reported* morbidity.

> **Discourses**: Where media discourses highlight female mental health problems, women are more likely to recognise symptoms of mental illness. The question once again is the extent to which gender differences in mental health are real differences or simply the outcome of a greater female willingness to embrace the idea of mental illness (an **artefact** explanation).

## Structural and material factors

Patterns of gender morbidity and, in particular, mortality are sensitive to social inequalities; both male and female morbidity and mortality rates correlate significantly with social class, with a general trend towards lower rates in higher classes. There are a range of material reasons for these patterns.

**Inter-class differences** focus around the effects of:

> poverty
> substandard and overcrowded housing
> unemployment

These correlate with a range of lifestyle factors:

> smoking
> alcohol intake
> poor diet

This, however, is only part of the explanation. **Intra-class differences** between men and women can't be adequately explained by material factors alone, since they are *shared* by men and women of the *same class*. To understand why women have higher morbidity, we must look more closely at gender relationships *within* social classes.

**Material** differences include the following:

> **Diet**: Spencer (1996) suggests that, where family income is tight, working-class mothers are more likely to go without food, or to eat bulky but unhealthy food, to ensure their children (and partner) eat reasonably well.

> **Essential services**, such as gas and electricity: These are often limited by poverty. Where women are more likely to spend most of their time within the home, this can contribute to a cold, unhealthy environment that leaves them vulnerable to a range of illnesses.

> **Substandard housing** that is cold and damp: Such conditions are similarly likely to adversely affect female morbidity.

A **structural factor** that contributes to greater female morbidity in working-class families (and also extends into the middle classes) is a female **double shift**. Where women are expected to be both paid employees and unpaid domestic labourers, they work long hours that leave them more vulnerable to physical morbidity.

Duncombe and Marsden (1993) also note a **triple shift** — the third element being emotional labour. Where women invest time and effort in the *psychological* well-being of family members, this leaves them more exposed to **mental morbidity** (such as depressive illnesses); they are more likely to neglect their own well-being for the sake of their partner and children. Nazroo et al. (1998), for example, found an increased risk of depression in women as a result of gendered role differences; in households 'where there was a clear distinction in roles between men and women', problems concerning 'children, housing and reproduction' were found to trigger depressive illnesses in women.

Another factor is **social capital**. Klinenberg (2003) has shown that higher levels of **social isolation** result in higher levels of morbidity. Home-bound working-class women, for example, are more likely to experience social isolation than professional middle-class women. In addition, **lone parenthood** is one of the most socially isolated and materially deprived family structures in our society, and the majority of these structures (around 90%) are headed by women. Where poverty and isolation have a strong association with ill health, this is one reason for higher rates of female morbidity.

### Evaluation

**Material factors** *alone* don't adequately explain why males and females of the *same* class display different rates of morbidity and mortality. To explain this situation we need to link different **gender roles** to material factors; *within social classes* material factors, such as poverty and deprivation, affect males and females differently.

Wilkinson and Pickett (2010) argue that increasing **living standards** do not go hand-in-glove with lower male morbidity and higher life expectancy beyond a certain point. Once certain material conditions have been met (such as access to clean water), there are no dramatic improvements in health. What matters in contemporary societies, they argue, is not unequal access to material resources but rather unequal access to **social resources**. In other words, **social exclusion** is the key to understanding health differences. Women of different social classes, for example, show higher rates of morbidity compared with men because they experience higher rates of exclusion within their particular class circles.

> **?**  What cultural factors influence the health of men rather than women?

# Ethnicity

Although ethnicity refers to **cultural differences** in areas like religion, family structures, beliefs, values and norms, this relatively simple statement hides a wide range of **definitional problems** that make it difficult to establish a strong relationship between ethnicity and health. These problems relate less to how an ethnic group defines itself — **subjectively**, on the basis of what group members believe or how other groups define different ethnicities, or **objectively** on the basis of some agreed criteria, such as country of origin — and more to how **official statistical definitions** converge and diverge.

A major problem here is that different studies and sources often use different definitions of ethnicity — and this makes comparisons between ethnic groups difficult (and possibly **invalid**). A further problem, as Steinbach (2009) notes, is that 'Ethnicity is not recorded on UK death certificates'; while mortality data use 'country of birth' as a useful alternative, this fails to adequately classify members of ethnic minorities born in the UK.

While keeping the limitations of classification and measurement firmly in mind, we can note a range of health differences between ethnic groups defined in terms of their 'historic country of origin'. Black British ethnicities, for example, are defined in terms of categories such as black Caribbean and black African.

## Morbidity

Cooper's (2002) examination of 'the self-reported health of men and women from white and minority ethnic groups in the UK' found the following:

➢ All ethnic minority groups had poorer health compared with whites.
➢ Morbidity was higher for many minority ethnic women than for their male counterparts.
➢ The highest morbidity for all adults occurred in the most disadvantaged groups, 'notably Pakistanis and Bangladeshis' — a finding replicated by Fitzpatrick et al. (2007).
➢ Class inequalities explained the 'health disadvantage experienced by minority ethnic men and women', but morbidity was higher for women than for men of the same class (something that mirrors gendered inequalities in morbidity found across all ethnic groups).

The Office for National Statistics (2005) reported that women from all ethnic groups were more likely than men to rate their health as 'not good'. Concerning **hospital admissions**, Fitzpatrick et al. (2007) note the following points:

➢ Asian ethnicities have higher rates of admission due to coronary heart disease.
➢ Asian and black Caribbean ethnicities have higher rates of diabetes.
➢ Asian ethnicities have above average hospitalisation for cataract surgery (diabetes is 'a known risk factor for cataracts').
➢ Black Africans are the largest ethnic group receiving HIV care. This group also has the highest rates of tuberculosis.

**?** Give examples of two morbidity differences between ethnic minority groups.

## Mortality

Kelly and Nazroo (2008) identify a range of ethnic differences in mortality rates, as follows.

**Non-white ethnic groups** have:
➢ lower mortality rates from respiratory disease and lung cancer
➢ higher mortality rates for conditions relating to diabetes

**Black Caribbean men** have:
➢ lower rates of mortality
➢ low rates of heart disease mortality
➢ high rates of stroke mortality

**Black Africans** have:
➢ high overall mortality rates
➢ high rates of stroke mortality
➢ low rates of heart disease mortality

**South Asians** have:
➢ high rates of heart disease mortality
➢ high rates of stroke mortality

Overall, there are wide variations in ethnic morbidity and mortality both across and within groups:
➢ **Across groups**: Pakistani and Bangladeshi men and women have the highest rates of disability, while non-white groups have higher rates for specific illnesses, such as diabetes.
➢ **Within groups**: Women have higher rates of morbidity but lower mortality, and age differences in morbidity exist within all ethnic groups.

## Explanations

### Artefact

This approach argues that the relationship between ethnicity and health is difficult to establish for several reasons:
➢ There are problems in defining 'ethnicity'.
➢ Different definitions are used by different studies, which makes comparisons difficult.
➢ There is a lack of official statistics about the morbidity and mortality of different ethnicities. Harding (2007), for example, argues that explanations of ethnic inequality in health are 'compromised by the lack of relevant data'.
➢ Misclassifications may occur. Nazroo and King (2002) argue that, while black Caribbeans have higher levels of treatment for psychosis, it doesn't follow that they have higher levels of mental illness; rather, it means that they are more likely to be prescribed treatment on the basis of the symptoms they express.

The main argument, therefore, is that we have little or no way of knowing if apparent relationships between ethnicity and health involve real differences or are simply the result of statistical artefact.

**Age** may be a complicating factor. The Office for National Statistics (2005) notes that 'Differences between minority ethnic groups and the general population may be partly due to their age differences'; that is, different ethnic groups may have different age profiles, and this may affect the patterns of health found. For example, some ethnic groups have much larger proportions of very old and very young members, which can adversely affect morbidity and mortality rates.

**Class** is also likely to be a complicating factor. A lack of definitional clarity or standardisation compounds the argument that 'ethnicity statistics' actually measure class differences. Pakistanis, for example, have the highest levels of morbidity and mortality, and are also the most deprived ethnic group in our society.

**?** **What problems do we have with defining ethnicity?**

### Evaluation

Artefact arguments have some validity because there are clearly major problems concerning:

➢ standardised definitions of ethnicity
➢ failures to standardise age profiles across ethnic groups
➢ the separation of class and gender variables from 'ethnic effects'

However, the Office for National Statistics (2005) notes that, where age differences *are* standardised, Pakistani and Bangladeshi ethnicities still report rates of ill health twice that of their white British counterparts. Similarly, where we can identify differences in morbidity and mortality between broadly defined ethnic groups (using, for example, country of origin as the baseline difference), it's logical to assume that refinements in measurement are more likely than not to reveal greater ethnic differences.

In addition, while ethnic class differences are significant, this doesn't mean we should ignore general ethnic differences in morbidity and mortality — especially when looking at differences in rates for specific forms of ill health, such as diabetes.

### Natural/social selection

Explanations of this kind focus on two areas:

➢ **Genetic disorders**: Some ethnic groups show a greater incidence of certain types of genetic disorder than others. Examples include sickle-cell anaemia in black African/Caribbean ethnicities and Tay-Sachs, a disease of the nervous system, in Jewish populations.
➢ **Mental health**: Ramon (2007) argues that genetic and biochemical explanations for ethnic differences in mental health tend to dominate psychiatric interpretations

— and since psychiatrists tend to be primary definers of mental health, they have a significant input to mental health decisions.

*Evaluation*

➤ **Genetic disorders**: While some ethnic groups do have a genetic predisposition for certain types of disease, these are not sufficient to account for the broad differences found between ethnic groups in our society.

➤ **Mental health**: Ramon (2007) argues that different patterns of mental health among ethnic groups can be explained by **social**, rather than **genetic**, causes. Morgan et al. (2008), for example, found a strong relationship between class and mental disorders in the black Caribbean working-class population. The most disadvantaged in the black population developed greater mental health problems in later life.

### Cultural/behavioural factors

These explanations focus on two main variables: lifestyle choices and behavioural choices.

In considering **lifestyle choices**, the focus is on a range of practices that promote or inhibit good health:

➤ **Risky health behaviours** such as smoking and alcohol consumption: Asian ethnicities tend to smoke less and consume less alcohol than their white counterparts (with certain exceptions — Bangladeshi men, for example, smoke more).

➤ **Dietary differences**: Higgins and Dale (2011) found that Pakistani and Bangladeshi women, as well as men from most ethnic minorities, were more likely to eat five portions of fruit or vegetables a day than their white counterparts. Some Asian ethnicities consume higher than average amounts of dairy products.

➤ **Physical exercise**: Higgins and Dale (2011) found that levels of physical exercise were lower for Pakistani and Bangladeshi men and women, and for Indian and Chinese women.

Fitzpatrick et al. (2007) note that Irish and Scottish ethnicities have the highest mortality rates from all causes of death — which suggests that cultural behaviours play a significant part in rates of morbidity and mortality.

In terms of **behavioural choices**, this approach considers such areas as the extent to which different ethnic groups make use of medical services. Stuart (2008),

Ethnic groups often differ in their dietary patterns

for example, notes how 'Low take-up of services among black and minority ethnic communities' is often explained in terms of 'cultural differences' such as:

➢ language barriers
➢ lack of interest
➢ alternative services

Stuart, however, suggests different reasons for ethnic minorities receiving, in the main, poorer-quality care:

➢ social and physical isolation
➢ poor communication between some ethnic groups
➢ lack of interpreting services
➢ interaction difficulties with GPs, receptionists and hospital staff
➢ difficulties registering with GPs

### Evaluation

**Lifestyle choices** are significant for some specific forms of ill health, such as cancer rates among different ethnic groups. Particular cultural practices can be important: for example, very few Bangladeshi women smoke. However, apart from particular practices of that kind, it's not clear how individual ethnic lifestyle choices have an overall effect on morbidity and mortality rates.

**Equality of opportunity** is an issue. Minority groups are often criticised for a failure to take up free, readily available health services, and a similar criticism is levelled at the white working class. This assumes, however, that every individual is equally positioned to take advantage of these services.

Stuart (2008) points out that when a cultural factor such as 'language differences' is raised as an explanation for low take-up, the implication is that the problem lies with the individual rather than the service. When take-up is seen as a matter of behavioural choice, there is a strong element of **victim blaming** and of expecting individuals to adapt themselves to health services rather than the other way around. An alternative view would recognise the need for the service to adapt, for example by providing interpreters.

### Structural and material factors

As artefact explanations point out, one of the problems with explaining different ethnic morbidity and mortality rates is the influence of social class. This is especially pertinent when the **demographic profile** of many ethnic minorities is one where they are *generally* over-represented in the lowest social classes:

➢ Asian ethnicities are most likely to feature in the *least wealthy* 10% of the UK population, while Chinese ethnicities are most likely to appear in the *wealthiest* 10%.
➢ Self and Zealey (2007) report that Asian and black African ethnicities are most likely to experience low incomes.

➤ Berthoud (1998) identifies Pakistanis and Bangladeshis as being among the very poorest in our society.

Given that class is an important factor in morbidity and mortality, one dimension to this approach suggests that poorer levels of health among ethnic minority groups are related to **material deprivation** — higher levels of poverty and poor housing, lower levels of employment and income, riskier work environments and the like.

A further dimension involves **social deprivation** — some groups have greater difficulties in taking advantage of health services than others. This kind of social deprivation involves:

➤ not knowing one's health rights
➤ not accessing health services (such as a GP)
➤ not establishing and maintaining relationships with health services and carers

Social deprivation correlates with material deprivation, with the working classes experiencing higher levels of both.

Furthermore, this approach argues that ethnic minority groups face an added problem of racism. This racism is sometimes **overt**, but increasingly **covert** in the form of **cultural racism**. This is seen in the idea that an ethnic minority culture is to blame for their unequal treatment — that, for example, an inability to speak 'standard English' is a feature of ethnic minority groups that prevents them from accessing health services.

Cultural racism places the blame for 'discrimination' on those who are victimised — in terms of a 'failure to integrate', for instance — rather than locating it in the culture and practice of a dominant majority culture. Fitzpatrick et al. (2007), for example, found that Asian minorities reported the worst levels of patient experience when dealing with doctors and hospitals.

### Evaluation

Harriss (2007) concludes that 'much of the variation in self-reported health between and within black and minority ethnic groups can be explained by differences in socio-economic status':

➤ higher rates of poverty and unemployment
➤ lower levels of income and of benefits take-up

However, Harriss also suggests that this picture is complicated by an 'interplay of factors affecting ethnic health':

➤ the long-term impact of migration
➤ racism and discrimination
➤ poor delivery and take-up of healthcare
➤ differences in culture and lifestyles
➤ biological susceptibility

**Exam-style questions**

1 Identify and explain two ways in which patterns of ill health are influenced by social class. (17 marks)

2 Identify and explain two ways in which patterns of ill health are influenced by gender. (17 marks)

3 Outline and evaluate the view that class inequalities in health are caused by structural factors. (33 marks)

4 Outline and evaluate the view that ethnic inequalities in health are caused by structural factors. (33 marks)

5 Outline and evaluate the view that social class inequalities in health are caused by cultural factors. (33 marks)

6 Outline and evaluate the view that gender inequalities in health are caused by structural factors. (33 marks)

# The social construction of mental illness and disability

## Definitions, diagnosis and trends of mental illness

### Definitions and diagnosis

Before we look at trends in mental illness and explanations for those trends, we need to think about how mental illness is defined. This is not as straightforward as it might appear because, as Busfield (1996) argues, 'mental disorder stands in a difficult and precarious position between' the following:

➤ **physical illness** — where objective criteria can be defined and measured
➤ **deviance** — where notions of what is 'acceptable' behaviour involve moral and subjective decision-making

Concepts of mental illness are, therefore, subject to a long-running dispute between health professionals and social theorists 'as to where the boundaries should be set'. In other words, mental illness is a **contested concept** — it has no clear, unequivocal, objective definition. Rather, as Busfield (1986) argues, different groups define, measure and treat mental illness in different ways. We can illustrate this by comparing three different types of **diagnostic model**: medical, psychological and sociological.

**?** Why might mental illness be difficult to define?

### The medical model

This model has three significant features.

The first is **objectivity**. As with its physical counterpart, mental illness is a real, objective condition.

The second feature concerns **causality**. Causes are internal to the body, the major ones being genetic and biochemical; chemical imbalances in the brain, for example, *cause* abnormal behaviours. Causes are definable by mental health practitioners — those with scientific knowledge and understanding of mental health.

The third feature concerns **treatment**. A range of methods can be successful — from surgical intervention or chemical procedures (using drugs to control or resolve biochemical imbalances) to, ultimately perhaps, gene manipulation. Treatments are **external** in that the patient plays no part in their diagnosis or cure; this is managed by health professionals, with the patient expected to play the **sick role**.

Mental illness is part of the same continuum as physical illness and can be approached in the same way. Just as the body can have a normal or abnormal state (healthy or ill), the mind can similarly be normal or abnormal (mentally healthy or ill). The objective of treatment, therefore, is the removal of the causes of an abnormal state and the restoration of a normal state of mental health.

### Psychological models

These models are many and varied, but we can identify three common features, in terms of objectivity/subjectivity, causality and treatment.

Some forms of mental illness, such as schizophrenia, may have biochemical causes and can be treated **objectively**, through the use of drugs or surgical procedures. Others, however, require a more **subjective** approach, for example involving discussion and therapy. Kinderman (2005) suggests that one subjective approach 'examines the events of people's lives to discover how they've interpreted and reacted to these'.

**Causality** ranges from genetic and biochemical factors to current or childhood traumas; these causes are internal and specific to each individual, and each manifestation needs a specific form of intervention. The majority of these interventions are collaborative; the health professional and the patient work together to identify the problems that have caused the illness.

**Treatment** is always possible, but the patient is not always 'cured'. Some forms of psychological intervention simply help individuals cope with or manage their illness. While individual cures are desirable, this approach also focuses on the prevention of future illnesses.

### Sociological models

The focus of sociological models is not the individual as such, but rather the social and material conditions under which they live. The causes of mental illness are *external* to the individual, either in the **material conditions** of the victim's life (**structural** approaches) or the **social processes** that lead to them being labelled 'mentally ill' (**interactionist approaches**). We will describe and evaluate each approach in more detail later in the chapter.

## Trends

In this section we can outline some basic trends in mental illness based on the categories of class, gender and ethnicity.

### Social class

Ortega and Larson (2000) argue that the inverse relationship between class and mental disorder (the higher the class, the lower the level of disorder) 'is now so well established that it has almost acquired the status of a sociological law'. This observation is supported by a variety of statistical evidence. The Centre for Social Justice (2011), for example, found that adults from the lowest 20% of household incomes, when compared with the richest 10%, are:

➤ three times more likely to have a common mental disorder
➤ nine times more likely to have psychotic disorders (more serious forms of mental illness which may involve delusions and hallucinations)

Similarly, in terms of the long-term risk of developing a mental illness, the National Centre for Social Research (2011) found that:

➤ the poorest 20% in England were at greater risk than the richest 20%
➤ manual workers (both male and female) have a higher risk than non-manual workers

These findings are supported by *longer-term* trends:

➤ Eaton's (1974) review of 17 mental health studies showed that those with the lowest incomes were at the highest risk of developing schizophrenia.
➤ Eaton and Harrison's (2001) review of 13 additional studies confirmed this relationship.
➤ Muntaner et al. (2004) similarly found that higher levels of schizophrenia were associated with lower-income groups.

### Gender

As McManus et al. (2009) suggest, women are more likely than men to develop milder forms of mental illness. The National Centre for Social Research (2011) noted that rates of these were higher for women across all classes, income levels and age groups. The higher risk of mental illness was related to social class, with the risk for the poorest 20% of women:

➤ 2.5 times higher than for the richest 20%
➤ 2 times higher than for those on average incomes

The general trend over the past 10 years is that levels of risk have stayed fairly consistent for both men and women. In 1999, for example, around 15% of men and 19% of women were at risk of developing mental illnesses; in 2009 the figures were 15% and 17% respectively.

Social class is an important factor in mental illness: women from manual backgrounds have the highest risk. However, its influence needs to be qualified in terms of gender and inequality:

➤ **Gender**: The risk of mental illness for women from *non-manual backgrounds* is equal to that of men from *manual backgrounds* — which suggests gender itself is a significant variable.

➤ **Inequality**: Kahn et al.'s (2000) American study found that lower income levels correlated with a higher risk of women developing mental illness (both the relationship and the trend are fairly consistent across Western societies). However, they identified a more significant pattern: the risk of female mental illness increased in line with **income inequality**. The greater the difference in earnings between those at the top and the bottom of society, the higher the level of risk.

### Ethnicity

Nazroo (1997) argues that there are higher rates of mental illness in ethnic minorities, both black and white, and particularly in Irish ethnicities. However, this has to be qualified by how we *measure* mental illness. In terms of diagnosis, 'the rate of psychosis was no greater among Caribbean men than among white men'; but in terms of treatment, 'Caribbeans, particularly young Caribbean men, are far more likely than whites to be receiving hospital treatment'.

In general, Nazroo suggests that 'ethnic minority status might increase the risk of mental illness, regardless of skin colour':

➤ Caribbeans 'had the highest rates of mental illness and were more likely to suffer depression than whites'.

➤ Irish and other minority whites (those born outside Britain) had similar rates to Caribbeans.

➤ Caribbean women had an increased risk if they were married or cohabiting.

Nazroo's study found the same pattern as most other research: the lower the social class, as measured by occupation and income, the higher the level of mental illness.

The Centre for Social Justice (2011) reports that, despite black and minority ethnic groups having a higher risk of serious (psychotic) mental illness, black people are more likely to:

➤ be turned away when they ask for help from mental health services

➤ have other problems wrongly attributed to mental health

➤ be admitted to hospital through a referral from the criminal justice system

➤ have mental health problems which are not detected by a doctor

In terms of common mental disorders, Weich et al. (2004) found higher rates among the elderly in ethnic minority groups. McManus et al. (2009) found higher rates for white, black and South Asian women — which again suggests the significance of gender, as well as class.

Hatloy (2010) reported higher levels of depressive illness among Pakistani and Indian women, and higher levels of anxiety illness among Irish men and Indian women.

These statistical relationships and trends suggest two things:

➢ An **inverse care law** applies in the case of ethnic minorities (and probably applies equally well to social class) whereby, as the Centre for Social Justice suggests, 'those who are in most need of support are the least likely to access the services which provide this support'.

➢ We need to be careful about how we interpret and explain statistical relationships since they are highly dependent on a range of complicating factors:
  ➢ how we define mental illness
  ➢ who defines mental illness
  ➢ the difference between diagnosis and treatment

> **?** Briefly explain the meaning of an 'inverse care law'.

# Sociological explanations for trends in mental illness

## Structural approaches

Structural approaches generally accept medical definitions of mental illness. They treat it as having an **objective** existence whose causes are to be found in **social and material conditions** external to the individual. Mental illness is a **social construction** in the sense that forces outside the individual combine to push them into mental illnesses that range from the relatively mild (such as anxiety or depression) to the relatively severe (such as those involving psychotic or delusional behaviour). The particular focus is on how social and material pressures are experienced by the individual as **stress**. We can discuss this in terms of two ideas: **social resources** and **social power**.

### Social resources

Social resources include such things as levels of education and income. The greater the social resources an individual possesses, the lower the likelihood of their developing a mental illness. This idea fits neatly with the statistical evidence we've outlined (the lower the class, the greater the risk of mental illness) and explains mental illness in terms of the extent to which individuals are exposed to stressful events and processes, such as unemployment and poverty. Turner et al. (1995), for example, argue that where the working class experience more stressful life events they develop higher levels of mental illness.

The relationship between social structure, stress and the individual can be explained in a variety of ways. One of the broadest is **strain theory**. This has its origins in the work of Merton (1938), who argued that every society sets goals for its members (such as the attainment of success and wealth) and provides legitimate means (such as paid work) through which they can be achieved. However, a society may fail to provide these means for everyone: most people in our society, for example, are never going to be wealthy and successful. This creates structural tensions that make the individual react in different ways to the 'denial of success'. One possible reaction is despair — the feeling that nothing the individual does can improve their life. This, in turn, leads to what Merton calls **retreatism**: the individual withdraws from society through alcoholism, drug abuse and, in some instances, mental illness.

More specifically, we can outline some concrete ways in which structural forces stress individuals.

The Centre for Social Justice (2011) argues that social deprivation — involving, for example, low or no income, substandard housing and unemployment — causes 'physical health problems which greatly increase the risk of mental illness'. The risk of mental illness is much higher for those who suffer 'chronic low level stress' stemming from the problems of 'coping with daily hardship and disadvantage'.

A more focused expression of this idea is the concept of the **positive feedback loop** (Figure 11.4), involving a circular relationship between the following factors:

➤ material conditions — living in a deprived neighbourhood
➤ social conditions — educational failure and family breakdown
➤ psychological conditions — social isolation

These conditions create poorer physical health, which increases the risk of mental illness.

**Stress theory**, based on the pioneering work of Selye (1956), argues that certain 'life events' are more stressful than others. These events can be measured and ranked, using something like Holmes and Rahe's (1967) 'Social Readjustment Rating Scale'. See Table 11.5 for examples of ranked life events. The ranked events can be correlated with higher or lower levels of physical and mental illness. The greater the level of 'stressful events' in an individual's life, the more likely they are to develop mental illness.

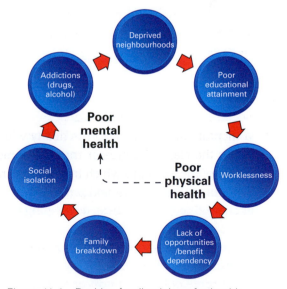

Figure 11.4   Positive feedback loop for health

Table 11.5   Examples of ranked life events

| Life event | Life change score |
|---|---|
| Death of partner | 100 |
| Imprisonment | 63 |
| Dismissal from work | 47 |
| Retirement | 45 |
| Change in financial status (e.g. unemployment) | 38 |
| Change in working hours or conditions | 20 |
| Minor violation of law | 11 |

*Source: Holmes and Rahe (1967)*

Those who scored 300 or more points on the complete scale of 43 life events were highly likely to develop physical or mental illnesses (Holmes and Rahe 1967). As Thoits (2010) puts it, the theory here is that 'pile-ups of stressors' produce high levels of psychological distress that result in the onset or recurrence of psychiatric disorders. However, she notes that only a relatively small percentage of those who scored highly on the scale actually developed mental illnesses.

McManus et al. (2009) found no real association between income and trauma; major traumas, such as death of a partner (100 points) and divorce (73), could strike equally across the class structure. However, they did find that lower-income households suffered higher levels of **post-traumatic stress disorder**, which suggests that some groups are better positioned to *resist* the effects of trauma and stress than others. This, as Thoits suggests, involves the ability to develop **buffers** that limit the effects of stressful life events. These are related to the idea of social power, discussed in the next section.

**?**   **Give an example of one source of strain in working-class life.**

### Social power

Social power involves the degree of control people feel they have over their own life, their work status and so forth. This version of structural theory argues that the crucial factor in the development of mental illness is not class (or indeed gender and ethnic) differences in *exposure* to stress, but rather differences in the ability to *cope* with such exposure. Different social classes have different access to resources that limit the likelihood of mental illness developing after exposure to stress.

Pearlin and Schooler (1978) argue that, in order to deal with the negative effects of various **life strains**, people employ a range of social and psychological **coping resources** — such as the ability to draw on others (especially close friends and family) as a source of help, comfort and reassurance. Those lower down the social scale have lower levels of **social capital** — access to social networks that might effectively act as 'buffers' against stressful life events. They also have lower levels of **social power**: they are less able to develop an active approach to dealing with stressful events. Those higher up the class scale are more used to solving problems in their everyday working lives and are therefore better positioned psychologically to take the steps required to preserve their mental health. Additional consequences of differences in social power include:

➢ negative attitudes towards psychiatric care
➢ the stigma of 'mental illness'
➢ a relative lack of access to psychiatric care

These ideas go some way towards explaining differences in diagnosis and treatment. If the lower classes, males and minority ethnic groups are more seriously mentally ill when they finally come into contact with the psychiatric services, they are more likely to be hospitalised. On this basis, Thoits (2010) suggests we need to refine the concept of exposure to stress, for several reasons:

➢ Ethnic minority groups have greater exposure to stress created through racial discrimination.
➢ Stressors are cumulative 'over the life course and across generations', and the gap between the 'advantaged and the disadvantaged' is affected by class factors. The lower classes are likely to suffer a greater accumulation of stressful life events and do not have the resources available that act as buffers against the impact of such events. For example, although both working-class and middle-class individuals could suffer unemployment, the latter are likely to have accumulated resources such as personal savings, insurance, a network of contacts and educational qualifications that make finding new work easier.
➢ Class factors are significant because 'the impacts of stressors on health and well-being are reduced when people have high levels of mastery, self-esteem or social support' — something that is more likely to be the case in the middle and upper classes.

> **?** How do the middle classes have more social power than the working classes?

### Evaluation

An important strength of structural approaches is the ability to explain why mental illness occurs more frequently among **disadvantaged groups**; they provide an explanation for the **non-random distribution** of mental illness:

➢ **Social class**: Lower social classes experience greater strains and have a lower ability to cope with these strains.
➢ **Gender**: Higher rates of female mental illness are explained by the greater levels of stress that result from a combination of paid and domestic employment — what Muntaner et al. (2004) term the 'double burden of home and work stress'. In basic terms, the 'pressure to cope' is much greater for women because they experience more stress through the dual action of class and patriarchy. Women not in paid employment are also more likely to be cut off from wider social networks, as are

single parents (the majority of whom are women), and this means they can muster fewer 'coping resources' at times of great personal stress.

➤ **Ethnicity**: Many ethnic minority groups in our society suffer a 'double disadvantage' in the sense of being more likely to experience both poverty and discrimination — both of which are significant sources of stress.

This general approach is not, however, without its critics. The **natural selection** approach (sometimes called **diathesis–stress theory**) argues that some individuals or groups have a greater predisposition towards mental illness than others. This disposition might be:

➤ genetic — a product of certain gene combinations
➤ biological — due to a chemical imbalance in the brain
➤ social — involving, for example, inadequate childhood socialisation or a mentally ill parent
➤ psychological — stemming, for instance, from an undiagnosed childhood trauma

However, the argument here is that 'stress' is merely the **trigger** for mental illness, not its cause — it is only when a 'predisposed individual' is placed under stress that their predisposition comes to the fore.

Another criticism comes from the **social selection** approach. While structural theories argue that low social class is a *cause* of mental illness, the 'drift hypothesis' suggests the reverse — mental illness causes individuals to 'drift down' the class structure because they find it impossible to retain work and earn an income.

A further criticism of structural approaches comes from interactionist approaches.

## Interactionist approaches

Interactionist sociologists take a different approach to understanding mental illness from their structural counterparts (Table 11.6).

Table 11.6 Structuralist and interactionist assumptions about mental illness

| Structuralist assumptions | Interactionist assumptions |
| --- | --- |
| Mental illness is a real, objectively defined condition. | Mental illness is a subjective condition created by the official labelling of some behaviours as 'mentally ill'. |
| Mental illness can be statistically measured and quantified. | Statistical measurements are no more than the quantification of official labelling processes. What is being quantified, therefore, is not 'mental illness' itself, but rather how certain behaviours are socially defined. |
| The non-random distribution of mental illness in terms of class, gender and ethnicity is explained by the different social and material conditions that act on differently placed individuals. | The non-random distribution of mental illness is explained by a greater willingness of medical professionals to label the relatively powerless (lower social classes, women and ethnic minorities) as mentally ill. |

Interactionist approaches see mental illness as socially constructed in terms of the way behaviour is so **labelled**. If the label and status 'mentally ill' did not exist, mental illness would not exist — the behaviour would be called something else and people would relate to it in a different way.

Mental illness is seen as behaviour that deviates from the norm of mental health. Following Becker's (1963) argument, the way to understand deviance is not to focus on what people *do*, because different people can display exactly the same behaviour but be *treated differently*. Busfield (1996) expresses this neatly when she argues that 'men's mental life and behaviour…are more likely to be regulated through attributions of wrongdoing, women's through attributions of mental disorder' — or, to put this more colloquially, 'Men are bad; women are mad'.

The argument here is that deviance (mental illness in this case) is not a quality of the act (what someone does) but a quality of how someone reacts to what someone does — and the most significant 'reactors' in terms of mental illness are medical professionals, those who have the power to attach the label of mental illness to some forms of behaviour.

Interactionists are also concerned with **regulation**. If 'mental illness' is little more than a label applied to certain types of behaviour, interactionists want to understand how and why, as Busfield (1996) suggests, *similar* behaviours come to be regulated *differently*.

Foucault (1961), although by no means an interactionist, touches on these matters when he argues that 'madness', as we now think of it, is related to two ideas:

➢ **Reason**: The development of scientific thinking in the eighteenth century led to the idea that the natural world was ordered and rational — it obeyed certain physical laws that could be identified and explained. This led to the view that if rationality was a normal state then anything **irrational** must be **abnormal** — hence the idea of 'madness' to describe some forms of behaviour that were 'not normal'.

➢ **Control**: Where some forms of behaviour are seen as abnormal, they have to be controlled, and in the spirit of scientific development of the age these controls became ever more elaborate. They focused initially on controlling the **bodies** of those behaving irrationally and abnormally, **institutionalised** through confinement and separation from normal society. Prisons became the norm for criminals, mental institutions and asylums the norm for those labelled mad. A professional class developed who had a vested interest in ensuring that only they had the power to define abnormality, and that 'madness' was given a rational reading and explanation.

These notions of reason and control illustrate the interactionist idea that no behaviour is inherently deviant; what's significant is how people react to and label different forms of behaviour. The focus of interest, therefore, is explaining how behaviour comes to be defined as 'mad'. For Foucault, as for many interactionists, 'madness' is not an objective medical condition; it is a subjective social category defined by powerful vested interests.

We can explore this idea further by considering different ways in which interactionists have theorised mental illness.

### The myth of mental illness?

Szasz (1961) argues that mental illness is a condition constructed by psychiatric professionals who apply an official medical label to behaviours that deviate from commonsense notions of normality. Szasz (1998) further suggests that we should see mental illness as a **metaphor** or metaphorical disease that has no biological origin or basis. Rather it is simply a convenient way to categorise 'thoughts, feelings, and behaviours' considered by some to be socially undesirable: 'Individuals with brain diseases (bad brains) or kidney diseases (bad kidneys) are literally sick. Individuals with mental diseases (bad behaviours) are metaphorically sick.'

Szasz argues that labelling certain types of 'undesirable behaviour' as mental illness provides a justification for **social control** — either physical or chemical incarceration (the latter involving the control of behaviour through the use of drugs). In this way, people whose behaviour is considered problematic for a ruling elite (the working classes, ethnic minorities) can be legally and justifiably controlled through the agency of the medical profession.

A contemporary extension of this view focuses on the **medicalisation of self and society**. This involves two broad ideas.

The first idea concerns '**problems of the self**', and the way we are encouraged to seek medical solutions to such problems (to deal with various traumas, for example). In this way a wide range of 'normal behavioural responses', from 'depression' through 'anxiety' to 'panic', are labelled 'mental illnesses'. These 'illnesses' (and the bodies to which they are attached) are then controlled through a range of treatments, from talking therapies to drugs.

The second idea concerns various behaviours labelled as '**problems for society**', from the misbehaviour of children to female crime. These are seen as medical conditions requiring treatment. Davis (2010), for example, reports the increasing use of Ritalin to treat attention deficit hyperactivity disorder (ADHD), a condition that first appeared in the mid-1980s. She notes that:

> ...professionals have argued over the use of such drugs. Some believe they treat a legitimate problem. Others, such as Dr Gwynedd Lloyd, refuse to acknowledge ADHD is even a medical condition. 'You can't do a blood test to check whether you've got ADHD — it's diagnosed through a behavioural checklist... Getting out of your seat and running about is an example — half the kids in a school could qualify under that criterion. I know a lot of children have genuine difficulties, and some of these are biological, but most are social and cultural.'

For interactionists, the medicalisation of self and society owes more to the power of medical professionals to label behaviour as 'mental illness' than to any real increase in this condition. This was demonstrated in an experiment carried out by Rosenhan (1973). It was designed to discover if doctors could correctly diagnose mental illness. If they could not, he argued, this would tell us something very important about the relationship between mental illness and labelling — that mental illness is not an objective but a subjective condition; that it is whatever medical professionals claim it to be.

Rosenhan and seven of his students became pseudopatients: they pretended to be suffering from some form of 'mental illness'. They got themselves admitted to 12 hospitals on the basis that they were hearing a voice saying 'hollow, empty, thud'. This was interpreted by the hospital staff as a symptom of schizophrenia. Taylor (forthcoming) writes:

> Once admitted to the hospital the pseudopatients stopped faking the symptom and behaved normally. When asked by the staff how they were feeling, they said they were fine, the symptom had disappeared and could they please be released... [However,] the pseudopatients remained in hospital for between 7 and 52 days. It seemed behaving normally was not enough to get out of a mental hospital, you had to accept the diagnosis first...and they were all finally released with a diagnosis of schizophrenia in remission.

The implication of this experiment is that 'mental illness' only exists because we begin with a label (and a set of characteristics we associate with it) that we then apply to particular forms of behaviour. This process reverses cause and effect; rather than a cause (mental illness) coming *before* the label (the effect), the effect (labelling) comes *before* the cause. In other words, we only *know* behaviour is mental illness because that's how medical professionals label it. Rather than an objective, quantifiable medical condition producing a specific label ('schizophrenia'), the label defines the condition.

**? Why should we see mental illness as 'a myth'?**

A contemporary example cited by the Centre for Social Justice (2011) is that while black Caribbeans don't show greater levels of psychosis than any other group, the police are more likely to refer them for treatment. In addition,

> ...staff in mental health hospitals are more likely to perceive them as potentially dangerous and psychiatrists are more likely to consider this group as potentially dangerous to others. It is therefore possible that African Caribbean people are more likely to be diagnosed with psychosis *because of bias among those who treat them*.

Similarly, Scheff (1999) argues that we can explain class differences in mental illness not as *real* differences resulting from differential exposure to structural strains, but rather as *artefact* differences: the tendency for middle-class professionals to label as mentally ill a disproportionate number of the powerless (those who are less able to challenge medical labelling). Scheff further argues that labelling processes create a **self-fulfilling prophecy** that contributes to the confirmation of the original label. Once a label has been successfully applied:

➤ The individual is encouraged to acknowledge their illness in order to be 'cured'.
➤ The individual is rewarded for behaving as a 'good patient'. Scheff argues that we frequently learn the 'stereotypical behaviours of mental illness' from an early age, through the media and so forth.
➤ Once discharged, the individual has acquired a **master status** as 'mentally ill' that affects how others behave towards them.
➤ This reinforces the mentally ill identity — and may have real psychological consequences, stemming from feelings of rejection, social isolation, an inability to secure employment and so on.

**?** Are class differences in mental illness *real* differences?

### Evaluation

While interactionist theories have sensitised us to a range of significant ideas about how mental illness is socially constructed, these approaches are not without their criticisms:

➤ While it is conceivable that a range of behaviours should not be treated as mental illness, this doesn't necessarily mean mental illness doesn't exist — particularly those types that can be traced to clear genetic or biological causes. By suggesting mental illness is 'just a label', we risk denying help to those who may be suffering from a real, definable condition.
➤ Labelling doesn't successfully explain why some forms of mental illness (but not others) are distributed equally across class, gender and ethnic groups. If mental illness were simply an artefact, we would expect to see far higher levels among the working classes and far lower levels among the higher classes.
➤ The idea that labelling is itself a 'cause' of mental illness doesn't explain why people should present themselves with symptoms (some extremely serious) in the first place, prior to any labelling process. This suggests that defining mental illness is a more complex process than interactionist approaches imply.

# Disability

The social construction of disability refers to the way different societies interpret the meaning of physical and mental impairments. For example, notions of disability in our society frequently carry with them the meaning of damage — 'the disabled' are not only different but also *inferior* to those who are not disabled. In other words, through a failure to meet cultural notions of a 'normal' physical or mental state, disability is seen as a **damaged status**, undesirable and hence **stigmatised**.

More generally, Table 11.7 illustrates changing concepts of disability over time. It shows how the disabled have been treated in line with changing ideas about the causes of physical and mental impairment.

Table 11.7   Changing concepts of disability

| Treatment | Cause |
|---|---|
| ANCIENT GREECE AND ROME (5TH CENTURY BC) | |
| Greece: Infanticide widely practised; sometimes obligatory for 'imperfect children'. | Metaphysical (not explicitly linked to physical causes), e.g. disability as a punishment for sin. |
| Rome: Infanticide practised for the 'sickly' or weak'. Those with no visible impairment at birth harshly treated as adults. Physically impaired (such as deaf or blind) considered objects of curiosity or ridicule and sometimes made to fight 'for the amusement of the public' in Roman Games. | Physiological: Wealthy Romans attempted 'cures' for physical and mental impairments using hydrotherapy and fitness regimes. |
| EARLY CHRISTIAN (2ND CENTURY AD) | |
| Exclusion: the physically and mentally impaired separated from 'normal society'. Some notion of caring for the disabled, directly or indirectly, through giving alms (such as money and food). | Disability seen as ungodly and the consequence of immorality, wrongdoing and sin. |
| MEDIEVAL EUROPE (15TH CENTURY) | |
| Exclusion from society with the disabled relying on 'Christian charity'. Some severely disabled admitted to hospitals for the 'poor, sick and bedridden'. Some religious groups advocated infanticide. | Religious notions of the link between disability, impurity and sin. Also the link between disability and the Devil (the disabled were 'living proof' of Satan's power). Disability sometimes seen as punishment for mother's involvement in witchcraft. |
| 17TH-CENTURY EUROPE | |
| Introduction of some government aid for 'deserving poor' (such as the disabled). Impairment as source of amusement and ridicule; 'idiots' often kept by the wealthy. Physically disabled frequently put on show with mental asylums (such as Bedlam) open to the public. | Notions of disability still related to ideas about sin, but not as strongly as in the past. Scientific ideas start to develop about the physiological basis of disabilities. |
| 19TH-CENTURY EUROPE | |
| Development of modern ideas about disability. Physically and mentally disabled excluded through institutionalisation (in hospitals and asylums). Establishment of 'charities for the disabled', run by the able-bodied. | Greater understanding of medical causes of disability. Initially physical, but gradual development of the idea of mental illness (through the work of Freud, for example). |

*Source: adapted from Barnes (1997)*

We can examine contemporary ideas about disability by outlining two models developed by Oliver (1983): the individual or medical model, and the social model.

## The individual or medical model

This model sees disability in terms of two ideas:

➤ **Individual**: Disability is 'inherent in the individual' and it is their responsibility to cope with and overcome the limitations of their condition. This also 'promotes the notion that it is the disabled individual who must adapt to the way society is constructed and organised'.

➤ **Medical**: The disabled are 'defined by their illness or medical condition' and are dependent on others for care and/or cure. Both of these situations are medicalised, in the sense that 'proper care' needs to follow medical guidelines and the ultimate solution to the 'disability problem' is a medical cure.

Under this model the disabled individual, rather than the way society is organised, is seen as 'the problem'. As Oliver argues, the inability of the disabled to live a 'normal life' stems from their physical and/or psychological condition, and the 'solution' to this problem is twofold:

➤ **Care**: In the short term at least, the disabled have to be looked after by others. The objective is to ensure that they participate as fully as possible in social relationships, albeit with limitations imposed by their condition.

➤ **Cure**: In the long term the aim is to find a medical cure for the disabling condition.

As Oliver notes, both solutions suggest that disability is a 'personal tragedy' and also carry with them notions of **non-culpable forms of deviance** — the disabled are different. The perception of disability as deviance is reinforced by the medical model, Oliver argues, because it gives power to medical professionals and takes it away from the disabled individual:

➤ It confirms the view of disability as something different and undesirable; disability is seen as a '**broken condition**' that needs to be fixed.

➤ It teaches the disabled to depend on others. To 'cope' with their disability, the disabled must '**learn helplessness**' — they must allow others to take control of their lives and environment if they are to be 'helped' to overcome their limitations.

In general terms, the medical model serves three specific functions:

➤ **Individualising deviance**: It places responsibility for disability on the individual, who must learn to both cope and submit to care.

➤ **Boundary setting**: By defining some people as abnormal or deviant, the model also defines the 'boundaries of normality'.

➤ **Normalisation**: Definitions of abnormality are reinforced because the model aims to 'normalise the disabled' through the **medicalisation** of their condition.

> **?** What is *one* feature of the medical model of disability?

## Evaluation

➤ **Stereotypes and stigma**: Defining the disabled as different stigmatises this identity as something undesirable and unfortunate. As the disabled are forced to fit, as best they can, into 'normal society', this group — although defined more by their differences than their similarities — are stereotyped by notions of abnormality.

➤ **Discrimination**: The disabled are subject to punitive **social controls** which are not extended to the able-bodied. These controls determine where they can go, what they can do, who they can associate with — and even, on occasion, whether they're allowed to be born.

➤ **Self-fulfilling prophecies**: By treating the disabled as different and incapable, the medical model emphasises the negative aspects of disability. This, in turn, makes the disabled see themselves as helpless.

➤ **Separation**: The model sets the disabled apart from the abled, for example in special schools. This reinforces the notion of difference they aim to resolve.

➤ **Medicalisation**: Oliver argues that disability is not a medical condition, but a **social state**. We should view disability as an aspect of 'normality' and treat the disabled accordingly — both in interpersonal terms, for instance through the removal of stigmatising language, and in environmental terms, by finding ways to realign the environment to allow the disabled to enjoy the same rights and freedoms as the abled.

## The social model

This model argues that disability is a problem for society, rather than the individual. This idea is expressed in the distinction made by UPIAS (1976) between impairment and disability:

➤ **Impairment** refers to the lack of something, such as a limb, that inhibits the normal functioning of the body (or mind).

➤ **Disability** refers to restrictions caused by the way societies are organised for the benefit of the able-bodied (a simple example being steps, rather than ramps, as a way of entering buildings).

This distinction changes the focus of disability away from the individual and the problems *they* cause society, and towards the society and the problems *it* causes the impaired.

It is also important because it changes our interpretation of 'disabled'. Rather than defining it **negatively** as 'not abled', it is possible to define it **positively** as 'differently abled' (**diffabled**). This, in turn, suggests that 'disability' and 'ability' are dimensions of the same process. Just as the 'abled-bodied' display differences in ability (some being more mobile than others, for instance), the same is true of impairment.

> **?** **What is the main difference between impairment and disability?**

The social model argues, therefore, that in any society where large numbers of people have physical and mental impairments, the onus is on society to adjust to this situation. If the design of the built environment makes access for people with mobility problems an issue, the solution is not to exclude them; rather it is to change the environment to enable their inclusion. In this respect, Oliver (1990) suggests that the social model has a number of characteristics:

➤ Disability is seen as a '**failure of society**', not the individual, when it fails 'to provide appropriate services and adequately ensure the needs of disabled people are fully taken into account'.

➤ **Inclusion**, rather than exclusion, is seen as the key to engaging with disability. The social model argues that differently-abled people should be able to 'participate in activities on an equal footing'. This involves removing various barriers to inclusion:

➤ **Material**: Someone in a wheelchair is only 'disabled' in an environment that does not allow full mobility and access.

➤ **Non-material**: It is also important to deal with problems that stem from seeing the disabled as not just different but in some way inferior (**negative stereotyping**).

➤ **Discrimination** against the impaired is seen as institutionalised. Society 'disables people, through designing everything to meet the needs of the majority of people who are not disabled'.

David Kilpatrick/Alamy

The built environment can be designed to maximise access and mobility for disabled people

## Evaluation

➤ **Disabled identities**: The social model assumes that those with impairments see themselves as having a common identity as disabled — but many disabled people reject this notion. Insisting on a single 'disabled identity' simply reflects the power relationships present in the medical model, with the definitions of medical professionals replaced by those of 'society' or various interest groups.

➤ **Design**: Finkelstein (1981) argues that modifying physical environments to allow 'total inclusion' is 'an unsustainable myth' — removing barriers for one form of impairment may, for example, generate barriers to other forms. In addition, Shakespeare and Watson (2002) argue, 'If someone has an impairment which causes constant pain, how can the social environment be implicated?'

➤ **Outdated**: Shakespeare and Watson (2002) argue that the social model is an 'outdated ideology' for three reasons:

➤ **Denial of difference**: The model denies there is any real difference (aside from that created 'by society') between the disabled and the abled — yet disabled individuals may live with pain and disability not experienced by the able-bodied.

This model, by denying difference, takes away from the disabled an important part of their identity.

> **Impairment or disability?**: The model argues that the former is a creation of bodily difference while the latter is socially created. However, by focusing on impairment the social model argues that physical and mental differences are actually *more* significant than the medical model suggests.

> **Only and always disabled?**: By arguing that society is the cause of disability, the model assumes that individuals are either disabled (and always will be) or they are not (and never will be). However, many people experience impairment in less dramatic terms, often moving through 'different states of ability' (as with gradual loss of eyesight with age).

---

**Exam-style questions**

**1** Identify and explain two ways in which disability can be seen as socially constructed. (17 marks)

**2** Identify and explain two ways in which mental illness is related to gender. (17 marks)

**3** Identify and explain two ways in which mental illness is influenced by ethnicity. (17 marks)

**4** Outline and evaluate the view that disability is socially constructed. (33 marks)

**5** Outline and evaluate interactionist views of mental illness. (33 marks)

---

# The role of health professionals in society

## Sociological explanations

We've referred at various points to the role played by **medical professionals** in areas like the diagnosis and treatment of illness and impairment. In this section we will examine their role in more detail, from a range of sociological perspectives.

### Functionalism

For functionalists society is seen as a **social system**, organised around a general **value consensus**, where the constituent parts (**institutions** such as the family, education and health) contribute to the overall maintenance and reproduction of the system. In this respect, functionalists generally consider healthcare in terms of two types of role:

> the **general role** played by the health institution in the overall social system

> the **specific individual roles** that need to be performed within the institution for it to function successfully

These two types of role are important because societies can only function successfully if individuals are prevented from following their own self-interests; people must be encouraged to cooperate and behave in ways that are reasonable, consistent and broadly predictable. We will consider these roles further in the following subsections.

## The role of health systems

For Parsons (1937) the role of any institution is defined by four **functional prerequisites** — the things that must happen if it is to successfully play its part in society:

- **Goal attainment**: People must be given goals to achieve and some way of moving towards their attainment. For the health system, these goals might include curing the sick or caring for those who cannot be cured.
- **Adaptation**: There needs to be some way for people to achieve institutional goals and this might include setting up a system of:
  - people — such as health professionals (surgeons, doctors and nurses)
  - places — health facilities such as surgeries, hospitals, care homes and hospices
- **Integration**: People have to be motivated to achieve health goals. Examples might include:
  - **Economic motivators** such as a **career structure** for health professionals: Doctors and consultants in Britain, for example, are among some of the highest income earners. Average annual GP earnings, according to the Health and Social Care Information Centre (2011), are currently £97,500. The lower-paid nursing staff enjoy significant levels of **social status** compared with other employees with similar salaries.
  - **Cultural motivators**: For functionalists, an important integrating mechanism is the **collective orientation** of health professionals — the idea that they put the interests of the community and patients above their own interests. Doctors, for example, take the **Hippocratic Oath** (under which they promise to act **ethically**), undergo years of rigorous training and have their competence monitored by the General Medical Council. In addition, doctors belong to the British Medical Association, a professional association that sets out standards of behaviour, ethical practices and so forth.
- **Latency**: This represents a way of managing **conflicts**. All institutions develop rules of behaviour, and ways of rewarding conformity and punishing deviance. The General Medical Council, for example, has the power to remove doctors from the medical register, which means they are no longer allowed to practise medicine (60 doctors suffered this punishment in 2007).

Functional prerequisites for institutions

**G** oal attainment
**A** daptation
**I** ntegration
**L** atency

**?** How are health professionals motivated to achieve healthcare goals?

### The role of health professionals

For the health system to perform its general social role of returning the ill to health, roles within this institution need to be carefully specified and their relationship managed. One way of organising health roles is through **hierarchies** of knowledge and power. The system is kept moving towards its goals through a top-down organisation whereby those who occupy the most **functionally important** positions (doctors and consultants) are given the most power and receive the greatest rewards.

In addition, health professionals play an important **gatekeeping role** that operates on two levels:

➤ **Primary care**: Dixon et al. (1998) note that access to care is filtered through a hierarchy of levels, with an initial gatekeeping role played by the GP; this involves making an initial diagnosis and then a decision about whether the patient should be referred 'up the system' to specialist practitioners. This role, Forrest (2003) argues, is designed to ensure healthcare services are matched to healthcare needs.

➤ **General care**: The broader gatekeeping role involves making decisions about whether individuals should be officially defined as 'sick', and therefore exempt from their usual social responsibilities.

A further aspect of the professional role is the idea of **universalism**: the sick are treated ethically and equally, regardless of cultural characteristics such as class, gender and ethnicity, on the basis of their health needs. In return for the patient's trust, doctors are required to act in the interests of the patient, with the objective of returning them to health. Ethical behaviour is paramount in this relationship, not simply because it is a dependent one (where the health professional is dealing with vulnerable individuals) but also because health professionals are given powers over patients (to examine them, record and distribute personal information about their condition and so forth) based on the idea of trust.

Overall, therefore, the roles of the healthcare system and professionals within that system are seen in terms of their functional organisation to fulfil certain **needs and purposes**. For society to function in a stable and orderly manner, institutions such as work, education and the family need healthy individuals, and the purpose of the health system is to ensure this need is met.

**?** **Give an example of one aspect of the professional healthcare role.**

### Evaluation

➤ **Functional importance**: The high incomes and statuses of doctors and consultants are justified on the basis that they are objectively more functionally important to the health institution, but we can only judge this value subjectively. Nursing staff, for example, are functionally important too — since the system couldn't function without them — but they have much lower pay and status than doctors.

➤ **Dysfunctions**: As we've seen, Illich (1976) argues that health professionals can perform their roles dysfunctionally by actually making people ill (**iatrogenesis**).

➤ **Social closure**: Some argue that professional bodies (such as the BMA) and regulators act as a 'closed shop' to protect professional interests (such as high incomes) by limiting entrance into the profession, rather than serving the public interest. This suggests the system is not necessarily meritocratic and therefore not necessarily functional.

➤ **Alternatives**: The assumption that the current organisation of health systems around a biomedical model is functional means that alternative models of health are seen as dysfunctional.

## Marxism

The focus for Marxist perspectives is on **conflicts** surrounding the role of health professionals, based around two ideas:

➤ Capitalist societies are class societies based around the fundamental conflict between a ruling and a subject class. The underlying logic of this relationship is the pursuit of (private) profit based around competition and social and economic inequalities.

➤ A ruling class has a clear interest in ensuring a fit and healthy workforce that can be exploited for **profit**, especially if the workers themselves effectively pay to maintain their health — through income and consumption taxes to fund the collective approach of the NHS, or private health insurance to fund the individualistic approach of the US healthcare system.

The key idea, for Marxists, is that in capitalist societies the role of health professionals is shaped by conflicts across three dimensions: economic, political and ideological. These are discussed below.

### Economics: medicine as production and consumption

Bambra et al. (2005) argue that in capitalist societies health is a commodity — something to be bought and sold — and the role of health professionals is to service this market. The area of greatest profitability is not community protection and prevention but individual cure.

The argument here is that the major improvements to general public health in any society (as measured by things like average life expectancy) occur through a series of relatively simple measures — such as the provision of clean water — and once these are achieved there is a diminishing rate of return and profit on 'medical improvements'. Only by switching the focus to 'individual cures for individual ailments' can profits be continually created — and this is where, Navarro (1989) argues, '**corporate medicine**' comes to the fore.

For large corporate interests to exploit medical care for profit — through drug sales, the provision of private insurance or servicing the needs of a national health service — they need to develop relationships at all levels of health provision: from dealing directly with governments, through research and development that produces new products for sale to health professionals, to advertising that reaches directly into the hearts and minds of consumers.

Thus the economic dimension promotes a **biomedical model** of health, with the belief that higher levels of individual health are achievable through better drugs or improved surgical techniques. It also promotes the **ideology** of healthcare as something to be bought — both as a society, through building hospitals, organising health services and the like, and individually, through the consumption of a vast range of health products, from 'cold cures' to slimming pills.

### Politics: medicine as social control (part 1)

For Marxists, health professionals play key roles in:

➤ creating healthy workers who are a continued source of profit
➤ controlling definitions of health and illness
➤ deciding who is ill and who is healthy
➤ defining new disorders (which can be treated by new and profitable drugs)

In general, therefore, the **gate-keeping** role played by health professionals is a form of '**soft policing**' — making the day-to-day decisions about individual health and illness that contribute to the continued operation of capitalist society. Healthcare professionals are locked into this political and economic system through high salaries and the high statuses that come with increasing **specialisation**; certain groups, such as surgeons and consultants, are able to place a very high value on their knowledge and skills precisely because of the individualisation and **commodification** of medical services. ('Commodification' refers to the process of turning something into a commodity.)

The political role of healthcare professionals, and specifically those who occupy senior roles in the **medical hierarchy**, is a powerful one. This professional group sits at the centre of an important relationship: they hold the trust of the general public (those whom they nominally serve) and they are courted by corporations seeking to provide medical services to both individuals and governments. Navarro (1989) argues that the power of health professionals stems from their **monopoly control** over two areas:

➤ **The production of medical knowledge**: Health professionals have created a system of training and registration that restricts entry into the profession.
➤ **The provision of health services**: Only suitably trained, qualified and registered staff are allowed to administer these services.

This control has, in turn, shaped two processes: the **social organisation** of medicine, and the **division of labour** within medical institutions. Both processes, Marxists argue, have been shaped in the interests of healthcare professionals rather than the interests of the people they nominally serve.

### Ideology: medicine as social control (part 2)

Althusser (1972) argues that medicine is an **ideological state apparatus**: the means through which people are socialised to accept a range of ideas beneficial to a ruling class. These include the idea that health is an individual, not a collective, problem, and the belief that curative medicine is superior to all other forms. The real causes of ill health, such as poverty and social inequality, are obscured by this ideology.

Navarro (1979) suggests that health professionals, because they are involved in promoting these ideas, are **ideological agents of social control**. 'Health' is promoted as the outcome of **individual lifestyle choices** (concerning diet, exercise and so forth), **random chance** or **individual weaknesses** — whereas, for Marxists, it should be seen as the result of unequal **life chances**, the long-term effects of **economic exploitation** and the willingness of a ruling class to promote its interests (and health) at the expense of the majority of workers.

Marxism

**P** olitics
**I** deology
**E** conomics

> **?** How is medicine a form of social control?

### Evaluation

➤ **Left functionalism**: Some forms of Marxism simply replace the functionalist idea that the role of health professionals benefits society as a whole with the idea that they provide various benefits to a ruling class.

➤ **Capitalism**: By focusing on the 'general logic' underpinning capitalist societies (the pursuit of private profit), Marxists underplay the many significant differences between such societies. Health provision in America, for example, follows very different principles from that in Britain. Turner (1987), from a Weberian perspective (see below), argues that we need to understand the **diversity** of medical systems in capitalist societies.

➤ **Professional roles**: Marxism overplays the role of healthcare professionals as **agents of social and ideological control**. We could argue, for example, that professional medicine plays a key role in protecting the public from harm by insisting on the proper scientific scrutiny of the claims made by corporations and pharmaceutical companies.

➤ **Health**: The advances made in medical science are important and beneficial to large numbers of people who would otherwise experience greater suffering.

## Weberian approaches

Weberian approaches focus on the relationship between **social structures** and **social actions**. They seek to understand how the nature of organisational structures influences the behaviour of individuals and groups within those structures — and, for our current purpose, how **social status** is negotiated within organisations. In particular, this approach explores the idea of professional status as a means of protecting the self-interests of doctors as an **elite group** of medical practitioners.

Weber (1905) argued that the development of modern societies was influenced by the concept of **rationalisation**. Ideas about organising behaviour **efficiently** and **productively** to achieve certain organisational goals, such as providing medical care for the greatest number of individuals, are implemented through:

➢ **institutions** — such as work
➢ **practices** — the various roles people play within an organisation

In modern societies, **rational organisation** is generally expressed in terms of **bureaucracy**, an organisational form that Ritzer (1996) describes as follows:

➢ **Large-scale**: It involves big, complex institutional structures.
➢ **Goal-orientated**: It exists to achieve certain clearly defined aims.
➢ **Rule-orientated**: 'People have certain responsibilities and must act in accord with rules and written regulations.'
➢ **Hierarchical**: It is arranged in levels, with those at the top (and at each successive level) having more power, influence and importance than those lower down.

A further key feature noted by Borthwick et al. (2009) is that **status** within bureaucracies is **achieved** (through particular merits and demonstrations of knowledge and skills) rather than **ascribed** (given).

If we combine these elements of bureaucratic organisation in relation to the British health system, we can understand the role of healthcare professionals as part of a **hierarchical status system**. The object of interest, for Weberian sociologists, is how and why certain groups achieve, maintain and enhance status within an organisation. We therefore need to understand professional groups within the health system as **status groups**, primarily organised to protect the standing and interests of their *members*. This is achieved by doctors in two ways: **specialisation** and **status hierarchies**.

## Specialisation

Status groups stake out clear areas of knowledge, skills and expertise. These need to be exclusively owned by a group if they are to restrict entry and, in consequence, raise their status and income. One way to do this is through the increasing **specialisation** of the medical role (neurologists, paediatricians, urologists and so on). By raising the level of expertise, healthcare professionals create **barriers** to professional entry by:

➢ claiming exclusive knowledge
➢ increasing the need for long and expensive training
➢ establishing monopoly practices

These barriers are complemented by a range of practices designed to consolidate the exclusive and economically valuable status of healthcare professionals:

➢ **strict regulation**, preferably by a 'neutral' organisation such as the state (and the General Medical Council, in Britain), that requires alternative medical practices to pass strict tests to be admitted into the medical canon

➤ **self-governance** by a professional association (such as the British Medical Association) which sets standards to keep all members of the status group in line

➤ **specialised training** and testing, through university degrees and medical doctorates that exclude all but a small minority of potential entrants, while enhancing the claim to exclusive knowledge and skills

This does have certain advantages for those dealing with professional groups — for example, a patient can expect to be treated **ethically** and have their health assessed **objectively** by someone who has attained an objectively defined level of medical competence. However, professional status within an organisational hierarchy also has wide-ranging benefits for those playing the professional role. These include **privileges**, as Allsop and Saks (2002) note, such as the ability to:

➤ set their own behavioural and ethical rules
➤ define standards of competence
➤ define exclusive areas of practice

Bureaucratic organisation combines with claims for professional expertise to create, for Weberians, a very effective system of **professional closure**. Alexander (2005) characterises this as a form of **social exclusion**: by restricting and controlling their membership, a group creates an artificial shortage of expertise which is then translated into a range of rewards (such as high levels of status, power and income) exclusively enjoyed by the group members.

Professional closure has the additional advantage of making it difficult for **alternative** forms of medical knowledge and expertise to develop. It is based on a biomedical model of health that is the basis of health professionals' claim to exclusive knowledge and skills. If this model is effectively challenged, then so too is the professional claim to closure.

### Status hierarchies

In their day-to-day interaction with patients and other, competing healthcare professionals, especially nursing staff, doctors must work to maintain their **status** against the claims of these groups. Stein (1967) initially noted how doctors and nurses played an elaborate 'game' designed to protect the doctor's status while acknowledging that much of the day-to-day care of patients was done by lower-status (and much lower-paid) nurses:

> One rarely hears a nurse say 'Doctor, I would recommend...'. A physician hearing a recommendation of that nature would gape in amazement at the effrontery of the nurse... Nevertheless...nurses make recommendations of more import every hour and physicians willingly and respectfully consider them.

When Stein et al. (1990) revisited 'the **doctor–nurse game**', they found that their relationship had evolved. This was partly a result of nurses seeking to enhance their own status by restricting entrance through higher educational qualifications and by creating a new range of professional roles that edged into the territory once exclusively occupied by doctors. Radcliffe (2000), however, takes a different view:

> For all the jostling for position over the past 20 years little has changed. This is primarily because the power in the relationship is mediated by the patient. If in doubt ask the patient who is in control. The public may love its angels but it holds its medics in awe.

In a similar vein, Foucault (1973) notes the power of the **clinical gaze**. The medical institution and senior health professionals (as a powerful group within that institution) exercise **power** through their **moral authority** over patients: they have the ability both to explain problems, such as illness, and to provide solutions to those problems.

**?** How do status groups protect the standing and interests of healthcare professionals?

### Evaluation
Criticisms of the Weberian approach turn on how we interpret the concept of professionalism. While this status clearly confers advantages on those who have it, it also provides benefits for those who require medical services:
- trained and competent medical staff
- ethical behaviour governed by a code of conduct strictly policed by both professional associations and the state
- higher standards of behaviour and care

**Barriers** to entry can also serve the public by ensuring that those who offer medical services are properly qualified and that the service has been tested and assessed as effective, or at least not harmful.

**Alternatives** to the biomedical model, such as homeopathy or aromatherapy, may find it difficult to break into the health service, although, as we will see, it's not impossible. On the other hand, bureaucratisation and professionalism ensure that competing medical claims have to be scientifically assessed.

**Preventative medicine**, at least in the British healthcare model, has assumed increasing significance in recent years. It's difficult to see how this could occur if, as the Weberian approach claims, it's not in the interests of professional status groups to promote anything other than a curative approach to medicine.

## Feminism

Feminist perspectives have focused on two ways in which women are **marginalised**: within the medical profession, and as objects of medical attention.

### Women and the medical profession

The **historical origins** of female marginalisation within the health profession are traced, by writers such as Ehrenreich and English (1972), to women's role as 'healers' in the Middle Ages (the fourteenth and fifteenth centuries in particular). The developing, male-only medical profession used accusations of witchcraft against female folk-healers to 'remove the competition'.

**Contemporary perspectives** on male domination emphasise the following aspects:

➤ **Vertical segregation**: The medical profession is characterised by distinct layers of power, income and authority, with the higher level (doctors and consultants) overwhelmingly male and the lower level (nursing staff) overwhelmingly female.

➤ **Professional closure**: This results in female exclusion from the higher-status positions.

Female voices are marginalised further by the need to defer to male professionals of higher status even in situations where their greater everyday knowledge, experience and skills mean that they have more understanding of patient care and needs.

### Women as objects of medical attention

A second strand to feminist arguments concerns male medical control over female bodies and minds.

In terms of **bodies**, one area of concern is the '**medicalisation of childbirth**': it is argued that women are subjected to a range of processes, from hospital deliveries to Caesarean operations, that owe more to the convenience of health professionals than to the interests of the women involved.

**Medical interventions** in areas of specifically female life, such as menstruation, pregnancy and childbirth, were once handled privately, within the family. The extension of male medical influence into these areas is interpreted as a desire to both control female behaviour and extend medical practice into profitable areas of the marketplace.

There is also concern about control over female **minds**. Across both class and ethnic categories, women suffer higher levels of mental disorder than men. Feminists suggest two explanations for this:

➤ Health professionals are more willing to classify (or **label**) females as mentally ill because of **patriarchal** notions of 'female fallibility', such as the idea that women are more prone to common mental disorders simply because they are women.

➤ The causes of female illness, both mental and physical, are **social**, not medical. The dual roles of women in contemporary societies, as both paid employees and unpaid domestic workers, place greater stresses and strains on women's minds and bodies.

These two ideas are bound up in the concept of **medicalisation** — the idea that healthcare professionals are more likely to use medical labels for behaviour that deviates from conventional norms about how women are supposed to behave. As Busfield (1996) puts it, there is an assumption that 'Men are bad; women are mad'.

One further aspect of feminist concern relates to **informal care** within family groups. The argument here is that major responsibilities for both physical and mental healthcare are increasingly passed on to women by the medical profession. While women do most of the additional work, they receive little help, credit or financial remuneration.

> **?** How are women marginalised by the healthcare profession?

### Evaluation

While feminism makes a significant contribution to our understanding of the role of healthcare professionals by highlighting a range of '**malestream biases**' within the medical profession, this approach has attracted a range of criticisms. There are significant doubts about two major areas of feminist argument: historical developments and contemporary society.

In terms of **history**, there has been dispute over the feminist claim that the female 'healing role' was taken over by men, and specifically by a male medical profession, as the result of a deliberate (and literal) witch-hunt. Burns (2003), for example, argues that the picture in England was more complicated than feminists have suggested. When the state wanted witches persecuted, medical authorities were often invoked in evidence against them; however, in periods when witches were not officially persecuted, medical authorities were often used in their *defence*. More significantly, Burns argues that by the seventeenth century, when a coherent medical profession began to emerge, there was 'a remarkable succession of increasingly radical physician *opponents* of witch-hunting'.

Other criticisms concern feminist analysis of **contemporary society**. While the medical profession, especially at the highest levels, has historically been male-dominated, it doesn't necessarily follow that this is still the case. A recent report by the Royal College of Physicians (2009) notes that women:

➢ made up 57% of acceptances for medical school
➢ are likely to become the majority of NHS GPs by 2013
➢ are likely to become the majority of all NHS doctors sometime after 2017
➢ accounted for over 60% of specialist training acceptances into general practice, paediatrics, public health medicine, and obstetrics and gynaecology

Another criticism concerns the focus on **patriarchy**. Rather than seeing medical power in patriarchal terms, an alternative is to see it in **class** terms. Since lower-class males, for example, suffer similar experiences to women at the hands of health professionals, we should see healthcare in terms of **professional power**, whether wielded by men or by women. This then becomes the central way of explaining health inequalities, the medicalisation of deviant behaviours and the like.

# The rise of complementary/alternative medicine

In this section we will discuss complementary and alternative medicine, considering the ways in which they present a challenge to conventional medicine. We can note first that complementary and alternative medicine are defined less in terms of the *type* of medical treatment or service being provided and more in terms of their *relationship* to the **dominant form** of medical practice in society (the biomedical model).

## Complementary medicine

'Complementary medicine' refers to treatment or services used *in conjunction with* (as 'a complement to') conventional forms of medicine. They normally belong to one of three types (although, in practice, they may be combined):

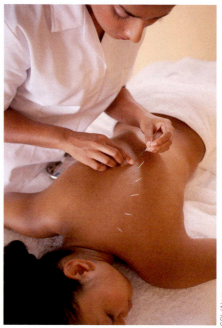

Acupuncture is gaining popularity in Western countries

➢ **Mind and body practices** include:
  ➢ **acupuncture** — a traditional Chinese medical practice that uses very thin metal needles inserted into the skin, for example to relieve pain
  ➢ **meditation** techniques such as yoga
➢ **Natural products** include a variety of herbal medicines and vitamins used as dietary supplements. **Probiotic** foods (such as live yogurts) are probably some of the most well-known.
➢ **Body-based practices** involve a range of manipulative techniques designed to relieve conditions such as back pain. Two common examples are chiropractic services and massage.

## Alternative medicine

'Alternative medicine' refers to treatment or services used *in place of* conventional medicine. Some of the best-known or most widely used are the following:

➢ **Homeopathy**: This involves treating illness using the principle of 'like cures like': a substance that would cause illness in a healthy person is used, in very minute doses, to treat someone who is ill, on the basis that the 'harmful' substance stimulates the body's natural defence mechanisms.
➢ **Naturopathy**: This is again based on the idea of stimulating the body's natural defence mechanisms to prevent and overcome illness. It uses diet and exercise, discourages 'unhealthy practices', and employs various forms of natural therapy to 'remove the barriers to self-healing'.

> **Aromatherapy**: This uses 'essential oils' (plant extracts) as a way of altering people's health.

**?** What is the difference between complementary and alternative medicine?

## Complement or challenge?

It may seem obvious that, by definition, complementary medicine does not threaten the conventional medical model while alternative medicine does. However, the situation is not quite so simple. Despite their differences, complementary/alternative medicines (CAMs) challenge conventional forms of medicine in three ways, which we can consider under the headings of causality, organisation and treatment.

### Causality

CAMs can be distinguished from conventional Western forms of medicine in terms of the way each views the relationship between **mind and body**. Conventional biomedicine separates 'the mind' from 'the body' when treating illness. The mind (or how people feel) is seen as having no direct impact on health; the focus is on the search for, and treatment of, the **physical causes** of ill health. The emphasis is generally on cure rather than prevention, although this depends to some extent on the nature of different health systems.

CAM represents a challenge to conventional medicine in that it generally takes a different view of mind and body. It argues that the mind and the body are connected, such that when the two are working 'in harmony' the body's natural defence mechanisms are enhanced; this gives people greater protection against disease and greater ability to recover from illness. Rather than focusing on symptoms and locating causes in particular parts of the body, this view adopts a **holistic approach** to treatment — one that looks at the 'whole person' (mind, body, emotions and 'spirit') as a way of understanding and treating ailments.

### Organisation

Alternative medicines in particular present a challenge to conventional forms of medicine in terms of the relationship between practitioners and patients:

> **Conventional medicine** is **bureaucratically** organised and involves a clear, formal separation between the practitioner (doctor) and patient — the latter requires the former to cure their illness. Partly because of the focus on physical causality, the doctor is not particularly interested in the patient beyond any factors (diet, lifestyle and the like) that might impact on treatment and recovery.

> **Alternative medicine** emphasises **holistic** treatment (treatment based on an understanding of the 'whole person'). In this approach, the treatment of the *person* is as significant as the treatment of the *ailment*. This means that the relationship between practitioner and patient is non-bureaucratic, less hierarchical and less formal.

### Treatment

As we've suggested, one way CAM challenges conventional biomedicine is through a focus on holistic (mind and body) treatment. This, in turn, produces a range of specific differences in the way health and illness are treated. While conventional medicine focuses on the use of various, mainly synthetic, drugs and invasive surgical practices (such as heart surgery), CAM focuses on the idea of 'natural drugs' and non-invasive methods.

The two approaches are not inevitably opposed. Conventional medicine, for example, frequently uses naturally occurring drugs, such as quinine for the treatment of malaria and opiates for pain relief. It also uses 'alternative techniques', such as massage, as part of its overall healthcare package. However, many alternative forms of medicine are philosophically opposed to synthetic drug treatments and invasive surgical techniques.

CAM

**C** ausality
**O** rganisation
**T** reatment

> **?** How does alternative medicine challenge the power of healthcare professionals?

## The empire fights back

One arena in which the 'alternative challenge' to conventional medicine has been played out in recent times is the **scientific testing** of CAM claims to be a valuable alternative to conventional treatments. We will consider two aspects of the 'alternative challenge': the opposition between 'natural' and 'artificial' medicine, and the issue of effectiveness.

### Natural versus artificial medicine

One of the criticisms levelled at alternative approaches such as homeopathy is that the label 'natural' is subtly confused in the mind of the consumer or patient with 'good'. This involves the idea that if something 'occurs naturally' it is automatically beneficial. The reverse, of course, is also the case — anything 'unnatural' (such as a synthetic drug) is, by definition, 'bad'. Conventional medicine points out that something natural is not automatically beneficial or harmless, just as something synthetic is not automatically harmful. The death cap mushroom, for example, is a 'naturally occurring substance' that, if consumed, can cause death (the clue is in the name).

### Effectiveness

Homeopathy is one of the largest and most popular alternative medicine practices. It involves a market worth, Sample (2008) reports, '£38m in 2007 and expected to reach £46m by 2012'. It has been subjected to a range of scientific testing:

➤ Linde et al.'s (1998) review of a large number of clinical tests found no evidence that homeopathy was an effective treatment 'for any single clinical condition'. However, they did conclude that homeopathic treatment had some beneficial effects as a **placebo**, as many people reported feeling better after treatment. (A placebo is a treatment which has no inherent therapeutic value, but can have a beneficial effect simply as a result of a patient's belief in the treatment.)

➢ Ernst et al.'s (2007) review of the evidence for the effectiveness of homeopathy in the treatment of children and adolescents similarly found little difference between the effects of homeopathic treatment and placebo treatments. They concluded that, while homeopathy was largely harmless, it carried the danger of 'delaying effective treatment or diagnosis'.

➢ Ernst (2010) concluded that, while there are currently around 200 clinical trials of homeopathic medicine, 'the totality of this evidence fails to show that homeopathic remedies work'.

Despite the lack of scientific validation of the clinical effectiveness of complementary and alternative medicine, there is little doubt it has become established as part of the **cultural health system** — the overall system of healthcare, conventional and alternative — in British society. Siahpush (1998) suggests three reasons for this:

➢ dissatisfaction with the health outcomes of conventional medicine, for example when there are unpleasant side-effects of conventional drug treatments or when conventional treatments have failed

➢ dissatisfaction with doctor–patient interaction and relationships, for example among those wanting greater involvement in their diagnosis and treatment

➢ the existence of value systems (such as 'New Age' beliefs) that fit with the philosophical underpinnings of alternative medicine

**Exam-style questions**

1 Identify and explain two reasons for the growth of alternative medicine. (17 marks)

2 Outline and evaluate the functionalist view of the role of health professionals. (33 marks)

3 Outline and evaluate the view that health professionals have too much power in the contemporary UK. (33 marks)

4 Outline and evaluate sociological views on the role of medical professionals in society. (33 marks)

# Index